JUL 2 7 2005

# A VINDICATION OF THE RIGHTS OF MEN

and

# A VINDICATION OF THE RIGHTS OF WOMAN

A VINDICATION OF THE RIGHTS OF MEN,

IN A LETTER TO THE RIGHT HONOURABLE

*EDMUND BURKE*;

OCCASIONED BY HIS REFLECTIONS ON THE
REVOLUTION IN FRANCE

and

A VINDICATION OF THE RIGHTS OF WOMAN:

WITH STRICTURES ON POLITICAL AND
MORAL SUBJECTS

*by Mary Wollstonecraft*

*Edited by D.L. Macdonald and Kathleen Scherf*

broadview literary texts

**Canadian Cataloguing in Publication Data**

Wollstonecraft, Mary, 1759-1797
    A vindication of the rights of men ; A vindication of the rights of woman

(Broadview Literary Texts)
Includes bibliographical references and index.
ISBN 1-55111-088-1

1. Human rights.   2. Liberty.   3. Burke, Edmund, 1729?-1797. Reflections on the revolution in France.   4. France – History – Revolution, 1789-1799 – Causes.   5. Women's rights – Great Britain.   6. Women – Education – Great Britain.   7. Women – History – 19th century.   8. Feminism.
I. Macdonald, David Lorne, 1955- .
II. Scherf, Kathleen, 1960-  .   III. Wollstonecraft, Mary, 1759-1797.
Vindication of the rights of woman.   IV. Title.   V. Series.

JC571.W873 1997    323    C97-930849-6

305. 4 (0941)

Broadview Press
Post Office Box 1243, Peterborough, Ontario, Canada K9J 7H5

in the United States of America:
3576 California Road, Orchard Park, NY 14127

in the United Kingdom:
B.R.A.D. Book Representation & Distribution Ltd.,
244A, London Road, Hadleigh, Essex SS7 2DE

Broadview Press is grateful to Professor Eugene Benson for advice on editorial matters for the Broadview Literary Texts series.

Broadview Press gratefully acknowledges the support of the Canada Council, the Ontario Arts Council, and the Ministry of Canadian Heritage.

Book design by George Kirkpatrick

PRINTED IN CANADA

# Contents

# Acknowledgements

We are grateful to the Clarendon Press of Oxford University Press for permission to quote from Edmund Burke's *Reflections on the Revolution in France* (Appendix A.4), edited by L.G. Mitchell and William B. Todd, in volume 8 (1989) of *The Writings and Speeches of Edmund Burke*, general editor Paul Langford. We are grateful to Wollstonecraft's previous editors – Miriam Brody, Ulrich H. Hardt, Richard Holmes, Gary Kelly, Carol Poston, Janet Todd and Marilyn Butler, Sylvana Tomaselli, and Ralph M. Wardle – for their readings and annotations, which have often contributed to our own.

We would like to thank the many librarians who have assisted us, especially at the University of Calgary and the British Library. Mical Moser was of great assistance in collating texts, doing library searches, reading documents in French, checking our translation of Olympe de Gouges, and helping to compile the index. Roberta Jackson read the introduction and helped to check the final copy. Greg Doran helped to read proofs and checked the references. We are also grateful for the assistance of Bruce Barker-Benfield, James A. Black, Helen Buss, Michael Dewar, Paula Gaber, Bruce Graver, Miriam Y. Holden, Mary Jacobus, Marie Loughlin, Anne McWhir, Jeanne Moskal, Mitzi Myers, David Oakleaf, Donald H. Reiman, Charles E. Robinson, Vivienne Rundle, Goran Stanivukovic, Janis Svilpis, and Ted Underwood.

Our part in this book is dedicated to Roberta Jackson and Dan Silk: "true voluptuousness must proceed from the mind – for what can equal the sensations produced by mutul affection, supported by mutual respect?" (340).

# Introduction

A few years ago, one of the editors of this book gave a lecture on Mary Wollstonecraft at a community centre for senior citizens. Before explaining her ideas, he gave a short sketch of her life, including the well-known story of how, as a girl, she used to sleep on the landing outside her parents' bedroom, so that, if her father flew into one of his drunken rages during the night, she could come between them, and receive on her own body the blows intended for her mother (Godwin 206). At this point, he was interrupted by a small, very elderly, and frail-looking woman, who shouted – who knows from what depth of feeling? – "She should have shot the bastard!" Another year, he taught *A Vindication of the Rights of Woman* in his undergraduate course in Romantic literature. Some students find the book hard going (the main purpose of this edition is to make it more accessible), but it filled one young woman with delight. "This is the best book I ever read!" she exclaimed. "It says that men and women should love each other *for their minds!*" Wollstonecraft is an author whose life and work still speak powerfully to women and men today.

## 1. The Writing of the *Vindications*

Mary Wollstonecraft's two great vindications of human rights were inspired by what seemed to many at the time a moment of unprecedented human possibility (Myers, "Politics" 119). As William Wordsworth would recall in 1805:

> Not favoured spots alone, but the whole Earth,
> The beauty wore of promise – that which sets
> (To take an image which was felt, no doubt,
> Among the bowers of Paradise itself)
> The budding rose above the rose full blown.
> What temper at the prospect did not wake
> To happiness unthought of? (*The Prelude* 10.702-8)[1]

Even contemporaries whose tempers did not wake to unthought-of happiness at the prospect agreed about its global significance. In 1790, Edmund Burke reflected: "It looks to me as if I were in a great crisis, not of the affairs of France alone but of all Europe, perhaps of more than Europe. All circumstances taken together, the French revolution is the most astonishing that has hitherto happened in the world" (*Writings* 8: 60; see below, 82n).

For British radicals, this moment of opportunity seems to have begun in earnest with the campaign to abolish the Atlantic slave trade. (The American Revolution, though inspiring, does not seem to have had quite the same impact: it was a revolution of which even Edmund Burke could approve.) The Society for Effecting the Abolition of the Slave Trade was founded in 1787; its famous slogan – "Am I not a man and a brother?" – emphasized the universality of its claims. As a writer, Wollstonecraft lent the campaign her support; for example, she wrote a favourable review of *The Interesting Narrative of the Life of Olaudah Equiano, or Gustavus Vassa, the African* (1789; see Appendix A.1) for the *Analytical Review*, pointing out that Equiano's account of "the treatment of male and female slaves, on the voyage, and in the West Indies, ... make[s] the blood turn its course" (*Works* 7: 100-1).[2] In *A Vindication of the Rights of Men*, she repeatedly denounced the slave trade as an abuse of the property rights that conservatives like Burke were anxious to protect (44, 86), vividly described the sufferings it entailed – "Hell stalks abroad; – the lash resounds on the slave's naked sides; and the sick wretch, who can no longer earn the sour bread of unremitting labour, steals to a ditch to bid the world a long good night" (95-96,) – and called on Parliament to abolish it (86-87). She returned to the subject in *A Vindication of the Rights of Woman*, extending the concept boldly to the relations between men and women (see Macdonald), and arguing that "slavery will have its constant effect, degrading the master and the abject dependent" (104).

The apogee of the moment of opportunity – the inspiration of Wordsworth's rhapsody and Burke's diatribe – was the early phase of the French Revolution. British radicals welcomed this event both as a belated equivalent of Britain's own Glorious Revolution, almost exactly one hundred years earlier, and as an unprecedented new beginning.[3] Radical thinking about the new beginning tended to focus on the *Declaration Of The Rights Of Men And Of Citizens* promulgated by the National Assembly in 1789 (Appendix A.2). When Wollstonecraft's mentor, the Presbyterian minister and scientist Richard Price, composed a sermon for the Revolution Society – that is, the society dedicated to commemorating the Glorious Revolution of 1688 – on 4 November 1789, he clearly had the French Revolution in mind. Although he published his sermon as *A Discourse on the Love of Our Country* (Appendix A.3), he argued that this love should be tempered with the "UNIVERSAL BENEVOLENCE" taught by Christ, "which is an unspeakably nobler principle than any partial affections" such as patriotism (358). Like Wordsworth and Burke, he saw the Revolution as an event of global significance; in a passage that gave great offense to Burke, he compared himself, an aging radical contemplating the nascent Revolution, to the aged Simeon contemplating the infant Christ: "What an eventful period is this! I am thankful that I have lived to it; and I could almost say, *Lord, now lettest thou thy servant depart in peace, for mine eyes have seen thy salvation*" (370; Luke 2: 29-30). Wollstonecraft praised Price's sermon, in the *Analytical Review*, for "breath[ing] the animated sentiments of ardent virtue in a simple, unaffected, nay, even negligent style" (*Works* 7: 185-87).

Price received a more famous, and more critical, review on 1 November 1790. Burke's magisterial *Reflections on the Revolution in France* (Appendix A.4) is, in part, a critique of *A Discourse on the Love of Our Country*. Wollstonecraft's reply, *A Vindication of the Rights of Men*, is, in part, a vindication of Richard Price.

Wollstonecraft read the *Reflections* upon its publication; she was infuriated by this attack on the principles she had so fervently embraced. Encouraged by her publisher, Joseph Johnson (another mentor), she immediately sat down to compose a reply to Burke. She wrote quickly and passionately, stalled only by a "temporary fit of torpor and indolence" (Godwin 230), during which she entertained doubts about publishing her reply. She confessed these doubts to Johnson, who did not press her to finish if it would cause her discomfort, even though half the sheets were already printed. Johnson was acutely aware of the topicality of Wollstonecraft's reply to Burke, and he was eager to have it in print as soon as possible (as individual manuscript sheets were completed, he had them set, printed, and corrected), so that his indulgence was a generous one. Wollstonecraft, buoyed by his understanding and confidence, completed the work, and only a few weeks after the appearance of Burke's *Reflections*, Johnson published the first edition of *A Vindication of the Rights of Men* – one of the first responses to Burke (Wardle 111-12). The title page did not bear the author's name.

The first edition appeared in early December 1790; the second, this time credited to Wollstonecraft, on 14 December. Wollstonecraft made the corrections for the second edition on the sheets for the first; had there been more time, she would have been able to publish a single "correct" edition, but both Johnson and Wollstonecraft were keen to capitalize on the controversy aroused by Burke's book. According to Gerald P. Tyson, "Only six weeks elapsed from the appearance of Burke's *Reflections* in November to the second 'corrected' edition of Wollstonecraft's answer" (126).[4]

The reviews were divided, predictably, along party lines (see Appendix D.1). Johnson's own *Analytical Review* praised it, of course; so did the *English Review*, the *Monthly Review*, and the *New Annual Register*. The conservative *Critical Review*, the *General Magazine*, and the *Gentleman's Magazine* all attacked it, especially for its critique of the class system, which (in the words of the *General Magazine*), threatened to "bring all to the most perfect equality, and, by establishing absolute democracy, annihilate every species of subordination, and introduce anarchy, in the room of order" (Appendix D.1.iv). Burke himself claimed not to have read it (*Correspondence* 6: 214), but his ignorance of her critique of his *Reflections* did not prevent him from describing Wollstonecraft (in 1795) as one of "that Clan of desperate, Wicked, and mischievously ingenious Women, who have brought, or are likely to bring Ruin and shame upon all those that listen to them" (*Correspondence* 8: 304).

Almost all the reviews (including Burke's remark) have one striking feature in common: they all comment on a woman's venturing to write in the most emphatically masculine genre of all, the political treatise (see Poovey 56-57). The *Analytical Review*, noting the appearance both of the first *Vindication* and of Catharine Macaulay Graham's *Observations on the Reflections of the Right Hon. Edmund Burke* (1790), remarked: "how deeply must it wound the feelings of a *chivalrous knight*, who owes the fealty of 'proud submission and dignified obedience' to the fair sex, to perceive that two of the boldest of his adversaries are women!" (Appendix D.1.i). The *English Review* conceded that "The language may be thought by some too bold and pointed for a female pen; but when women undertake to write on masculine subjects, and reason as Miss Wollstonecraft does, we wish their language to be free from all female *prettinesses*, and to express with energy and perspicuity, the ideas they mean to convey" (Appendix D.1.iii). The *Critical Review*, which reviewed the anonymous first edition, had to add a last-minute footnote, excusing its error – "It has been observed in an old play, that minds have no sex; and in truth we did not discover this Defender of the Rights of *Man* to be a *Woman*" – and apologizing because "a Lady should have been addressed with more respect" (Appendix D.1.ii). The *General Magazine* complained that "The title and subject of this lady's performance have furnished the prurient wags, who feed the public mind, by diurnal lucubrations, with many a clumsy jest, and many a pointless sarcasm," and worried that "These jokes, low, lascivious, and poor as they are, may have helped to sell the pamphlet" (Appendix D.1.iv). The *Gentleman's Magazine* indulged in jests and sarcasms of precisely this kind: "T H E *rights of men* asserted by a fair lady! The age of chivalry cannot be over, or the sexes have changed their ground.... We should be sorry to raise a horse-laugh against a fair lady; but we were always taught to suppose that the *rights of women* were the proper theme of the female sex" (Appendix D.1.v). It is not hard to imagine that these responses to the first *Vindication* helped to inspire the second.

As Wollstonecraft herself insists ("I plead for my sex – not for myself" [101]), the inspiration of *A Vindication of the Rights of Woman* was not primarily personal. If the first *Vindication* was a response to Burke's *Reflections*, the second was a response to the *Rapport sur l'instruction publique* presented to the National Assembly by Charles-Maurice de Talleyrand-Périgord (1754-1838) in September 1791 (Appendix B.1), and particularly to Talleyrand's admission: "One half of the human race excluded by the other from all participation in government; persons native in fact and foreign in law in the land which nevertheless saw their birth; landowners without direct influence and without representation: those are political phenomena which, on abstract principles, it seems impossible to explain" (Talleyrand 118; see below, 103). The *Declaration of the Rights of Men* had been precisely that – no more (Schröder 263-65).[5] The refusal of the Revolution to extend those rights to women was a betrayal of the abstract (in Talleyrand's terms) or universal (in our terms) principles on which it was founded. (In fact, women lost under the Revolution some of the gains they had made during the ancien régime [Kates xix-xx, 273].)

Wollstonecraft was not the only feminist to make this point. In 1790, Marie-Jean de Caritat, marquis de Condorcet (1743-94), the famous mathematician, member of the Académie Française, and perpetual secretary of the Académie Royale des Sciences, published his essay "On the Admission of Women to the Rights of Citizenship." In 1791, the novelist and playwright Olympe de Gouges (1748-93) published *The Rights of Woman*. There is no evidence that Wollstonecraft was familiar with either work, but Gouges's pamphlet, especially, has some fascinating points of contact with the second *Vindication*. It is dedicated to Marie Antoinette (in tones very different from Burke's rhapsodies over the injured queen); it stresses the importance of education and enhanced professional opportunities for women; it compares the positions of women and slaves and analyses the corrupting effects of arbitrary power. For these reasons, and because it has never, so far as we know, been translated in its entirety,[6] we have included it here (Appendix A.5) – including even its postscript, a denunciation of Parisian taxi-drivers, which gives a vivid picture of the frustrations faced by a woman of letters in Revolutionary France. Both Condorcet and Gouges perished in the Terror: Condorcet poisoned himself in prison, much to the delight of Edmund Burke (*Correspondence* 8: 304); and Gouges, who had argued, "woman has the right to mount the scaffold; she should equally have the right to mount the Tribune," went to the guillotine. The *Feuille du salut public* commented on her death: "She wanted to be a statesman, and it seems the law has punished this conspiratress for having forgotten the virtues befitting her sex" (Woshinsky 1).

Wollstonecraft was well qualified to respond to Talleyrand's report: she had run a school and worked as a governess; she had published an educational treatise (*Thoughts on the Education of Daughters*, 1787), a book of children's stories (*Original Stories*, 1788), and an educational anthology (*The Female Reader*, 1789). In November 1790, she had reviewed *Letters on Education* (Appendix B.2), by Catharine Macaulay Graham (1731-91), praising it enthusiastically but concluding on a muted note that it "displays a degree of sound reason and profound thought which either through defective organs, or a mistaken education, seldom appears in female productions" (*Works* 7: 321-22). By 1792, she had decided that the second cause was responsible; Johnson's *Analytical Review* described the second *Vindication*, accordingly, as "an elaborate *treatise* of *female education*" (Appendix D.2.i).

On 6 October 1791, Wollstonecraft wrote to William Roscoe that she was working on a book (*Letters* 203); she wrote to him again on 3 January 1792 that she had been "very much engrossed by writing and printing my vindication of the Rights of Woman.... I shall give the last sheet to the printer to day" (205). *A Vindication of the Rights of Woman* must have been printed the same way as her previous *Vindication*; Wollstonecraft's January letter to Roscoe continues "I intend to finish the next volume before I begin to print, for it is not pleasant to have the Devil coming for the conclusion of a sheet before it is written" (206).[7] As with the first *Vindication*, Wollstonecraft must have handed in manuscript sheets and received printed sheets to correct. By February 1792, the book was in circulation throughout the British Isles. It was translated into French, and three American editions appeared between 1792 and 1794. Wollstonecraft and her book became so well known that Johnson brought out a revised second edition later in 1792 – not much later: there exists at least one copy (Goldsmith 15366) combining the preliminaries of the first edition and the body of the second, suggesting that composition and revision might have overlapped.

The first reviews appeared in March. Wollstonecraft had learned from the negative reviews of the first *Vindication*; the second is in some ways even more radical than the first, but she took care to moderate its rhetoric, and its reviews were almost unanimously favourable (see Appendix D.2). Modern critics sometimes assume that the second *Vindication* was greeted with a storm of outrage; they may be thinking of the outrage that followed her death in 1797, and the publication of her husband's *Memoirs of the Author of a Vindication of the Rights of Woman* in 1798. Godwin described her life, including her love affair with Gilbert Imlay, her suicide attempts, and her agonizing death, with great dignity but also with utter frankness; reactionary critics pounced. Perhaps the most revolting was Richard Polwhele, who declared (anonymously):

> she was given up to her "heart's lusts," and let "to follow her own imaginations," that the fallacy of her doctrines and the effects of an irreligious conduct, might be manifested to the world; and ... she died a death that strongly marked the distinction of the sexes, by pointing out the destiny of women, and the diseases to which they are liable.... (29-30)

Polwhele's tirade ironically recalls the obituary on Gouges in the revolutionary *Feuille du salut public*. But the disastrous reception of Godwin's *Memoirs* in the reactionary climate of 1798 should not be allowed to obscure the success of the *Vindication* in the last days of the moment of opportunity. (In February 1793, France declared war on Britain, and the moment was over.)

The one negative review, in the *Critical Review*, is unpleasant enough, though its actual arguments, as R.M. Janes points out, are tellingly feeble (296-97). It begins by arguing that Wollstonecraft has unwittingly subjected the radical cause to a *reductio ad absurdum*: "reasoning on the boasted principles of the Rights of Man, she finds they lead very clearly to the object of her work, a Vindication of the Rights of Woman; and, by the absurdity of many of her conclusions, shows, while we admit the reasoning, that the premises must be, in some respects, fallacious" (Appendix D.2.ii). Two contemporary parodies made the same point even more blatantly: *A Sketch of the Rights of Boys and Girls*, by "Launcelot Light and Laetitia Lookabout," and *A Vindication of the Rights of Brutes* (anonymous, but attributed to Thomas Taylor) sarcastically suggested that if the rights of men were to be extended to women, they might as well be extended to children, and even to animals. Taylor concludes:

> It only now remains (and this must be the province of some abler hand) to demonstrate the same great truth in a similar manner, of vegetables, minerals, and even the most apparently

contemptible clod of earth; that thus this sublime theory being copiously and accurately discussed, and its truth established by an indisputable series of facts, government may be entirely subverted, subordination abolished, and all things every where, and in every respect, be common to all. (103)

One can only hope that the pseudonymous Light and Lookabout, and the anonymous Taylor, are turning in their unmarked graves now that we have well-organized movements for the rights of children and animals. And yet, in an important sense, they were right: the insistence of feminists like Wollstonecraft and Gouges that the revolutionaries take seriously their own universalist claims is partly responsible for the rise of these modern movements;[8] it is partly responsible for our current sense, so uncannily and so unwittingly anticipated by Taylor, that we share a planet of limited resources with a wide variety of living creatures, all of which need to be treated with respect if we are to survive. If we do survive, Wollstonecraft will be partly responsible.[9]

## 2. A Reading of the *Vindications*

The two *Vindications* differ in emphasis, as their different titles suggest. The first is concerned with *men* (and women), in society, and with the relations between different classes. Written and published within a month of the appearance of Burke's *Reflections*, it is a work of practical politics, an intervention in what Marilyn Butler has called the Revolution Controversy. The second *Vindication* is concerned with *woman* (and man), in the abstract. It is a work of psychological and metaphysical (or, as Wollstonecraft's subtitle calls it, "moral"), as well as political, theory. In the first *Vindication*, Wollstonecraft habitually refers to her "fellow-citizens"; in the second, to her "fellow-creatures."

This difference is only one of emphasis. The arguments of the two works overlap to a substantial extent; and to the extent that they do differ, they complement each other. *A Vindication of the Rights of Men* is already centrally concerned with the rights of women. As Mitzi Myers ("Politics" 119-20) and Harriet Devine Jump (60) have pointed out, Wollstonecraft is at least as concerned with the attitudes underlying Burke's arguments as with the specifics of those arguments; and

she subjects those attitudes to two interrelated critiques: "the socioe-
conomic and the moral-aesthetic" (Myers, "Politics" 120-21). As Virginia Sapiro has pointed out (200), Wollstonecraft is aware not only
that Burke discusses the Revolution in highly gendered terms, but
that his discussion is shaped throughout by the aesthetic categories
developed in his famous earlier book, *A Philosophical Enquiry into the
Origin of our Ideas of the Sublime and Beautiful* (1757), categories that are
themselves highly gendered (cf. Paulson 81-84). The sublime is masculine; the beautiful, feminine; the sublime is associated with power,
and it inspires respect, admiration, and even fear; the beautiful is associated with weakness, and it inspires love. "There is a wide difference
between admiration and love. The sublime, which is the cause of the
former, always dwells on great objects, and terrible; the latter on small
ones, and pleasing; we submit to what we admire, but we love what
submits to us" (Burke, *Philosophical Enquiry* 103). Wollstonecraft begins
her argument, accordingly, by redefining Burke's terms, making them
less gendered and more equal: "truth, in morals, has ever appeared to
me the essence of the sublime; and, in taste, simplicity the only criterion of the beautiful" (35). Halfway through the book, they have
become not just equal but virtually identical: "simplicity [that is, the
beautiful] ... in works of taste, is but a synonymous word for truth
[that is, the sublime]" (61; Sapiro 200). This identification allows Wollstonecraft to combine beauty with conventionally masculine qualities,
to "prove that there is a beauty in virtue, a charm in order" (81), just
as, in the second *Vindication*, she combines such feminine qualities as
"Gentleness of manners, forbearance and long-suffering" with the
sublime (143).

Such a combination of the masculine and the feminine would
have horrified Burke, who characterizes the women of Paris, who
marched on Versailles on 5 October 1789, as androgynous monsters
who had taken on the masculine terrors of the sublime, "the horrid
yells, and shrilling screams, and frantic dances, and infamous contumelies, and all the unutterable abominations of the furies of hell, in
the abused shape of the vilest of women" (*Writings* 8: 122; Appendix
A.4.i). Claudia L. Johnson suggests that Burke actually downplays the
importance of the women in this passage (38-39); that is not the
impression of Wollstonecraft, who singles out the passage for criti-

cism, particularly on the basis of its class snobbery: "Probably you mean women who gained a livelihood by selling vegetables or fish, who never had had any advantages of education" (62; cf. Paulson 80-81). But she also realizes that his celebration of the beauty of womanhood – his famous praise of Marie Antoinette – is actually a form of degradation. In fact, it is the form of degradation with which the second *Vindication* is centrally concerned (Paulson 84).

Burke's homage is degrading because it is based on rank and physical attractiveness, and "The respect ... which is paid to wealth and mere personal charms, is a true north-east blast, that blights the tender blossoms of affection and virtue" (278). The respect paid to wealth is degrading because it places women in a false position – on a pedestal – which effectively isolates them and denies them what Wollstonecraft considers the essential opportunity for self-improvement: "A king is always a king – and a woman always a woman: his authority and her sex, ever stand between them and rational converse" (171-72). Wollstonecraft's concern with the degrading consequences of rank explains one of the differences between the two *Vindications*: in the first, she speaks movingly of the hardships of men and women of the working class – for example, the women who marched on Versailles; in the second, she argues that working-class women are, in some ways, better off than their social superiors:

> With respect to virtue, to use the word in a comprehensive sense, I have seen most in low life. Many poor women maintain their children by the sweat of their brow, and keep together families that the vices of the fathers would have scattered abroad; but gentlewomen are too indolent to be actively virtuous, and are softened rather than refined by civilization. (196)

The respect paid to beauty is even worse than that paid to rank, because it is based on purely physical attributes, and so it not only leads women to over-value their bodies, but actually affects their minds: "Taught from their infancy that beauty is woman's sceptre, the mind shapes itself to the body, and, roaming round its gilt cage, only seeks to adorn its prison" (157). This process is what we would now call the social construction of gender; it is the way that "females ... are made women of" (245-46): Wollstonecraft distinguishes clearly between sex and gender, "females" and "women," and insists that women are made, not born (Jump 73). She has some harsh things to say about women in the second *Vindication*; she admits that she is as hard on them as "the severest satirist"; but always as a protest at what has been made of them. If they are "the weakest as well as the most oppressed half of the species" (145), their weakness is a product of their oppression, not a justification of it (Kelly 108). As Myers points out, some of the specifics of Wollstonecraft's programme (e.g., her demands for coeducation, economic independence, wider professional opportunities, civil and political rights) still seem progressive, while some of her concessions (e.g., that most women's most important roles will remain domestic and maternal) now seem conservative ("Reform" 206-7). Her critique of the social construction of gender remains radical, in the strict sense: it goes to the root of the matter.

The confinement of women to the physical is a denial of what Wollstonecraft considers their fundamental right. She derives her concept of natural rights from the concept of a just and reasonable God; Gary Kelly argues that a paragraph linking her respect for rights and her fear of God (66) is "the central passage in the [first] *Vindication*" (Kelly 96), and the idea is equally central to the second. In this, Wollstonecraft follows Locke, but there is a significant difference between their arguments. According to Locke, human beings have rights because they have duties: they are "the Servants of one Sovereign Master, sent into the World by his order and about his business" (*Two Treatises* 289), and no-one may rightfully interfere with that business. Although Wollstonecraft frequently refers to the relationship between rights and duties (101, 282, 284), her central argument is that human beings have rights because they have immortal souls, and their central right is to improve those souls:

> if woman be allowed to have an immortal soul, she must have, as the employment of life, an understanding to improve. And when, to render the present state more complete, though every thing proves it to be but a fraction of a mighty sum, she is incited by present gratification to forget her grand destination, nature is counteracted, or she was born only to procreate and rot. (180)

Wollstonecraft's protest against the confinement of women to the physical is associated, as Poovey has pointed out, with a certain suspicion of sexuality; in denying that women are "born only to procreate and rot," Wollstonecraft sometimes seems to want to deny that they are sexual beings at all (Poovey 74-77; cf. Johnson 41-43, Paulson 85).[10] Moreover, as Myers puts it, "her ultimate frame of reference is non-secular" ("Reform" 205): her argument is otherworldly in a way that sometimes distracts her from her concern with the condition of women in this world: "the only hopes worth cherishing" are hopes for the afterlife, for which this "life is merely an education" (236). She does not, however, simply dismiss this world; she insists that "Men will not become moral when they only build airy castles in a future world to compensate for the disappointments which they meet with in this; if they turn their thoughts from relative duties to religious reveries" (242). The first *Vindication* makes the point more emphatically, describing Burke's suggestion that the poor should seek consolation in the thought of heaven for their sufferings on earth as "contemptible hard hearted sophistry," and telling him firmly: "It is, Sir, *possible* to render the poor happier in this world, without depriving them of the consolation which you gratuitously grant them in the next" (92). Ideally, for Wollstonecraft, the claims of the two worlds are in harmony, and "the plan of life which enables us to carry some knowledge and virtue into another world, is the one best calculated to ensure content in this" (227).

This point is not always clear to modern readers. Even Virginia Sapiro, in *A Vindication of Political Virtue* (1992), one of the best books on Wollstonecraft, though she mentions Wollstonecraft's views on immortality (50), comes to the conclusion that *A Vindication of the Rights of Woman*, despite its title, is not primarily about rights at all (118): Wollstonecraft, according to Sapiro, "rarely discussed legal rights and privileges without drawing the focus to their impact on the development of virtue" (119). Yet Wollstonecraft insists that the development of virtue is the most important right of all, indeed the only really fundamental right; and even readers who do not share her belief that it is a preparation for the next world should be able to respect her insistence that women have a right to the development of virtue – or, as we might put it, to the greatest possible fulfilment of their potential as human beings (Myers, "Politics" 119).

A certain ambivalence is among Wollstonecraft's most striking characteristics as a political thinker. As Sapiro points out, she belongs to both the Lockean and the republican tradition (xx); she recognizes the claims of both reason and passion (xxi); and she argues on grounds both of rights and of utility (85-86).

She also presents herself as the antagonist both of Burke (in the first *Vindication*) and of Rousseau (in the second). It would be hard to imagine a political writer of the eighteenth century picking two more important – or more different – targets (Johnson 32; Kelly 126; Paulson 62-65). Moreover, Wollstonecraft is ambivalent about both of them. She continues her critique of Burke's aesthetics in *Letters Written during a Short Residence in Sweden, Norway, and Denmark* (1796), but at the same time, her experience of the Scandinavian landscape continues to be shaped by those aesthetics. She deplores Rousseau's account of the development of women, but she largely endorses his account of the development of men, in order to "extend it to women" (Sapiro 282-83); above all, she values him as an "energetic advocate for immortality" (120).

Wollstonecraft was also ambivalent about the literary movement she helped to inaugurate; the reflections on the Romantic imagination that are scattered through the second *Vindication* correspond to the critique of the politics of representation in the first. It was not until the Victorian period that the writing of her own period was called "Romantic." Wollstonecraft herself, like most of her contemporaries, tends to use the word pejoratively; in the first *Vindication*, she defines it as referring to "false, or rather artificial, feelings" (61), and she complains that Burke has "inflame[d his] imagination, instead of enlightening [his] understanding" (37; cf. Boulton 168-69). In the second, she argues that "a romantic kind of delicacy" made Rousseau "practise self-denial" instead of satisfying his sexual appetite, with the result that "he debauched his imagination, and reflecting on the sensations to which fancy gave force, he traced them in the most glowing colours, and sunk them deep into his soul" (214). This treats Rousseau's imagination as primarily, though not entirely, the venue of his masturbatory fantasies. Other passages about the imagination, though still ambivalent, place the emphasis on its positive potential.[11]

In a discussion of the benefits of deluded ambition, she argues:

> the very excess of these blind impulses, pampered by that lying, yet constantly trusted guide, the imagination, ... [by] preparing them for some other state, render[s] short-sighted mortals wiser without their own concurrence; or, what comes to the same thing, when they were pursuing some imaginary present good. (237)

Despite its lying and pampering, then, the imagination helps prepare us for the other world; this anticipates Wordsworth's claim, in the great apostrophe to the imagination in *The Prelude*, that it gives us the sense that

> Our destiny, our nature, and our home
> Is with infinitude, and only there;
> With hope it is, hope that can never die,
> Effort, and expectation, and desire,
> And something evermore about to be. (6.538-42)

Kelly argues that the technique of Wollstonecraft's *Letters Written During a Short Residence in Sweden, Norway, and Denmark* (1796) "prefigures the method of Wordsworth's 'Tintern Abbey'" (187); but the *Vindication* already prefigures Wordsworth. The Romantic sublime may be a fundamentally masculine mode (Jump 124), but it is not one that this Romantic feminist denies herself.

If Wollstonecraft's sense of the metaphysical ends of the imagination is Wordsworthian (or vice versa), her sense of its operations is Coleridgean (or vice versa); it is a power that "struggles to idealize and to unify," to create artworks that are organic wholes (Coleridge 167). The great sculptors of classical Greece may have combined the physical features of many different models in a single statue, but because of "the ebullition of an heated fancy ... a whole was produced – a model of that grand simplicity, of those concurring energies, which arrest our attention and command our reverence" (314-15). Artworks not informed by the imagination (which, conventionally for the eighteenth century but confusingly for us post-Coleridgeans,

Wollstonecraft tends to call the "fancy") are like the products of what Coleridge calls the fancy, which "has no other counters to play with but fixities and definites" (Coleridge 167). Thus Wollstonecraft complains about "the studied attitudes of some modern pictures, copied with tasteless servility after the antiques; – the soul is left out, and none of the parts are tied together by what may properly be termed character" (223) – or by what Coleridge might term the imagination.

Wollstonecraft's sense of poets as heroes, and benefactors of humanity, is similarly Romantic: "These are the glowing minds that concentrate pictures for their fellow-creatures; forcing them to view with interest the objects reflected from the impassioned imagination, which they passed over in nature." The reason that humanity needs its poets is that "The generality of people cannot see or feel poetically, they want fancy"; that is, they lack imagination; "but when an author lends them his eyes they can see as he saw, and be amused by images they could not select, though lying before them" (245). This anticipates both Wordsworth's claim that the *Lyrical Ballads* "choose incidents and situations from common life, and ... throw over them a certain colouring of imagination" (*Poems* 1: 869) in order to "counteract" the "multitude of causes, unknown to former times, [which] are now acting with a combined force to blunt the discriminating powers of the mind" (872-73), and Coleridge's account of the purpose of Wordsworth's poems: "to give the charm of novelty to things of every day, ... by awakening the mind's attention from the lethargy of custom and directing it to the loveliness and the wonders of the world before us; an inexhaustible treasure, but for which, in consequence of the film of familiarity and selfish solicitude, we have eyes yet see not, ears that hear not, and hearts that neither feel nor understand" (169).[12]

Wollstonecraft's favourite poet-heroes are the favourites of the Romantic movement, Shakespeare and Milton (150). She is also, in a typically Romantic (but not stereotypically feminine) way, unembarrassed about assuming the role herself (Kelly 110-11). After outlining her ideas for the reform of the educational system and explaining the effects they are likely to have on students, she exclaims: "My imagination darts forward with benevolent fervour to greet these amiable and respectable groups, in spite of the sneering of cold hearts, who are at liberty to utter, with frigid self-importance, the damning epithet –

romantic" (314).[13] Such a passage suggests the connection between the political and aesthetic arguments of both *Vindications*, and the source of Wollstonecraft's greatness as a political thinker: she had the courage to imagine.[14]

## 3. A Note on the Texts

Wollstonecraft produced the first two editions of each of the *Vindications* in a single burst of creativity; in each case, the first edition served her as a rough draft, which she revised to produce the second. Gary Kelly prefers the first edition of the first *Vindication*, as the text in which Wollstonecraft first found her voice (236–37 n. 8); our impression is that in this edition she was still searching for the voice she found in the second. Wollstonecraft's revisions provide her second edition with better grammar, spelling, and accuracy of quotation; better style; and greater clarity or specificity. They allow her to avoid ambiguity about key concepts; to expand her case; and to substantiate it by adding footnotes identifying quotations from Burke, or containing new quotations. They make her argument more human in focus and use less personification – which, as Wordsworth says in the Preface to *Lyrical Ballads*, amounts to the same thing (*Poems* 1: 873). They make her attack on Burke more personal, but her references to herself less personal, than in the anonymous first edition. Accordingly, we have chosen the second edition as our copytext, emending it only to correct obvious typographical errors.[15]

The differences between the first and second editions of the second *Vindication* are not so extensive, but, as Carol Poston and Janet Todd have pointed out, the revisions not only improve the grammar and style, they also clarify and strengthen Wollstonecraft's feminist message. Johnson issued a third edition in 1796; Ulrich Hardt, who up to this point has carried out the most extensive textual work on *A Vindication of the Rights of Woman*, suggests that Wollstonecraft had nothing to do with the 95 variants (17 substantives, 78 accidentals) he has found between the second and third editions (2). He explains all of them away as compositor's errors in setting type from the second edition. Hardt argues that no textual evidence exists to link Wollstonecraft to the third edition, and furthermore, that "it would have been inconvenient for Mary Wollstonecraft to oversee the printing of the 1796 edition" (3), since she was busy with her travels and suicide attempts. It is true that 1795 was not a good year for Wollstonecraft, but 1796 was much better – she published *Letters Written During a Short Residence in Sweden, Norway, and Denmark*, began her affair with Godwin, and conceived her second child. While we agree that many of the variants between the second and third editions seem to be compositor's errors, this is not so obviously the case with all of them. A number change the reading of the second edition back to that of the first, as though undoing revisions – or correcting compositor's errors – in the second. And the removal of the words "VOL. I" from the title page and "END OF THE FIRST VOLUME" from the last page is obviously an acknowledgement that the second volume was never going to appear. Moreover, there is also no textual evidence proving Wollstonecraft had *nothing* to do with the printing and publication of the third edition. Her letters through 1795 indicate that she endured financial hardship during this period of her life; she would have surely welcomed and perhaps participated in the republication of her best-known work. In any case, the 1796 third edition was the last publication of *A Vindication of the Rights of Woman* which appeared during Wollstonecraft's life, and so it is the last with any claim to authority. Whether or not Wollstonecraft was involved in the production of the third edition, however, it is clearly an afterthought; like all other Wollstonecraft scholars, we have based our edition on the second.[16]

Hardt's edition of the second *Vindication* is guided by the strict principles of the Greg-Bowers school of scientific scholarly editing. He takes the first edition as his copytext in order to preserve the integrity of authorial accidentals, and splices in substantive variants from the second edition, which he regards as the last of the editions to display authorial intent. He has produced, therefore, a classic Greg-Bowers eclectic text, one which Wollstonecraft never wrote, but which Donald S. Taylor, in his Foreword to Hardt's text, describes as "as close as we are likely to get to the text of *A Vindication* that she would have wished to be final" (vii). Hardt's text is also, apparently, "clearly more faithful to the author's intentions than any single previous edition – even the two 1792 editions in which, on his showing,

Wollstonecraft had an active part" (vii–viii).

We do not wish to rehearse here the arguments against "ideal" texts and the impossibility of assessing authorial intent; such arguments have been well-documented over the past twenty years. Unlike Hardt, however, we claim no definitive knowledge of Wollstonecraft's final intentions for her text; indeed, the speed of writing, the carelessness of the correcting and printing process – in which she was completely immersed from September 1791 to January 1792 – and her documented intention to write a second volume (*Letters* 206) indicate to us that she herself was probably unsure of what her final intentions were. The character and tone of *A Vindication of the Rights of Woman* do not readily reflect any vision of a "final" intention, as the book's flavour is that of an immediate and urgent response. Our copytext is the second edition Wollstonecraft actually saw through the press, not an ideal construction; we have emended it (with reference to the other editions) only to correct obvious typographical errors.[17]

In our copytexts, quotations are usually, but not consistently, enclosed in single quotation marks; we have used double quotation marks throughout, in accordance with Broadview's house style. In the first *Vindication*, footnotes are indicated by superscript letters; in the second, by asterisks, daggers, etc. We have used superscript numbers throughout, in accordance with Broadview's house style. Editorial footnotes are distinguished from Wollstonecraft's own by being enclosed in square brackets.

In our footnotes, we have identified as many of Wollstonecraft's quotations and allusions as we could, though no doubt we have also missed many. As recently as 1979, Ralph Wardle could say:

> Obviously Mary Wollstonecraft was an avid reader, but she was no scholar. The current of new and fresh ideas that she encountered at Johnson's shop seems not to have inspired her to any very thorough investigation of the seminal works in the areas she was exploring.... When she cited an authority ... she usually did so only to reject his theories wholesale. (Wollstonecraft, *Collected Letters* 39)

Wollstonecraft was certainly denied the advantages of a formal education, but she was proud of the education she had managed to give herself, and she was not averse to showing it off. Her presentation of herself as learned might even be described as a part of her feminist argument – a demonstration that a woman could acquire, and use, learning, even under the unfavourable circumstances of the 1790s. Her knowledge of the authors she cites is more extensive, and her dialogue with them is more complex and subtle, than Wardle gives her credit for. We hope that this edition will make the essentially dialogical quality of her work accessible to modern readers.

## Notes

1.  In its context in *The Prelude*, this passage actually refers to Thermidor; but Wordsworth also published it separately under the title "French Revolution As It Appeared to Enthusiasts at Its Commencement" (*Poems* 1: 636-37).

2.  In their Prefatory Note to Wollstonecraft's "Contributions to the *Analytical Review* 1788-1797," Janet Todd and Marilyn Butler, the editors of her *Works*, note that the attribution of reviews in the *Analytical* must be speculative, since they are either "anonymous or signed with initials." Todd and Butler explain their principles of attribution clearly and cogently (*Works* 7: 14-18), and it seems impossible, in the short term, to improve on them, so we have followed them.

    Unfortunately, Todd and Butler's edition, which is indispensable and should be definitive, is not textually reliable. In *A Vindication of the Rights of Men*, for example, they print "the silent majesty of misery" (47) as "the silent majority of misery" (*Works* 5: 17), apparently because of a memory of the Nixon years; "the common stock" (85) as "the common flock" (5: 49), apparently because of a misreading of the long *s*; and "exalts the man above his fellows" (98) as "exalts the man above his elbows" (5: 60), for no apparent reason.

3.  Reactions to the Revolution were various, even among radicals. For good surveys, see Boulton, *The Language of Politics in the Age of Wilkes and Burke* 75-96, and Butler, *Burke, Paine, Godwin, and the Revolution Controversy*.

4. Unfortunately, Mary Wollstonecraft did not keep a journal, or if she did, it has disappeared. The absence of her journal, combined with the destruction of Joseph Johnson's publishing records, makes precise dating of her drafts impossible. However, through her letters, the records of variants generated by textual collation, and, to a lesser extent, Godwin's memoir, editors have been able to identify the order of versions for both *Vindications*.

5. Even the Abolition movement seemed more concerned, at least in its rhetoric, with men and brothers than with women and sisters.

6. Most of it is available in Darline Gay Levy, Harriet Branson Applewhite, and Mary Durham Johnson, eds., *Women in Revolutionary Paris 1789-1795: Selected Documents Translated with Notes and Commentary* (Urbana: U of Illinois P, 1979) 87-96.

7. A "devil" is a printer's assistant. Wollstonecraft's surviving notes for the second volume are in Appendix C.

8. Wollstonecraft's own universalism has its limits, of course, as her disparaging references to Islam, for example, suggest.

9. See Jonathan Bate, *Romantic Ecology: Wordsworth and the Environmental Tradition* (London: Routledge, 1991), and Keith Thomas, *Man and the Natural World: A History of the Modern Sensibility* (New York: Pantheon Books, 1983) 50, 172, 301-2.

10. Jump speculates that Wollstonecraft's attitude towards sexuality was affected by her desire to establish a Platonic relationship with the married artist Henry Fuseli (66-67).

11. The *Vindication* is also an imaginative work in the sense that Wollstonecraft frequently supports her argument with exemplary anecdotes, like the tale of the two widows (161-65) and the withering satirical portrait of the three daughters (331-32). Myers compares the good widow to Mrs. Mason, the central character of *Original Stories*; Wollstonecraft prepared the second edition of her children's book shortly before beginning the second *Vindication* ("Impeccable Governesses" 40).

12. Similarly, Kelly argues that Wollstonecraft's late essay "On Poetry" (1797) "anticipates the preface to *Lyrical Ballads*" (203; cf. Jump 152-54); but Wordsworth's famous advocacy of "the real language of men" (867) is already anticipated both by Wollstonecraft's advocacy of simplicity of style in the Introduction

to the *Vindication* (109; cf. Conger 93-94, 125) and, in a more complex way, by her critique of the sexist "language of men" in Chapter IV (168).

13. Sure enough, even the sympathetic *Monthly Review* described some of Wollstonecraft's "projects" as "romantic" (see Appendix D.2.iii).

14. For a recent discussion of the politics of the imagination, see Martha C. Nussbaum, *Poetic Justice: The Literary Imagination and Public Life* (Boston: Beacon Press, 1995).

15. We were able to examine (in microfilm) only two copies of the first edition, one housed at the British Library (T.1102[3]), the other in the collection of Miriam Y. Holden. A collation of these two revealed no differences between them, so we believe the first edition text to be stable. Unfortunately, we could examine only one copy of the second edition – our copytext – again housed at the British Library (1486.k.4); readers of the present text should be aware that we have been unable to collate this copy against any others, so that other states of this edition may exist.

16. We collated copies of the first edition at the University of Toronto (D-10/1654 RBSC) and at Smith College, Northampton, Mass.; the Goldsmith College copy (15366) combining the preliminaries (i-xix) of the first and the body (1-452) of the second edition; a British Library copy (C.133.e.7) and a Goldsmith copy (15367) of the second edition; and a British Library copy (Cup.403.w.16) of the third.

17. This includes a missing word ("to") in the last line of the second poem by Barbauld quoted on page 168; since it was present in the first edition, we consider its omission from the second an obvious error.

# Mary Wollstonecraft: A Brief Chronology

1756: marriage of Edward John Wollstonecraft (born 1736) and Elizabeth Dickson (c. 1740).

1757: birth of Edward (Ned) Wollstonecraft.

1759: birth of Mary Wollstonecraft (27 April) in London .

1761: birth of Henry Woodstock Wollstonecraft.

1763: birth of Elizabeth (Eliza) Wollstonecraft.

1765: birth of Everina (Averina) Wollstonecraft.

1768: birth of James Wollstonecraft.

1770: birth of Charles Wollstonecraft.

1775: MW's first meeting with Fanny Blood.

1778: first job, as a paid companion to Mrs. Dawson, in Windsor and Bath.

1780 mother's illness; MW returns home to nurse her.

1782: death of her mother (19 April); MW goes to live with Fanny Blood and family; marriage of Eliza to Meredith Bishop.

1783: birth of Eliza's daughter (10 August?); second job, at MW's own school, in Islington.

1784: postpartum depression of Eliza (January); MW removes Eliza from Bishop's house; school moved to Newington Green; meeting with Richard Price.

1785: marriage of Fanny Blood to Hugh Skeys in Lisbon (February); MW's trip to Lisbon; birth of Fanny Blood Skeys's child (November); death of Fanny Blood Skeys.

1786: return to London; failure of the school; third job, as governess to Kingsborough children in Mitchelstown, Ireland.

1787: publication of her first book, *Thoughts on the Education of Daughters*, by Joseph Johnson; dismissed by Lady Kingsborough in Bristol (August); return to London; fourth job, as translator, reader, reviewer, and editorial assistant for Johnson's *Analytical Review*.

1788: publication of her first novel, *Mary: A Fiction*, her children's book, *Original Stories from Real Life*, and *Of the*

*Importance of Religious Opinions*, her translation from the French of Jacques Necker.

1789: publication of her anthology, *The Female Reader*.

1790: publication of *Young Grandison*, her translation from the Dutch of Maria Geertruida van de Werken de Cambon; writing and publication of *A Vindication of the Rights of Men* (November); temporary adoption of Ann (seven-year-old relative of Hugh Skeys).

1790-91: publication of *Elements of Morality, for the Use of Children*, her translation from the German of Christian Gotthilf Salzmann.

1791: second edition of *Original Stories*; begins writing *A Vindication of the Rights of Woman* (September); meeting with William Godwin (November).

1792: publication of *A Vindication of the Rights of Woman* (January); meeting with Talleyrand (February); planned trip to Paris with Johnson and Henry and Sophia Fuseli; emotional crisis with Henry Fuseli; departure for Paris, alone (December).

1793: meeting with Gilbert Imlay, who registers her at U.S. embassy as his wife; publication of *The Emigrants* (attributed to Imlay, possibly by MW).

1794: birth of MW's first daughter, Fanny, in Le Havre (14 May); publication of *An Historical and Moral View of the Origin and Progress of the French Revolution*.

1795: return to London (April); first suicide attempt (May); journey to Scandinavia (June); return (September); second suicide attempt (October).

1796: publication of *Letters Written During a Short Residence in Sweden, Norway, and Denmark* (January); affair with Godwin.

1797: marriage to Godwin (29 March); birth of second daughter, Mary (30 August); death of MW (10 September).

1798: publication of *Posthumous Works of the Author of a Vindication of the Rights of Woman*, edited by Godwin, and of Godwin's *Memoirs of the Author of a Vindication of the Rights of Woman*.

A

# VINDICATION

OF THE

# RIGHTS OF MEN,

IN A

# LETTER

TO THE RIGHT HONOURABLE

*EDMUND BURKE*;

OCCASIONED BY          .

## HIS REFLECTIONS

ON THE

## REVOLUTION IN FRANCE.

By *MARY WOLLSTONECRAFT.*

THE SECOND EDITION.

# ADVERTISEMENT.

Mr. Burke's Reflections on the French Revolution first engaged my attention as the transient topic of the day; and reading it more for amusement than information, my indignation was roused by the sophistical arguments, that every moment crossed me, in the questionable shape of natural feelings and common sense.

Many pages of the following letter were the effusions of the moment; but, swelling imperceptibly to a considerable size, the idea was suggested of publishing a short vindication of *the Rights of Men*.[1]

Not having leisure or patience to follow this desultory writer through all the devious tracks in which his fancy has started fresh game, I have confined my strictures, in a great measure, to the grand principles at which he has levelled many ingenious arguments in a very specious garb.

---

1   [See Appendix A.2.]

A

# LETTER

TO THE

*Right Honourable EDMUND BURKE.*

SIR,

IT is not necessary, with courtly insincerity, to apologise to you for thus intruding on your precious time, nor to profess that I think it an honour to discuss an important subject with a man whose literary abilities have raised him to notice in the state. I have not yet learned to twist my periods, nor, in the equivocal idiom of politeness, to disguise my sentiments, and imply what I should be afraid to utter: if, therefore, in the course of this epistle, I chance to express contempt, and even indignation, with some emphasis, I beseech you to believe that it is not a flight of fancy; for truth, in morals, has ever appeared to me the essence of the sublime; and, in taste, simplicity the only criterion of the beautiful.[1] But I war not with an individual when I contend for the *rights of men* and the liberty of reason. You see I do not condescend to cull my words to avoid the invidious phrase, nor shall I be prevented from giving a manly definition of it, by the flimsy ridicule which a lively fancy has interwoven with the present acceptation of the term. Reverencing the rights of humanity, I shall dare to assert them; not intimidated by the horse laugh that you have raised, or waiting till time has wiped away the compassionate tears which you have elaborately laboured to excite.

From the many just sentiments interspersed through the letter before me, and from the whole tendency of it, I should believe you to be a good, though a vain man, if some circumstances in your conduct did not render the inflexibility of your integrity doubtful; and for this vanity a knowledge of human nature enables me to discover such

---

1 [Throughout, Wollstonecraft is concerned not only with Burke's *Reflections on the Revolution in France* (1790), but with his *A Philosophical Enquiry into the Origin of our Ideas of the Sublime and the Beautiful* (1757). We cite the 2nd ed. (1759), ed. Adam Phillips (Oxford: Oxford UP, 1990).]

extenuating circumstances, in the very texture of your mind, that I am ready to call it amiable, and separate the public from the private character.

I know that a lively imagination renders a man particularly calculated to shine in conversation and in those desultory productions where method is disregarded; and the instantaneous applause which his eloquence extorts is at once a reward and a spur. Once a wit and always a wit, is an aphorism that has received the sanction of experience; yet I am apt to conclude that the man who with scrupulous anxiety endeavours to support that shining character, can never nourish by reflection any profound, or, if you please, metaphysical passion. Ambition becomes only the tool of vanity, and his reason, the weather-cock of unrestrained feelings, is only employed to varnish over the faults which it ought to have corrected.

Sacred, however, would the infirmities and errors of a good man be, in my eyes, if they were only displayed in a private circle; if the venial fault only rendered the wit anxious, like a celebrated beauty, to raise admiration on every occasion, and excite emotion, instead of the calm reciprocation of mutual esteem and unimpassioned respect. Such vanity enlivens social intercourse, and forces the little great man to be always on his guard to secure his throne; and an ingenious man, who is ever on the watch for conquest, will, in his eagerness to exhibit his whole store of knowledge, furnish an attentive observer with some useful information, calcined by fancy and formed by taste.

And though some dry reasoner might whisper that the arguments were superficial, and should even add, that the feelings which are thus ostentatiously displayed are often the cold declamation of the head, and not the effusions of the heart – what will these shrewd remarks avail, when the witty arguments and ornamental feelings are on a level with the comprehension of the fashionable world, and a book is found very amusing? Even the Ladies, Sir, may repeat your sprightly sallies, and retail in theatrical attitudes many of your sentimental exclamations. Sensibility is the *manie* of the day, and compassion the virtue which is to cover a multitude of vices, whilst justice is left to mourn in sullen silence, and balance truth in vain.

In life, an honest man with a confined understanding is frequently the slave of his habits and the dupe of his feelings, whilst the man with a clearer head and colder heart makes the passions of others bend to his interest; but truly sublime is the character that acts from principle, and governs the inferior springs of activity without slackening their vigour; whose feelings give vital heat to his resolves, but never hurry him into feverish eccentricities.

However, as you have informed us that respect chills love,[1] it is natural to conclude, that all your pretty flights arise from your pampered sensibility; and that, vain of this fancied pre-eminence of organs, you foster every emotion till the fumes, mounting to your brain, dispel the sober suggestions of reason. It is not in this view surprising, that when you should argue you become impassioned, and that reflection inflames your imagination, instead of enlightening your understanding.

Quitting now the flowers of rhetoric, let us, Sir, reason together;[2] and, believe me, I should not have meddled with these troubled waters, in order to point out your inconsistencies, if your wit had not burnished up some rusty, baneful opinions, and swelled the shallow current of ridicule till it resembled the flow of reason, and presumed to be the test of truth.

I shall not attempt to follow you through "horse-way and foot-path;"[3] but, attacking the foundation of your opinions, I shall leave the superstructure to find a centre of gravity on which it may lean till some strong blast puffs it into air; or your teeming fancy, which the ripening judgment of sixty years has not tamed,[4] produces another Chinese erection,[5] to stare, at every turn, the plain country people in the face, who bluntly call such an airy edifice – a folly.

The birthright of man, to give you, Sir, a short definition of this disputed right, is such a degree of liberty, civil and religious, as is compatible with the liberty of every other individual with whom he is united in a social compact, and the continued existence of that compact.[6]

Liberty, in this simple, unsophisticated sense, I acknowledge, is a fair idea that has never yet received a form in the various govern-

---

1   [Burke, *Philosophical Enquiry* 101; 3.10.]
2   [Isaiah 1: 18.]
3   [Shakespeare, *King Lear* 4.1.56.]
4   [Burke was sixty-one.]
5   [A pagoda.]
6   [See the *Declaration of the Rights of Men and of Citizens* iv, Appendix A.2; and Price, *Discourse* 20-21, Appendix A.3.]

ments that have been established on our beauteous globe; the demon of property has ever been at hand to encroach on the sacred rights of men, and to fence round with awful pomp laws that war with justice. But that it results from the eternal foundation of right – from immutable truth – who will presume to deny, that pretends to rationality – if reason has led them to build their morality[1] and religion on an everlasting foundation – the attributes of God?

I glow with indignation when I attempt, methodically, to unravel your slavish paradoxes, in which I can find no fixed first principle to refute; I shall not, therefore, condescend to shew where you affirm in one page what you deny in another; and how frequently you draw conclusions without any previous premises: – it would be something like cowardice to fight with a man who had never exercised the weapons with which his opponent chose to combat, and irksome to refute sentence after sentence in which the latent spirit of tyranny appeared.

I perceive, from the whole tenor of your Reflections, that you have a mortal antipathy to reason; but, if there is any thing like argument, or first principles, in your wild declamation, behold the result: – that we are to reverence the rust of antiquity, and term the unnatural customs, which ignorance and mistaken self-interest have consolidated, the sage fruit of experience: nay, that, if we do discover some errors, our *feelings* should lead us to excuse, with blind love, or unprincipled filial affection, the venerable vestiges of ancient days. These are gothic notions of beauty – the ivy is beautiful, but, when it insidiously destroys the trunk from which it receives support, who would not grub it up?

Further, that we ought cautiously to remain for ever in frozen inactivity, because a thaw, whilst it nourishes the soil, spreads a temporary inundation; and the fear of risking any personal present convenience should prevent a struggle for the most estimable advantages. This is sound reasoning, I grant, in the mouth of the rich and short-sighted.

---

1   As religion is included in my idea of morality, I should not have mentioned the term without specifying all the simple ideas which that comprehensive word generalizes; but as the charge of atheism has been very freely banded about in the letter I am considering, I wish to guard against misrepresentation.

Yes, Sir, the strong gained riches, the few have sacrificed the many to their vices; and, to be able to pamper their appetites, and supinely exist without exercising mind or body, they have ceased to be men. – Lost to the relish of true pleasure, such beings would, indeed, deserve compassion, if injustice was not softened by the tyrant's plea – necessity;[1] if prescription was not raised as an immortal boundary against innovation. Their minds, in fact, instead of being cultivated, have been so warped by education, that it may require some ages to bring them back to nature, and enable them to see their true interest, with that degree of conviction which is necessary to influence their conduct.

The civilization which has taken place in Europe has been very partial, and, like every custom that an arbitrary point of honour has established, refines the manners at the expence of morals, by making sentiments and opinions current in conversation that have no root in the heart, or weight in the cooler resolves of the mind. – And what has stopped its progress? – hereditary property – hereditary honours. The man has been changed into an artificial monster by the station in which he was born, and the consequent homage that benumbed his faculties like the torpedo's touch; – or a being, with a capacity of reasoning, would not have failed to discover, as his faculties unfolded, that true happiness arose from the friendship and intimacy which can only be enjoyed by equals; and that charity is not a condescending distribution of alms, but an intercourse of good offices and mutual benefits, founded on respect for justice and humanity.

Governed by these principles, the poor wretch, whose *inelegant* distress extorted from a mixed feeling of disgust and animal sympathy present relief, would have been considered as a man, whose misery demanded a part of his birthright, supposing him to be industrious; but should his vices have reduced him to poverty, he could only have addressed his fellow-men as weak beings, subject to like passions, who ought to forgive, because they expect to be forgiven, for suffering the impulse of the moment to silence the suggestions of conscience, or reason, which you will; for, in my view of things, they are synonymous terms.

Will Mr. Burke be at the trouble to inform us, how far we are to go back to discover the rights of men, since the light of reason is such

---

1    [Milton, *Paradise Lost* 4.393-94.]

a fallacious guide that none but fools trust to its cold investigation?

In the infancy of society, confining our view to our own country, customs were established by the lawless power of an ambitious individual; or a weak prince was obliged to comply with every demand of the licentious barbarous insurgents, who disputed his authority with irrefragable arguments at the point of their swords; or the more specious requests of the Parliament, who only allowed him conditional supplies.

Are these the venerable pillars of our constitution? And is Magna Charta to rest for its chief support on a former grant, which reverts to another, till chaos becomes the base of the mighty structure – or we cannot tell what? – for coherence, without some pervading principle of order, is a solecism.[1]

Speaking of Edward the IIId. Hume observes, that "he was a prince of great capacity, not governed by favourites, not led astray by any unruly passion, sensible that nothing could be more essential to his interests than to keep on good terms with his people: yet, on the whole, it appears that the government, at best, was only a barbarous monarchy, not regulated by any fixed maxims, or bounded by any certain or undisputed rights, which in practice were regularly observed. The King conducted himself by one set of principles; the Barons by another; the Commons by a third; the Clergy by a fourth. All these systems of government were opposite and incompatible: each of them prevailed in its turn, as incidents were favourable to it: a great prince rendered the monarchical power predominant: the weakness of a king gave reins to the aristocracy: a superstitious age saw the clergy triumphant: the people, for whom chiefly government was instituted, and who chiefly deserve consideration, were the weakest of the whole."[2]

And just before that most auspicious aera, the fourteenth century, during the reign of Richard II. whose total incapacity to manage the reins of power, and keep in subjection his haughty Barons, rendered

---

1 [Burke, *Reflections*; *Writings* 8: 81-82. Magna Charta, signed (reluctantly) by King John in 1215, had come to be interpreted as limiting the absolute power of the Crown and protecting its subjects from oppression.]

2 [David Hume (1711-76), *The History of England from the Invasion of Julius Caesar to the Revolution in 1688* (1778), 6 vols. (Indianapolis: Liberty Classics, 1983) 2: 283-84; 2.16.]

him a mere cypher; the House of Commons, to whom he was obliged frequently to apply, not only for subsidies but assistance to quell
the insurrections that the contempt in which he was held naturally
produced, gradually rose into power; for whenever they granted supplies to the King, they demanded in return, though it bore the name
of petition, a confirmation, or the renewal of former charters, which
had been infringed, and even utterly disregarded by the King and his
seditious Barons, who principally held their independence of the
crown by force of arms, and the encouragement which they gave to
robbers and villains, who infested the country, and lived by rapine and
violence.

To what dreadful extremities were the poorer sort reduced, their
property, the fruit of their industry, being entirely at the disposal of
their lords, who were so many petty tyrants!

In return for the supplies and assistance which the king received
from the commons, they demanded privileges, which Edward, in his
distress for money to prosecute the numerous wars in which he was
engaged during the greater part of his reign, was constrained to grant
them; so that by degrees they rose to power, and became a check on
both king and nobles. Thus was the foundation of our liberty established, chiefly through the pressing necessities of the king, who was
more intent on being supplied for the moment, in order to carry on
his wars and ambitious projects, than aware of the blow he gave to
kingly power, by thus making a body of men feel their importance,
who afterwards might strenuously oppose tyranny and oppression,
and effectually guard the subject's property from seizure and confiscation. Richard's weakness completed what Edward's ambition began.

At this period, it is true, Wickliffe opened a vista for reason by
attacking some of the most pernicious tenets of the church of Rome;[1]
still the prospect was sufficiently misty to authorize the question –
Where was the dignity of thinking of the fourteenth century?

A Roman Catholic, it is true, enlightened by the reformation,
might, with singular propriety, celebrate the epoch that preceded it, to
turn our thoughts from former atrocious enormities; but a Protestant
must acknowledge that this faint dawn of liberty only made the sub-

---

1 [John Wycliffe (c. 1329-84), English reformer, challenged the authority of the
Church in his lectures (Oxford, 1379-80) and in *De Eucharistia* (1381).]

siding darkness more visible;[1] and that the boasted virtues of that century all bear the stamp of stupid pride and headstrong barbarism. Civility was then called condescension, and ostentatious almsgiving humanity; and men were content to borrow their virtues, or, to speak with more propriety, their consequence, from posterity, rather than undertake the arduous task of acquiring it for themselves.

The imperfection of all modern governments must, without waiting to repeat the trite remark, that all human institutions are unavoidably imperfect, in a great measure have arisen from this simple circumstance, that the constitution, if such an heterogeneous mass deserve that name, was settled in the dark days of ignorance, when the minds of men were shackled by the grossest prejudices and most immoral superstition. And do you, Sir, a sagacious philosopher, recommend night as the fittest time to analyze a ray of light?

Are we to seek for the rights of men in the ages when a few marks were the only penalty imposed for the life of a man, and death for death when the property of the rich was touched? when — I blush to discover the depravity of our nature — when a deer was killed! Are these the laws that it is natural to love, and sacrilegious to invade? — Were the rights of men understood when the law authorized or tolerated murder? — or is power and right the same in your creed?

But in fact all your declamation leads so directly to this conclusion, that I beseech you to ask your own heart, when you call yourself a friend of liberty, whether it would not be more consistent to style yourself the champion of property, the adorer of the golden image which power has set up? — And, when you are examining your heart, if it would not be too much like mathematical drudgery, to which a fine imagination very reluctantly stoops, enquire further, how it is consistent with the vulgar notions of honesty, and the foundation of morality — truth; for a man to boast of his virtue and independence, when he cannot forget that he is at the moment enjoying the wages of falsehood[2]; and that, in a skulking, unmanly way, he has secured himself a pension of fifteen hundred pounds per annum on the Irish establishment? Do honest men, Sir, for I am not rising to the refined

---

1  [Milton, *Paradise Lost* 1.63.]
2  See Mr. Burke's Bills for oeconomical reform. [*Speech . . . to the House of Commons on the 11th February 1780; Works* 2: 268-71, 358-62.]

principle of honour, ever receive the reward of their public services, or secret assistance, in the name of *another?*[1]

But to return from a digression which you will more perfectly understand than any of my readers – on what principle you, Sir, can justify the reformation, which tore up by the roots an old establishment, I cannot guess – but, I beg your pardon, perhaps you do not wish to justify it – and have some mental reservation to excuse you, to yourself, for not openly avowing your reverence.[2] Or, to go further back; – had you been a Jew – you would have joined in the cry, crucify him! – crucify him! The promulgator of a new doctrine, and the violator of old laws and customs, that not melting, like ours, into darkness and ignorance, rested on Divine authority, must have been a dangerous innovator, in your eyes, particularly if you had not been informed that the Carpenter's Son was of the stock and lineage of David. But there is no end to the arguments which might be deduced to combat such palpable absurdities, by shewing the manifest inconsistencies which are necessarily involved in a direful train of false opinions.

It is necessary emphatically to repeat, that there are rights which men inherit at their birth, as rational creatures, who were raised above the brute creation by their improvable faculties; and that, in receiving these, not from their forefathers but, from God, prescription can never undermine natural rights.

A father may dissipate his property without his child having any right to complain; – but should he attempt to sell him for a slave, or fetter him with laws contrary to reason; nature, in enabling him to discern good from evil, teaches him to break the ignoble chain, and not to believe that bread becomes flesh, and wine blood, because his parents swallowed the Eucharist with this blind persuasion.

There is no end to this implicit submission to authority – some where it must stop, or we return to barbarism; and the capacity of improvement, which gives us a natural sceptre on earth, is a cheat, an ignis-fatuus, that leads us from inviting meadows into bogs and

---

1  [In fact, Burke would not be granted a pension until 1794.]
2  [Wollstonecraft exploits the suspicion that Burke was a crypto-Catholic, educated by Jesuits: Protestants accused Jesuits of practising deception by giving apparently straightforward statements a "mental reservation" inaccessible to their hearers.]

dunghills. And if it be allowed that many of the precautions, with which any alteration was made, in our government, were prudent, it rather proves its weakness than substantiates an opinion of the soundness of the stamina, or the excellence of the constitution.

But on what principle Mr. Burke could defend American independence,[1] I cannot conceive; for the whole tenor of his plausible arguments settles slavery on an everlasting foundation. Allowing his servile reverence for antiquity, and prudent attention to self-interest, to have the force which he insists on, the slave trade ought never to be abolished; and, because our ignorant forefathers, not understanding the native dignity of man, sanctioned a traffic that outrages every suggestion of reason and religion, we are to submit to the inhuman custom, and term an atrocious insult to humanity the love of our country, and a proper submission to the laws by which our property is secured.[2] – Security of property! Behold, in a few words, the definition of English liberty. And to this selfish principle every nobler one is sacrificed. – The Briton takes place of the man, and the image of God is lost in the citizen! But it is not that enthusiastic flame which in Greece and Rome consumed every sordid passion: no, self is the focus; and the disparting rays rise not above our foggy atmosphere. But softly – it is only the property of the rich that is secure; the man who lives by the sweat of his brow has no asylum from oppression; the strong man may enter – when was the castle of the poor sacred? and the base informer steal him from the family that depend on his industry for subsistence.

Fully sensible as you must be of the baneful consequences that inevitably follow this notorious infringement on the dearest rights of men, and that it is an infernal blot on the very face of our immaculate constitution, I cannot avoid expressing my surprise that when you recommended our form of government as a model, you did not caution the French against the arbitrary custom of pressing men for the sea service.[3] You should have hinted to them, that property in England is much more secure than liberty, and not have concealed that the liberty of an honest mechanic – his all – is often sacrificed to secure the

---

1    [Burke, *Speech on . . . Conciliation with America* (22 March 1775); *Works* 2: 99-186.]
2    [See Appendix A.1.]
3    [Impressment, a form of forcible conscription into the navy, lasted until 1815.]

property of the rich. For it is a farce to pretend that a man fights *for his country, his hearth, or his altars*, when he has neither liberty nor property. – His property is in his nervous arms – and they are compelled to pull a strange rope at the surly command of a tyrannic boy, who probably obtained his rank on account of his family connections, or the prostituted vote of his father, whose interest in a borough, or voice as a senator, was acceptable to the minister.

Our penal laws punish with death the thief who steals a few pounds; but to take by violence, or trepan, a man, is no such heinous offence. – For who shall dare to complain of the venerable vestige of the law that rendered the life of a deer more sacred than that of a man? But it was the poor man with only his native dignity who was thus oppressed – and only metaphysical sophists and cold mathematicians can discern this insubstantial form; it is a work of abstraction – and a *gentleman* of lively imagination must borrow some drapery from fancy before he can love or pity a *man*. – Misery, to reach your heart, I perceive, must have its cap and bells; your tears are reserved, very *naturally* considering your character, for the declamation of the theatre, or for the downfall of queens, whose rank alters the nature of folly, and throws a graceful veil over vices that degrade humanity; whilst the distress of many industrious mothers, whose *helpmates* have been torn from them, and the hungry cry of helpless babes, were vulgar sorrows that could not move your commiseration, though they might extort an alms. "The tears that are shed for fictitious sorrow are admirably adapted," says Rousseau, "to make us proud of all the virtues which we do not possess."[1]

The baneful effects of the despotic practice of pressing we shall, in all probability, soon feel; for a number of men, who have been taken from their daily employments, will shortly be let loose on society, now that there is no longer any apprehension of a war.

The vulgar, and by this epithet I mean not only to describe a class of people, who, working to support the body, have not had time to

---

1  [Rousseau, *Politics and the Arts: Letter to M. d'Alembert on the Theatre* (1758), trans. Allan Bloom (Ithaca: Cornell UP, 1968) 25. Cf. *Original Stories; Works* 4: 403, 443; and Catharine Macaulay Graham, *Letters on Education. With Observations on Religious and Metaphysical Subjects* (London: C. Dilly, 1790) 308-9, 312. Wollstonecraft reviewed Macaulay's book enthusiastically in the *Analytical Review* (*Works* 7: 309-22), and she recommends it in the second *Vindication* (231 n.).]

cultivate their minds; but likewise those who, born in the lap of affluence, have never had their invention sharpened by necessity are, nine out of ten, the creatures of habit and impulse.

If I were not afraid to derange your nervous system by the bare mention of a metaphysical enquiry, I should observe, Sir, that self-preservation is, literally speaking, the first law of nature; and that the care necessary to support and guard the body is the first step to unfold the mind, and inspire a manly spirit of independence. The mewing babe in swaddling-clothes, who is treated like a superior being, may perchance become a gentleman; but nature must have given him uncommon faculties if, when pleasure hangs on every bough, he has sufficient fortitude either to exercise his mind or body in order to acquire personal merit. The passions are necessary auxiliaries of reason: a present impulse pushes us forward, and when we discover that the game did not deserve the chace, we find that we have gone over much ground, and not only gained many new ideas, but a habit of thinking. The exercise of our faculties is the great end, though not the goal we had in view when we started with such eagerness.

It would be straying still further into metaphysics to add, that this is one of the strongest arguments for the natural immortality of the soul. – Every thing looks like a means, nothing like an end, or point of rest, when we can say, now let us sit down and enjoy the present moment; our faculties and wishes are proportioned to the present scene; we may return without repining to our sister clod. And, if no conscious dignity whisper that we are capable of relishing more refined pleasures, the thirst of truth appears to be allayed; and thought, the faint type of an immaterial energy, no longer bounding it knows not where, is confined to the tenement that affords it sufficient variety. – The rich man may then thank his God that he is not like other men[1] – but when is retribution to be made to the miserable, who cry day and night for help, and there is no one at hand to help them? And not only misery but immorality proceeds from this stretch of arbitrary authority. The vulgar have not the power of emptying their mind of the only ideas they imbibed whilst their hands were employed; they cannot quickly turn from one kind of life to another. Pressing them

---

1   [Luke 18: 11.]

entirely unhinges their minds; they acquire new habits, and cannot return to their old occupations with their former readiness; consequently they fall into idleness, drunkenness, and the whole train of vices which you stigmatise as gross.

A government that acts in this manner cannot be called a good parent, nor inspire natural (habitual is the proper word) affection, in the breasts of children who are thus disregarded.

The game laws are almost as oppressive to the peasantry as press-warrants to the mechanic. In this land of liberty what is to secure the property of the poor farmer when his noble landlord chooses to plant a decoy field near his little property? Game devour the fruit of his labour; but fines and imprisonment await him if he dare to kill any – or lift up his hand to interrupt the pleasure of his lord.[1] How many families have been plunged, in the *sporting* countries, into misery and vice for some paltry transgression of these coercive laws, by the natural consequence of that anger which a man feels when he sees the reward of his industry laid waste by unfeeling luxury? – when his children's bread is given to dogs!

You have shewn, Sir, by your silence on these subjects, that your respect for rank has swallowed up the common feelings of humanity; you seem to consider the poor as only the live stock of an estate, the feather of hereditary nobility. When you had so little respect for the silent majesty of misery, I am not surprised at your manner of treating an individual whose brow a mitre will never grace, and whose popularity may have wounded your vanity – for vanity is ever sore. Even in France, Sir, before the revolution, literary celebrity procured a man the treatment of a gentleman; but you are going back for your credentials of politeness to more distant times. – Gothic affability is the mode you think proper to adopt, the condescension of a Baron, not the civility of a liberal man. Politeness is, indeed, the only substitute for humanity; or what distinguishes the civilised man from the unlettered savage? and he who is not governed by reason should square his behaviour by an arbitrary standard; but by what rule your attack on

---

1 [Under the game laws, which remained in effect until 1831, only members of certain classes could kill game. A "decoy field" was planted to attract game; naturally, the game would also be attracted to the crops on neighbouring farms. Cf. Rousseau, *Emile* 352-53.]

Dr. Price[1] was regulated we have yet to learn.

I agree with you, Sir, that the pulpit is not the place for political discussions,[2] though it might be more excusable to enter on such a subject, when the day was set apart merely to commemorate a political revolution, and no stated duty was encroached upon. I will, however, wave this point, and allow that Dr. Price's zeal may have carried him further than sound reason can justify. I do also most cordially coincide with you, that till we can see the remote consequences of things, present calamities must appear in the ugly form of evil, and excite our commiseration. The good that time slowly educes from them may be hid from mortal eye, or dimly seen; whilst sympathy compels man to feel for man, and almost restrains the hand that would amputate a limb to save the whole body. But, after making this concession, allow me to expostulate with you, and calmly hold up the glass which will shew you your partial feelings.

In reprobating Dr. Price's opinions you might have spared the man; and if you had had but half as much reverence for the grey hairs of virtue as for the accidental distinctions of rank, you would not have treated with such indecent familiarity and supercilious contempt, a member of the community whose talents and modest virtues place him high in the scale of moral excellence. I am not accustomed to look up with vulgar awe, even when mental superiority exalts a man above his fellows; but still the sight of a man whose habits are fixed by piety and reason, and whose virtues are consolidated into goodness, commands my homage – and I should touch his errors with a tender hand when I made a parade of my sensibility. Granting, for a moment, that Dr. Price's political opinions are Utopian reveries, and that the world is not yet sufficiently civilized to adopt such a sublime system of morality; they could, however, only be the reveries of a benevolent mind. Tottering on the verge of the grave, that worthy man in his whole life never dreamt of struggling for power or riches; and, if a glimpse of the glad dawn of liberty rekindled the fire of youth in his veins, you, who could not stand the fascinating glance of a *great* Lady's

---

1   [Richard Price (1723-91), whose sermon *A Discourse on the Love of our Country* (1789; see Appendix A.3) provoked Burke's *Reflections*.]

2   [Burke, *Reflections*; *Writings* 8: 62. Price had already conceded the point in *Discourse* 2; see Appendix A.3.]

eyes,[1] when neither virtue nor sense beamed in them, might have pardoned his unseemly transport, – if such it must be deemed.

I could almost fancy that I now see this respectable old man, in his pulpit, with hands clasped, and eyes devoutly fixed, praying with all the simple energy of unaffected piety; or, when more erect, inculcating the dignity of virtue, and enforcing the doctrines his life adorns; benevolence animated each feature, and persuasion attuned his accents; the preacher grew eloquent, who only laboured to be clear; and the respect that he extorted, seemed only the respect due to personified virtue and matured wisdom. – Is this the man you brand with so many opprobrious epithets? he whose private life will stand the test of the strictest enquiry – away with such unmanly sarcasms, and puerile conceits. – But, before I close this part of my animadversions, I must convict you of wilful misrepresentation and wanton abuse.

Dr. Price, when he reasons on the necessity of men attending some place of public worship, concisely obviates an objection that has been made in the form of an apology,[2] by advising those, who do not approve of our Liturgy, and cannot find any mode of worship out of the church, in which they can conscientiously join, to establish one for themselves.[3] This plain advice you have tortured into a very different meaning, and represented the preacher as actuated by a dissenting phrensy, recommending dissensions, "not to diffuse truth, but to spread contradictions[4]." A simple question will silence this impertinent declamation. – What is truth? A few fundamental truths meet the first enquiry of reason, and appear as clear to an unwarped mind, as that air and bread are necessary to enable the body to fulfil its vital functions; but the opinions which men discuss with so much heat must be simplified and brought back to first principles; or who can discriminate the vagaries of the imagination, or scrupulosity of weakness, from the verdict of reason? Let all these points be demonstrated, and not determined by arbitrary authority and dark traditions, lest a

---

1   [Burke, *Reflections*; *Writings* 8: 126. See Appendix A.4.i.]
2   [Augustus Henry Fitzroy, Duke of Grafton (1735-1811), *Hints, &c. Submitted to the Serious Attention of the Clergy, Nobility and Gentry, Newly Assembled, by a Layman, a Friend to the True Principles of the Constitution in the Church & State, and to Civil and Religious Liberty* (1789); see Price, *Discourse* 17n., Appendix A.3.]
3   [Price, *Discourse on the Love of our Country* (1789) 18; Appendix A.3.]
4   Page 15. [Burke, *Reflections*; *Writings* 8: 63; Price, *Discourse* 18; see Appendix A.3.]

dangerous supineness should take place; for probably, in ceasing to enquire, our reason would remain dormant, and delivered up, without a curb, to every impulse of passion, we might soon lose sight of the clear light which the exercise of our understanding no longer kept alive. To argue from experience, it should seem as if the human mind, averse to thought, could only be opened by necessity; for, when it can take opinions on trust, it gladly lets the spirit lie quiet in its gross tenement. Perhaps the most improving exercise of the mind, confining the argument to the enlargement of the understanding, is the restless enquiries that hover on the boundary, or stretch over the dark abyss of uncertainty. These lively conjectures are the breezes that preserve the still lake from stagnating. We should be aware of confining all moral excellence to one channel, however capacious; or, if we are so narrow-minded, we should not forget how much we owe to chance that our inheritance was not Mahometism; and that the iron hand of destiny, in the shape of deeply rooted authority, has not suspended the sword of destruction over our heads. But to return to the misrepresentation.

¹Blackstone, to whom Mr. Burke pays great deference,² seems to agree with Dr. Price, that the succession of the King of Great Britain depends on the choice of the people, or that they have a power to cut

---

1   "The doctrine of *hereditary* right does by no means imply an *indefeasible* right to the throne. No man will, I think, assert this, that has considered our laws, constitution, and history, without prejudice, and with any degree of attention. It is unquestionably in the breast of the supreme legislative authority of this kingdom, the King and both Houses of Parliament, to defeat this hereditary right; and, by particular entails, limitations, and provisions, to exclude the immediate heir, and vest the inheritance in any one else. This is strictly consonant to our laws and constitution; as may be gathered from the expression so frequently used in our statute books, of `the King's Majesty, his heirs, and successors.' In which we may observe that, as the word `heirs' necessarily implies an inheritance, or hereditary right, generally subsisting in `the royal person;' so the word successors, distinctly taken, must imply that this inheritance may sometimes be broken through; or, that there may be a successor, without being the heir of the king."

I shall not, however, rest in something like a subterfuge, and quote, as partially as you have done, from Aristotle. Blackstone has so cautiously fenced round his opinion with provisos, that it is obvious he thought the letter of the law leaned towards your side of the question—but a blind respect for the law is not a part of my creed. [William Blackstone (1723-80), *Commentaries on the Laws of England* (1765-69) 188; 1.3. Burke, *Reflections*; *Writings* 8: 174, cites Aristotle, *Politics* 4.4.]

2   [Burke, *Reflections*; *Writings* 8: 82.]

it off; but this power, as you have fully proved, has been cautiously exerted, and might with more propriety be termed a *right* than a power. Be it so! – yet when you elaborately cited precedents to shew that our forefathers paid great respect to hereditary claims, you might have gone back to your favourite epoch, and shewn their respect for a church that fulminating laws have since loaded with opprobrium. The preponderance of inconsistencies, when weighed with precedents, should lessen the most bigotted veneration for antiquity, and force men of the eighteenth century to acknowledge, that our *canonized forefathers*[1] were unable, or afraid, to revert to reason, without resting on the crutch of authority; and should not be brought as a proof that their children are never to be allowed to walk alone.

When we doubt the infallible wisdom of our ancestors, it is only advancing on the same ground to doubt the sincerity of the law, and the propriety of that servile appellation – OUR SOVEREIGN LORD THE KING.[2] Who were the dictators of this adulatory language of the law? Were they not courtly parasites and worldly priests? Besides, whoever at divine service, whose feelings were not deadened by habit, or their understandings quiescent, ever repeated without horror the same epithets applied to a man and his Creator? If this is confused jargon – say what are the dictates of sober reason, or the criterion to distinguish nonsense?

You further sarcastically animadvert on the consistency of the democratists, by wresting the obvious meaning of a common phrase, *the dregs of the people;*[3] or your contempt for poverty may have led you into an error. Be that as it may, an unprejudiced man would have directly perceived the single sense of the word, and an old Member of Parliament could scarcely have missed it. He who had so often felt the pulse of the electors needed not have gone beyond his own experience to discover that the dregs alluded to were the vicious, and not the lower class of the community.

Again, Sir, I must doubt your sincerity or your discernment. – You have been behind the curtain; and, though it might be difficult to

---

1  [Burke, *Reflections*; *Writings* 8: 85.]
2  [Burke, *Reflections*; *Writings* 8: 78–80.]
3  [Price, *A Discourse on the Love of our Country* (1789) 42n., Appendix A.3; Burke, *Reflections*; *Writings* 8: 107.]

bring back your sophisticated heart to nature and make you feel like a man, yet the awestruck confusion in which you were plunged must have gone off when the vulgar emotion of wonder, excited by finding yourself a Senator, had subsided. Then you must have seen the clogged wheels of corruption continually oiled by the sweat of the laborious poor, squeezed out of them by unceasing taxation. You must have discovered that the majority in the House of Commons was often purchased by the crown, and that the people were oppressed by the influence of their own money, extorted by the venal voice of a packed representation.

You must have known that a man of merit cannot rise in the church, the army, or navy, unless he has some interest in a borough; and that even a paltry exciseman's place can only be secured by electioneering interest. I will go further, and assert that few Bishops, though there have been learned and good Bishops, have gained the mitre without submitting to a servility of dependence that degrades the man. – All these circumstances you must have known, yet you talk of virtue and liberty, as the vulgar talk of the letter of the law; and the polite of propriety. It is true that these ceremonial observances produce decorum; the sepulchres are white-washed,[1] and do not offend the squeamish eyes of high rank; but virtue is out of the question when you only worship a shadow, and worship it to secure your property.

Man has been termed, with strict propriety, a microcosm, a little world in himself. – He is so; – yet must, however, be reckoned an ephemera, or, to adopt your figure of rhetoric, a summer's fly.[2] The perpetuation of property in our families is one of the privileges you most warmly contend for; yet it would not be very difficult to prove that the mind must have a very limited range that thus confines its benevolence to such a narrow circle, which, with great propriety, may be included in the sordid calculations of blind self-love.

A brutal attachment to children has appeared most conspicuous in parents who have treated them like slaves, and demanded due homage for all the property they transferred to them, during their lives. It has led them to force their children to break the most sacred ties; to do

---

1 [Matthew 23: 27.]
2 [Burke, *Reflections; Writings* 8: 145.]

violence to a natural impulse, and run into legal prostitution to increase wealth or shun poverty; and, still worse, the dread of parental malediction has made many weak characters violate truth in the face of Heaven; and, to avoid a father's angry curse, the most sacred promises have been broken. It appears to be a natural suggestion of reason, that a man should be freed from implicit obedience to parents and private punishments, when he is of an age to be subject to the jurisdiction of the laws of his country; and that the barbarous cruelty of allowing parents to imprison their children, to prevent their contaminating their noble blood by following the dictates of nature when they chose to marry, or for any misdemeanor that does not come under the cognizance of public justice, is one of the most arbitrary violations of liberty.[1]

Who can recount all the unnatural crimes which the *laudable, interesting* desire of perpetuating a name has produced?[2] The younger children have been sacrificed to the eldest son; sent into exile, or confined in convents, that they might not encroach on what was called, with shameful falsehood, the *family* estate. Will Mr. Burke call this parental affection reasonable or virtuous? – No; it is the spurious offspring of over-weening, mistaken pride – and not that first source of civilization, natural parental affection, that makes no difference between child and child, but what reason justifies by pointing out superior merit.

Another pernicious consequence which unavoidably arises from this artificial affection is, the insuperable bar which it puts in the way of early marriages. It would be difficult to determine whether the minds or bodies of our youth are most injured by this impediment. Our young men become selfish coxcombs, and gallantry with modest women, and intrigues with those of another description, weaken both mind and body, before either has arrived at maturity. The character of a master of a family, a husband, and a father, forms the citizen imperceptibly, by producing a sober manliness of thought, and orderly behaviour; but, from the lax morals and depraved affections of the lib-

---

1  [Under the *ancien régime*, persons could be imprisoned without trial through the use of *lettres de cachets*. Parents sometimes obtained them to prevent their children from making unsuitable marriages; see Wordsworth, *The Prelude* (1805) 9.555-934.]
2  [Burke, *Reflections*; *Writings* 8: 102.]

ertine, what results? – a finical man of taste, who is only anxious to secure his own private gratifications, and to maintain his rank in society.

The same system has an equally pernicious effect on female morals. – Girls are sacrificed to family convenience, or else marry to settle themselves in a superior rank, and coquet, without restraint, with the fine gentleman whom I have already described. And to such lengths has this vanity, this desire of shining, carried them, that it is not now necessary to guard girls against imprudent love matches; for if some widows did not now and then *fall* in love, Love and Hymen would seldom meet, unless at a village church.

I do not intend to be sarcastically paradoxical when I say, that women of fashion take husbands that they may have it in their power to coquet, the grand business of genteel life, with a number of admirers, and thus flutter the spring of life away, without laying up any store for the winter of age, or being of any use to society. Affection in the marriage state can only be founded on respect – and are these weak beings respectable? Children are neglected for lovers, and we express surprise that adulteries are so common! A woman never forgets to adorn herself to make an impression on the senses of the other sex, and to extort the homage which it is gallant to pay, and yet we wonder that they have such confined understandings!

Have ye not heard that we cannot serve two masters?[1] an immoderate desire to please contracts the faculties, and immerges, to borrow the idea of a great philosopher, the soul in matter, till it becomes unable to mount on the wing of contemplation.[2]

It would be an arduous task to trace all the vice and misery that arise in society from the middle class of people apeing the manners of the great. All are aiming to procure respect on account of their property; and most places are considered as sinecures that enable men to start into notice. The grand concern of three parts out of four is to contrive to live above their equals, and to appear to be richer than they are. How much domestic comfort and private satisfaction is sacrificed to this irrational ambition! It is a destructive mildew that blights the fairest virtues; benevolence, friendship, generosity, and all

---

1   [Matthew 6: 24; Luke 16: 13.]
2   [Plato, *Phaedrus* 246c.]

those endearing charities which bind human hearts together, and the pursuits which raise the mind to higher contemplations, all that were not cankered in the bud by the false notions that "grew with its growth and strengthened with its strength,"[1] are crushed by the iron hand of property!

Property, I do not scruple to aver it, should be fluctuating, which would be the case, if it were more equally divided amongst all the children of a family; else it is an everlasting rampart, in consequence of a barbarous feudal institution, that enables the elder son to over-power talents and depress virtue.

Besides, an unmanly servility, most inimical to true dignity of character is, by this means, fostered in society. Men of some abilities play on the follies of the rich, and mounting to fortune as they degrade themselves, they stand in the way of men of superior talents, who cannot advance in such crooked paths, or wade through the filth which *parasites* never boggle at. Pursuing their way straight forward, their spirit is either bent or broken by the rich man's contumelies,[2] or the difficulties they have to encounter.

The only security of property that nature authorizes and reason sanctions is, the right a man has to enjoy the acquisitions which his talents and industry have acquired; and to bequeath them to whom he chooses. Happy would it be for the world if there were no other road to wealth or honour; if pride, in the shape of parental affection, did not absorb the man, and prevent friendship from having the same weight as relationship. Luxury and effeminacy would not then intro-duce so much idiotism into the noble families which form one of the pillars of our state: the ground would not lie fallow, nor would undi-rected activity of mind spread the contagion of restless idleness, and its concomitant, vice, through the whole mass of society.

Instead of gaming they might nourish a virtuous ambition, and love might take place of the gallantry which you, with knightly fealty, venerate. Women would probably then act like mothers, and the fine lady, become a rational woman, might think it necessary to superin-tend her family and suckle her children, in order to fulfil her part of the social compact. But vain is the hope, whilst great masses of prop-

---

1 [Pope, *An Essay on Man* 2.136.]
2 [Cf. Shakespeare, *Hamlet* 3.1.71.]

erty are hedged round by hereditary honours; for numberless vices, forced in the hot-bed of wealth, assume a sightly form to dazzle the senses and cloud the understanding. The respect paid to rank and fortune damps every generous purpose of the soul, and stifles the natural affections on which human contentment ought to be built. Who will venturously ascend the steeps of virtue, or explore the great deep for knowledge, when *the one thing needful*,[1] attained by less arduous exertions, if not inherited, procures the attention man naturally pants after, and vice "loses half its evil by losing all its grossness[2]." – What a sentiment to come from a moral pen!

A surgeon would tell you that by skinning over a wound you spread disease through the whole frame; and, surely, they indirectly aim at destroying all purity of morals, who poison the very source of virtue, by smearing a sentimental varnish over vice, to hide its natural deformity. Stealing, whoring, and drunkenness, are gross vices, I presume, though they may not obliterate every moral sentiment, and have a vulgar brand that makes them appear with all their native deformity; but overreaching, adultery, and coquetry, are venial offences, though they reduce virtue to an empty name, and make wisdom consist in saving appearances.

"On this scheme of things[3] a king *is* but a man; a queen *is* but a woman; a woman *is* but an animal, and an animal not of the highest order." – All true, Sir; if she is not more attentive to the duties of humanity than queens and fashionable ladies in general are. I will still further accede to the opinion you have so justly conceived of the spirit which begins to animate this age. – "All homage paid to the sex in general, as such, and without distinct views, is to be regarded as *romance* and folly." Undoubtedly; because such homage vitiates them, prevents their endeavouring to obtain solid personal merit; and, in short, makes those beings vain inconsiderate dolls, who ought to be prudent mothers and useful members of society. "Regicide and sacrilege are but fictions of superstition corrupting jurisprudence, by destroying its simplicity. The murder of a king, or a queen, or a bishop,

---

1  [Cf. Luke 10: 42.]
2  Page 113. [Burke, *Reflections*; *Writings* 8: 127. See Appendix A.4.i.]
3  As you ironically observe, p. 114. [Burke, *Reflections*; *Writings* 8: 128 (Appendix A.4.i).]

are only common homicide."[1] – Again I agree with you; but you perceive, Sir, that by leaving out the word *father*, I think the whole extent of the comparison invidious.

You further proceed grossly to misrepresent Dr. Price's meaning; and, with an affectation of holy fervour, express your indignation at his profaning a beautiful rapturous ejaculation, when alluding to the King of France's submission to the National Assembly[2]; he rejoiced to hail a glorious revolution, which promised an universal diffusion of liberty and happiness.[3]

Observe, Sir, that I called your piety affectation. – A rant to enable you to point your venomous dart, and round your period. I speak with warmth, because, of all hypocrites, my soul most indignantly spurns a religious one; – and I very cautiously bring forward such a heavy charge, to strip you of your cloak of sanctity. Your speech at the time the bill for a regency was agitated now lies before me. – *Then* you could in direct terms, to promote ambitious or interested views, exclaim without any pious qualms – "Ought they to make a mockery of him, putting a crown of thorns on his head, a reed in his hand, and dressing him in a raiment of purple, cry, Hail! King of the British!"[4] Where was your sensibility when you could utter this cruel mockery, equally insulting to God and man? Go hence, thou slave of impulse, look into the private recesses of thy heart, and take not a mote from thy brother's eye, till thou hast removed the beam from thine own.[5]

Of your partial feelings I shall take another view, and shew that

---

1 [Burke, *Reflections*; *Writings* 8: 128 (Appendix A.4.i). The italics are Wollstonecraft's; and, as she implies, Burke includes parricide in his list of uncommon homicide.]

2 In July, when he first submitted to his people; and not the mobbing triumphal catastrophe in October, which you chose, to give full scope to your declamatory powers.

3 [Price, *Discourse* 49-50 (Appendix A.3); Burke, *Reflections*, *Writings* 8: 115-16, 117 (Appendix A.4.i); Catharine Macaulay Graham, *Observations on the Reflections of the Right Hon. Edmund Burke, on the Revolution in France, in a Letter to the Right Hon. the Earl of Stanhope* (London: C. Dilly, 1790) 19-27, 53-56. The biblical allusion to which Burke objects is to Luke 2: 29-32.]

4 [Burke, *Speech . . . to the House of Commons on the 9th of February 1789.* Wollstonecraft recalls Burke's behaviour during the crisis precipitated by the insanity of George III (1738-1820) in 1788-89. The biblical allusion to which Wollstonecraft objects is to the mockery of Christ: Matthew 27: 28-29; Mark 15: 17-19; Luke 23: 11; John 19: 2-3.]

5 [Matthew 7: 3.]

"following nature, which is," you say, "wisdom without reflection, and *above it*"[1] – has led you into great inconsistences, to use the softest phrase. When, on a late melancholy occasion, a very important question was agitated, with what indecent warmth did *you* treat a woman, for I shall not lay any stress on her title, whose conduct in life has deserved praise, though not, perhaps, the servile elogiums which have been lavished on the queen.[2] But sympathy, and you tell us that you have a heart of flesh, was made to give way to party spirit and the feelings of a man, not to allude to your romantic gallantry, to the views of the statesman. When you descanted on the horrors of the 6th of October, and gave a glowing, and, in some instances, a most exaggerated description of that infernal night, without having troubled yourself to clean your palette, you might have returned home and indulged us with a sketch of the misery you personally aggravated.

With what eloquence might you not have insinuated, that the sight of unexpected misery and strange reverse of fortune makes the mind recoil on itself; and, pondering, traced the uncertainty of all human hope, the frail foundation of sublunary grandeur! What a climax lay before you. A father torn from his children, – a husband from an affectionate wife, – a man from himself! And not torn by the resistless stroke of death, for time would then have lent its aid to mitigate remediless sorrow; but that living death, which only kept hope alive in the corroding form of suspense, was a calamity that called for all your pity.

The sight of august ruins, of a depopulated country – what are they to a disordered soul! when all the faculties are mixed in wild confusion. It is then indeed we tremble for humanity – and, if some wild fancy chance to cross the brain, we fearfully start, and pressing our hand against our brow, ask if we are yet men? – if our reason is undisturbed? – if judgment hold the helm? Marius might sit with dignity on the ruins of Carthage,[3] and the wretch in the Bastille, who longed in vain to see the human face divine,[4] might yet view the

---

1  [Burke, *Reflections*; *Writings* 8: 83.]
2  [Burke, *Speech . . . to the House of Commons on the 6th of February 1789*.]
3  [Gaius Marius (157-86 B.C.), defeated by Sulla in 88 B.C., fled to Africa, where he was refused entry by the governor of Carthage. He sat among the ruins of the old city to emphasize how low he had fallen.]
4  [A possible allusion to Blake, "The Divine Image" 10-11, 15.]

operations of his own mind, and vary the leaden prospect by new combinations of thought: poverty, shame, and even slavery, may be endured by the virtuous man – he has still a world to range in[1] – but the loss of reason appears a monstrous flaw in the moral world, that eludes all investigation, and humbles without enlightening.

In this state was the King, when you, with unfeeling disrespect, and indecent haste, wished to strip him of all his hereditary honours. – You were so eager to taste the sweets of power, that you could not wait till time had determined, whether a dreadful delirium would settle into a confirmed madness; but, prying into the secrets of Omnipotence, you thundered out that God had *hurled him from his throne*, and that it was the most insulting mockery to recollect that he had been a king, or to treat him with any particular respect on account of his former dignity.[2] – And who was the monster whom Heaven had thus awfully deposed, and smitten with such an angry blow? Surely as harmless a character as Lewis XVIth; and the queen of Great Britain,[3] though her heart may not be enlarged by generosity, who will presume to compare her character with that of the queen of France?[4]

Where then was the infallibility of that extolled instinct which rises above reason? was it warped by vanity, or *hurled* from its throne by self-interest? To your own heart answer these questions in the sober hours of reflection – and, after reviewing this gust of passion, learn to respect the sovereignty of reason.

I have, Sir, been reading, with a scrutinizing, comparative eye, several of your insensible and profane speeches during the King's illness. I disdain to take advantage of a man's weak side, or draw consequences from an unguarded transport – A lion preys not on carcasses! But on this occasion you acted systematically. It was not the passion of the moment, over which humanity draws a veil: no; what but the odious maxims of Machiavelian policy could have led you to have searched in the very dregs of misery for forcible arguments to support your party? Had not vanity or interest steeled your heart, you would have been shocked at the cold insensibility which could carry a man

---

1   [Cf. Shakespeare, *Coriolanus* 3.3.136.]
2   [Burke, *Speech . . . to the House of Commons on the 9th of February 1789.*]
3   [Charlotte Sophia (1738-1818).]
4   [Marie Antoinette (1755-93).]

to those dreadful mansions, where human weakness appears in its most awful form to *calculate* the chances against the King's recovery. Impressed as *you are* with respect for royalty, I am astonished that you did not tremble at every step, lest Heaven should avenge on your guilty head the insult offered to its vicegerent. But the conscience that is under the direction of transient ebullitions of feeling, is not very tender or consistent, when the current runs another way.

Had you been in a philosophizing mood, had your heart or your reason been at home, you might have been convinced, by ocular demonstration,[1] that madness is only the absence of reason. – The ruling angel leaving its seat, wild anarchy ensues. You would have seen that the uncontrouled imagination often pursues the most regular course in its most daring flight; and that the eccentricities are boldly relieved when judgment no longer officiously arranges the sentiments, by bringing them to the test of principles. You would have seen every thing out of nature in that strange chaos of levity and ferocity, and of all sorts of follies jumbled together. You would have seen in that monstrous tragi-comic scene the most opposite passions necessarily succeed, and sometimes mix with each other in the mind; alternate contempt and indignation; alternate laughter and tears; alternate scorn and horror[2]. – This is a true picture of that chaotic state of mind, called madness; when reason gone, we know not where, the wild elements of passion clash, and all is horror and confusion. You might have heard the best turned conceits, flash following flash, and doubted whether the rhapsody was not eloquent, if it had not been delivered in an equivocal language, neither verse nor prose, if the sparkling periods had not stood alone, wanting force because they wanted concatenation.

It is a proverbial observation, that a very thin partition divides wit and madness.[3] Poetry therefore naturally addresses the fancy, and the language of passion is with great felicity borrowed from the heightened picture which the imagination draws of sensible objects concentred by impassioned reflection. And, during this "fine phrensy,"[4]

---

1   [Cf. Shakespeare, *Othello* 3.3.360.]
2   This quotation is not marked with inverted commas, because it is not exact. P. 11. [Burke, *Reflections*; *Writings* 8: 60.]
3   [Dryden, *Absalom and Achitophel* (1681) 1.163.]
4   [Shakespeare, *A Midsummer Night's Dream* 5.1.12.]

reason has no right to rein-in the imagination, unless to prevent the introduction of supernumerary images; if the passion is real, the head will not be ransacked for stale tropes and cold rodomontade. I now speak of the genuine enthusiasm of genius, which, perhaps, seldom appears, but in the infancy of civilization; for as this light becomes more luminous reason clips the wing of fancy – the youth becomes a man.

Whether the glory of Europe is set, I shall not now enquire; but probably the spirit of romance and chivalry is in the wane; and reason will gain by its extinction.

From observing several cold romantic characters I have been led to confine the term romantic to one definition – false, or rather artificial, feelings. Works of genius are read with a prepossession in their favour, and sentiments imitated, because they were fashionable and pretty, and not because they were forcibly felt.

In modern poetry the understanding and memory often fabricate the pretended effusions of the heart, and romance destroys all simplicity; which, in works of taste, is but a synonymous word for truth. This romantic spirit has extended to our prose, and scattered artificial flowers over the most barren heath; or a mixture of verse and prose producing the strangest incongruities. The turgid bombast of some of your periods fully proves these assertions; for when the heart speaks we are seldom shocked by hyperbole, or dry raptures.

I speak in this decided tone, because from turning over the pages of your late publication, with more attention than I did when I first read it cursorily over; and comparing the sentiments it contains with your conduct on many important occasions, I am led very often to doubt your sincerity, and to suppose that you have said many things merely for the sake of saying them well; or to throw some pointed obloquy on characters and opinions that jostled with your vanity.

It is an arduous task to follow the doublings of cunning, or the subterfuges of inconsistency; for in controversy, as in battle, the brave man wishes to face his enemy, and fight on the same ground. Knowing, however, the influence of a ruling passion, and how often it assumes the form of reason when there is much sensibility in the heart, I respect an opponent, though he tenaciously maintains opinions in which I cannot coincide; but, if I once discover that many of those opinions are empty rhetorical flourishes, my respect is soon changed into that pity which borders on contempt; and the mock dignity and haughty stalk, only reminds me of the ass in the lion's skin.[1]

A sentiment of this kind glanced across my mind when I read the following exclamation. "Whilst the royal captives, who followed in the train, were slowly moved along, amidst the horrid yells, and shrilling screams, and frantic dances, and infamous contumelies, and all the unutterable abominations of the furies of hell, in the abused shape of the vilest of women[2]." Probably you mean women who gained a livelihood by selling vegetables or fish, who never had had any advantages of education; or their vices might have lost part of their abominable deformity, by losing part of their grossness. The queen of France – the great and small vulgar, claim our pity; they have almost insuperable obstacles to surmount in their progress towards true dignity of character; still I have such a plain downright understanding that I do not like to make a distinction without a difference. But it is not very extraordinary that *you* should, for throughout your letter you frequently advert to a sentimental jargon, which has long been current in conversation, and even in books of morals, though it never received the *regal* stamp of reason. A kind of mysterious instinct is *supposed* to reside in the soul, that instantaneously discerns truth, without the tedious labour of ratiocination. This instinct, for I know not what other name to give it, has been termed *common sense*, and more frequently *sensibility*; and, by a kind of *indefeasible* right, it has been *supposed*, for rights of this kind are not easily proved, to reign paramount over the other faculties of the mind, and to be an authority from which there is no appeal.

This subtle magnetic fluid, that runs round the whole circle of society, is not subject to any known rule, or, to use an obnoxious phrase, in spite of the sneers of mock humility, or the timid fears of some well-meaning Christians, who shrink from any freedom of

---

1  [See *Aesop's Fables. With Instructive Morals and Reflections, Abstracted from All Party Considerations, Adapted to All Capacities; and Design'd to Promote Religion, Morality, and Universal Benevolence*, ed. Samuel Richardson (London: J.F. and C. Rivington, et al., 1740) 133; Fable 170. The ass gives himself away by braying.]

2  Page 106. [Burke, *Reflections*; *Writings* 8: 122 (Appendix A.4.i).]

thought, lest they should rouse the old serpent, to the *eternal fitness of things*.[1] It dips, we know not why, granting it to be an infallible instinct, and, though supposed always to point to truth, its pole-star, the point is always shifting, and seldom stands due north.

It is to this instinct, without doubt, that you allude, when you talk of the "moral constitution of the heart." To it, I allow, for I consider it as a congregate of sensations and passions, *Poets* must apply, "who have to deal with an audience not yet graduated in the school of the rights of men."[2] They must, it is clear, often cloud the understanding, whilst they move the heart by a kind of mechanical spring; but that "in the theatre the first intuitive glance"[3] of feeling should discriminate the form of truth, and see her fair proportion, I must beg leave to doubt. Sacred be the feelings of the heart! concentred in a glowing flame, they become the sun of life; and, without his invigorating impregna-tion, reason would probably lie in helpless inactivity, and never bring forth her only legitimate offspring – virtue. But to prove that virtue is really an acquisition of the individual, and not the blind impulse of unerring instinct, the bastard vice has often been begotten by the same father.

In what respect are we superior to the brute creation, if intellect is not allowed to be the guide of passion? Brutes hope and fear, love and hate; but, without a capacity to improve, a power of turning these pas-sions to good or evil, they neither acquire virtue nor wisdom. – Why? Because the Creator has not given them reason[4].

But the cultivation of reason is an arduous task, and men of lively fancy, finding it easier to follow the impulse of passion, endeavour to persuade themselves and others that it is most *natural*. And happy is it for those, who indolently let that heaven-lighted spark rest like the ancient lamps in sepulchres, that some virtuous habits, with which the reason of others shackled them, supplies its place. – Affection for par-ents, reverence for superiors or antiquity, notions of honour, or that worldly self-interest that shrewdly shews them that honesty is the best

---

1   [Fielding, *Tom Jones* (1749) Book 4, chap. 4; Macaulay, *Letters* 381, 405, 453.]
2   [Burke, *Reflections*; *Writings* 8: 132.]
3   [Burke, *Reflections*; *Writings* 8: 132.]
4   I do not now mean to discuss the intricate subject of their mortality; reason may, perhaps, be given to them in the next stage of existence, if they are to mount in the scale of life, like men, by the medium of death. [Cf. Macaulay, *Letters* 1-2, 356-57.]

policy: all proceed from the reason for which they serve as substitutes; – but it is reason at second-hand.

Children are born ignorant, consequently innocent; the passions, are neither good nor evil dispositions, till they receive a direction, and either bound over the feeble barrier raised by a faint glimmering of unexercised reason, called conscience, or strengthen her wavering dictates till sound principles are deeply rooted, and able to cope with the headstrong passions that often assume her awful form. What moral purpose can be answered by extolling good dispositions, as they are called, when these good dispositions are described as instincts: for instinct moves in a direct line to its ultimate end, and asks not for guide or support. But if virtue is to be acquired by experience, or taught by example, reason, perfected by reflection, must be the director of the whole host of passions, which produce a fructifying heat, but no light, that you would exalt into her place. – She must hold the rudder, or, let the wind blow which way it list, the vessel will never advance smoothly to its destined port; for the time lost in tacking about would dreadfully impede its progress.

In the name of the people of England, you say, "that we know *we* have made no discoveries; and we think that no discoveries are to be made in morality; nor many in the great principles of government, nor in the ideas of liberty, which were understood long before we were born, altogether as well as they will be after the grave has heaped its mould upon our presumption, and the silent tomb shall have imposed its law on our pert loquacity. In England we have not yet been completely emboweled of our natural entrails; we still feel within us, and we cherish and cultivate those inbred sentiments which are the faithful guardians, the active monitors of our duty, the true supporters of all liberal and manly morals[1]." – What do you mean by inbred sentiments? From whence do they come? How were they bred? Are they the brood of folly, which swarm like the insects on the banks of the Nile, when mud and putrefaction have enriched the languid soil? Were these *inbred* sentiments faithful guardians of our duty when the church was an asylum for murderers, and men worshipped bread as a God? when slavery was authorized by law to fasten her fangs on human flesh, and the iron eat into the very soul? If these sen-

---

1    Page 128. [Burke, *Reflections*; *Writings* 8: 137.]

timents are not acquired, if our passive dispositions do not expand into virtuous affections and passions, why are not the Tartars in the first rude horde endued with sentiments white and *elegant* as the driven snow? Why is passion or heroism the child of reflection, the consequence of dwelling with intent contemplation on one object? The appetites are the only perfect inbred powers that I can discern; and they like instincts have a certain aim, they can be satisfied – but improveable reason has not yet discovered the perfection it may arrive at – God forbid!

First, however, it is necessary to make what we know practical. Who can deny, that has marked the slow progress of civilization, that men may become more virtuous and happy without any new discovery in morals? Who will venture to assert that virtue would not be promoted by the more extensive cultivation of reason? If nothing more is to be done, let us eat and drink, for to-morrow we die – and die for ever![1] Who will pretend to say, that there is as much happiness diffused on this globe as it is capable of affording? as many social virtues as reason would foster, if she could gain the strength she is able to acquire even in this imperfect state; if the voice of nature was allowed to speak audibly from the bottom of the heart, and the *native* unalienable rights of men were recognized in their full force; if factitious merit did not take place of genuine acquired virtue, and enable men to build their enjoyment on the misery of their fellow creatures; if men were more under the dominion of reason than opinion, and did not cherish their prejudices "because they were prejudices[2]?" I am not, Sir, aware of your sneers, hailing a millennium, though a state of greater purity of morals may not be a mere poetic fiction; nor did my fancy ever create a heaven on earth, since reason threw off her swaddling clothes. I perceive, but too forcibly, that happiness, literally speaking, dwells not here; – and that we wander to and fro in a vale of darkness as well as tears. I perceive that my passions pursue objects that the imagination enlarges, till they become only a sublime idea that shrinks from the enquiry of sense, and mocks the experimental philosophers who would confine this spiritual phlogiston in their

---

1  [Isaiah 22: 13.]
2  Page 129. [Burke, *Reflections*; *Writings* 8: 138 (Appendix A.4.ii).]

material crucibles.[1] I know that the human understanding is deluded with vain shadows, and that when we eagerly pursue any study, we only reach the boundary set to human enquiries. – Thus far shalt thou go, and no further, says some stern difficulty; and the *cause* we were pursuing melts into utter darkness. But these are only the trials of contemplative minds, the foundation of virtue remains firm. – The power of exercising our understanding raises us above the brutes; and this exercise produces that "primary morality," which you term "untaught feelings."[2]

If virtue be an instinct, I renounce all hope of immortality; and with it all the sublime reveries and dignified sentiments that have smoothed the rugged path of life: it is all a cheat, a lying vision; I have disquieted myself in vain; for in my eye all feelings are false and spurious, that do not rest on justice as their foundation, and are not concentred by universal love.

I reverence the rights of men. – Sacred rights! for which I acquire a more profound respect, the more I look into my own mind; and, professing these heterodox opinions, I still preserve my bowels; my heart is human, beats quick with human sympathies – and I FEAR God!

I bend with awful reverence when I enquire on what my fear is built. – I fear that sublime power, whose motive for creating me must have been wise and good; and I submit to the moral laws which my reason deduces from this view of my dependence on him. – It is not his power that I fear – it is not to an arbitrary will, but to unerring *reason* I submit. – Submit – yes; I disregard the charge of arrogance, to the law that regulates his just resolves; and the happiness I pant after must be the same in kind, and produced by the same exertions as his – though unfeigned humility overwhelms every idea that would presume to compare the goodness which the most exalted created being could acquire, with the grand source of life and bliss.

This fear of God makes me reverence myself. – Yes, Sir, the regard I

---

1  [Phlogiston, a "subtle fluid," was believed to make matter inflammable. When Joseph Priestley (1733-1804) discovered oxygen, he called it "dephlogisticated air," in the belief that combustion did not consist of the oxidation of fuel, but of the phlogistication of air.]
2  [Burke, *Reflections*; *Writings* 8: 138 (Appendix A.4.ii).]

have for honest fame, and the friendship of the virtuous, falls far short of the respect which I have for myself. And this, enlightened self-love, if an epithet the meaning of which has been grossly perverted will convey my idea, forces me to see; and, if I may venture to borrow a prostituted term, to *feel*, that happiness is reflected, and that, in communicating good, my soul receives its noble aliment. – I do not trouble myself, therefore, to enquire whether this is the fear the *people* of England feel: – and, if it be *natural* to include all the modifications which you have annexed – it is not[1].

Besides, I cannot help suspecting that, if you had the *enlightened* respect for yourself, which you affect to despise, you would not have said that the constitution of our church and state, formed, like most other modern ones, by degrees, as Europe was emerging out of barbarism, was formed "under the auspices, and was confirmed by the sanctions, of religion and piety."[2] You have turned over the historic page; have been hackneyed in the ways of men, and must know that private cabals and public feuds, private virtues and vices, religion and superstition, have all concurred to foment the mass and swell it to its present form; nay more, that it in part owes its sightly appearance to bold rebellion and insidious innovation. Factions, Sir, have been the leaven, and private interest has produced public good.

These general reflections are not thrown out to insinuate that virtue was a creature of yesterday: No; she had her share in the grand drama. I guard against misrepresentation; but the man who cannot modify general assertions, has scarcely learned the first rudiments of reasoning. I know that there is a great portion of virtue in the Romish church, yet I should not choose to neglect clothing myself with a garment of my own righteousness, depending on a kind donative of works of supererogation. I know that there are many clergymen, of all denominations, wise and virtuous; yet I have not that respect for the whole body, which, you say, characterizes our nation, "emanating from a certain plainness and directness of understanding."[3] – Now we are stumbling on *inbred* feelings and secret lights

---

1   *Vide* Reflections, p. 128. "We fear God; we look up with *awe* to kings; with *affection* to parliaments; with *duty* to magistrates; with *reverence* to priests; and with *respect* to nobility." [Burke, *Reflections*; *Writings* 8: 137; Wollstonecraft's italics.]
2   [Burke, *Reflections*; *Writings* 8: 141.]
3   [Burke, *Reflections*; *Writings* 8: 141.]

again – or, I beg your pardon, it may be the furbished up face which you choose to give to the argument.

It is a well-known fact, that when *we*, the people of England, have a son whom we scarcely know what to do with – *we* make a clergyman of him. When a living is in the gift of a family, a son is brought up to the church; but not always with hopes full of immortality. "Such sublime principles are *not constantly* infused into persons of exalted birth;" they sometimes think of "the paltry pelf of the moment¹" – and the vulgar care of preaching the gospel, or practising self-denial, is left to the poor curates, who, arguing on your ground, cannot have, from the scanty stipend they receive, "very high and worthy notions of their function and destination."² This consecration *for ever*; a word, that from lips of flesh is big with a mighty nothing, has not purged the *sacred temple* from all the impurities of fraud, violence, injustice, and tyranny. Human passions still lurk in her *sanctum sanctorum*;³ and, without the profane exertions of reason, vain would be her ceremonial ablutions; morality would still stand aloof from this national religion, this ideal consecration of a state; and men would rather choose to give the goods of their body, when on their death beds, to clear the narrow way to heaven, than restrain the mad career of passions during life.

Such a curious paragraph occurs in this part of your letter, that I am tempted to transcribe it⁴, and must beg you to elucidate it, if I misconceive your meaning.

The only way in which the people interfere in government, reli-

---

1 Page 137. [Burke, *Reflections*; *Writings* 8: 143.]

2 [Burke, *Reflections*; *Writings* 8: 143.]

3 ["Holy of holies": the inner sanctuary of the Tabernacle (Exodus 26: 31-34).]

4 "When the people have emptied themselves of all the lust of selfish will, which without religion it is utterly impossible they ever should; when they are conscious that they exercise, and exercise perhaps in an higher link of the order of delegation, the power, which to be legitimate must be according to that eternal immutable law, in which will and reason are the same, they will be more careful how they place power in base and incapable hands. In their nomination to office, they will not appoint to the exercise of authority as to a pitiful job, but as to an holy function; not according to their sordid selfish interest, nor to their wanton caprice, nor to their arbitrary will; but they will confer that power (which any man may well tremble to give or to receive) on those only, in whom they may discern that predominant proportion of active virtue and wisdom, taken together and fitted to the charge, such, as in the great and inevitable mixed mass of human imperfections and infirmities, is to be found." P. 140. [Burke, *Reflections*; *Writings* 8: 145.]

gious or civil, is in electing representatives. And, Sir, let me ask you, with manly plainness – are these *holy* nominations? Where is the booth of religion? Does she mix her awful mandates, or lift her persuasive voice, in those scenes of drunken riot and beastly gluttony? Does she preside over those nocturnal abominations which so evidently tend to deprave the manners of the lower class of people? The pestilence stops not here – the rich and poor have one common nature, and many of the great families, which, on this side adoration, you venerate, date their misery, I speak of stubborn matters of fact, from the thoughtless extravagance of an electioneering frolic. – Yet, after the effervescence of spirits, raised by opposition, and all the little and tyrannic arts of canvassing are over – quiet souls! they only intend to march rank and file to say YES – or NO.

Experience, I believe, will shew that sordid interest, or licentious thoughtlessness, is the spring of action at most elections. – Again, I beg you not to lose sight of my modification of general rules. So far are the people from being habitually convinced of the sanctity of the charge they are conferring, that the venality of their votes must admonish them that they have no right to expect disinterested conduct. But to return to the church, and the habitual conviction of the people of England.

So far are the people from being "habitually convinced that no evil can be acceptable, either in the act or the permission, to him whose essence is good[1];" that the sermons which they hear are to them almost as unintelligible as if they were preached in a foreign tongue. The language and sentiments rising above their capacities, very orthodox Christians are driven to fanatical meetings for amusement, if not for edification. The clergy, I speak of the body, not forgetting the respect and affection which I have for individuals, perform the duty of their profession as a kind of fee-simple, to entitle them to the emoluments accruing from it; and their ignorant flock think that merely going to church is meritorious.

So defective, in fact, are our laws, respecting religious establishments, that I have heard many rational pious clergymen complain, that they had no method of receiving their stipend that did not clog their endeavours to be useful; whilst the lives of many less conscien-

---

1 Page 140. [Burke, *Reflections*; *Writings* 8: 145.]

tious rectors are passed in litigious disputes with the people they engaged to instruct; or in distant cities, in all the ease of luxurious idleness.

But you return to your old firm ground. – *Art thou there, Truepenny?*[1] Must we swear to secure property, and make assurance doubly sure,[2] to give your perturbed spirit rest?[3] Peace, peace to the manes of thy patriotic phrensy, which contributed to deprive some of thy fellow-citizens of their property in America: another spirit now walks abroad to secure the property of the church.[4] – The tithes are safe! – We will not say for ever – because the time may come, when the traveller may ask where proud London stood? when its *temples*, its laws, and its trade, may be buried in one common ruin, and only serve as a by-word to point a moral,[5] or furnish senators, who wage a wordy war, on the other side of the Atlantic, with tropes to swell their thundering bursts of eloquence.

Who shall dare to accuse you of inconsistency any more, when you have so staunchly supported the despotic principles which agree so perfectly with the unerring interest of a large body of your fellow-citizens; not the largest – for when you venerate parliaments – I presume it is not the majority, as you have had the presumption to dissent, and loudly explain your reasons. – But it was not my intention, when I began this letter, to descend to the minutiae of your conduct, or to weigh your infirmities in a balance; it is only some of your pernicious opinions that I wish to hunt out of their lurking holes; and to shew you to yourself, stripped of the gorgeous drapery in which you have enwrapped your tyrannic principles.

That the people of England respect the national establishment I do not deny; I recollect the melancholy proof which they gave, in this very century, of their *enlightened* zeal and reasonable affection. I likewise know that, according to the dictates of a *prudent* law, in a commercial state, truth is reckoned a libel; yet I acknowledge, having never made my humanity give place to Gothic gallantry, that I should

---

1   [Shakespeare, *Hamlet* 1.5.150.]
2   [Shakespeare, *Macbeth* 4.1.83.]
3   [Shakespeare, *Hamlet* 1.5.182.]
4   [The confiscation of church property by the revolutionary government is one of Burke's central themes in *Reflections*; see *Writings* 8: 151, 154–60, 162–73, 200–12.]
5   [Johnson, *The Vanity of Human Wishes* 222.]

have been better pleased to have heard that Lord George Gordon was confined on account of the calamities which he brought on his country, than for a *libel* on the queen of France.[1]

But one argument which you adduce to strengthen your assertion, appears to carry the preponderancy towards the other side.

You observe that "our education is so formed as to confirm and fix this impression, (respect for the religious establishment); and that our education is in a manner wholly in the hands of ecclesiastics, and in all stages from infancy to manhood[2]." Far from agreeing with you, Sir, that these regulations render the clergy a more useful and respectable body, experience convinces me that the very contrary is the fact. In schools and colleges they may, in some degree, support their dignity within the monastic walls; but, in paying due respect to the parents of the young nobility under their tutorage, they do not forget, obsequiously, to respect their noble patrons. The little respect paid, in great houses, to tutors and chaplains proves, Sir, the fallacy of your reasoning. It would be almost invidious to remark, that they sometimes are only modern substitutes for the jesters of Gothic memory, and serve as whetstones for the blunt wit of the noble peer who patronizes them; and what respect a boy can imbibe for a *butt*, at which the shaft of ridicule is daily glanced, I leave those to determine who can distinguish depravity of morals under the specious mask of refined manners.

Besides, the custom of sending clergymen to travel with their noble pupils, as humble companions, instead of exalting, tends inevitably to degrade the clerical character: it is notorious that they meanly submit to the most servile dependence, and gloss over the most capricious follies, to use a soft phrase, of the boys to whom they look up for preferment. An airy mitre dances before them, and they wrap their sheep's clothing more closely about them, and make their spirits bend till it is prudent to claim the rights of men and the honest freedom of speech of an Englishman. How, indeed, could they venture to reprove for his vices their patron: the clergy only give the true

---

1  [Burke, *Reflections*; *Writings* 8: 135. Gordon (1751-93) was acquitted of high treason after having instigated the anti-Catholic "Gordon Riots" of June 1780. He was imprisoned for life in 1787 for a libel on British justice and on Marie Antoinette.]
2  Page 148. [Burke, *Reflections*; *Writings* 8: 149.]

feudal emphasis to this word. It has been observed, by men who have not superficially investigated the human heart, that when a man makes his spirit bend to any power but reason, his character is soon degraded, and his mind shackled by the very prejudices to which he submits with reluctance. The observations of experience have been carried still further; and the servility to superiors, and tyranny to inferiors, said to characterize our clergy, have rationally been supposed to arise naturally from their associating with the nobility. Among unequals there can be no society;[1] – giving a manly meaning to the term; from such intimacies friendship can never grow; if the basis of friendship is mutual respect, and not a commercial treaty. Taken thus out of their sphere, and enjoying their tithes at a distance from their flocks, is it not natural for them to become courtly parasites, and intriguing dependents on great patrons, or the treasury? Observing all this – for these things have not been transacted in the dark – our young men of fashion, by a common, though erroneous, association of ideas, have conceived a contempt for religion, as they sucked in with their milk a contempt for the clergy.

The people of England, Sir, in the thirteenth and fourteenth centuries, I will not go any further back to insult the ashes of departed popery, did not settle the establishment, and endow it with princely revenues, to make it proudly rear its head, as a part of the constitutional body, to guard the liberties of the community; but, like some of the laborious commentators on Shakespeare, you have affixed a meaning to laws that chance, or, to speak more philosophically, the interested views of men, settled, not dreaming of your ingenious elucidations.

What, but the rapacity of the only men who exercised their reason, the priests, secured such vast property to the church, when a man gave his perishable substance to save himself from the dark torments of purgatory; and found it more convenient to indulge his depraved appetites, and pay an exorbitant price for absolution, than listen to the suggestions of reason, and work out his own salvation: in a word, was not the separation of religion from morality the work of the priests, and partly achieved in those *honourable* days which you so piously deplore?

---

1   [Milton, *Paradise Lost* 8.383–84.]

That civilization, that the cultivation of the understanding, and refinement of the affections, naturally make a man religious, I am proud to acknowledge. – What else can fill the aching void in the heart, that human pleasures, human friendships can never fill? What else can render us resigned to live, though condemned to ignorance? – What but a profound reverence for the model of all perfection, and the mysterious tie which arises from a love of goodness? What can make us reverence ourselves, but a reverence for that Being, of whom we are a faint image? That mighty Spirit moves on the waters – confusion hears his voice, and the troubled heart ceases to beat with anguish, for trust in Him bade it be still.[1] Conscious dignity may make us rise superior to calumny, and sternly brave the winds of adverse fortune, – raised in our own esteem by the very storms of which we are the sport[2] – but when friends are unkind, and the heart has not the prop on which it fondly leaned, where can a tender suffering being fly but to the Searcher of hearts? and, when death has desolated the present scene, and torn from us the friend of our youth – when we walk along the accustomed path, and, almost fancying nature dead, ask, Where art thou who gave life to these well-known scenes? when memory heightens former pleasures to contrast our present prospects – there is but one source of comfort within our reach; – and in this sublime solitude the world appears to contain only the Creator and the creature, of whose happiness he is the source. – These are human feelings; but I know not of any common nature or common relation amongst men but what results from reason. The common affections and passions equally bind brutes together; and it is only the continuity of those relations that entitles us to the denomination of rational creatures; and this continuity arises from reflection – from the operations of that reason which you contemn with flippant disrespect.

If then it appears, arguing from analogy, that reflection must be the natural foundation of *rational* affections, and of that experience which enables one man to rise above another, a phenomenon that has never been seen in the brute creation, it may not be stretching the argument further than it will go to suppose, that those men who are obliged to

---

1 [Genesis 1: 2; Mark 4: 39; Milton, *Paradise Lost* 7.210-17.]
2 [Cf. Shakespeare, *King Lear* 3.2.1-24, 4.1.36-37.]

exercise their reason have the most reason, and are the persons pointed out by Nature to direct the society of which they make a part, on any extraordinary emergency.

Time only will shew whether the general censure, which you afterwards qualify, if not contradict, and the unmerited contempt that you have ostentatiously displayed of the National Assembly, be founded on reason, the offspring of conviction, or the spawn of envy. Time may shew, that this obscure throng knew more of the human heart and of legislation than the profligates of rank, emasculated by hereditary effeminacy.

It is not, perhaps, of very great consequence who were the founders of a state; savages, thieves, curates, or practitioners in the law. It is true, you might sarcastically remark, that the Romans had always a *smack* of the old leaven, and that the private robbers, supposing the tradition to be true, only became public depredators.[1] You might have added, that their civilization must have been very partial, and had more influence on the manners than morals of the people; or the amusements of the amphitheatre would not have remained an everlasting blot not only on their humanity, but on their refinement, if a vicious elegance of behaviour and luxurious mode of life is not a prostitution of the term. However, the thundering censures which you have cast with a ponderous arm, and the more playful bushfiring of ridicule, are not arguments that will ever depreciate the National Assembly, for applying to their understanding rather than to their imagination, when they met to settle the newly acquired liberty of the state on a solid foundation.

If you had given the same advice to a young history painter of abilities, I should have admired your judgment, and re-echoed your sentiments[2]. Study, you might have said, the noble models of antiquity, till your imagination is inflamed; and, rising above the vulgar practice

---

1 [Burke, *Reflections*; *Writings* 8: 165; Price, *Discourse* 6; see Appendix A.3.]
2 Page 51. "If the last generations of your country appeared without much lustre in your eyes, you might have passed them by, and derived your claims from a more early race of ancestors. Under a pious predilection to those ancestors, your imaginations would have realized in them a standard of virtue and wisdom, beyond the vulgar practice of the hour: and you would have risen with the example to whose imitation you aspired. Respecting your forefathers, you would have been taught to respect yourselves." [Burke, *Reflections*; *Writings* 8: 86.]

of the hour, you may imitate without copying those great originals. A glowing picture, of some interesting moment, would probably have been produced by these natural means; particularly if one little circumstance is not overlooked, that the painter had noble models to revert to, calculated to excite admiration and stimulate exertion.

But, in settling a constitution that involved the happiness of millions, that stretch beyond the computation of science, it was, perhaps, necessary for the Assembly to have a higher model in view than the *imagined* virtues of their forefathers; and wise to deduce their respect for themselves from the only legitimate source, respect for justice. Why was it a duty to repair an ancient castle, built in barbarous ages, of Gothic materials? Why were the legislators obliged to rake amongst heterogeneous ruins; to rebuild old walls, whose foundations could scarcely be explored, when a simple structure might be raised on the foundation of experience, the only valuable inheritance our forefathers could bequeath?[1] Yet of this bequest we can make little use till we have gained a stock of our own; and even then, their inherited experience would rather serve as light-houses, to warn us against dangerous rocks or sand-banks, than as finger-posts that stand at every turning to point out the right road.

Nor was it absolutely necessary that they should be diffident of themselves when they were dissatisfied with, or could not discern the *almost obliterated* constitution of their ancestors[2]. They should first have been convinced that our constitution was not only the best modern, but the best possible one; and that our social compact was the surest foundation of all the *possible* liberty a mass of men could enjoy, that the human understanding could form. They should have been certain that our representation answered all the purposes of representation; and that an established inequality of rank and property secured the liberty of the whole community, instead of rendering it a sounding epithet of subjection, when applied to the nation at large. They should

---

1    [Burke, *Reflections*; *Writings* 8: 85.]
2    Page 53. "If diffident of yourselves, and not clearly discerning the almost obliterated constitution of your ancestors, you had looked to your neighbours in this land, who had kept alive the ancient principles and models of the old common law of Europe meliorated and adapted to its present state—by following wise examples you would have given new examples of wisdom to the world." [Burke, *Reflections*; *Writings* 8: 87.]

have had the same respect for our House of Commons that you, vauntingly, intrude on us, though your conduct throughout life has spoken a very different language; before they made a point of not deviating from the model which first engaged their attention.

That the British House of Commons is filled with every thing illustrious in rank, in descent, in hereditary, and acquired opulence, may be true, – but that it contains every thing respectable in talents, in military, civil, naval, and political distinction, is very problematical. Arguing from natural causes, the very contrary would appear to the speculatist to be the fact; and let experience say whether these speculations are built on sure ground.

It is true you lay great stress on the effects produced by the bare idea of a liberal descent[1]; but from the conduct of men of rank, men of discernment would rather be led to conclude, that this idea obliterated instead of inspiring native dignity, and substituted a factitious pride that disemboweled the man. The liberty of the rich has its ensigns armorial to puff the individual out with insubstantial honours; but where are blazoned the struggles of virtuous poverty? Who, indeed, would dare to blazon what would blur the pompous monumental inscription you boast of, and make us view with horror, as monsters in human shape, the superb gallery of portraits proudly set in battle array?

But to examine the subject more closely. Is it among the list of possibilities that a man of rank and fortune *can* have received a good education? How can he discover that he is a man, when all his wants are instantly supplied, and invention is never sharpened by necessity? Will he labour, for every thing valuable must be the fruit of laborious exertions, to attain knowledge and virtue, in order to merit the affection of his equals, when the flattering attention of sycophants is a more luscious cordial?

Health can only be secured by temperance; but is it easy to persuade a man to live on plain food even to recover his health, who has

---

1  Page 49. "Always acting as if in the presence of canonized forefathers, the spirit of freedom, leading in itself to misrule and excess, is tempered with an awful gravity. This idea of a liberal descent inspires us with a sense of habitual native dignity, which prevents that upstart insolence almost inevitably adhering to and disgracing those who are the first acquirers of any distinction!" [Burke, *Reflections*; *Writings* 8: 85.]

been accustomed to fare sumptuously every day? Can a man relish the simple food of friendship, who has been habitually pampered by flattery? And when the blood boils, and the senses meet allurements on every side, will knowledge be pursued on account of its abstract beauty? No; it is well known that talents are only to be unfolded by industry, and that we must have made some advances, led by an inferior motive, before we discover that they are their own reward.

But *full blown* talents *may*, according to your system, be hereditary, and as independent of ripening judgment, as the inbred feelings that, rising above reason, naturally guard Englishmen from error. Noble franchises! what a grovelling mind must that man have, who can pardon his step-dame Nature for not having made him at least a lord?

And who will, after your description of senatorial virtues,[1] dare to say that our House of Commons has often resembled a bear-garden; and appeared rather like a committee of *ways and means* than a dignified legislative body, though the concentrated wisdom and virtue of the whole nation blazed in one superb constellation? That it contains a dead weight of benumbing opulence I readily allow, and of ignoble ambition; nor is there any thing surpassing belief in a supposition that the raw recruits, when properly drilled by the minister, would gladly march to the Upper House to unite hereditary honours to fortune. But talents, knowledge, and virtue, must be a part of the man, and cannot be put, as robes of state often are, on a servant or a block, to render a pageant more magnificent.

Our House of Commons, it is true, has been celebrated as a school of eloquence, a hot-bed for wit, even when party intrigues narrow the understanding and contract the heart; yet, from the few proficients it has accomplished, this inferior praise is not of great magnitude: nor of great consequence, Mr. Locke would have added, who was ever of opinion that eloquence was oftener employed to make "the worse appear the better part," than to support the dictates of cool judgment.[2] However, the greater number who have gained a seat by their fortune and hereditary rank, are content with their pre-eminence, and

---

1 [Burke, *Reflections*; *Writings* 8: 95.]
2 [Cf. Locke, *An Essay Concerning Human Understanding* (1689), ed. Peter H. Nidditch (Oxford: Clarendon P, 1975) 508; 3.10.34. The words in quotation marks are not from Locke; they are part of the accusation against Socrates: Plato, *Apology* 19b.]

struggle not for more hazardous honours. But you are an exception; you have raised yourself by the exertion of abilities, and thrown the automatons of rank into the back ground. Your exertions have been a generous contest for secondary honours, or a grateful tribute of respect due to the noble ashes that lent a hand to raise you into notice, by introducing you into the house of which you have ever been an ornament, if not a support. But, unfortunately, you have lately lost a great part of your popularity: members were tired of listening to declamation, or had not sufficient taste to be amused when you ingeniously wandered from the question, and said certainly many good things, if they were not to the present purpose. You were the Cicero of one side of the house for years;[1] and then to sink into oblivion, to see your blooming honours fade before you, was enough to rouse all that was human in you – and make you produce the impassioned *Reflections* which have been a glorious revivification of your fame. – Richard is himself again![2] He is still a great man, though he has deserted his post, and buried in elogiums, on church establishments, the enthusiasm that forced him to throw the weight of his talents on the side of liberty and natural rights, when the *will*[3] of the nation oppressed the Americans.

There appears to be such a mixture of real sensibility and fondly cherished romance in your composition, that the present crisis carries you out of yourself; and since you could not be one of the grand movers, the next *best* thing that dazzled your imagination was to be a conspicuous opposer. Full of yourself, you make as much noise to convince the world that you despise the revolution, as Rousseau did to persuade his contemporaries to let him live in obscurity.

Reading your Reflections warily over, it has continually and forcibly struck me, that had you been a Frenchman, you would have been, in spite of your respect for rank and antiquity, a violent revolutionist; and deceived, as you now probably are, by the passions that cloud your reason, have termed your romantic enthusiasm an enlightened love of your country, a benevolent respect for the rights of men.

---

1    [The oratorical genius of Marcus Tullius Cicero (106-43 B.C.) was proverbial.]
2    [Colley Cibber, *The Tragical History of King Richard III* (1700) 5.3.]
3    Page 6. "Being a citizen of a particular state, and bound up in a considerable degree, by its *public will*," &c. [Burke, *Reflections*; *Writings* 8: 56.]

Your imagination would have taken fire, and have found arguments, full as ingenious as those you now offer, to prove that the constitution, of which so few pillars remained, that constitution which time had almost obliterated, was not a model sufficiently noble to deserve close adherence. And, for the English constitution, you might not have had such a profound veneration as you have lately acquired; nay, it is not impossible that you might have entertained the same opinion of the English Parliament, that you professed to have during the American war.

Another observation which, by frequently occurring, has almost grown into a conviction, is simply this, that had the English in general reprobated the French revolution, you would have stood forth alone, and been the avowed Goliah of liberty.[1] But, not liking to see so many brothers near the throne of fame, you have turned the current of your passions, and consequently of your reasoning, another way. Had Dr. Price's sermon not lighted some sparks very like envy in your bosom, I shrewdly suspect that he would have been treated with more candour; nor is it charitable to suppose that any thing but personal pique and hurt vanity could have dictated such bitter sarcasms and reiterated expressions of contempt as occur in your Reflections.

But without fixed principles even goodness of heart is no security from inconsistency, and mild affectionate sensibility only renders a man more ingeniously cruel, when the pangs of hurt vanity are mistaken for virtuous indignation, and the gall of bitterness for the milk of Christian charity.

Where is the dignity, the infallibility of sensibility, in the fair ladies, whom, if the voice of rumour is to be credited, the captive negroes curse in all the agony of bodily pain, for the unheard of tortures they invent? It is probable that some of them, after the sight of a flagellation, compose their ruffled spirits and exercise their tender feelings by the perusal of the last imported novel. — How true these tears are to nature, I leave you to determine. But these ladies may have read your Enquiry concerning the origin of our ideas of the Sublime and Beautiful, and, convinced by your arguments, may have laboured to be pretty, by counterfeiting weakness.[2]

---

1   [1 Samuel 17: 4-54.]
2   [Burke, *Philosophical Enquiry* 100 (3.9), 105-6 (3.16).]

You may have convinced them that *littleness* and *weakness* are the very essence of beauty; and that the Supreme Being, in giving women beauty in the most supereminent degree, seemed to command them, by the powerful voice of Nature, not to cultivate the moral virtues that might chance to excite respect, and interfere with the pleasing sensations they were created to inspire. Thus confining truth, fortitude, and humanity, within the rigid pale of manly morals, they might justly argue, that to be loved, woman's high end and great distinction! they should "learn to lisp, to totter in their walk, and nick-name God's creatures."[1] Never, they might repeat after you, was any man, much less a woman, rendered amiable by the force of those exalted qualities, fortitude, justice, wisdom, and truth; and thus forewarned of the sacrifice they must make to those austere, unnatural virtues, they would be authorized to turn all their attention to their persons, systematically neglecting morals to secure beauty. – Some rational old woman indeed might chance to stumble at this doctrine, and hint, that in avoiding atheism you had not steered clear of the mussulman's creed;[2] but you could readily exculpate yourself by turning the charge on Nature, who made our idea of beauty independent of reason. Nor would it be necessary for you to recollect, that if virtue has any other foundation than worldly utility, you have clearly proved that one half of the human species, at least, have not souls; and that Nature, by making women *little, smooth, delicate, fair* creatures,[3] never designed that they should exercise their reason to acquire the virtues that produce opposite, if not contradictory, feelings. The affection they excite, to be uniform and perfect, should not be tinctured with the respect which moral virtues inspire, lest pain should be blended with pleasure, and admiration disturb the soft intimacy of love. This laxity of morals in the female world is certainly more captivating to a libertine imagination than the cold arguments of reason, that give no sex to virtue. If beautiful weakness be interwoven in a woman's frame, if the chief business of her life be (as you insinuate) to inspire love, and Nature

---

1    [An amalgam of Shakespeare, *Hamlet* 3.1.144-45 and Burke, *Philosophical Enquiry* 100; 3.9. Cf. Macaulay, *Letters* 48.]
2    [Wollstonecraft shared the common Enlightenment misconception that Islam denied women souls.]
3    [Burke, *Philosophical Enquiry* 102-6; 3.13-16.]

has made an eternal distinction between the qualities that dignify a rational being and this animal perfection, her duty and happiness in this life must clash with any preparation for a more exalted state. So that Plato and Milton were grossly mistaken in asserting that human love led to heavenly, and was only an exaltation of the same affection;[1] for the love of the Deity, which is mixed with the most profound reverence, must be love of perfection, and not compassion for weakness.

To say the truth, I not only tremble for the souls of women, but for the good natured man, whom every one loves. The *amiable* weakness of his mind is a strong argument against its immateriality, and seems to prove that beauty relaxes the *solids* of the soul as well as the body.

It follows then immediately, from your own reasoning, that respect and love are antagonist principles; and that, if we really wish to render men more virtuous, we must endeavour to banish all enervating modifications of beauty from civil society. We must, to carry your argument a little further, return to the Spartan regulations, and settle the virtues of men on the stern foundation of mortification and self-denial; for any attempt to civilize the heart, to make it humane by implanting reasonable principles, is a mere philosophic dream. If refinement inevitably lessens respect for virtue, by rendering beauty, the grand tempter, more seductive; if these relaxing feelings are incompatible with the nervous exertions of morality, the sun of Europe is not set; it begins to dawn, when cold metaphysicians try to make the head give laws to the heart.

But should experience prove that there is a beauty in virtue, a charm in order, which necessarily implies exertion, a depraved sensual taste may give way to a more manly one – and *melting* feelings to rational satisfactions. Both may be equally natural to man; the test is their moral difference, and that point reason alone can decide.

Such a glorious change can only be produced by liberty. Inequality of rank must ever impede the growth of virtue, by vitiating the mind that submits or domineers; that is ever employed to procure nourishment for the body, or amusement for the mind. And if this grand example be set by an assembly of unlettered clowns, if they can produce a crisis that may involve the fate of Europe, and "more than

---

1  [Plato, *Symposium* 210a-211c; Milton, *Paradise Lost* 8.589-92.]

Europe[1]," you must allow us to respect unsophisticated reason, and reverence the active exertions that were not relaxed by a fastidious respect for the beauty of rank, or a dread of the deformity produced by any *void* in the social structure.

After your contemptuous manner of speaking of the National Assembly, after descanting on the coarse vulgarity of their proceedings,[2] which, according to your own definition of virtue, is a proof of its genuineness;[3] was it not a little inconsistent, not to say absurd, to assert, that a dozen people of quality were not a sufficient counterpoise to the vulgar mob with whom they condescended to associate?[4] Have we half a dozen leaders of eminence in our House of Commons, or even in the fashionable world? yet the sheep obsequiously pursue their steps with all the undeviating sagacity of instinct.

In order that liberty should have a firm foundation, an acquaintance with the world would naturally lead cool men to conclude that it must be laid, knowing the weakness of the human heart, and the "deceitfulness of riches,"[5] either by *poor* men, or philosophers, if a sufficient number of men, disinterested from principle, or truly wise, could be found. Was it natural to expect that sensual prejudices should give way to reason, or present feelings to enlarged views? – No; I am afraid that human nature is still in such a weak state, that the abolition of titles,[6] the corner-stone of despotism, could only have been the work of men who had no titles to sacrifice. The National Assembly, it is true, contains some honourable exceptions; but the majority had not such powerful feelings to struggle with, when reason led them to respect the naked dignity of virtue.

Weak minds are always timid. And what can equal the weakness of mind produced by servile flattery, and the vapid pleasures that neither hope nor fear seasoned? Had the constitution of France been new

---

1   Page 11. "It looks to me as if I were in a great crisis, not of the affairs of France alone but of all Europe, perhaps of more than Europe. All circumstances taken together, the French revolution is the most astonishing that has hitherto happened in the world." [Burke, *Reflections*; *Writings* 8: 60.]

2   [Burke, *Reflections*; *Writings* 8: 131.]

3   [Burke, *A Vindication of Natural Society* (1756); *Works* 1: 66. In fact, this work is an ironic exercise in "the abuse of reason" (1: 7).]

4   [Burke, *Reflections*; *Writings* 8: 103.]

5   [Matthew 13: 22.]

6   [The National Assembly abolished hereditary titles on 19 June 1790.]

modelled, or more cautiously repaired, by the lovers of elegance and beauty, it is natural to suppose that the imagination would have erected a fragile temporary building; or the power of one tyrant, divided amongst a hundred, might have rendered the struggle for liberty only a choice of masters. And the glorious *chance* that is now given to human nature of attaining more virtue and happiness than has hitherto blessed our globe, might have been sacrificed to a meteor of the imagination, a bubble of passion. The ecclesiastics, indeed, would probably have remained in quiet possession of their sinecures; and your gall might not have been mixed with your ink on account of the daring sacrilege that brought them more on a level. The nobles would have had bowels for their younger sons, if not for the misery of their fellow-creatures. An august mass of property would have been transmitted to posterity to guard the temple of superstition, and prevent reason from entering with her officious light. And the pomp of religion would have continued to impress the senses, if she were unable to subjugate the passions.

Is hereditary weakness necessary to render religion lovely? and will her form have lost the smooth delicacy that inspires love, when stripped of its Gothic drapery? Must every grand model be placed on the pedestal of property? and is there no beauteous proportion in virtue, when not clothed in a sensual garb?

Of these questions there would be no end, though they lead to the same conclusion; – that your politics and morals, when simplified, would undermine religion and virtue to set up a spurious, sensual beauty, that has long debauched your imagination, under the specious form of natural feelings.

And what is this mighty revolution in property? The present incumbents only are injured, or the hierarchy of the clergy, an ideal part of the constitution, which you have personified, to render your affection more tender. How has posterity been injured by a distribution of the property snatched, perhaps, from innocent hands, but accumulated by the most abominable violation of every sentiment of justice and piety? Was the monument of former ignorance and iniquity to be held sacred, to enable the present possessors of enormous benefices to *dissolve* in indolent pleasures? Was not their convenience, for they have not been turned adrift on the world, to give place to a just partition of the land belonging to the state? And did not the respect due to the natural equality of man require this triumph over Monkish rapacity? Were those monsters to be reverenced on account of their antiquity, and their unjust claims perpetuated to their ideal children, the clergy, merely to preserve the sacred majesty of Property inviolate, and to enable the Church to retain her pristine splendor? Can posterity be injured by individuals losing the chance of obtaining great wealth, without meriting it, by its being diverted from a narrow channel, and disembogued into the sea that affords clouds to water all the land? Besides, the clergy not brought up with the expectation of great revenues will not feel the loss; and if bishops should happen to be chosen on account of their personal merit, religion may be benefited by the vulgar nomination.

The sophistry of asserting that Nature leads us to reverence our civil institutions from the same principle that we venerate aged individuals, is a palpable fallacy "that is so like truth, it will serve the turn as well." And when you add, "that we have chosen our nature rather than our speculations, our breasts rather than our inventions[1]," the pretty jargon seems equally unintelligible.

But it was the downfall of the visible power and dignity of the church that roused your ire; you could have excused a little squeezing of the individuals to supply present exigencies; the actual possessors of the property might have been oppressed with something like impunity, if the church had not been spoiled of its gaudy trappings. You love the church, your country, and its laws, you repeatedly tell us, because they deserve to be loved; but from you this is not a panegyric: weakness and indulgence are the only incitements to love and confidence that you can discern,[2] and it cannot be denied that the tender mother you venerate deserves, on this score, all your affection.

It would be as vain a task to attempt to obviate all your passionate

---

1 Page 50. "We procure reverence to our civil institutions on the principle upon which nature teaches us to revere individual men; on account of their age; and on account of those from whom they are descended. All your sophisters cannot produce any thing better adapted to preserve a rational and manly freedom than the course that we have pursued; who have chosen our nature rather than our speculations, our breasts rather than our inventions, for the great conservatories and magazines of our rights and privileges." [Burke, *Reflections; Writings* 8: 85.]

2 [Burke, *Philosophical Enquiry* 103; 3.13.]

objections, as to unravel all your plausible arguments, often illustrated by known truths, and rendered forcible by pointed invectives. I only attack the foundation. On the natural principles of justice I build my plea for disseminating the property artfully said to be appropriated to religious purposes, but, in reality, to support idle tyrants, amongst the society whose ancestors were cheated or forced into illegal grants. Can there be an opinion more subversive of morality, than that time sanctifies crimes, and silences the blood that calls out for retribution, if not for vengeance? If the revenue annexed to the Gallic church was greater than the most bigoted protestant would now allow to be its reasonable share, would it not have been trampling on the rights of men to perpetuate such an arbitrary appropriation of the common stock, because time had rendered the fraudulent seizure venerable? Besides, if Reason had suggested, as surely she must, if the imagination had not been allowed to dwell on the fascinating pomp of ceremonial grandeur, that the clergy would be rendered both more virtuous and useful by being put more on a par with each other, and the mass of the people it was their duty to instruct; – where was there room for hesitation? The charge of presumption, thrown by you on the most reasonable innovations, may, without any violence to truth, be retorted on every reformation that has meliorated our condition, and even on the improvable faculty that gives us a claim to the pre-eminence of intelligent beings.

Plausibility, I know, can only be unmasked by shewing the absurdities it glosses over, and the simple truths it involves with specious errors. Eloquence has often confounded triumphant villany; but it is probable that it has more frequently rendered the boundary that separates virtue and vice doubtful. – Poisons may be only medicines in judicious hands; but they should not be administered by the ignorant, because they have sometimes seen great cures performed by their powerful aid.[1]

The many sensible remarks and pointed observations which you have mixed with opinions that strike at our dearest interests, fortify those opinions, and give them a degree of strength that renders them formidable to the wise, and convincing to the superficial. It is impossible to read half a dozen pages of your book without admiring your

1   [Cf. Plato, *Phaedrus* 268a–c, 270b–c.]

ingenuity, or indignantly spurning your sophisms. Words are heaped on words, till the understanding is confused by endeavouring to disentangle the sense, and the memory by tracing contradictions. After observing a host of these contradictions, it can scarcely be a breach of charity to think that you have often sacrificed your sincerity to enforce your favourite arguments, and called in your judgment to adjust the arrangement of words that could not convey its dictates.

A fallacy of this kind, I think, could not have escaped you when you were treating the subject that called forth your bitterest animadversions, the confiscation of the ecclesiastical revenue. Who of the vindicators of the rights of men ever ventured to assert, that the clergy of the present day should be punished on account of the intolerable pride and inhuman cruelty of many of their predecessors[1]? No; such a thought never entered the mind of those who warred with inveterate prejudices. A desperate disease required a powerful remedy. Injustice had no right to rest on prescription; nor has the character of the present clergy any weight in the argument.

You find it very difficult to separate policy from justice: in the political world they have frequently been separated with shameful dexterity. To mention a recent instance. According to the limited views of timid, or interested politicians, an abolition of the infernal slave trade would not only be unsound policy, but a flagrant infringement of the laws (which are allowed to have been infamous) that induced the planters to purchase their estates. But is it not consonant with justice, with the common principles of humanity, not to mention Christianity, to abolish this abominable mischief?[2] There is not one argument, one invective, levelled by you at the confiscators of the church revenue, which could not, with the strictest propriety, be applied by the planters and negro-drivers to our Parliament, if it glo-

---

1   *Vide* Page 210. [Burke, *Reflections*; *Writings* 8: 191.]

2   "When men are encouraged to go into a certain mode of life by the existing laws, and protected in that mode as in a lawful occupation—when they have accommodated *all their ideas, and all their habits to it,*" &c.—"I am sure it is unjust in legislature, by an arbitrary act, to offer a sudden violence to their minds and their feelings; forcibly to degrade them from their state and condition, and to stigmatize with shame and infamy that character and those customs which before had been made the measure of their happiness." Page 230. [Burke, *Reflections*; *Writings* 8: 205; Wollstonecraft's italics. See Appendix A.1.]

riously dared to shew the world that British senators were men: if the natural feelings of humanity silenced the cold cautions of timidity, till this stigma on our nature was wiped off, and all men were allowed to enjoy their birth-right – liberty, till by their crimes they had authorized society to deprive them of the blessing they had abused.[1]

The same arguments might be used in India, if any attempt were made to bring back things to nature, to prove that a man ought never to quit the cast that confined him to the profession of his lineal forefathers. The Bramins would doubtless find many ingenious reasons to justify this debasing, though venerable prejudice;[2] and would not, it is to be supposed, forget to observe that time, by interweaving the oppressive law with many useful customs, had rendered it for the present very convenient, and consequently legal.[3] Almost every vice that has degraded our nature might be justified by shewing that it had been productive of *some* benefit to society: for it would be as difficult to point out positive evil as unallayed good, in this imperfect state. What indeed would become of morals, if they had no other test than prescription? The manners of men may change without end; but, wherever reason receives the least cultivation – wherever men rise above brutes, morality must rest on the same base. And the more man discovers of the nature of his mind and body, the more clearly he is convinced, that to act according to the dictates of reason is to conform to the law of God.

The test of honour may be arbitrary and fallacious, and, retiring into subterfuge, elude close enquiry; but true morality shuns not the day, nor shrinks from the ordeal of investigation. Most of the happy revolutions that have taken place in the world have happened when weak princes held the reins they could not manage; but are they, on that account, to be canonized as saints or demi-gods, and pushed forward to notice on the throne of ignorance? Pleasure wants a zest, if experience cannot compare it with pain; but who courts pain to heighten his pleasures? A transient view of society will further illus-

---

1   [See Appendix A.1.]
2   [See Appendix A.4.ii.]
3   [In the other great cause of his later career, the impeachment of Warren Hastings, Governor-General of India (1787-95), Burke argued that Western standards of legality should be applied to the government of the East. Hastings was acquitted.]

trate arguments which appear so obvious that I am almost ashamed to produce illustrations. How many children have been taught oeconomy, and many other virtues, by the extravagant thoughtlessness of their parents; yet a good education is allowed to be an inestimable blessing. The tenderest mothers are often the most unhappy wives; but can the good that accrues from the private distress that produces a sober dignity of mind justify the inflictor? Right or wrong may be estimated according to the point of sight, and other adventitious circumstances; but, to discover its real nature, the enquiry must go deeper than the surface, and beyond the local consequences that confound good and evil together. The rich and weak, a numerous train, will certainly applaud your system, and loudly celebrate your pious reverence for authority and establishments – they find it pleasanter to enjoy than to think; to justify oppression than correct abuses. – *The rights of men* are grating sounds that set their teeth on edge; the impertinent enquiry of philosophic meddling innovation. If the poor are in distress, they will make some *benevolent* exertions to assist them; they will confer obligations, but not do justice. Benevolence is a very amiable specious quality; yet the aversion which men feel to accept a right as a favour, should rather be extolled as a vestige of native dignity, than stigmatized as the odious offspring of ingratitude. The poor consider the rich as their lawful prey; but we ought not too severely to animadvert on their ingratitude. When they receive an alms they are commonly grateful at the moment; but old habits quickly return, and cunning has ever been a substitute for force.

That both physical and moral evil were not only foreseen, but entered into the scheme of Providence, when this world was contemplated in the Divine mind, who can doubt, without robbing Omnipotence of a most exalted attribute? But the business of the life of a good man should be, to separate light from darkness; to diffuse happiness, whilst he submits to unavoidable misery. And a conviction that there is much unavoidable wretchedness, appointed by the grand Disposer of all events, should not slacken his exertions: the extent of what is possible can only be discerned by God. The justice of God may be vindicated by a belief in a future state; but, only by believing that evil is educing good for the individual, and not for an imaginary whole. The happiness of the whole must arise from the happiness of

the constituent parts, or the essence of justice is sacrificed to a supposed grand arrangement. And that may be good for the whole of a
creature's existence, that disturbs the comfort of a small portion. The
evil which an individual suffers for the good of the community is partial, it must be allowed, if the account is settled by death. – But the
partial evil which it suffers, during one stage of existence, to render
another stage more perfect, is strictly just. The Father of all only can
regulate the education of his children. To suppose that, during the
whole or part of its existence, the happiness of any individual is sacrificed to promote the welfare of ten, or ten thousand, other beings – is
impious. But to suppose that the happiness, or animal enjoyment, of
one portion of existence is sacrificed to improve and ennoble the
being itself, and render it capable of more perfect happiness, is not to
reflect on either the goodness or wisdom of God.

It may be confidently asserted that no man chooses evil, because it
is evil; he only mistakes it for happiness, the good he seeks. And the
desire of rectifying these mistakes, is the noble ambition of an enlightened understanding, the impulse of feelings that Philosophy invigo-
rates. To endeavour to make unhappy men resigned to their fate, is the
tender endeavour of short-sighted benevolence, of transient yearnings
of humanity; but to labour to increase human happiness by extirpat-
ing error, is a masculine godlike affection. This remark may be carried
still further. Men who possess uncommon sensibility, whose quick
emotions shew how closely the eye and heart are connected, soon
forget the most forcible sensations. Not tarrying long enough in the
brain to be subject to reflection, the next sensations, of course, obliterate them. Memory, however, treasures up these proofs of native
goodness; and the being who is not spurred on to any virtuous act,
still thinks itself of consequence, and boasts of its feelings. Why?
Because the sight of distress, or an affecting narrative, made its blood
flow with more velocity, and the heart, literally speaking, beat with
sympathetic emotion. We ought to beware of confounding mechanical instinctive sensations with emotions that reason deepens, and justly terms the feelings of *humanity*. This word discriminates the active
exertions of virtue from the vague declamation of sensibility.

The declaration of the National Assembly, when they recognized
the rights of men, was calculated to touch the humane heart – the

downfall of the clergy, to agitate the pupil of impulse. On the watch to find fault, faults met your prying eye; a different prepossession might have produced a different conviction.

When we read a book that supports our favourite opinions, how eagerly do we suck in the doctrines, and suffer our minds placidly to reflect the images that illustrate the tenets we have previously embraced. We indolently acquiesce in the conclusion, and our spirit animates and corrects the various subjects. But when, on the contrary, we peruse a skilful writer, with whom we do not coincide in opinion, how attentive is the mind to detect fallacy. And this suspicious coolness often prevents our being carried away by a stream of natural eloquence, which the prejudiced mind terms declamation – a pomp of words! We never allow ourselves to be warmed; and, after contending with the writer, are more confirmed in our opinion; as much, perhaps, from a spirit of contradiction as from reason. A lively imagination is ever in danger of being betrayed into error by favourite opinions, which it almost personifies, the more effectually to intoxicate the understanding. Always tending to extremes, truth is left behind in the heat of the chace, and things are viewed as positively good, or bad, though they wear an equivocal face.

Some celebrated writers have supposed that wit and judgment were incompatible; opposite qualities, that, in a kind of elementary strife, destroyed each other:[1] and many men of wit have endeavoured to prove that they were mistaken. Much may be adduced by wits and metaphysicians on both sides of the question. But, from experience, I am apt to believe that they do weaken each other, and that great quickness of comprehension, and facile association of ideas, naturally preclude profundity of research. Wit is often a lucky hit; the result of a momentary inspiration. We know not whence it comes, and it blows where it lists.[2] The operations of judgment, on the contrary, are cool and circumspect; and coolness and deliberation are great enemies to enthusiasm. If wit is of so fine a spirit, that it almost evaporates when translated into another language, why may not the temperature have an influence over it? This remark may be thought derogatory to the inferior qualities of the mind: but it is not a hasty one; and I mention

---

1    [Burke, *Philosophical Enquiry*, "Introduction on Taste" 17; Locke, *Essay* 156; 2.11.2.]
2    [John 3: 8.]

it as a prelude to a conclusion I have frequently drawn, that the cultivation of reason damps fancy. The blessings of Heaven lie on each side; we must choose, if we wish to attain any degree of superiority, and not lose our lives in laborious idleness. If we mean to build our knowledge or happiness on a rational basis, we must learn to distinguish the *possible*, and not fight against the stream. And if we are careful to guard ourselves from imaginary sorrows and vain fears, we must also resign many enchanting illusions: for shallow must be the discernment which fails to discover that raptures and ecstasies arise from error. – Whether it will always be so, is not now to be discussed; suffice it to observe, that Truth is seldom arrayed by the Graces; and if she charms, it is only by inspiring a sober satisfaction, which takes its rise from a calm contemplation of proportion and simplicity. But, though it is allowed that one man has by nature more fancy than another, in each individual there is a spring-tide when fancy should govern and amalgamate materials for the understanding; and a graver period, when those materials should be employed by the judgment. For example, I am inclined to have a better opinion of the heart of an *old* man, who speaks of Sterne as his favourite author, than of his understanding. There are times and seasons for all things: and moralists appear to me to err, when they would confound the gaiety of youth with the seriousness of age; for the virtues of age look not only more imposing, but more natural, when they appear rather rigid. He who has not exercised his judgment to curb his imagination during the meridian of life, becomes, in its decline, too often the prey of childish feelings. Age demands respect; youth love: if this order is disturbed, the emotions are not pure; and when love for a man in his grand climacteric takes place of respect, it, generally speaking, borders on contempt. Judgment is sublime, wit beautiful; and, according to your own theory, they cannot exist together without impairing each other's power.[1] The predominancy of the latter, in your endless Reflections, should lead hasty readers to suspect that it may, in a great degree, exclude the former.

But, among all your plausible arguments, and witty illustrations, your contempt for the poor always appears conspicuous, and rouses my indignation. The following paragraph in particular struck me, as

1   [Burke, *Philosophical Enquiry*, "Introduction on Taste" 17; Locke, *Essay* 156; 2.11.2.]

breathing the most tyrannic spirit, and displaying the most factitious feelings. "Good order is the foundation of all good things. To be enabled to acquire, the people, without being servile, must be tractable and obedient. The magistrate must have his reverence, the laws their authority. The body of the people must not find the principles of natural subordination by art rooted out of their minds. They *must* respect that property of which they *cannot* partake. *They must labour to obtain what by labour can be obtained; and when they find, as they commonly do, the success disproportioned to the endeavour, they must be taught their consolation in the final proportions of eternal justice.* Of this consolation, whoever deprives them, deadens their industry, and strikes at the root of all acquisition as of all conservation. He that does this, is the cruel oppressor, the merciless enemy, of the poor and wretched; at the same time that, by his wicked speculations, he exposes the fruits of successful industry, and the accumulations of fortune," (ah! there's the rub)[1] "to the plunder of the negligent, the disappointed, and the unprosperous[2]."

This is contemptible hard-hearted sophistry, in the specious form of humility, and submission to the will of Heaven. – It is, Sir, *possible* to render the poor happier in this world, without depriving them of the consolation which you gratuitously grant them in the next. They have a right to more comfort than they at present enjoy; and more comfort might be afforded them, without encroaching on the pleasures of the rich: not now waiting to enquire whether the rich have any right to exclusive pleasures. What do I say? – encroaching! No; if an intercourse were established between them, it would impart the only true pleasure that can be snatched in this land of shadows, this hard school of moral discipline.

I know, indeed, that there is often something disgusting in the distresses of poverty, at which the imagination revolts, and starts back to exercise itself in the more attractive Arcadia of fiction. The rich man builds a house, art and taste give it the highest finish. His gardens are planted, and the trees grow to recreate the fancy of the planter, though the temperature of the climate may rather force him to avoid the dangerous damps they exhale, than seek the umbrageous retreat.

---

1  [Shakespeare, *Hamlet* 3.1.65.]
2  Page 351. [Burke, *Reflections; Writings* 8: 290.]

Every thing on the estate is cherished but man; – yet, to contribute to the happiness of man, is the most sublime of all enjoyments. But if, instead of sweeping pleasure-grounds, obelisks, temples, and elegant cottages, as *objects* for the eye, the heart was allowed to beat true to nature, decent farms would be scattered over the estate, and plenty smile around. Instead of the poor being subject to the griping hand of an avaricious steward, they would be watched over with fatherly solicitude, by the man whose duty and pleasure it was to guard their happiness, and shield from rapacity the beings who, by the sweat of their brow, exalted him above his fellows.

I could almost imagine I see a man thus gathering blessings as he mounted the hill of life; or consolation, in those days when the spirits lag, and the tired heart finds no pleasure in them. It is not by squandering alms that the poor can be relieved, or improved – it is the fostering sun of kindness, the wisdom that finds them employments calculated to give them habits of virtue, that meliorates their condition. Love is only the fruit of love; condescension and authority may produce the obedience you applaud; but he has lost his heart of flesh who can see a fellow-creature humbled before him, and trembling at the frown of a being, whose heart is supplied by the same vital current, and whose pride ought to be checked by a consciousness of having the same infirmities.

What salutary dews might not be shed to refresh this thirsty land, if men were more *enlightened!* Smiles and premiums might encourage cleanliness, industry, and emulation. – A garden more inviting than Eden would then meet the eye, and springs of joy murmur on every side. The clergyman would superintend his own flock, the shepherd would then love the sheep he daily tended; the school might rear its decent head, and the buzzing tribe, let loose to play, impart a portion of their vivacious spirits to the heart that longed to open their minds, and lead them to taste the pleasures of men. Domestic comfort, the civilizing relations of husband, brother, and father, would soften labour, and render life contented.

Returning once from a despotic country[1] to a part of England well cultivated, but not very picturesque – with what delight did I not observe the poor man's garden! – The homely palings and twining

---

1  [Portugal, which Wollstonecraft visited in 1785.]

woodbine, with all the rustic contrivances of simple, unlettered taste, was a sight which relieved the eye that had wandered indignant from the stately palace to the pestiferous hovel, and turned from the awful contrast into itself to mourn the fate of man, and curse the arts of civilization!

Why cannot large estates be divided into small farms? these dwellings would indeed grace our land. Why are huge forests still allowed to stretch out with idle pomp and all the indolence of Eastern grandeur? Why does the brown waste meet the traveller's view, when men want work? But commons cannot be enclosed without *acts of parliament* to increase the property of the rich![1] Why might not the industrious peasant be allowed to steal a farm from the heath? This sight I have seen; – the cow that supported the children grazed near the hut, and the cheerful poultry were fed by the chubby babes, who breathed a bracing air, far from the diseases and the vices of cities. Domination blasts all these prospects; virtue can only flourish amongst equals, and the man who submits to a fellow-creature, because it promotes his worldly interest, and he who relieves only because it is his duty to lay up a treasure in heaven,[2] are much on a par, for both are radically degraded by the habits of their life.

In this great city, that proudly rears its head, and boasts of its population and commerce, how much misery lurks in pestilential corners, whilst idle mendicants assail, on every side, the man who hates to encourage impostors, or repress, with angry frown, the plaints of the poor! How many mechanics, by a flux of trade or fashion, lose their employment; whom misfortunes, not to be warded off, lead to the idleness that vitiates their character and renders them afterwards averse to honest labour! Where is the eye that marks these evils, more gigantic than any of the infringements of property, which you piously deprecate? Are these remediless evils? And is the humane heart satisfied with turning the poor over to *another* world, to receive the blessings this could afford? If society was regulated on a more enlarged plan; if man was contented to be the friend of man, and did not seek to bury the sympathies of humanity in the servile appellation

---

1   [At the beginning of the eighteenth century, half the land in England was common land; by the middle of the nineteenth, it had almost all been enclosed.]

2   [Matthew 6: 20.]

of master; if, turning his eyes from ideal regions of taste and elegance, he laboured to give the earth he inhabited all the beauty it is capable of receiving, and was ever on the watch to shed abroad all the happiness which human nature can enjoy; – he who, respecting the rights of men, wishes to convince or persuade society that this is true happiness and dignity, is not the cruel *oppressor* of the poor, nor a short-sighted philosopher – HE fears God and loves his fellow-creatures. – Behold the whole duty of man! – the citizen who acts differently is a sophisticated being.

Surveying civilized life, and seeing, with undazzled eye, the polished vices of the rich, their insincerity, want of natural affections, with all the specious train that luxury introduces, I have turned impatiently to the poor, to look for man undebauched by riches or power – but, alas! what did I see? a being scarcely above the brutes, over which he tyrannized; a broken spirit, worn-out body, and all those gross vices which the example of the rich, rudely copied, could produce. Envy built a wall of separation, that made the poor hate, whilst they bent to their superiors; who, on their part, stepped aside to avoid the loathsome sight of human misery.

What were the outrages of a day[1] to these continual miseries? Let those sorrows hide their diminished head before the tremendous mountain of woe that thus defaces our globe! Man preys on man; and you mourn for the idle tapestry that decorated a gothic pile, and the dronish bell that summoned the fat priest to prayer. You mourn for the empty pageant of a name, when slavery flaps her wing, and the sick heart retires to die in lonely wilds, far from the abodes of men. Did the pangs you felt for insulted nobility, the anguish that rent your heart when the gorgeous robes were torn off the idol human weakness had set up, deserve to be compared with the long-drawn sigh of melancholy reflection, when misery and vice are thus seen to haunt our steps, and swim on the top of every cheering prospect? Why is our fancy to be appalled by terrific perspectives of a hell beyond the grave? – Hell stalks abroad; – the lash resounds on the slave's naked sides; and the sick wretch, who can no longer earn the sour bread of unremitting labour, steals to a ditch to bid the world a long good

---

1  The 6th of October.

night[1] – or, neglected in some ostentatious hospital, breathes his last amidst the laugh of mercenary attendants.

Such misery demands more than tears – I pause to recollect myself; and smother the contempt I feel rising for your rhetorical flourishes and infantine sensibility.

------------------------------------------------------------

Taking a retrospective view of my hasty answer, and casting a cursory glance over your *Reflections*, I perceive that I have not alluded to several reprehensible passages, in your elaborate work; which I marked for censure when I first perused it with a steady eye. And now I find it almost impossible candidly to refute your sophisms, without quoting your own words, and putting the numerous contradictions I observed in opposition to each other. This would be an effectual refutation; but, after such a tedious drudgery, I fear I should only be read by the patient eye that scarcely wanted my assistance to detect the flagrant errors. It would be a tedious process to shew, that often the most just and forcible illustrations are warped to colour over opinions *you* must *sometimes* have secretly despised; or, at least, have discovered, that what you asserted without limitation, required the greatest. Some subjects of exaggeration may have been superficially viewed: depth of judgment is, perhaps, incompatible with the predominant features of your mind. Your reason may have often been the dupe of your imagination; but say, did you not sometimes angrily bid her be still, when she whispered that you were departing from strict truth? Or, when assuming the awful form of conscience, and only smiling at the vagaries of vanity, did she not austerely bid you recollect your own errors, before you lifted the avenging stone?[2] Did she not sometimes wave her hand, when you poured forth a torrent of shining sentences, and beseech you to concatenate them – plainly telling you that the impassioned eloquence of the heart was calculated rather to affect than dazzle the reader, whom it hurried along to conviction? Did she not anticipate the remark of the wise, who drink not at a shallow sparkling stream, and tell you that they would discover when, with the dignity of sincerity, you supported an opinion that only appeared to you with one

---

1   [See Appendix A.1.]
2   [ John 8: 7.]

face; or, when superannuated vanity made you torture your invention? – But I forbear.

I have before animadverted on our method of electing representatives, convinced that it debauches both the morals of the people and the candidates, without rendering the member really responsible, or attached to his constituents; but, amongst your other contradictions, you blame the National Assembly for expecting any exertions from the servile principle of responsibility, and afterwards insult them for not rendering themselves responsible.[1] Whether the one the French have adopted will answer the purpose better, and be more than a shadow of representation, time only can shew. In theory it appears more promising.

Your real or artificial affection for the English constitution seems to me to resemble the brutal affection of some weak characters. They think it a duty to love their relations with a blind, indolent tenderness, that *will not* see the faults it might assist to correct, if their affection had been built on rational grounds. They love they know not why, and they will love to the end of the chapter.

Is it absolute blasphemy to doubt of the omnipotence of the law, or to suppose that religion might be more pure if there were fewer baits for hypocrites in the church? But our manners, you tell us, are drawn from the French, though you had before celebrated our native plainness[2]. If they were, it is time we broke loose from dependance – – Time that Englishmen drew water from their own springs; for, if manners are not a painted substitute for morals, we have only to cultivate our reason, and we shall not feel the want of an arbitrary model. Nature will suffice; but I forget myself: – Nature and Reason, according to your system, are all to give place to authority; and the gods, as

---

1   [Burke, *Reflections*; *Writings* 8: 234-37, 249.]
2   Page 118. "It is not clear, whether in England we learned those grand and decorous principles, and manners, of which considerable traces yet remain, from you, or whether you took them from us. But to you, I think, we trace them best. You seem to me to be—*gentis incunabula nostrae*. France has always more or less influenced manners in England; and when your fountain is choaked up and polluted, the stream will not run long, or not run clear with us, or perhaps with any nation. This gives all Europe, in my opinion, but too close and connected a concern in what is done in France." [Burke, *Reflections*; *Writings* 8: 131. The Latin means "the cradle of our race" (Virgil, *Aeneid* 3.105).]

Shakespeare makes a frantic wretch exclaim, seem to kill us for their sport, as men do flies.[1]

Before I conclude my cursory remarks, it is but just to acknowledge that I coincide with you in your opinion respecting the *sincerity* of many modern philosophers.[2] Your consistency in avowing a veneration for rank and riches deserves praise; but I must own that I have often indignantly observed that some of the *enlightened* philosophers, who talk most vehemently of the native rights of men, borrow many noble sentiments to adorn their conversation, which have no influence on their conduct. They bow down to rank, and are careful to secure property; for virtue, without this adventitious drapery, is seldom very respectable in their eyes – nor are they very quick-sighted to discern real dignity of character when no sounding name exalts the man above his fellows. – But neither open enmity nor hollow homage destroys the intrinsic value of those principles which rest on an eternal foundation, and revert for a standard to the immutable attributes of God.

THE END.

---

1    [Shakespeare, *King Lear* 4.1.36-37.]
2    [Burke, *Reflections*; *Writings* 8: 114.]

A

# VINDICATION

OF THE

# RIGHTS OF WOMAN:

WITH

# STRICTURES

ON

# POLITICAL AND MORAL SUBJECTS.

BY MARY WOLLSTONECRAFT.

VOL. I.

THE SECOND EDITION.

# M. TALLEYRAND-PÉRIGORD,

## LATE BISHOP OF AUTUN.[1]

SIR,

HAVING read with great pleasure a pamphlet which you have lately published,[2] I dedicate this volume to you; to induce you to reconsider the subject, and maturely weigh what I have advanced respecting the rights of woman and national education: and I call with the firm tone of humanity; for my arguments, Sir, are dictated by a disinterested spirit – I plead for my sex – not for myself. Independence I have long considered as the grand blessing of life, the basis of every virtue – and independence I will ever secure by contracting my wants, though I were to live on a barren heath.

It is then an affection for the whole human race that makes my pen dart rapidly along to support what I believe to be the cause of virtue: and the same motive leads me earnestly to wish to see woman placed in a station in which she would advance, instead of retarding, the progress of those glorious principles that give a substance to morality. My opinion, indeed, respecting the rights and duties of woman, seems to flow so naturally from these simple principles, that I think it scarcely possible, but that some of the enlarged minds who formed your admirable constitution, will coincide with me.

In France there is undoubtedly a more general diffusion of knowledge than in any part of the European world, and I attribute it, in a great measure, to the social intercourse which has long subsisted

---

1    [Charles-Maurice de Talleyrand-Périgord (1754-1838) was made Bishop of Autun in 1788. As minister of finance in the French revolutionary government, he initiated the confiscation of church property that so exercised Burke. He resigned his bishopric in January 1791 and was excommunicated that April.]

2    [*Rapport sur l'instruction publique, fait au nom du Comité de Constitution à l'Assemblée Nationale, les 10, 11, et 19 Septembre 1791, par M. de Talleyrand-Périgord, Ancien Évêque d'Autun.* Talleyrand prepared the report with the help of such distinguished thinkers as Condorcet and Laplace.]

between the sexes. It is true, I utter my sentiments with freedom, that in France the very essence of sensuality has been extracted to regale the voluptuary, and a kind of sentimental lust has prevailed, which, together with the system of duplicity that the whole tenour of their political and civil government taught, have given a sinister sort of sagacity to the French character, properly termed finesse; from which naturally flow a polish of manners that injures the substance, by hunting sincerity out of society. – And, modesty, the fairest garb of virtue! has been more grossly insulted in France than even in England, till their women have treated as *prudish* that attention to decency, which brutes instinctively observe.

Manners and morals are so nearly allied that they have often been confounded; but, though the former should only be the natural reflection of the latter, yet, when various causes have produced factitious and corrupt manners, which are very early caught, morality becomes an empty name. The personal reserve, and sacred respect for cleanliness and delicacy in domestic life, which French women almost despise, are the graceful pillars of modesty; but, far from despising them, if the pure flame of patriotism have reached their bosoms, they should labour to improve the morals of their fellow-citizens, by teaching men, not only to respect modesty in women, but to acquire it themselves, as the only way to merit their esteem.

Contending for the rights of woman, my main argument is built on this simple principle, that if she be not prepared by education to become the companion of man, she will stop the progress of knowledge and virtue; for truth must be common to all, or it will be inefficacious with respect to its influence on general practice. And how can woman be expected to co-operate unless she know why she ought to be virtuous? unless freedom strengthen her reason till she comprehend her duty, and see in what manner it is connected with her real good? If children are to be educated to understand the true principle of patriotism, their mother must be a patriot; and the love of mankind, from which an orderly train of virtues spring, can only be produced by considering the moral and civil interest of mankind; but the education and situation of woman, at present, shuts her out from such investigations.

In this work I have produced many arguments, which to me were conclusive, to prove that the prevailing notion respecting a sexual[1] character was subversive of morality, and I have contended, that to render the human body and mind more perfect, chastity must more universally prevail, and that chastity will never be respected in the male world till the person of a woman is not, as it were, idolized, when little virtue or sense embellish it with the grand traces of mental beauty, or the interesting simplicity of affection.

Consider, Sir, dispassionately, these observations – for a glimpse of this truth seemed to open before you when you observed, "that to see one half of the human race excluded by the other from all participation of government, was a political phaenomenon that, according to abstract principles, it was impossible to explain."[2] If so, on what does your constitution rest? If the abstract rights of man[3] will bear discussion and explanation, those of woman, by a parity of reasoning, will not shrink from the same test: though a different opinion prevails in this country, built on the very arguments which you use to justify the oppression of woman – prescription.

Consider, I address you as a legislator, whether, when men contend for their freedom, and to be allowed to judge for themselves respecting their own happiness, it be not inconsistent and unjust to subjugate women, even though you firmly believe that you are acting in the manner best calculated to promote their happiness? Who made man the exclusive judge, if woman partake with him the gift of reason?

In this style, argue tyrants of every denomination, from the weak king to the weak father of a family; they are all eager to crush reason; yet always assert that they usurp its throne only to be useful. Do you not act a similar part, when you *force* all women, by denying them civil and political rights, to remain immured in their families groping in the dark? for surely, Sir, you will not assert, that a duty can be binding which is not founded on reason? If indeed this be their destination, arguments may be drawn from reason: and thus augustly supported, the more understanding women acquire, the more they will be

---

1    [Wollstonecraft almost always uses this word to mean "gender-specific."]
2    [Talleyrand, *Rapport* 118 (Appendix B.1.ii). The French constitution of 1791 recognized only men over 25 as citizens; French women did not get the vote until 1944.]
3    [See Appendix A.2.]

attached to their duty – comprehending it – for unless they comprehend it, unless their morals be fixed on the same immutable principle as those of man, no authority can make them discharge it in a virtuous manner. They may be convenient slaves, but slavery will have its constant effect, degrading the master and the abject dependent.

But, if women are to be excluded, without having a voice, from a participation of the natural rights of mankind, prove first, to ward off the charge of injustice and inconsistency, that they want reason – else this flaw in your NEW CONSTITUTION will ever shew that man must, in some shape, act like a tyrant, and tyranny, in whatever part of society it rears its brazen front, will ever undermine morality.

I have repeatedly asserted, and produced what appeared to me irrefragable arguments drawn from matters of fact, to prove my assertion, that women cannot, by force, be confined to domestic concerns; for they will, however ignorant, intermeddle with more weighty affairs, neglecting private duties only to disturb, by cunning tricks, the orderly plans of reason which rise above their comprehension.

Besides, whilst they are only made to acquire personal accomplishments, men will seek for pleasure in variety, and faithless husbands will make faithless wives; such ignorant beings, indeed, will be very excusable when, not taught to respect public good, nor allowed any civil rights, they attempt to do themselves justice by retaliation.

The box of mischief thus opened in society, what is to preserve private virtue, the only security of public freedom[1] and universal happiness?

Let there be then no coercion *established* in society, and the common law of gravity prevailing, the sexes will fall into their proper places. And, now that more equitable laws are forming your citizens, marriage may become more sacred: your young men may choose wives from motives of affection, and your maidens allow love to root out vanity.

---

1 [Wollstonecraft often seems to allude, and always ironically, to the subtitle of Bernard Mandeville (1670-1733), *The Fable of the Bees; or, Private Vices, Public Benefits* (1714). In disparaging him, she follows Catharine Macaulay Graham, *Letters on Education. With Observations on Religious and Metaphysical Subjects* (London: C. Dilly, 1790) 33, 186, 277-78. Wollstonecraft reviewed Macaulay's book enthusiastically in the *Analytical Review* (*Works* 7: 309-22), and she recommends it later in the *Vindication* (231n.). Cf. Price, *Discourse* 5, 43, Appendix A.3.]

The father of a family will not then weaken his constitution and debase his sentiments, by visiting the harlot, nor forget, in obeying the call of appetite, the purpose for which it was implanted.[1] And, the mother will not neglect her children to practise the arts of coquetry, when sense and modesty secure her the friendship of her husband.

But, till men become attentive to the duty of a father, it is vain to expect women to spend that time in their nursery which they, "wise in their generation,"[2] choose to spend at their glass; for this exertion of cunning is only an instinct of nature to enable them to obtain indirectly a little of that power of which they are unjustly denied a share: for, if women are not permitted to enjoy legitimate rights, they will render both men and themselves vicious, to obtain illicit privileges.

I wish, Sir, to set some investigations of this kind afloat in France; and should they lead to a confirmation of my principles, when your constitution is revised the Rights of Woman may be respected, if it be fully proved that reason calls for this respect, and loudly demands JUSTICE for one half of the human race.

I am, Sir,

Your's respectfully,<br>M. W.

---

1  [This is the first of several warnings that sensual over-indulgence is bad for the health.]
2  [Luke 16: 8.]

# ADVERTISEMENT.

WHEN I began to write this work, I divided it into three parts, supposing that one volume would contain a full discussion of the arguments which seemed to me to rise naturally from a few simple principles; but fresh illustrations occurring as I advanced, I now present only the first part to the public.

Many subjects, however, which I have cursorily alluded to, call for particular investigation, especially the laws relative to women, and the consideration of their peculiar duties. These will furnish ample matter for a second volume, which in due time will be published, to elucidate some of the sentiments, and complete many of the sketches begun in the first.[1]

---

1   [The second volume was never written; most critics assume its place was taken by Wollstonecraft's unfinished novel *Maria; or, The Wrongs of Woman* (1798), which devotes considerable attention to "the laws relative to women." But see the "Hints" posthumously published by Godwin, Appendix C.]

# CONTENTS.

# INTRODUCTION.

AFTER considering the historic page, and viewing the living world with anxious solicitude, the most melancholy emotions of sorrowful indignation have depressed my spirits, and I have sighed when obliged to confess, that either nature has made a great difference between man and man, or that the civilization which has hitherto taken place in the world has been very partial. I have turned over various books written on the subject of education, and patiently observed the conduct of parents and the management of schools; but what has been the result? – a profound conviction that the neglected education of my fellow-creatures is the grand source of the misery I deplore; and that women, in particular, are rendered weak and wretched by a variety of concurring causes, originating from one hasty conclusion. The conduct and manners of women, in fact, evidently prove that their minds are not in a healthy state; for, like the flowers which are planted in too rich a soil, strength and usefulness are sacrificed to beauty; and the flaunting leaves, after having pleased a fastidious eye, fade, disregarded on the stalk, long before the season when they ought to have arrived at maturity. – One cause of this barren blooming I attribute to a false system of education, gathered from the books written on this subject by men who, considering females rather as women than human creatures, have been more anxious to make them alluring mistresses than affectionate wives and rational mothers; and the understanding of the sex has been so bubbled by this specious homage, that the civilized women of the present century, with a few exceptions, are only anxious to inspire love, when they ought to cherish a nobler ambition, and by their abilities and virtues exact respect.

In a treatise, therefore, on female rights and manners, the works which have been particularly written for their improvement must not be overlooked; especially when it is asserted, in direct terms, that the minds of women are enfeebled by false refinement; that the books of instruction, written by men of genius, have had the same tendency as more frivolous productions; and that, in the true style of Mahometanism, they are treated as a kind of subordinate beings, and not as a part of the human species, when improveable reason is allowed to be the dignified distinction which raises men above the brute creation, and puts a natural sceptre in a feeble hand.

Yet, because I am a woman, I would not lead my readers to suppose that I mean violently to agitate the contested question respecting the equality or inferiority of the sex; but as the subject lies in my way, and I cannot pass it over without subjecting the main tendency of my reasoning to misconstruction, I shall stop a moment to deliver, in a few words, my opinion. – In the government of the physical world it is observable that the female in point of strength is, in general, inferior to the male. This is the law of nature; and it does not appear to be suspended or abrogated in favour of woman.[1] A degree of physical superiority cannot, therefore, be denied – and it is a noble prerogative! But not content with this natural pre-eminence, men endeavour to sink us still lower, merely to render us alluring objects for a moment; and women, intoxicated by the adoration which men, under the influence of their senses, pay them, do not seek to obtain a durable interest in their hearts, or to become the friends of the fellow creatures who find amusement in their society.

I am aware of an obvious inference: – from every quarter have I heard exclamations against masculine women; but where are they to be found? If by this appellation men mean to inveigh against their ardour in hunting, shooting, and gaming, I shall most cordially join in the cry; but if it be against the imitation of manly virtues, or, more properly speaking, the attainment of those talents and virtues, the exercise of which ennobles the human character, and which raise females in the scale of animal being, when they are comprehensively termed mankind; – all those who view them with a philosophic eye must, I should think, wish with me, that they may every day grow more and more masculine.

This discussion naturally divides the subject. I shall first consider women in the grand light of human creatures, who, in common with men, are placed on this earth to unfold their faculties; and afterwards I shall more particularly point out their peculiar designation.

I wish also to steer clear of an error which many respectable writers have fallen into; for the instruction which has hitherto been

---

1  [Cf. Macaulay, *Letters* 206 (Appendix B.2).]

addressed to women, has rather been applicable to *ladies*, if the little indirect advice, that is scattered through Sandford and Merton,[1] be excepted; but, addressing my sex in a firmer tone, I pay particular attention to those in the middle class, because they appear to be in the most natural state. Perhaps the seeds of false-refinement, immorality, and vanity, have ever been shed by the great. Weak, artificial beings, raised above the common wants and affections of their race, in a premature unnatural manner, undermine the very foundation of virtue, and spread corruption through the whole mass of society! As a class of mankind they have the strongest claim to pity; the education of the rich tends to render them vain and helpless, and the unfolding mind is not strengthened by the practice of those duties which dignify the human character. – They only live to amuse themselves, and by the same law which in nature invariably produces certain effects, they soon only afford barren amusement.[2]

But as I purpose taking a separate view of the different ranks of society, and of the moral character of women, in each, this hint is, for the present, sufficient; and I have only alluded to the subject, because it appears to me to be the very essence of an introduction to give a cursory account of the contents of the work it introduces.

My own sex, I hope, will excuse me, if I treat them like rational creatures, instead of flattering their *fascinating* graces, and viewing them as if they were in a state of perpetual childhood, unable to stand alone. I earnestly wish to point out in what true dignity and human happiness consists – I wish to persuade women to endeavour to acquire strength, both of mind and body, and to convince them that the soft phrases, susceptibility of heart, delicacy of sentiment, and refinement of taste, are almost synonymous with epithets of weakness, and that those beings who are only the objects of pity and that kind of love, which has been termed its sister, will soon become objects of contempt.[3]

Dismissing then those pretty feminine phrases, which the men condescendingly use to soften our slavish dependence, and despising

---

1 [Thomas Day (1748-89), *The History of Sandford and Merton*, 3 vols. (1783-89). Wollstonecraft reviewed the third volume for the *Analytical Review* (*Works* 7: 174-76).]
2 [Cf. Jean-Jacques Rousseau (1712-78), *Emile* (1762) 85; Macaulay, *Letters* 66-68. Macaulay, however, addresses her *Letters* to the "opulent" (v, 171, 223-34, 236-37).]
3 [Cf. *Original Stories*; *Works* 4: 381.]

that weak elegancy of mind, exquisite sensibility, and sweet docility of manners, supposed to be the sexual characteristics of the weaker vessel, I wish to shew that elegance is inferior to virtue, that the first object of laudable ambition is to obtain a character as a human being, regardless of the distinction of sex; and that secondary views should be brought to this simple touchstone.

This is a rough sketch of my plan; and should I express my conviction with the energetic emotions that I feel whenever I think of the subject, the dictates of experience and reflection will be felt by some of my readers. Animated by this important object, I shall disdain to cull my phrases or polish my style; – I aim at being useful, and sincerity will render me unaffected; for, wishing rather to persuade by the force of my arguments, than dazzle by the elegance of my language, I shall not waste my time in rounding periods, or in fabricating the turgid bombast of artificial feelings, which, coming from the head, never reach the heart.[1] – I shall be employed about things, not words! – and, anxious to render my sex more respectable members of society, I shall try to avoid that flowery diction which has slided from essays into novels, and from novels into familiar letters and conversation.

These pretty superlatives, dropping glibly from the tongue, vitiate the taste, and create a kind of sickly delicacy that turns away from simple unadorned truth; and a deluge of false sentiments and overstretched feelings, stifling the natural emotions of the heart, render the domestic pleasures insipid, that ought to sweeten the exercise of those severe duties, which educate a rational and immortal being for a nobler field of action.[2]

The education of women has, of late, been more attended to than formerly; yet they are still reckoned a frivolous sex, and ridiculed or pitied by the writers who endeavour by satire or instruction to improve them. It is acknowledged that they spend many of the first years of their lives in acquiring a smattering of accomplishments;[3] meanwhile strength of body and mind are sacrificed to libertine notions of beauty, to the desire of establishing themselves, – the only way women can rise in the world, – by marriage. And this desire mak-

---

1    [Cf. *Original Stories; Works* 4: 359, 450.]
2    [Cf. *Original Stories; Works* 4: 437.]
3    [Cf. *Original Stories; Works* 4: 435; and Macaulay, *Letters* 61-62.]

ing mere animals of them, when they marry they act as such children may be expected to act: – they dress; they paint, and nickname God's creatures.[1] – Surely these weak beings are only fit for a seraglio! – Can they be expected to govern a family with judgment, or take care of the poor babes whom they bring into the world?

If then it can be fairly deduced from the present conduct of the sex, from the prevalent fondness for pleasure which takes place of ambition and those nobler passions that open and enlarge the soul; that the instruction which women have hitherto received has only tended, with the constitution of civil society, to render them insignificant objects of desire – mere propagators of fools! – if it can be proved that in aiming to accomplish them, without cultivating their understandings, they are taken out of their sphere of duties, and made ridiculous and useless when the short-lived bloom of beauty is over,[2] I presume that *rational* men will excuse me for endeavouring to persuade them to become more masculine and respectable.

Indeed the word masculine is only a bugbear: there is little reason to fear that women will acquire too much courage or fortitude, for their apparent inferiority with respect to bodily strength, must render them, in some degree, dependent on men in the various relations of life; but why should it be increased by prejudices that give a sex to virtue, and confound simple truths with sensual reveries?

Women are, in fact, so much degraded by mistaken notions of female excellence, that I do not mean to add a paradox when I assert, that this artificial weakness produces a propensity to tyrannize, and gives birth to cunning, the natural opponent of strength, which leads them to play off those contemptible infantine airs that undermine esteem even whilst they excite desire. Let men become more chaste and modest, and if women do not grow wiser in the same ratio, it will be clear that they have weaker understandings. It seems scarcely nec-

---

1  [Shakespeare, *Hamlet* 3.1.142-46. Cf. Burke, *Philosophical Enquiry* 100 (3.9); Macaulay, *Letters* 48.]

2  A lively writer, I cannot recollect his name, asks what business women turned of forty have to do in the world? [Wollstonecraft may be thinking of a remark made by Lord Merton, a character in Frances Burney (1752-1840), *Evelina; or, The History of a Young Lady's Entrance into the World* (1778), ed. Edward A. Bloom (London: Oxford UP, 1968) 275; Vol. 3, letter 1.]

essary to say, that I now speak of the sex in general. Many individuals have more sense than their male relatives; and, as nothing preponderates where there is a constant struggle for an equilibrium, without it has naturally more gravity, some women govern their husbands without degrading themselves, because intellect will always govern.

# VINDICATION

OF THE

# RIGHTS OF WOMAN.

## PART I.

# CHAP. I.

## THE RIGHTS AND INVOLVED DUTIES
## OF MANKIND CONSIDERED.

In the present state of society it appears necessary to go back to first principles in search of the most simple truths, and to dispute with some prevailing prejudice every inch of ground. To clear my way, I must be allowed to ask some plain questions, and the answers will probably appear as unequivocal as the axioms on which reasoning is built; though, when entangled with various motives of action, they are formally contradicted, either by the words or conduct of men.

In what does man's pre-eminence over the brute creation consist? The answer is as clear as that a half is less than the whole; in Reason.

What acquirement exalts one being above another? Virtue, we spontaneously reply.

For what purpose were the passions implanted? That man by struggling with them might attain a degree of knowledge denied to the brutes; whispers Experience.[1]

Consequently the perfection of our nature and capability of happiness, must be estimated by the degree of reason, virtue, and knowledge, that distinguish the individual, and direct the laws which bind society: and that from the exercise of reason, knowledge and virtue naturally flow, is equally undeniable, if mankind be viewed collectively.

The rights and duties of man thus simplified, it seems almost impertinent to attempt to illustrate truths that appear so incontrovertible; yet such deeply rooted prejudices have clouded reason, and such spurious qualities have assumed the name of virtues, that it is necessary to pursue the course of reason as it has been perplexed and involved in error, by various adventitious circumstances, comparing the simple axiom with casual deviations.

---

1   [Cf. the dialogue of personifications in Macaulay, *Letters* 75.]

Men, in general, seem to employ their reason to justify prejudices, which they have imbibed, they can scarcely trace how, rather than to root them out.[1] The mind must be strong that resolutely forms its own principles; for a kind of intellectual cowardice prevails which makes many men shrink from the task, or only do it by halves. Yet the imperfect conclusions thus drawn, are frequently very plausible, because they are built on partial experience, on just, though narrow, views.

Going back to first principles, vice skulks, with all its native deformity, from close investigation; but a set of shallow reasoners are always exclaiming that these arguments prove too much, and that a measure rotten at the core may be expedient. Thus expediency is continually contrasted with simple principles, till truth is lost in a mist of words, virtue, in forms, and knowledge rendered a sounding nothing, by the specious prejudices that assume its name.

That the society is formed in the wisest manner, whose constitution is founded on the nature of man, strikes, in the abstract, every thinking being so forcibly, that it looks like presumption to endeavour to bring forward proofs; though proof must be brought, or the strong hold of prescription will never be forced by reason; yet to urge prescription as an argument to justify the depriving men (or women) of their natural rights, is one of the absurd sophisms which daily insult common sense.

The civilization of the bulk of the people of Europe is very partial; nay, it may be made a question, whether they have acquired any virtues in exchange for innocence, equivalent to the misery produced by the vices that have been plastered over unsightly ignorance, and the freedom which has been bartered for splendid slavery. The desire of dazzling by riches, the most certain pre-eminence that man can obtain, the pleasure of commanding flattering sycophants, and many other complicated low calculations of doting self-love, have all contributed to overwhelm the mass of mankind, and make liberty a convenient handle for mock patriotism. For whilst rank and titles are held of the utmost importance, before which Genius "must hide its diminished head,"[2] it is, with a few exceptions, very unfortunate for a

---

1    [Burke, *Reflections*; *Writings* 8: 138; Appendix A.4.ii; cf. *Original Stories*; *Works* 4: 361.]
2    [Milton, *Paradise Lost* 4.35.]

nation when a man of abilities, without rank or property, pushes himself forward to notice. – Alas! what unheard of misery have thousands suffered to purchase a cardinal's hat for an intriguing obscure adventurer, who longed to be ranked with princes, or lord it over them by seizing the triple crown![1]

Such, indeed, has been the wretchedness that has flowed from hereditary honours, riches, and monarchy, that men of lively sensibility have almost uttered blasphemy in order to justify the dispensations of providence. Man has been held out as independent of his power who made him, or as a lawless planet darting from its orbit to steal the celestial fire of reason; and the vengeance of heaven, lurking in the subtile flame, like Pandora's pent up mischiefs, sufficiently punished his temerity, by introducing evil into the world.[2]

Impressed by this view of the misery and disorder which pervaded society, and fatigued with jostling against artificial fools, Rousseau became enamoured of solitude, and, being at the same time an optimist, he labours with uncommon eloquence to prove that man was naturally a solitary animal.[3] Misled by his respect for the goodness of God, who certainly – for what man of sense and feeling can doubt it! – gave life only to communicate happiness, he considers evil as positive, and the work of man; not aware that he was exalting one attribute at the expence of another, equally necessary to divine perfection.

Reared on a false hypothesis his arguments in favour of a state of nature are plausible, but unsound. I say unsound; for to assert that a state of nature is preferable to civilization, in all its possible perfection, is, in other words, to arraign supreme wisdom; and the paradoxical exclamation, that God has made all things right, and that error has been introduced by the creature, whom he formed,[4] knowing what

---

1  [The papal tiara.]
2  [In the Greek myth, Prometheus stole fire from heaven for the benefit of humanity. Zeus punished the theft by sending Pandora, the first woman, whose curiosity led her to open the "box of mischief," thus introducing evil into human life.]
3  [Rousseau expresses his love of solitude in *Confessions* (1781–88) Books 8 and 9, esp. 343, 374, 384, 407–8. Wollstonecraft reviewed the second part, which includes these books (*Works* 7: 228–34). He explains his theory that humans are naturally solitary in *Discourse on the Origin and Foundations of Inequality among Men* (1755).]
4  [This is a paraphrase of the first sentence of Book 1 of Rousseau, *Emile* 37.]

he formed, is as unphilosophical as impious.

When that wise Being who created us and placed us here, saw the fair idea, he willed, by allowing it to be so, that the passions should unfold our reason, because he could see that present evil would produce future good. Could the helpless creature whom he called from nothing break loose from his providence, and boldly learn to know good by practising evil, without his permission? No. – How could that energetic advocate for immortality argue so inconsistently?[1] Had mankind remained for ever in the brutal state of nature, which even his magic pen cannot paint as a state in which a single virtue took root, it would have been clear, though not to the sensitive unreflecting wanderer, that man was born to run the circle of life and death, and adorn God's garden for some purpose which could not easily be reconciled with his attributes.

But if, to crown the whole, there were to be rational creatures produced, allowed to rise in excellence by the exercise of powers implanted for that purpose; if benignity itself thought fit to call into existence a creature above the brutes[2], who could think and improve himself, why should that inestimable gift, for a gift it was, if man was so created as to have a capacity to rise above the state in which sensation produced brutal ease, be called, in direct terms, a curse?[3] A curse it might be reckoned, if the whole of our existence were bounded by our continuance in this world; for why should the gracious fountain of life[4] give us passions, and the power of reflecting, only to imbitter our days and inspire us with mistaken notions of dignity? Why should he lead us from love of ourselves to the sublime emotions which the discovery of his wisdom and goodness excites, if these feelings were not set in motion to improve our nature, of which they make a part[5],

---

1  [See "Profession of Faith of the Savoyard Vicar," in Rousseau, *Emile*, esp. 282-85.]
2  Contrary to the opinion of anatomists, who argue by analogy from the formation of the teeth, stomach, and intestines, Rousseau will not allow a man to be a carnivorous animal. And, carried away from nature by a love of system, he disputes whether man be a gregarious animal, though the long and helpless state of infancy seems to point him out as particularly impelled to pair, the first step towards herding. [Rousseau, *Emile* 57-59, 153-55. Macaulay agrees with Rousseau (*Letters* 38).]
3  [Cf. Macaulay, *Letters* 384, 386.]
4  [Psalms 36: 9; Proverbs 14: 27.]
5  What would you say to a mechanic whom you had desired to make a watch to point out the hour of the day, if, to shew his ingenuity, he added wheels to make it

and render us capable of enjoying a more godlike portion of happiness? Firmly persuaded that no evil exists in the world that God did not design to take place, I build my belief on the perfection of God.

Rousseau exerts himself to prove that all *was* right originally: a crowd of authors that all *is* now right: and I, that all will *be* right.

But, true to his first position, next to a state of nature, Rousseau celebrates barbarism, and apostrophizing the shade of Fabricius,[1] he forgets that, in conquering the world, the Romans never dreamed of establishing their own liberty on a firm basis, or of extending the reign of virtue. Eager to support his system, he stigmatizes, as vicious, every effort of genius; and, uttering the apotheosis of savage virtues, he exalts those to demi-gods, who were scarcely human – the brutal Spartans, who, in defiance of justice and gratitude, sacrificed, in cold blood, the slaves who had shewn themselves heroes to rescue their oppressors.[2]

Disgusted with artificial manners and virtues, the citizen of Geneva,[3] instead of properly sifting the subject, threw away the wheat with the chaff,[4] without waiting to inquire whether the evils which his ardent soul turned from indignantly, were the consequence of civilization or the vestiges of barbarism. He saw vice trampling on virtue, and the semblance of goodness taking place of the reality; he saw tal-

---

a repeater, &c. that perplexed the simple mechanism; should he urge, to excuse himself – had you not touched a certain spring, you would have known nothing of the matter, and that he should have amused himself by making *an experiment* without doing you any harm: would you not retort fairly upon him, by insisting that if he had not added those needless wheels and springs, the accident could not have happened? [A "repeater" was a watch that could strike the hour. The watch-maker analogy was a commonplace of eighteenth-century natural religion; cf. Rousseau, *Emile* 275.]

1  [Rousseau apostrophizes the shade of Gaius Fabricius (third century B.C.), the virtuous Roman, who urged his countrymen to conquer the world, in *Discourse on the Sciences and Arts* (1750) 45-46.]

2  [During the Peloponnesian War, the Spartans invited their slaves to pick out those who had most distinguished themselves in fighting against the Athenians; two thousand were chosen. Instead of giving them their freedom, as they had promised, the Spartans murdered them, on the grounds that they were the most high-spirited and likely to rebel (Thucydides, *The Peloponnesian War* 4.14.81). For Rousseau's praise, see *Discourse on the Sciences and Arts* 43.]

3  [This is how Rousseau identifies himself on the title pages of both *Discourses*, and of the *Letter to M. d'Alembert on the Theatre* (1758); see also *Confessions* 365-66, 368-69.]

4  [Matthew 3: 12.]

ents bent by power to sinister purposes, and never thought of tracing the gigantic mischief up to arbitrary power, up to the hereditary distinctions that clash with the mental superiority that naturally raises a man above his fellows. He did not perceive that regal power, in a few generations, introduces idiotism into the noble stem, and holds out baits to render thousands idle and vicious.

Nothing can set the regal character in a more contemptible point of view, than the various crimes that have elevated men to the supreme dignity. – Vile intrigues, unnatural crimes, and every vice that degrades our nature, have been the steps to this distinguished eminence; yet millions of men have supinely allowed the nerveless limbs of the posterity of such rapacious prowlers to rest quietly on their ensanguined thrones[1].

What but a pestilential vapour[2] can hover over society when its chief director is only instructed in the invention of crimes, or the stupid routine of childish ceremonies? Will men never be wise? – will they never cease to expect corn from tares, and figs from thistles?[3]

It is impossible for any man, when the most favourable circumstances concur, to acquire sufficient knowledge and strength of mind to discharge the duties of a king, entrusted with uncontrouled power; how then must they be violated when his very elevation is an insuperable bar to the attainment of either wisdom or virtue; when all the feelings of a man are stifled by flattery, and reflection shut out by pleasure! Surely it is madness to make the fate of thousands depend on the caprice of a weak fellow creature, whose very station sinks him *necessarily* below the meanest of his subjects![4] But one power should not be thrown down to exalt another – for all power inebriates weak man; and its abuse proves that the more equality there is established

---

1  Could there be a greater insult offered to the rights of man than the beds of justice in France, when an infant was made the organ of the detestable Dubois! [The "lits de justice" were ceremonial meetings of the French king and *parlement*, or high court. When Louis XV became king at the age of five, the duc d'Orléans was made regent, and the duc's former tutor, Guillaume Cardinal Dubois (1656-1723), gained considerable influence at court. In 1789, Wollstonecraft had reviewed a biography of Dubois (*Works* 7: 137-41).]

2  [Cf. *Hamlet* 2.2.299.]

3  [Matthew 7: 16, 13: 24-30; Luke 6: 44.]

4  [Cf. Macaulay, *Letters* 66-67, 224.]

among men, the more virtue and happiness will reign in society. But this and any similar maxim deduced from simple reason, raises an outcry – the church or the state is in danger, if faith in the wisdom of antiquity is not implicit; and they who, roused by the sight of human calamity, dare to attack human authority, are reviled as despisers of God, and enemies of man. These are bitter calumnies, yet they reached one of the best of men[1], whose ashes still preach peace, and whose memory demands a respectful pause, when subjects are discussed that lay so near his heart.——

After attacking the sacred majesty of Kings, I shall scarcely excite surprise by adding my firm persuasion[2] that every profession, in which great subordination of rank constitutes its power, is highly injurious to morality.

A standing army, for instance, is incompatible with freedom; because subordination and rigour are the very sinews of military discipline; and despotism is necessary to give vigour to enterprizes that one will directs. A spirit inspired by romantic notions of honour, a kind of morality founded on the fashion of the age, can only be felt by a few officers, whilst the main body must be moved by command, like the waves of the sea; for the strong wind of authority pushes the crowd of subalterns forward, they scarcely know or care why, with headlong fury.

Besides, nothing can be so prejudicial to the morals of the inhabitants of country towns as the occasional residence of a set of idle superficial young men, whose only occupation is gallantry, and whose polished manners render vice more dangerous, by concealing its deformity under gay ornamental drapery. An air of fashion, which is but a badge of slavery, and proves that the soul has not a strong individual character, awes simple country people into an imitation of the vices, when they cannot catch the slippery graces, of politeness. Every corps is a chain of despots, who, submitting and tyrannizing without exercising their reason, become dead weights of vice and folly on the community. A man of rank or fortune, sure of rising by interest, has

1   Dr. Price. [Richard Price (1723-91), attacked by Burke in *Reflections on the Revolution in France* (1790; see Appendix A.4) for his sermon *A Discourse on the Love of our Country* (1789; see Appendix A.3).]
2   [Cf. William Blake (1757-1827), *The Marriage of Heaven and Hell* (1790?) plate 12.]

nothing to do but to pursue some extravagant freak; whilst the needy *gentleman*, who is to rise, as the phrase turns, by his merit, becomes a servile parasite or vile pander.

Sailors, the naval gentlemen, come under the same description, only their vices assume a different and a grosser cast. They are more positively indolent, when not discharging the ceremonials of their station; whilst the insignificant fluttering of soldiers may be termed active idleness. More confined to the society of men, the former acquire a fondness for humour and mischievous tricks; whilst the latter, mixing frequently with well-bred women, catch a sentimental cant. – But mind is equally out of the question, whether they indulge the horse-laugh, or polite simper.

May I be allowed to extend the comparison to a profession where more mind is certainly to be found; for the clergy have superior opportunities of improvement, though subordination almost equally cramps their faculties? The blind submission imposed at college to forms of belief serves as a novitiate to the curate, who must obsequiously respect the opinion of his rector or patron, if he mean to rise in his profession. Perhaps there cannot be a more forcible contrast than between the servile dependent gait of a poor curate and the courtly mien of a bishop. And the respect and contempt they inspire render the discharge of their separate functions equally useless.

It is of great importance to observe that the character of every man is, in some degree, formed by his profession. A man of sense may only have a cast of countenance that wears off as you trace his individuality, whilst the weak, common man has scarcely ever any character,[1] but what belongs to the body; at least, all his opinions have been so steeped in the vat consecrated by authority, that the faint spirit which the grape of his own vine yields cannot be distinguished.

Society, therefore, as it becomes more enlightened, should be very careful not to establish bodies of men who must necessarily be made foolish or vicious by the very constitution of their profession.

In the infancy of society, when men were just emerging out of barbarism, chiefs and priests, touching the most powerful springs of savage conduct, hope and fear, must have had unbounded sway. An

---

1  [Possibly an ironic allusion to Pope, "Epistle II. To a Lady. Of the Characters of Women" (1735) 2.]

aristocracy, of course, is naturally the first form of government. But, clashing interests soon losing their equipoise, a monarchy and hierarchy break out of the confusion of ambitious struggles, and the foundation of both is secured by feudal tenures. This appears to be the origin of monarchical and priestly power, and the dawn of civilization. But such combustible materials cannot long be pent up; and, getting vent in foreign wars and intestine insurrections, the people acquire some power in the tumult, which obliges their rulers to gloss over their oppression with a shew of right. Thus, as wars, agriculture, commerce, and literature, expand the mind, despots are compelled, to make covert corruption hold fast the power which was formerly snatched by open force[1]. And this baneful lurking gangrene is most quickly spread by luxury and superstition, the sure dregs of ambition. The indolent puppet of a court first becomes a luxurious monster, or fastidious sensualist, and then makes the contagion which his unnatural state spread, the instrument of tyranny.

It is the pestiferous purple which renders the progress of civilization a curse, and warps the understanding, till men of sensibility doubt whether the expansion of intellect produces a greater portion of happiness or misery. But the nature of the poison points out the antidote; and had Rousseau mounted one step higher in his investigation, or could his eye have pierced through the foggy atmosphere, which he almost disdained to breathe, his active mind would have darted forward to contemplate the perfection of man in the establishment of true civilization, instead of taking his ferocious flight back to the night of sensual ignorance.

---

1  Men of abilities scatter seeds that grow up and have a great influence on the forming opinion; and when once the public opinion preponderates, through the exertion of reason, the overthrow of arbitrary power is not very distant.

# CHAP. II.

## THE PREVAILING OPINION OF A SEXUAL CHARACTER DISCUSSED.

To account for, and excuse the tyranny of man, many ingenious arguments have been brought forward to prove, that the two sexes, in the acquirement of virtue, ought to aim at attaining a very different character: or, to speak explicitly, women are not allowed to have sufficient strength of mind to acquire what really deserves the name of virtue. Yet it should seem, allowing them to have souls, that there is but one way appointed by Providence to lead *mankind* to either virtue or happiness.

If then women are not a swarm of ephemeron triflers, why should they be kept in ignorance under the specious name of innocence? Men complain, and with reason, of the follies and caprices of our sex, when they do not keenly satirize our headstrong passions and groveling vices. – Behold, I should answer, the natural effect of ignorance! The mind will ever be unstable that has only prejudices to rest on, and the current will run with destructive fury when there are no barriers to break its force. Women are told from their infancy, and taught by the example of their mothers, that a little knowledge of human weakness, justly termed cunning, softness of temper, *outward* obedience, and a scrupulous attention to a puerile kind of propriety, will obtain for them the protection of man; and should they be beautiful, every thing else is needless, for, at least, twenty years of their lives.

Thus Milton describes our first frail mother; though when he tells us that women are formed for softness and sweet attractive grace,[1] I cannot comprehend his meaning, unless, in the true Mahometan strain, he meant to deprive us of souls, and insinuate that we were beings only designed by sweet attractive grace, and docile blind obedience, to gratify the senses of man when he can no longer soar on

---

1 [Milton, *Paradise Lost* 4.297-98.]

the wing of contemplation.

How grossly do they insult us who thus advise us only to render ourselves gentle, domestic brutes! For instance, the winning softness so warmly, and frequently, recommended, that governs by obeying. What childish expressions, and how insignificant is the being – can it be an immortal one? who will condescend to govern by such sinister methods! "Certainly," says Lord Bacon, "man is of kin to the beasts by his body; and if he be not of kin to God by his spirit, he is a base and ignoble creature!"[1] Men, indeed, appear to me to act in a very unphilosophical manner when they try to secure the good conduct of women by attempting to keep them always in a state of childhood. Rousseau was more consistent when he wished to stop the progress of reason in both sexes, for if men eat of the tree of knowledge, women will come in for a taste;[2] but, from the imperfect cultivation which their understandings now receive, they only attain a knowledge of evil.

Children, I grant, should be innocent; but when the epithet is applied to men, or women, it is but a civil term for weakness. For if it be allowed that women were destined by Providence to acquire human virtues, and by the exercise of their understandings, that stability of character which is the firmest ground to rest our future hopes upon, they must be permitted to turn to the fountain of light, and not forced to shape their course by the twinkling of a mere satellite. Milton, I grant, was of a very different opinion; for he only bends to the indefeasible right of beauty, though it would be difficult to render two passages which I now mean to contrast, consistent. But into similar inconsistencies are great men often led by their senses.

> "To whom thus Eve with *perfect beauty* adorn'd.
> My Author and Disposer, what thou bidst
> *Unargued* I obey; so God ordains;
> God is *thy law, thou mine:* to know no more
> Is Woman's *happiest* knowledge and her *praise.*"[3]

---

1 [Francis Bacon (1561-1626), *Essays or Counsels Civil and Moral* (1625), Essay 16, "Of Atheism."]
2 [See Genesis 2-3.]
3 [Milton, *Paradise Lost* 4.634-38; Wollstonecraft's italics.]

These are exactly the arguments that I have used to children; but I have added, your reason is now gaining strength, and, till it arrives at some degree of maturity, you must look up to me for advice – then you ought to *think*, and only rely on God.

Yet in the following lines Milton seems to coincide with me; when he makes Adam thus expostulate with his Maker.

> "Hast thou not made me here thy substitute,
> And these inferior far beneath me set?
> Among *unequals* what society
> Can sort, what harmony or true delight?
> Which must be mutual, in proportion due
> Giv'n and receiv'd; but in *disparity*
> The one intense, the other still remiss
> Cannot well suit with either, but soon prove
> Tedious alike: of *fellowship* I speak
> Such as I seek, fit to participate
> All rational delight—"[1]

In treating, therefore, of the manners of women, let us, disregarding sensual arguments, trace what we should endeavour to make them in order to co-operate, if the expression be not too bold, with the supreme Being.[2]

By individual education, I mean, for the sense of the word is not precisely defined, such an attention to a child as will slowly sharpen the senses, form the temper, regulate the passions as they begin to ferment, and set the understanding to work before the body arrives at maturity; so that the man may only have to proceed, not to begin, the important task of learning to think and reason.

To prevent any misconstruction, I must add, that I do not believe that a private education can work the wonders which some sanguine writers have attributed to it. Men and women must be educated, in a great degree, by the opinions and manners of the society they live in. In every age there has been a stream of popular opinion that has carried all before it, and given a family character, as it were, to the centu-

---

1 [Milton, *Paradise Lost* 8.381-91; Wollstonecraft's italics.]
2 [Cf. Macaulay, *Letters* 402.]

ry. It may then fairly be inferred, that, till society be differently constituted, much cannot be expected from education. It is, however, sufficient for my present purpose to assert, that, whatever effect
circumstances have on the abilities, every being may become virtuous
by the exercise of its own reason; for if but one being was created
with vicious inclinations, that is positively bad, what can save us from
atheism? or if we worship a God, is not that God a devil?

Consequently, the most perfect education, in my opinion, is such
an exercise of the understanding as is best calculated to strengthen the
body and form the heart. Or, in other words, to enable the individual
to attain such habits of virtue as will render it independent. In fact, it
is a farce to call any being virtuous whose virtues do not result from
the exercise of its own reason. This was Rousseau's opinion respecting
men:[1] I extend it to women, and confidently assert that they have
been drawn out of their sphere by false refinement, and not by an
endeavour to acquire masculine qualities. Still the regal homage
which they receive is so intoxicating, that till the manners of the times
are changed, and formed on more reasonable principles, it may be
impossible to convince them that the illegitimate power, which they
obtain, by degrading themselves, is a curse, and that they must return
to nature and equality, if they wish to secure the placid satisfaction
that unsophisticated affections impart. But for this epoch we must
wait – wait, perhaps, till kings and nobles, enlightened by reason, and,
preferring the real dignity of man to childish state, throw off their
gaudy hereditary trappings: and if then women do not resign the arbitrary power of beauty – they will prove that they have *less* mind than
man.

I may be accused of arrogance; still I must declare what I firmly
believe, that all the writers who have written on the subject of female
education and manners from Rousseau to Dr. Gregory,[2] have contributed to render women more artificial, weak characters, than they
would otherwise have been; and, consequently, more useless members
of society. I might have expressed this conviction in a lower key; but I

1   [Cf. Rousseau, *Emile* 67, 89.]
2   [Rousseau, *Emile* Book 5; John Gregory (1724-73), *A Father's Legacy to his Daughters*
    (1774). Wollstonecraft included substantial excerpts from Gregory in *The Female
    Reader* (1789).]

am afraid it would have been the whine of affectation, and not the faithful expression of my feelings, of the clear result, which experience and reflection have led me to draw. When I come to that division of the subject, I shall advert to the passages that I more particularly disapprove of, in the works of the authors I have just alluded to; but it is first necessary to observe, that my objection extends to the whole purport of those books, which tend, in my opinion, to degrade one half of the human species, and render women pleasing at the expence of every solid virtue.

Though, to reason on Rousseau's ground, if man did attain a degree of perfection of mind when his body arrived at maturity, it might be proper, in order to make a man and his wife *one*, that she should rely entirely on his understanding; and the graceful ivy, clasping the oak that supported it, would form a whole in which strength and beauty would be equally conspicuous. But, alas! husbands, as well as their helpmates, are often only overgrown children; nay, thanks to early debauchery, scarcely men in their outward form – and if the blind lead the blind, one need not come from heaven to tell us the consequence.[1]

Many are the causes that, in the present corrupt state of society, contribute to enslave women by cramping their understandings and sharpening their senses. One, perhaps, that silently does more mischief than all the rest, is their disregard of order.

To do every thing in an orderly manner, is a most important precept, which women, who, generally speaking, receive only a disorderly kind of education, seldom attend to with that degree of exactness that men, who from their infancy are broken into method, observe. This negligent kind of guess-work, for what other epithet can be used to point out the random exertions of a sort of instinctive common sense, never brought to the test of reason? prevents their generalizing matters of fact – so they do to-day, what they did yesterday, merely because they did it yesterday.

This contempt of the understanding in early life has more baneful consequences than is commonly supposed; for the little knowledge which women of strong minds attain, is, from various circumstances, of a more desultory kind than the knowledge of men, and it is

---

1   [Matthew 15: 14. The speaker is Jesus, who has "come from heaven."]

acquired more by sheer observations on real life, than from comparing what has been individually observed with the results of experience generalized by speculation. Led by their dependent situation and domestic employments more into society, what they learn is rather by snatches; and as learning is with them, in general, only a secondary thing, they do not pursue any one branch with that persevering ardour necessary to give vigour to the faculties, and clearness to the judgment. In the present state of society, a little learning[1] is required to support the character of a gentleman; and boys are obliged to submit to a few years of discipline. But in the education of women, the cultivation of the understanding is always subordinate to the acquirement of some corporeal accomplishment; even while enervated by confinement and false notions of modesty, the body is prevented from attaining that grace and beauty which relaxed half-formed limbs never exhibit. Besides, in youth their faculties are not brought forward by emulation; and having no serious scientific study, if they have natural sagacity it is turned too soon on life and manners. They dwell on effects, and modifications, without tracing them back to causes; and complicated rules to adjust behaviour are a weak substitute for simple principles.

As a proof that education gives this appearance of weakness to females, we may instance the example of military men, who are, like them, sent into the world before their minds have been stored with knowledge or fortified by principles. The consequences are similar; soldiers acquire a little superficial knowledge, snatched from the muddy current of conversation, and, from continually mixing with society, they gain, what is termed a knowledge of the world; and this acquaintance with manners and customs has frequently been confounded with a knowledge of the human heart. But can the crude fruit of casual observation, never brought to the test of judgment, formed by comparing speculation and experience, deserve such a distinction? Soldiers, as well as women, practise the minor virtues with punctilious politeness. Where is then the sexual difference, when the education has been the same? All the difference that I can discern, arises from the superior advantage of liberty, which enables the former to see more of life.

---

1   [Cf. Pope, *An Essay on Criticism* (1711) 215.]

It is wandering from my present subject, perhaps, to make a political remark; but, as it was produced naturally by the train of my reflections, I shall not pass it silently over.

Standing armies can never consist of resolute, robust men; they may be well disciplined machines, but they will seldom contain men under the influence of strong passions, or with very vigorous faculties. And as for any depth of understanding, I will venture to affirm, that it is as rarely to be found in the army as amongst women; and the cause, I maintain, is the same. It may be further observed, that officers are also particularly attentive to their persons, fond of dancing, crowded rooms, adventures, and ridicule[1]. Like the *fair* sex, the business of their lives is gallantry. – They were taught to please, and they only live to please. Yet they do not lose their rank in the distinction of sexes, for they are still reckoned superior to women, though in what their superiority consists, beyond what I have just mentioned, it is difficult to discover.

The great misfortune is this, that they both acquire manners before morals, and a knowledge of life before they have, from reflection, any acquaintance with the grand ideal outline of human nature. The consequence is natural; satisfied with common nature, they become a prey to prejudices, and taking all their opinions on credit, they blindly submit to authority. So that, if they have any sense, it is a kind of instinctive glance, that catches proportions, and decides with respect to manners; but fails when arguments are to be pursued below the surface, or opinions analyzed.

May not the same remark be applied to women? Nay, the argument may be carried still further, for they are both thrown out of a useful station by the unnatural distinctions established in civilized life. Riches and hereditary honours have made cyphers of women to give consequence to the numerical figure; and idleness has produced a mixture of gallantry and despotism into society, which leads the very men who are the slaves of their mistresses to tyrannize over their sis-

---

1   Why should women be censured with petulant acrimony, because they seem to have a passion for a scarlet coat? Has not education placed them more on a level with soldiers than any other class of men? [See Jonathan Swift (1667-1745), "The Furniture of a Woman's Mind" (1727) 2. Wollstonecraft included several excerpts from Swift in *The Female Reader*.]

ters, wives, and daughters. This is only keeping them in rank and file, it is true. Strengthen the female mind by enlarging it, and there will be an end to blind obedience; but, as blind obedience is ever sought for by power, tyrants and sensualists are in the right when they endeavour to keep women in the dark, because the former only want slaves, and the latter a play-thing. The sensualist, indeed, has been the most dangerous of tyrants, and women have been duped by their lovers, as princes by their ministers, whilst dreaming that they reigned over them.

I now principally allude to Rousseau, for his character of Sophia is, undoubtedly, a captivating one, though it appears to me grossly unnatural;[1] however it is not the superstructure, but the foundation of her character, the principles on which her education was built, that I mean to attack; nay, warmly as I admire the genius of that able writer, whose opinions I shall often have occasion to cite, indignation always takes place of admiration, and the rigid frown of insulted virtue effaces the smile of complacency, which his eloquent periods are wont to raise, when I read his voluptuous reveries. Is this the man, who, in his ardour for virtue, would banish all the soft arts of peace, and almost carry us back to Spartan discipline? Is this the man who delights to paint the useful struggles of passion, the triumphs of good dispositions, and the heroic flights which carry the glowing soul out of itself? – How are these mighty sentiments lowered when he describes the pretty foot and enticing airs of his little favourite![2] But, for the present, I wave the subject, and, instead of severely reprehending the transient effusions of overweening sensibility, I shall only observe, that whoever has cast a benevolent eye on society, must often have been gratified by the sight of humble mutual love, not dignified by sentiment, or strengthened by a union in intellectual pursuits. The domestic trifles of the day have afforded matters for cheerful converse, and innocent caresses have softened toils which did not require great exercise of mind or stretch of thought: yet, has not the sight of this moderate felicity excited more tenderness than respect? An emotion similar to what we feel when children are playing, or animals sport-

1   [Rousseau, *Emile* Book 5.]
2   [Rousseau, *Emile* 393, 394, 398, 437.]

ing[1], whilst the contemplation of the noble struggles of suffering merit has raised admiration, and carried our thoughts to that world where sensation will give place to reason.

Women are, therefore, to be considered either as moral beings, or so weak that they must be entirely subjected to the superior faculties of men.

Let us examine this question. Rousseau declares that a woman should never, for a moment, feel herself independent, that she should be governed by fear to exercise her *natural* cunning, and made a coquetish slave in order to render her a more alluring object of desire, a *sweeter* companion to man, whenever he chooses to relax himself. He carries the arguments, which he pretends to draw from the indications of nature, still further, and insinuates that truth and fortitude, the corner stones of all human virtue, should be cultivated with certain restrictions, because, with respect to the female character, obedience is the grand lesson which ought to be impressed with unrelenting rigour.[2]

What nonsense! when will a great man arise with sufficient strength of mind to puff away the fumes which pride and sensuality have thus spread over the subject! If women are by nature inferior to men, their virtues must be the same in quality, if not in degree, or virtue is a relative idea; consequently, their conduct should be founded on the same principles, and have the same aim.[3]

Connected with man as daughters, wives, and mothers, their moral character may be estimated by their manner of fulfilling those simple duties; but the end, the grand end of their exertions should be to unfold their own faculties and acquire the dignity of conscious virtue. They may try to render their road pleasant; but ought never to forget, in common with man, that life yields not the felicity which can satis-

---

1   Similar feelings has Milton's pleasing picture of paradisiacal happiness ever raised in my mind; yet, instead of envying the lovely pair, I have, with conscious dignity, or Satanic pride, turned to hell for sublimer objects. In the same style, when viewing some noble monument of human art, I have traced the emanation of the Deity in the order I admired, till, descending from that giddy height, I have caught myself contemplating the grandest of all human sights; – for fancy quickly placed, in some solitary recess, an outcast of fortune, rising superior to passion and discontent.

2   [Rousseau, *Emile* 370.]

3   [Rousseau argues that men's and women's virtues are essentially different (*Emile* 363).]

fy an immortal soul. I do not mean to insinuate, that either sex should be so lost in abstract reflections or distant views, as to forget the affections and duties that lie before them, and are, in truth, the means appointed to produce the fruit of life; on the contrary, I would warmly recommend them, even while I assert, that they afford most satisfaction when they are considered in their true, sober light.

Probably the prevailing opinion, that woman was created for man, may have taken its rise from Moses's poetical story;[1] yet, as very few, it is presumed, who have bestowed any serious thought on the subject, ever supposed that Eve was, literally speaking, one of Adam's ribs, the deduction must be allowed to fall to the ground; or, only be so far admitted as it proves that man, from the remotest antiquity, found it convenient to exert his strength to subjugate his companion, and his invention to shew that she ought to have her neck bent under the yoke, because the whole creation was only created for his convenience or pleasure.

Let it not be concluded that I wish to invert the order of things; I have already granted, that, from the constitution of their bodies, men seem to be designed by Providence to attain a greater degree of virtue. I speak collectively of the whole sex; but I see not the shadow of a reason to conclude that their virtues should differ in respect to their nature. In fact, how can they, if virtue has only one eternal standard? I must therefore, if I reason consequentially, as strenuously maintain that they have the same simple direction, as that there is a God.

It follows then that cunning should not be opposed to wisdom, little cares to great exertions, or insipid softness, varnished over with the name of gentleness, to that fortitude which grand views alone can inspire.

I shall be told that woman would then lose many of her peculiar graces, and the opinion of a well known poet might be quoted to refute my unqualified assertion. For Pope has said, in the name of the whole male sex,

> "Yet ne'er so sure our passion to create,
> As when she touch'd the brink of all we hate."[2]

---

1 [Genesis 2: 18-25. Moses was believed to be the author of Genesis.]
2 [Pope, "Of the Characters of Women" 51-52.]

In what light this sally places men and women, I shall leave to the judicious to determine; meanwhile I shall content myself with observing, that I cannot discover why, unless they are mortal, females should always be degraded by being made subservient to love or lust.

To speak disrespectfully of love is, I know, high treason against sentiment and fine feelings; but I wish to speak the simple language of truth, and rather to address the head than the heart. To endeavour to reason love out of the world, would be to out Quixote Cervantes,[1] and equally offend against common sense; but an endeavour to restrain this tumultuous passion, and to prove that it should not be allowed to dethrone superior powers, or to usurp the sceptre which the understanding should ever coolly wield, appears less wild.

Youth is the season for love in both sexes; but in those days of thoughtless enjoyment provision should be made for the more important years of life, when reflection takes place of sensation. But Rousseau, and most of the male writers who have followed his steps, have warmly inculcated that the whole tendency of female education ought to be directed to one point: – to render them pleasing.[2]

Let me reason with the supporters of this opinion who have any knowledge of human nature, do they imagine that marriage can eradicate the habitude of life? The woman who has only been taught to please will soon find that her charms are oblique sunbeams, and that they cannot have much effect on her husband's heart when they are seen every day, when the summer is passed and gone. Will she then have sufficient native energy to look into herself for comfort, and cultivate her dormant faculties? or, is it not more rational to expect that she will try to please other men; and, in the emotions raised by the expectation of new conquests, endeavour to forget the mortification her love or pride has received? When the husband ceases to be a lover – and the time will inevitably come, her desire of pleasing will then grow languid, or become a spring of bitterness; and love, perhaps, the most evanescent of all passions, gives place to jealousy or vanity.

---

1   [An allusion to the impossibly idealistic hero of Miguel de Cervantes Saavedra (1547-1615), *Don Quixote* (1604-14). Burke compared Price to Don Quixote (*Reflections*; *Writings* 8: 58); in turn, radical writers and cartoonists applied the comparison to Burke, because of his lament for the age of chivalry (*Writings* 8: 17).]

2   [Rousseau, *Emile* 365.]

I now speak of women who are restrained by principle or preju-dice; such women, though they would shrink from an intrigue with real abhorrence, yet, nevertheless, wish to be convinced by the homage of gallantry that they are cruelly neglected by their husbands; or, days and weeks are spent in dreaming of the happiness enjoyed by congenial souls till their health is undermined and their spirits broken by discontent. How then can the great art of pleasing be such a neces-sary study? it is only useful to a mistress; the chaste wife, and serious mother, should only consider her power to please as the polish of her virtues, and the affection of her husband as one of the comforts that render her task less difficult and her life happier. – But, whether she be loved or neglected, her first wish should be to make herself respectable, and not to rely for all her happiness on a being subject to like infirmities with herself.

The worthy Dr. Gregory fell into a similar error. I respect his heart; but entirely disapprove of his celebrated Legacy to his Daugh-ters.

He advises them to cultivate a fondness for dress, because a fond-ness for dress, he asserts, is natural to them.[1] I am unable to compre-hend what either he or Rousseau mean, when they frequently use this indefinite term. If they told us that in a pre-existent state the soul was fond of dress, and brought this inclination with it into a new body, I should listen to them with a half smile, as I often do when I hear a rant about innate elegance. – But if he only meant to say that the exercise of the faculties will produce this fondness – I deny it. – It is not natural; but arises, like false ambition in men, from a love of power.

Dr. Gregory goes much further; he actually recommends dissimu-lation, and advises an innocent girl to give the lie to her feelings, and not dance with spirit, when gaiety of heart would make her feet elo-quent without making her gestures immodest.[2] In the name of truth and common sense, why should not one woman acknowledge that she can take more exercise than another?[3] or, in other words, that she has a sound constitution; and why, to damp innocent vivacity, is she

1    [Gregory, *Legacy* 55.]
2    [Gregory, *Legacy* 57-58.]
3    [Cf. Macaulay, *Letters* 60.]

darkly to be told that men will draw conclusions which she little thinks of? – Let the libertine draw what inference he pleases; but, I hope, that no sensible mother will restrain the natural frankness of youth by instilling such indecent cautions. Out of the abundance of the heart the mouth speaketh;[1] and a wiser than Solomon hath said, that the heart should be made clean, and not trivial ceremonies observed, which it is not very difficult to fulfil with scrupulous exact-ness when vice reigns in the heart.[2]

Women ought to endeavour to purify their heart;[3] but can they do so when their uncultivated understandings make them entirely dependent on their senses for employment and amusement, when no noble pursuit sets them above the little vanities of the day, or enables them to curb the wild emotions that agitate a reed over which every passing breeze has power? To gain the affections of a virtuous man is affectation necessary? Nature has given woman a weaker frame than man; but, to ensure her husband's affections, must a wife, who by the exercise of her mind and body whilst she was discharging the duties of a daughter, wife, and mother, has allowed her constitution to retain its natural strength, and her nerves a healthy tone, is she, I say, to con-descend to use art and feign a sickly delicacy in order to secure her husband's affection? Weakness may excite tenderness, and gratify the arrogant pride of man; but the lordly caresses of a protector will not gratify a noble mind that pants for, and deserves to be respected. Fondness is a poor substitute for friendship!

In a seraglio, I grant, that all these arts are necessary; the epicure must have his palate tickled, or he will sink into apathy; but have women so little ambition as to be satisfied with such a condition? Can they supinely dream life away in the lap of pleasure, or the languor of weariness, rather than assert their claim to pursue reasonable pleasures and render themselves conspicuous by practising the virtues which dignify mankind? Surely she has not an immortal soul who can loiter life away merely employed to adorn her person, that she may amuse the languid hours, and soften the cares of a fellow-creature who is

---

1   [Matthew 12: 34, Luke 6: 45.]
2   [Matthew 23: 25-28; Luke 11: 31-44. The speaker is Christ, wiser than Solomon (cf. Milton, *Paradise Regained* 2.205-6).]
3   [Matthew 5: 8.]

willing to be enlivened by her smiles and tricks, when the serious business of life is over.

Besides, the woman who strengthens her body and exercises her mind will, by managing her family and practising various virtues, become the friend, and not the humble dependent of her husband; and if she, by possessing such substantial qualities, merit his regard, she will not find it necessary to conceal her affection, nor to pretend to an unnatural coldness of constitution to excite her husband's passions. In fact, if we revert to history, we shall find that the women who have distinguished themselves have neither been the most beautiful nor the most gentle of their sex.

Nature, or, to speak with strict propriety, God, has made all things right; but man has sought him out many inventions to mar the work.[1] I now allude to that part of Dr. Gregory's treatise, where he advises a wife never to let her husband know the extent of her sensibility or affection.[2] Voluptuous precaution, and as ineffectual as absurd. – Love, from its very nature, must be transitory. To seek for a secret that would render it constant, would be as wild a search as for the philosopher's stone, or the grand panacea:[3] and the discovery would be equally useless, or rather pernicious, to mankind. The most holy band of society is friendship. It has been well said, by a shrewd satirist, "that rare as true love is, true friendship is still rarer."[4]

This is an obvious truth, and the cause not lying deep, will not elude a slight glance of inquiry.

Love, the common passion, in which chance and sensation take place of choice and reason, is, in some degree, felt by the mass of mankind; for it is not necessary to speak, at present, of the emotions that rise above or sink below love. This passion, naturally increased by suspense and difficulties, draws the mind out of its accustomed state, and exalts the affections; but the security of marriage, allowing the fever of love to subside, a healthy temperature is thought insipid, only

---

1   [Cf. Rousseau, *Emile* 37.]
2   [Gregory, *Legacy* 87-88.]
3   [Alchemists sought for two substances (or a substance with two properties): the philosopher's stone, which could transmute base metals into gold; and the elixir or panacea, which could prolong life indefinitely.]
4   [François, duc de La Rochefoucauld (1613-80), *Réflexions; ou, Sentences et maximes morales* (1678) no. 473.]

by those who have not sufficient intellect to substitute the calm tenderness of friendship, the confidence of respect, instead of blind admiration, and the sensual emotions of fondness.

This is, must be, the course of nature. – Friendship or indifference inevitably succeeds love. – And this constitution seems perfectly to harmonize with the system of government which prevails in the moral world. Passions are spurs to action, and open the mind; but they sink into mere appetites, become a personal and momentary gratification, when the object is gained, and the satisfied mind rests in enjoyment. The man who had some virtue whilst he was struggling for a crown, often becomes a voluptuous tyrant when it graces his brow; and, when the lover is not lost in the husband, the dotard, a prey to childish caprices, and fond jealousies, neglects the serious duties of life, and the caresses which should excite confidence in his children are lavished on the overgrown child, his wife.

In order to fulfil the duties of life, and to be able to pursue with vigour the various employments which form the moral character, a master and mistress of a family ought not to continue to love each other with passion. I mean to say, that they ought not to indulge those emotions which disturb the order of society, and engross the thoughts that should be otherwise employed. The mind that has never been engrossed by one object wants vigour – if it can long be so, it is weak.

A mistaken education, a narrow, uncultivated mind, and many sexual prejudices, tend to make women more constant than men; but, for the present, I shall not touch on this branch of the subject. I will go still further, and advance, without dreaming of a paradox, that an unhappy marriage is often very advantageous to a family, and that the neglected wife is, in general, the best mother. And this would almost always be the consequence if the female mind were more enlarged: for, it seems to be the common dispensation of Providence, that what we gain in present enjoyment should be deducted from the treasure of life, experience; and that when we are gathering the flowers of the day and revelling in pleasure, the solid fruit of toil and wisdom should not be caught at the same time. The way lies before us, we must turn to the right or left; and he who will pass life away in bounding from one pleasure to another, must not complain if he acquire neither wisdom nor respectability of character.

Supposing, for a moment, that the soul is not immortal, and that man was only created for the present scene, – I think we should have reason to complain that love, infantine fondness, ever grew insipid and palled upon the sense. Let us eat, drink, and love, for to-morrow we die,[1] would be, in fact, the language of reason, the morality of life; and who but a fool would part with a reality for a fleeting shadow? But, if awed by observing the improbable powers of the mind, we disdain to confine our wishes or thoughts to such a comparatively mean field of action; that only appears grand and important, as it is connected with a boundless prospect and sublime hopes, what necessity is there for falsehood in conduct, and why must the sacred majesty of truth be violated to detain a deceitful good that saps the very foundation of virtue? Why must the female mind be tainted by coquetish arts to gratify the sensualist, and prevent love from subsiding into friendship, or compassionate tenderness, when there are not qualities on which friendship can be built? Let the honest heart shew itself, and *reason* teach passion to submit to necessity; or, let the dignified pursuit of virtue and knowledge raise the mind above those emotions which rather imbitter than sweeten the cup of life, when they are not restrained within due bounds.

I do not mean to allude to the romantic passion, which is the concomitant of genius. – Who can clip its wing? But that grand passion not proportioned to the puny enjoyments of life, is only true to the sentiment, and feeds on itself. The passions which have been celebrated for their durability have always been unfortunate. They have acquired strength by absence and constitutional melancholy. – The fancy has hovered round a form of beauty dimly seen – but familiarity might have turned admiration into disgust; or, at least, into indifference, and allowed the imagination leisure to start fresh game. With perfect propriety, according to this view of things, does Rousseau make the mistress of his soul, Eloisa, love St. Preux, when life was fading before her; but this is no proof of the immortality of the passion.[2]

Of the same complexion is Dr. Gregory's advice respecting delicacy of sentiment, which he advises a woman not to acquire, if she have

---

1  [Isaiah 22: 13.]
2  [The heroine of Rousseau's *Julie; ou, La Nouvelle Héloise* (1761), faithfully married to Wolmar, confesses her love for St. Preux only on her deathbed.]

determined to marry.[1] This determination, however, perfectly consistent with his former advice, he calls *indelicate*, and earnestly persuades his daughters to conceal it, though it may govern their conduct: — as if it were indelicate to have the common appetites of human nature.

Noble morality! and consistent with the cautious prudence of a little soul that cannot extend its views beyond the present minute division of existence. If all the faculties of woman's mind are only to be cultivated as they respect her dependence on man; if, when a husband be obtained, she have arrived at her goal, and meanly proud rests satisfied with such a paltry crown, let her grovel contentedly, scarcely raised by her employments above the animal kingdom; but, if, struggling for the prize of her high calling, she look beyond the present scene, let her cultivate her understanding without stopping to consider what character the husband may have whom she is destined to marry. Let her only determine, without being too anxious about present happiness, to acquire the qualities that ennoble a rational being, and a rough inelegant husband may shock her taste without destroying her peace of mind. She will not model her soul to suit the frailties of her companion, but to bear with them: his character may be a trial, but not an impediment to virtue.

If Dr. Gregory confined his remark to romantic expectations of constant love and congenial feelings, he should have recollected that experience will banish what advice can never make us cease to wish for, when the imagination is kept alive at the expence of reason.

I own it frequently happens that women who have fostered a romantic unnatural delicacy of feeling, waste their[2] lives in *imagining* how happy they should have been with a husband who could love them with a fervid increasing affection every day, and all day. But they might as well pine married as single — and would not be a jot more unhappy with a bad husband than longing for a good one. That a proper education; or, to speak with more precision, a well stored mind, would enable a woman to support a single life with dignity, I grant; but that she should avoid cultivating her taste, lest her husband should occasionally shock it, is quitting a substance for a shadow. To say the truth, I do not know of what use is an improved taste, if the

---

1    [Gregory, *Legacy* 116-18.]
2    For example, the herd of Novelists.

individual be not rendered more independent of the casualties of life; if new sources of enjoyment, only dependent on the solitary operations of the mind, are not opened. People of taste, married or single, without distinction, will ever be disgusted by various things that touch not less observing minds. On this conclusion the argument must not be allowed to hinge; but in the whole sum of enjoyment is taste to be denominated a blessing?

The question is, whether it procures most pain or pleasure? The answer will decide the propriety of Dr. Gregory's advice, and shew how absurd and tyrannic it is thus to lay down a system of slavery; or to attempt to educate moral beings by any other rules than those deduced from pure reason, which apply to the whole species.

Gentleness of manners, forbearance and long-suffering, are such amiable Godlike qualities,[1] that in sublime poetic strains the Deity has been invested with them; and, perhaps, no representation of his goodness so strongly fastens on the human affections as those that represent him abundant in mercy and willing to pardon.[2] Gentleness, considered in this point of view, bears on its front all the characteristics of grandeur, combined with the winning graces of condescension; but what a different aspect it assumes when it is the submissive demeanour of dependence, the support of weakness that loves, because it wants protection; and is forbearing, because it must silently endure injuries; smiling under the lash at which it dare not snarl. Abject as this picture appears, it is the portrait of an accomplished woman, according to the received opinion of female excellence, separated by specious reasoners from human excellence. Or, they[3] kindly restore the rib, and make one moral being of a man and woman; not forgetting to give her all the "submissive charms."[4]

How women are to exist in that state where there is to be neither marrying nor giving in marriage,[5] we are not told. For though moralists have agreed that the tenor of life seems to prove that *man* is pre-

---

1  [Galatians 5: 22, Ephesians 4: 2.]
2  [Isaiah 55: 7.]
3  Vide Rousseau, and Swedenborg. [Rousseau, *Emile* 377; Emmanuel Swedenborg (1688-1772), *On Marriages in Heaven; and On the Nature of Heavenly Conjugal Love* (1768; trans. 1789), which Wollstonecraft reviewed (*Works* 7: 94-95).]
4  [Milton, *Paradise Lost* 4.498.]
5  [Matthew 22: 30; Mark 12: 25; Luke 20: 35.]

pared by various circumstances for a future state, they constantly concur in advising *woman* only to provide for the present. Gentleness, docility, and a spaniel-like affection are, on this ground, consistently recommended as the cardinal virtues of the sex; and, disregarding the arbitrary economy of nature, one writer has declared that it is masculine for a woman to be melancholy.[1] She was created to be the toy of man, his rattle, and it must jingle in his ears whenever, dismissing reason, he chooses to be amused.

To recommend gentleness, indeed, on a broad basis is strictly philosophical. A frail being should labour to be gentle. But when forbearance confounds right and wrong, it ceases to be a virtue; and, however convenient it may be found in a companion – that companion will ever be considered as an inferior, and only inspire a vapid tenderness, which easily degenerates into contempt. Still, if advice could really make a being gentle, whose natural disposition admitted not of such a fine polish, something towards the advancement of order would be attained; but if, as might quickly be demonstrated, only affectation be produced by this indiscriminate counsel, which throws a stumbling-block in the way of gradual improvement, and true melioration of temper, the sex is not much benefited by sacrificing solid virtues to the attainment of superficial graces, though for a few years they may procure the individuals regal sway.

As a philosopher, I read with indignation the plausible epithets which men use to soften their insults; and, as a moralist, I ask what is meant by such heterogeneous associations, as fair defects, amiable weaknesses, &c.?[2] If there be but one criterion of morals, but one archetype for man, women appear to be suspended by destiny, according to the vulgar tale of Mahomet's coffin;[3] they have neither the unerring instinct of brutes, nor are allowed to fix the eye of reason on a perfect model. They were made to be loved, and must not aim at respect, lest they should be hunted out of society as masculine.

---

1    [Unidentified; Poston suggests a (rather vague) allusion to Burke, *Philosophical Enquiry* (34n.8).]

2    [Milton, *Paradise Lost* 10.891; Pope, "Of the Characters of Women" 44 (misquoted).]

3    [According to the legend, Mohammed's coffin was suspended in midair by magnets. See Milton, *Eikonoklastes* (1649); Samuel Butler (1613-80), *Hudibras* (1663-78) 2.3.442, 3.2.605; Matthew Prior (1664-1721), *Alma; or, The Progress of the Mind* (1718) 2: 198-99.]

But to view the subject in another point of view. Do passive indolent women make the best wives? Confining our discussion to the present moment of existence, let us see how such weak creatures perform their part? Do the women who, by the attainment of a few superficial accomplishments, have strengthened the prevailing prejudice, merely contribute to the happiness of their husbands? Do they display their charms merely to amuse them? And have women, who have early imbibed notions of passive obedience, sufficient character to manage a family or educate children? So far from it, that, after surveying the history of woman, I cannot help, agreeing with the severest satirist, considering the sex as the weakest as well as the most oppressed half of the species. What does history disclose but marks of inferiority, and how few women have emancipated themselves from the galling yoke of sovereign man? – So few, that the exceptions remind me of an ingenious conjecture respecting Newton: that he was probably a being of a superior order, accidentally caged in a human body.[1] Following the same train of thinking, I have been led to imagine that the few extraordinary women who have rushed in eccentrical directions out of the orbit prescribed to their sex, were *male* spirits, confined by mistake in female frames. But if it be not philosophical to think of sex when the soul is mentioned, the inferiority must depend on the organs; or the heavenly fire, which is to ferment the clay, is not given in equal portions.

But avoiding, as I have hitherto done, any direct comparison of the two sexes collectively, or frankly acknowledging the inferiority of woman, according to the present appearance of things, I shall only insist that men have increased that inferiority till women are almost sunk below the standard of rational creatures. Let their faculties have room to unfold, and their virtues to gain strength, and then determine where the whole sex must stand in the intellectual scale. Yet let it be remembered, that for a small number of distinguished women I do not ask a place.

It is difficult for us purblind mortals to say to what height human discoveries and improvements may arrive when the gloom of despo-

---

1 [See James Thomson (1700-48), *A Poem Sacred to the Memory of Sir Isaac Newton* (1727); Pope, *An Essay on Man* (1733-34) 2.31-34; "Epitaph. Intended for Sir Isaac Newton, In Westminster-Abbey" (1730).]

tism subsides, which makes us stumble at every step; but, when morality shall be settled on a more solid basis, then, without being gifted with a prophetic spirit, I will venture to predict that woman will be either the friend or slave of man. We shall not, as at present, doubt whether she is a moral agent, or the link which unites man with brutes. But, should it then appear, that like the brutes they were principally created for the use of man, he will let them patiently bite the bridle, and not mock them with empty praise; or, should their rationality be proved, he will not impede their improvement merely to gratify his sensual appetites. He will not, with all the graces of rhetoric, advise them to submit implicitly their understanding to the guidance of man. He will not, when he treats of the education of women, assert that they ought never to have the free use of reason, nor would he recommend cunning and dissimulation to beings who are acquiring, in like manner as himself, the virtues of humanity.

Surely there can be but one rule of right, if morality has an eternal foundation, and whoever sacrifices virtue, strictly so called, to present convenience, or whose *duty* it is to act in such a manner, lives only for the passing day, and cannot be an accountable creature.

The poet then should have dropped his sneer when he says,

> "If weak women go astray,
> The stars are more in fault than they."[1]

For that they are bound by the adamantine chain of destiny is most certain, if it be proved that they are never to exercise their own reason, never to be independent, never to rise above opinion, or to feel the dignity of a rational will that only bows to God, and often forgets that the universe contains any being but itself and the model of perfection to which its ardent gaze is turned, to adore attributes that, softened into virtues, may be imitated in kind, though the degree overwhelms the enraptured mind.

If, I say, for I would not impress by declamation when Reason offers her sober light, if they be really capable of acting like rational creatures, let them not be treated like slaves; or, like the brutes who

---

1   [Prior, "Hans Carvel" (1700) 11-12.]

are dependent on the reason of man, when they associate with him; but cultivate their minds, give them the salutary, sublime curb of principle, and let them attain conscious dignity by feeling themselves only dependent on God. Teach them, in common with man, to submit to necessity, instead of giving, to render them more pleasing, a sex to morals.

Further, should experience prove that they cannot attain the same degree of strength of mind, perseverance, and fortitude, let their virtues be the same in kind, though they may vainly struggle for the same degree; and the superiority of man will be equally clear, if not clearer; and truth, as it is a simple principle, which admits of no modification, would be common to both. Nay, the order of society as it is at present regulated would not be inverted, for woman would then only have the rank that reason assigned her, and arts could not be practised to bring the balance even, much less to turn it.

These may be termed Utopian dreams. – Thanks to that Being who impressed them on my soul, and gave me sufficient strength of mind to dare to exert my own reason, till, becoming dependent only on him for the support of my virtue, I view, with indignation, the mistaken notions that enslave my sex.

I love man as my fellow; but his scepter, real, or usurped, extends not to me, unless the reason of an individual demands my homage; and even then the submission is to reason, and not to man. In fact, the conduct of an accountable being must be regulated by the operations of its own reason; or on what foundation rests the throne of God?

It appears to me necessary to dwell on these obvious truths, because females have been insulated, as it were; and, while they have been stripped of the virtues that should clothe humanity, they have been decked with artificial graces that enable them to exercise a short-lived tyranny. Love, in their bosoms, taking place of every nobler passion, their sole ambition is to be fair, to raise emotion instead of inspiring respect; and this ignoble desire, like the servility in absolute monarchies, destroys all strength of character. Liberty is the mother of virtue, and if women be, by their very constitution, slaves, and not allowed to breathe the sharp invigorating air of freedom, they must ever languish like exotics, and be reckoned beautiful flaws in nature.

As to the argument respecting the subjection in which the sex has ever been held, it retorts on man. The many have always been enthralled by the few; and monsters, who scarcely have shewn any discernment of human excellence, have tyrannized over thousands of their fellow-creatures. Why have men of superiour endowments submitted to such degradation? For, is it not universally acknowledged that kings, viewed collectively, have ever been inferior, in abilities and virtue, to the same number of men taken from the common mass of mankind – yet, have they not, and are they not still treated with a degree of reverence that is an insult to reason? China is not the only country where a living man has been made a God.[1] *Men* have submitted to superior strength to enjoy with impunity the pleasure of the moment – *women* have only done the same, and therefore till it is proved that the courtier, who servilely resigns the birthright of a man, is not a moral agent, it cannot be demonstrated that woman is essentially inferior to man because she has always been subjugated.

Brutal force has hitherto governed the world, and that the science of politics is in its infancy, is evident from philosophers scrupling to give the knowledge most useful to man that determinate distinction.

I shall not pursue this argument any further than to establish an obvious inference, that as sound politics diffuse liberty, mankind, including woman, will become more wise and virtuous.

---

1   [Cf. Price, *Discourse* 25; Appendix A.3.]

# CHAP. III.

## THE SAME SUBJECT CONTINUED.[1]

BODILY strength from being the distinction of heroes is now sunk into such unmerited contempt that men, as well as women, seem to think it unnecessary: the latter, as it takes from their feminine graces, and from that lovely weakness the source of their undue power; and the former, because it appears inimical to the character of a gentleman.

That they have both by departing from one extreme run into another, may easily be proved; but first it may be proper to observe, that a vulgar error has obtained a degree of credit, which has given force to a false conclusion, in which an effect has been mistaken for a cause.

People of genius have, very frequently, impaired their constitutions by study or careless inattention to their health, and the violence of their passions bearing a proportion to the vigour of their intellects, the sword's destroying the scabbard has become almost proverbial,[2] and superficial observers have inferred from thence, that men of genius have commonly weak, or, to use a more fashionable phrase, delicate constitutions. Yet the contrary, I believe, will appear to be the fact; for, on diligent inquiry, I find that strength of mind has, in most cases, been accompanied by superior strength of body, – natural soundness of constitution, – not that robust tone of nerves and vigour of muscles, which arise from bodily labour, when the mind is quiescent, or only directs the hands.

Dr. Priestley has remarked, in the preface to his biographical chart,[3] that the majority of great men have lived beyond forty-five. And, considering the thoughtless manner in which they have lavished their strength, when investigating a favourite science they have wasted the lamp of life, forgetful of the midnight hour; or, when, lost in poet-

---

1 [This is the title of nine of Macaulay's *Letters on Education*.]
2 [Rousseau, *Confessions* 209; Book 5.]
3 [Joseph Priestley (1733-1804), *A Description of a Chart of Biography* (1765) 25-26.]

ic dreams, fancy has peopled the scene, and the soul has been disturbed, till it shook the constitution, by the passions that meditation had raised; whose objects, the baseless fabric of a vision,[1] faded before the exhausted eye, they must have had iron frames. Shakspeare never grasped the airy dagger with a nerveless hand,[2] nor did Milton tremble when he led Satan far from the confines of his dreary prison.[3] – These were not the ravings of imbecility, the sickly effusions of distempered brains; but the exuberance of fancy, that "in a fine phrenzy" wandering,[4] was not continually reminded of its material shackles.

I am aware that this argument would carry me further than it may be supposed I wish to go; but I follow truth, and, still adhering to my first position, I will allow that bodily strength seems to give man a natural superiority over woman; and this is the only solid basis on which the superiority of the sex can be built. But I still insist, that not only the virtue, but the *knowledge* of the two sexes should be the same in nature, if not in degree, and that women, considered not only as moral, but rational creatures, ought to endeavour to acquire human virtues (or perfections) by the *same* means as men, instead of being educated like a fanciful kind of *half* being – one of Rousseau's wild chimeras[5].

---

1 [Shakespeare, *The Tempest* 4.1.151.]
2 [Shakespeare, *Macbeth* 2.1.33-49.]
3 [Milton, *Paradise Lost* 2.629-1055.]
4 [Shakespeare, *A Midsummer Night's Dream* 5.1.12.]
5 "Researches into abstract and speculative truths, the principles and axioms of sciences, in short, every thing which tends to generalize our ideas, is not the proper province of women; their studies should be relative to points of practice; it belongs to them to apply those principles which men have discovered; and it is their part to make observations, which direct men to the establishment of general principles. All the ideas of women, which have not the immediate tendency to points of duty, should be directed to the study of men, and to the attainment of those agreeable accomplishments which have taste for their object; for as to works of genius, they are beyond their capacity; neither have they sufficient precision or power of attention to succeed in sciences which require accuracy: and as to physical knowledge, it belongs to those only who are most active, most inquisitive; who comprehend the greatest variety of objects: in short, it belongs to those who have the strongest powers, and who exercise them most, to judge of the relations between sensible beings and the laws of nature. A woman who is naturally weak, and does not carry her ideas to any great extent, knows how to judge and make a proper estimate of those movements which she sets to work, in order to aid her weakness; and these movements are the passions of men. The mechanism she employs is much more powerful than

But, if strength of body be, with some shew of reason, the boast of men, why are women so infatuated as to be proud of a defect? Rousseau has furnished them with a plausible excuse, which could only have occurred to a man, whose imagination had been allowed to run wild, and refine on the impressions made by exquisite senses; – that they might, forsooth, have a pretext for yielding to a natural appetite without violating a romantic species of modesty, which gratifies the pride and libertinism of man.

Women, deluded by these sentiments, sometimes boast of their weakness, cunningly obtaining power by playing on the *weakness* of men; and they may well glory in their illicit sway, for, like Turkish bashaws,[1] they have more real power than their masters: but virtue is sacrificed to temporary gratifications, and the respectability of life to the triumph of an hour.

Women, as well as despots, have now, perhaps, more power than they would have if the world, divided and subdivided into kingdoms and families, were governed by laws deduced from the exercise of reason; but in obtaining it, to carry on the comparison, their character is

---

ours; for all her levers move the human heart. She must have the skill to incline us to do every thing which her sex will not enable her to do herself, and which is necessary or agreeable to her; therefore she ought to study the mind of man thoroughly, not the mind of man in general, abstractedly, but the dispositions of those men to whom she is subject, either by the laws of her country or by the force of opinion. She should learn to penetrate into their real sentiments from their conversation, their actions, their looks, and gestures. She should also have the art, by her own conversation, actions, looks, and gestures, to communicate those sentiments which are agreeable to them, without seeming to intend it. Men will argue more philosophically about the human heart; but women will read the heart of man better than they. It belongs to women, if I may be allowed the expression, to form an experimental morality, and to reduce the study of man to a system. Women have most wit, men have most genius; women observe, men reason: from the concurrence of both we derive the clearest light and the most perfect knowledge, which the human mind is, of itself, capable of attaining. In one word, from hence we acquire the most intimate acquaintance, both with ourselves and others, of which our nature is capable; and it is thus that art has a constant tendency to perfect those endowments which nature has bestowed. – The world is the book of women." *Rousseau's Emilius.* I hope my readers still remember the comparison, which I have brought forward, between women and officers. [Rousseau, *Emile* 386–87; Wollstonecraft quotes from *Emilius and Sophia; or, A New System of Education,* trans. William Kenrick (1763). Our references are to the translation by Allan Bloom (1979).]

1   [Or pashas, high-ranking officers of the Ottoman Empire.]

degraded, and licentiousness spread through the whole aggregate of society. The many become pedestal to the few. I, therefore, will venture to assert, that till women are more rationally educated, the progress of human virtue and improvement in knowledge must receive continual checks. And if it be granted that woman was not created merely to gratify the appetite of man, or to be the upper servant, who provides his meals and takes care of his linen, it must follow, that the first care of those mothers or fathers, who really attend to the education of females, should be, if not to strengthen the body, at least, not to destroy the constitution by mistaken notions of beauty and female excellence; nor should girls ever be allowed to imbibe the pernicious notion that a defect can, by any chemical process of reasoning, become an excellence. In this respect, I am happy to find, that the author of one of the most instructive books, that our country has produced for children, coincides with me in opinion; I shall quote his pertinent remarks to give the force of his respectable authority to reason[1].

---

1   A respectable old man gives the following sensible account of the method he pursued when educating his daughter. "I endeavoured to give both to her mind and body a degree of vigour, which is seldom found in the female sex. As soon as she was sufficiently advanced in strength to be capable of the lighter labours of husbandry and gardening, I employed her as my constant companion. Selene, for that was her name, soon acquired a dexterity in all these rustic employments, which I considered with equal pleasure and admiration. If women are in general feeble both in body and mind, it arises less from nature than from education. We encourage a vicious indolence and inactivity, which we falsely call delicacy; instead of hardening their minds by the severer principles of reason and philosophy, we breed them to useless arts, which terminate in vanity and sensuality. In most of the countries which I had visited, they are taught nothing of an higher nature than a few modulations of the voice, or useless postures of the body; their time is consumed in sloth or trifles, and trifles become the only pursuits capable of interesting them. We seem to forget, that it is upon the qualities of the female sex that our own domestic comforts and the education of our children must depend. And what are the comforts or the education which a race of beings, corrupted from their infancy, and unacquainted with all the duties of life, are fitted to bestow? To touch a musical instrument with useless skill, to exhibit their natural or affected graces to the eyes of indolent and debauched young men, to dissipate their husband's patrimony in riotous and unnecessary expences, these are the only arts cultivated by women in most of the polished nations I had seen. And the consequences are uniformly such as may be expected to proceed from such polluted sources, private misery and public servitude.

"But Selene's education was regulated by different views, and conducted upon severer principles; if that can be called severity which opens the mind to a sense of moral and religious duties, and most effectually arms it against the inevitable evils of life."

Mr. Day's Sandford and Merton, Vol. III. [3: 205-7.]

But should it be proved that woman is naturally weaker than man, whence does it follow that it is natural for her to labour to become still weaker than nature intended her to be?[1] Arguments of this cast are an insult to common sense, and savour of passion. The *divine right* of husbands, like the divine right of kings, may, it is to be hoped, in this enlightened age, be contested without danger, and, though conviction may not silence many boisterous disputants, yet, when any prevailing prejudice is attacked, the wise will consider, and leave the narrow-minded to rail with thoughtless vehemence at innovation.

The mother, who wishes to give true dignity of character to her daughter, must, regardless of the sneers of ignorance, proceed on a plan diametrically opposite to that which Rousseau has recommended with all the deluding charms of eloquence and philosophical sophistry: for his eloquence renders absurdities plausible, and his dogmatic conclusions puzzle, without convincing, those who have not ability to refute them.

Throughout the whole animal kingdom every young creature requires almost continual exercise, and the infancy of children, conformable to this intimation, should be passed in harmless gambols, that exercise the feet and hands, without requiring very minute direction from the head, or the constant attention of a nurse. In fact, the care necessary for self-preservation is the first natural exercise of the understanding, as little inventions to amuse the present moment unfold the imagination. But these wise designs of nature are counteracted by mistaken fondness or blind zeal. The child is not left a moment to its own direction, particularly a girl, and thus rendered dependent – dependence is called natural.

To preserve personal beauty, woman's glory! the limbs and faculties are cramped with worse than Chinese bands,[2] and the sedentary life which they are condemned to live, whilst boys frolic in the open air, weakens the muscles and relaxes the nerves. – As for Rousseau's remarks, which have since been echoed by several writers, that they have naturally, that is from their birth, independent of education, a

---

1   [Cf. Macaulay, *Letters* 24-25, 47-48.]
2   [An allusion to the practice of foot-binding. Cf. John Locke (1632-1704), *Some Thoughts concerning Education* (1693), ed. John W. and Jean S. Yolton (Oxford: Clarendon P, 1989) 91; para. 12; Macaulay, *Letters* 43-44.]

fondness for dolls, dressing, and talking – they are so puerile as not to merit a serious refutation.[1] That a girl, condemned to sit for hours together listening to the idle chat of weak nurses, or to attend at her mother's toilet, will endeavour to join the conversation, is, indeed, very natural; and that she will imitate her mother or aunts, and amuse herself by adorning her lifeless doll, as they do in dressing her, poor innocent babe! is undoubtedly a most natural consequence. For men of the greatest abilities have seldom had sufficient strength to rise above the surrounding atmosphere; and, if the page of genius have always been blurred by the prejudices of the age, some allowance should be made for a sex, who, like kings, always see things through a false medium.

Pursuing these reflections, the fondness for dress, conspicuous in women, may be easily accounted for, without supposing it the result of a desire to please the sex on which they are dependent. The absurdity, in short, of supposing that a girl is naturally a coquette, and that a desire connected with the impulse of nature to propagate the species, should appear even before an improper education has, by heating the imagination, called it forth prematurely, is so unphilosophical, that such a sagacious observer as Rousseau would not have adopted it, if he had not been accustomed to make reason give way to his desire of singularity, and truth to a favourite paradox.[2]

Yet thus to give a sex to mind was not very consistent with the principles of a man who argued so warmly, and so well, for the immortality of the soul.[3] – But what a weak barrier is truth when it stands in the way of an hypothesis! Rousseau respected – almost adored virtue – and yet he allowed himself to love with sensual fondness. His imagination constantly prepared inflammable fewel for his inflammable senses; but, in order to reconcile his respect for self-denial, fortitude, and those heroic virtues, which a mind like his could not coolly admire, he labours to invert the law of nature, and broaches a doctrine pregnant with mischief and derogatory to the character

---

1   [Rousseau, *Emile* 365, 367-68]
2   [Rousseau, *Emile* 365; he does, however, warn against a premature education (215). Macaulay also accuses Rousseau of a taste for paradoxes (*Letters* 205; Appendix B.2), which he concedes (*Emile* 93, 113).]
3   [Rousseau, *Emile* 282-85.]

of supreme wisdom.

His ridiculous stories, which tend to prove that girls are *naturally* attentive to their persons, without laying any stress on daily example, are below contempt. – And that a little miss should have such a correct taste as to neglect the pleasing amusement of making O's, merely because she perceived that it was an ungraceful attitude, should be selected with the anecdotes of the learned pig[1].

I have, probably, had an opportunity of observing more girls in their infancy than J. J. Rousseau – I can recollect my own feelings, and I have looked steadily around me; yet, so far from coinciding with him in opinion respecting the first dawn of the female character, I will venture to affirm, that a girl, whose spirits have not been damped by inactivity, or innocence tainted by false shame, will always be a romp, and the doll will never excite attention unless confinement allows her no alternative.[2] Girls and boys, in short, would play harmlessly together, if the distinction of sex was not inculcated long before nature makes any difference. – I will go further, and affirm, as an indisputable fact, that most of the women, in the circle of my observation, who have acted like rational creatures, or shewn any vigour of intellect, have accidentally been allowed to run wild – as some of the elegant formers of the fair sex would insinuate.

The baneful consequences which flow from inattention to health during infancy, and youth, extend further than is supposed – dependence of body naturally produces dependence of mind; and how can she be a good wife or mother, the greater part of whose time is employed to guard against or endure sickness? Nor can it be expected that a woman will resolutely endeavour to strengthen her constitution

---

1 "I once knew a young person who learned to write before she learned to read, and began to write with her needle before she could use a pen. At first, indeed, she took it into her head to make no other letter than the O: this letter she was constantly making of all sizes, and always the wrong way. Unluckily, one day, as she was intent on this employment, she happened to see herself in the looking-glass; when, taking a dislike to the constrained attitude in which she sat while writing, she threw away her pen, like another Pallas, and determined against making the O any more. Her brother was also equally averse to writing: it was the confinement, however, and not the constrained attitude, that most disgusted him." *Rousseau's Emilius.* [369. For the learned pig, see Sarah Trimmer (1741-1810), *Fabulous Histories* (1786) chap. 9; James Boswell (1740-1795), *Life of Johnson* (1791) November 1784.]
2 [In fact, Rousseau approves of exercise (within limits) for girls (*Emile* 366).]

and abstain from enervating indulgencies, if artificial notions of beauty, and false descriptions of sensibility, have been early entangled with her motives of action. Most men are sometimes obliged to bear with bodily inconveniencies, and to endure, occasionally, the inclemency of the elements; but genteel women are, literally speaking, slaves to their bodies, and glory in their subjection.

I once knew a weak woman of fashion, who was more than commonly proud of her delicacy and sensibility. She thought a distinguishing taste and puny appetite the height of all human perfection, and acted accordingly. – I have seen this weak sophisticated being neglect all the duties of life, yet recline with self-complacency on a sofa, and boast of her want of appetite as a proof of delicacy that extended to, or, perhaps, arose from, her exquisite sensibility: for it is difficult to render intelligible such ridiculous jargon. – Yet, at the moment, I have seen her insult a worthy old gentlewoman, whom unexpected misfortunes had made dependent on her ostentatious bounty, and who, in better days, had claims on her gratitude. Is it possible that a human creature could have become such a weak and depraved being, if, like the Sybarites,[1] dissolved in luxury, every thing like virtue had not been worn away, or never impressed by precept, a poor substitute, it is true, for cultivation of mind, though it serves as a fence against vice?

Such a woman is not a more irrational monster than some of the Roman emperors, who were depraved by lawless power. Yet, since kings have been more under the restraint of law, and the curb, however weak, of honour, the records of history are not filled with such unnatural instances of folly and cruelty, nor does the despotism that kills virtue and genius in the bud, hover over Europe with that destructive blast which desolates Turkey, and renders the men, as well as the soil, unfruitful.[2]

Women are every where in this deplorable state; for, in order to preserve their innocence, as ignorance is courteously termed, truth is hidden from them, and they are made to assume an artificial character

---

1  [The citizens of Sybaris, a Greek colony in Southern Italy, were proverbial for self-indulgence.]
2  [The simoom or samiel, a hot and allegedly unwholesome wind, here used as a symbol of despotism.]

before their faculties have acquired any strength. Taught from their infancy that beauty is woman's sceptre, the mind shapes itself to the body, and, roaming round its gilt cage, only seeks to adorn its prison. Men have various employments and pursuits which engage their attention, and give a character to the opening mind; but women, confined to one, and having their thoughts constantly directed to the most insignificant part of themselves, seldom extend their views beyond the triumph of the hour. But were their understanding once emancipated from the slavery to which the pride and sensuality of man and their short-sighted desire, like that of dominion in tyrants, of present sway, has subjected them, we should probably read of their weaknesses with surprise. I must be allowed to pursue the argument a little farther.

Perhaps, if the existence of an evil being were allowed, who, in the allegorical language of scripture, went about seeking whom he should devour,[1] he could not more effectually degrade the human character than by giving a man absolute power.

This argument branches into various ramifications. – Birth, riches, and every extrinsic advantage that exalt a man above his fellows, without any mental exertion, sink him in reality below them. In proportion to his weakness, he is played upon by designing men, till the bloated monster has lost all traces of humanity. And that tribes of men, like flocks of sheep, should quietly follow such a leader, is a solecism that only a desire of present enjoyment and narrowness of understanding can solve. Educated in slavish dependence, and enervated by luxury and sloth, where shall we find men who will stand forth to assert the rights of man; – or claim the privilege of moral beings, who should have but one road to excellence? Slavery to monarchs and ministers, which the world will be long in freeing itself from, and whose deadly grasp stops the progress of the human mind, is not yet abolished.

Let not men then in the pride of power, use the same arguments that tyrannic kings and venal ministers have used, and fallaciously assert that woman ought to be subjected because she has always been so. – But, when man, governed by reasonable laws, enjoys his natural

---

1  [1 Peter 5: 8.]

freedom, let him despise woman, if she do not share it with him; and, till that glorious period arrives, in descanting on the folly of the sex, let him not overlook his own.

Women, it is true, obtaining power by unjust means, by practising or fostering vice, evidently lose the rank which reason would assign them, and they become either abject slaves or capricious tyrants. They lose all simplicity, all dignity of mind, in acquiring power, and act as men are observed to act when they have been exalted by the same means.

It is time to effect a revolution in female manners – time to restore to them their lost dignity – and make them, as a part of the human species, labour by reforming themselves to reform the world. It is time to separate unchangeable morals from local manners. – If men be demi-gods – why let us serve them! And if the dignity of the female soul be as disputable as that of animals – if their reason does not afford sufficient light to direct their conduct whilst unerring instinct is denied – they are surely of all creatures the most miserable! and, bent beneath the iron hand of destiny, must submit to be a *fair defect* in creation. But to justify the ways of Providence respecting them,[1] by pointing out some irrefragable reason for thus making such a large portion of mankind accountable and not accountable, would puzzle the subtilest casuist.

The only solid foundation for morality appears to be the character of the supreme Being; the harmony of which arises from a balance of attributes; – and, to speak with reverence, one attribute seems to imply the *necessity* of another. He must be just, because he is wise, he must be good, because he is omnipotent.[2] For to exalt one attribute at the expence of another equally noble and necessary, bears the stamp of the warped reason of man – the homage of passion. Man, accustomed to bow down to power in his savage state, can seldom divest himself of this barbarous prejudice, even when civilization determines how much superior mental is to bodily strength; and his reason is clouded by these crude opinions, even when he thinks of the Deity. – His omnipotence is made to swallow up, or preside over his other

---

1    [Milton, *Paradise Lost* 10.891-92, 1.25-26.]
2    [Cf. Rousseau, *Emile* 277, 282; Macaulay, *Letters* 367-68, 379, 399; Price, *Discourse* 12; see Appendix A.3.]

attributes, and those mortals are supposed to limit his power irreverently, who think that it must be regulated by his wisdom.

I disclaim that specious humility which, after investigating nature, stops at the author. – The High and Lofty One, who inhabiteth eternity, doubtless possesses many attributes of which we can form no conception; but reason tells me that they cannot clash with those I adore – and I am compelled to listen to her voice.

It seems natural for man to search for excellence, and either to trace it in the object that he worships, or blindly to invest it with perfection, as a garment. But what good effect can the latter mode of worship have on the moral conduct of a rational being? He bends to power; he adores a dark cloud, which may open a bright prospect to him, or burst in angry, lawless fury, on his devoted head – he knows not why. And, supposing that the Deity acts from the vague impulse of an undirected will, man must also follow his own, or act according to rules, deduced from principles which he disclaims as irreverent. Into this dilemma have both enthusiasts and cooler thinkers fallen, when they laboured to free men from the wholesome restraints which a just conception of the character of God imposes.

It is not impious thus to scan the attributes of the Almighty: in fact, who can avoid it that exercises his faculties? For to love God as the fountain of wisdom, goodness, and power, appears to be the only worship useful to a being who wishes to acquire either virtue or knowledge. A blind unsettled affection may, like human passions, occupy the mind and warm the heart, whilst, to do justice, love mercy, and walk humbly with our God,[1] is forgotten. I shall pursue this subject still further, when I consider religion in a light opposite to that recommended by Dr. Gregory, who treats it as a matter of sentiment or taste.[2]

To return from this apparent digression. It were to be wished that women would cherish an affection for their husbands, founded on the same principle that devotion ought to rest upon. No other firm base is there under heaven – for let them beware of the fallacious light of sentiment; too often used as a softer phrase for sensuality. It follows then, I think, that from their infancy women should either be shut up

---

1   [Micah 6: 8.]
2   [Gregory, *Legacy* 13.]

like eastern princes, or educated in such a manner as to be able to think and act for themselves.

Why do men halt between two opinions, and expect impossibilities? Why do they expect virtue from a slave, from a being whom the constitution of civil society has rendered weak, if not vicious?

Still I know that it will require a considerable length of time to eradicate the firmly rooted prejudices which sensualists have planted; it will also require some time to convince women that they act contrary to their real interest on an enlarged scale, when they cherish or affect weakness under the name of delicacy, and to convince the world that the poisoned source of female vices and follies, if it be necessary, in compliance with custom, to use synonymous terms in a lax sense, has been the sensual homage paid to beauty:[1] – to beauty of features; for it has been shrewdly observed by a German writer, that a pretty woman, as an object of desire, is generally allowed to be so by men of all descriptions; whilst a fine woman, who inspires more sublime emotions by displaying intellectual beauty, may be overlooked or observed with indifference, by those men who find their happiness in the gratification of their appetites.[2] I foresee an obvious retort – whilst man remains such an imperfect being as he appears hitherto to have been, he will, more or less, be the slave of his appetites; and those women obtaining most power who gratify a predominant one, the sex is degraded by a physical, if not by a moral necessity.

This objection has, I grant, some force; but while such a sublime precept exists, as, "be pure as your heavenly Father is pure;"[3] it would seem that the virtues of man are not limited by the Being who alone could limit them; and that he may press forward without considering whether he steps out of his sphere by indulging such a noble ambition. To the wild billows it has been said, "thus far shalt thou go, and no further; and here shall thy proud waves be stayed."[4] Vainly then do they beat and foam, restrained by the power that confines the struggling planets in their orbits, matter yields to the great governing Spir-

---

1    [Cf. Macaulay, *Letters* 207 (Appendix B.2).]
2    [Immanuel Kant, *Observations on the Feeling of the Beautiful and Sublime* (1764), trans. John T. Goldthwait (Berkeley: U of California P, 1960) 86-90.]
3    [Matthew 5: 48; 1 John 3: 3.]
4    [Job 38: 11.]

it. – But an immortal soul, not restrained by mechanical laws and struggling to free itself from the shackles of matter, contributes to, instead of disturbing, the order of creation, when, co-operating with the Father of spirits, it tries to govern itself by the invariable rule that, in a degree, before which our imagination faints, regulates the universe.

Besides, if women be educated for dependence; that is, to act according to the will of another fallible being, and submit, right or wrong, to power, where are we to stop? Are they to be considered as vicegerents allowed to reign over a small domain, and answerable for their conduct to a higher tribunal, liable to error?

It will not be difficult to prove that such delegates will act like men subjected by fear, and make their children and servants endure their tyrannical oppression. As they submit without reason, they will, having no fixed rules to square their conduct by, be kind, or cruel, just as the whim of the moment directs; and we ought not to wonder if sometimes, galled by their heavy yoke, they take a malignant pleasure in resting it on weaker shoulders.

But, supposing a woman, trained up to obedience, be married to a sensible man, who directs her judgment without making her feel the servility of her subjection, to act with as much propriety by this reflected light as can be expected when reason is taken at second hand, yet she cannot ensure the life of her protector; he may die and leave her with a large family.

A double duty devolves on her; to educate them in the character of both father and mother; to form their principles and secure their property. But, alas! she has never thought, much less acted for herself. She has only learned to please¹ men, to depend gracefully on them; yet, encumbered with children, how is she to obtain another protec-

---

1  "In the union of the sexes, both pursue one common object, but not in the same manner. From their diversity in this particular, arises the first determinate difference between the moral relations of each. The one should be active and strong, the other passive and weak: it is necessary the one should have both the power and the will, and that the other should make little resistance.

"This principle being established, it follows that woman is expressly formed to please the man: if the obligation be reciprocal also, and the man ought to please in his turn, it is not so immediately necessary: his great merit is in his power, and he pleases merely because he is strong. This, I must confess, is not one of the refined

tor – a husband to supply the place of reason? A rational man, for we are not treading on romantic ground, though he may think her a pleasing docile creature, will not choose to marry a *family* for love, when the world contains many more pretty creatures. What is then to become of her? She either falls an easy prey to some mean fortune-hunter, who defrauds her children of their paternal inheritance, and renders her miserable; or becomes the victim of discontent and blind indulgence. Unable to educate her sons, or impress them with respect; for it is not a play on words to assert, that people are never respected, though filling an important station, who are not respectable; she pines under the anguish of unavailing impotent regret. The serpent's tooth enters into her very soul,[1] and the vices of licentious youth bring her with sorrow, if not with poverty also, to the grave.

This is not an overcharged picture; on the contrary, it is a very possible case, and something similar must have fallen under every attentive eye.

I have, however, taken it for granted, that she was well-disposed, though experience shews, that the blind may as easily be led into a ditch as along the beaten road.[2] But supposing, no very improbable conjecture, that a being only taught to please must still find her happiness in pleasing; – what an example of folly, not to say vice, will she be to her innocent daughters! The mother will be lost in the coquette, and, instead of making friends of her daughters, view them with eyes askance, for they are rivals – rivals more cruel than any other, because

---

maxims of love; it is, however, one of the laws of nature, prior to love itself.

"If woman be formed to please and be subjected to man, it is her place, doubtless, to render herself agreeable to him, instead of challenging his passion. The violence of his desires depends on her charms; it is by means of these she should urge him to the exertion of those powers which nature hath given him. The most successful method of exciting them, is, to render such exertion necessary by resistance; as, in that case, self-love is added to desire, and the one triumphs in the victory which the other obliged to acquire. Hence arise the various modes of attack and defence between the sexes; the boldness of one sex and the timidity of the other; and, in a word, that bashfulness and modesty with which nature hath armed the weak, in order to subdue the strong."

*Rousseau's Emilius.* [358.]

I shall make no other comment on this ingenious passage, than just to observe, that it is the philosophy of lasciviousness.

1 [Shakespeare, *King Lear* 1.4.297-98.]
2 [Matthew 15: 14.]

they invite a comparison, and drive her from the throne of beauty, who has never thought of a seat on the bench of reason.

It does not require a lively pencil, or the discriminating outline of a caricature, to sketch the domestic miseries and petty vices which such a mistress of a family diffuses. Still she only acts as a woman ought to act, brought up according to Rousseau's system. She can never be reproached for being masculine, or turning out of her sphere; nay, she may observe another of his grand rules, and, cautiously preserving her reputation free from spot, be reckoned a good kind of woman. Yet in what respect can she be termed good? She abstains, it is true, without any great struggle, from committing gross crimes; but how does she fulfil her duties? Duties! – in truth she has enough to think of to adorn her body and nurse a weak constitution.

With respect to religion, she never presumed to judge for herself; but conformed, as a dependent creature should, to the ceremonies of the church which she was brought up in, piously believing that wiser heads than her own have settled that business· – and not to doubt is her point of perfection. She therefore pays her tythe of mint and cummin – and thanks her God that she is not as other women are.[1] These are the blessed effects of a good education! These the virtues of man's help-mate[2]!

I must relieve myself by drawing a different picture.

Let fancy now present a woman with a tolerable understanding, for I do not wish to leave the line of mediocrity, whose constitution, strengthened by exercise, has allowed her body to acquire its full vigour; her mind, at the same time, gradually expanding itself to comprehend the moral duties of life, and in what human virtue and dignity consist.

Formed thus by the discharge of the relative duties of her station,

---

1 [Matthew 23: 23; Luke 18: 11.]

2 "O how lovely," exclaims Rousseau, speaking of Sophia, "is her ignorance! Happy is he who is destined to instruct her! She will never pretend to be the tutor of her husband, but will be content to be his pupil. Far from attempting to subject him to her taste, she will accommodate herself to his. She will be more estimable to him, than if she was learned: he will have a pleasure in instructing her." *Rousseau's Emilius.* [410; cf. 425-26.]

I shall content myself with simply asking, how friendship can subsist, when love expires, between the master and his pupil?

she marries from affection, without losing sight of prudence, and looking beyond matrimonial felicity, she secures her husband's respect before it is necessary to exert mean arts to please him and feed a dying flame, which nature doomed to expire when the object became familiar, when friendship and forbearance take place of a more ardent affection. – This is the natural death of love, and domestic peace is not destroyed by struggles to prevent its extinction. I also suppose the husband to be virtuous; or she is still more in want of independent principles.

Fate, however, breaks this tie. – She is left a widow, perhaps, without a sufficient provision; but she is not desolate! The pang of nature is felt; but after time has softened sorrow into melancholy resignation, her heart turns to her children with redoubled fondness, and anxious to provide for them, affection gives a sacred heroic cast to her maternal duties. She thinks that not only the eye sees her virtuous efforts from whom all her comfort now must flow, and whose approbation is life; but her imagination, a little abstracted and exalted by grief, dwells on the fond hope that the eyes which her trembling hand closed, may still see how she subdues every wayward passion to fulfil the double duty of being the father as well as the mother of her children. Raised to heroism by misfortunes, she represses the first faint dawning of a natural inclination, before it ripens into love, and in the bloom of life forgets her sex – forgets the pleasure of an awakening passion, which might again have been inspired and returned. She no longer thinks of pleasing, and conscious dignity prevents her from priding herself on account of the praise which her conduct demands. Her children have her love, and her brightest hopes are beyond the grave, where her imagination often strays.

I think I see her surrounded by her children, reaping the reward of her care. The intelligent eye meets hers, whilst health and innocence smile on their chubby cheeks, and as they grow up the cares of life are lessened by their grateful attention. She lives to see the virtues which she endeavoured to plant on principles, fixed into habits, to see her children attain a strength of character sufficient to enable them to endure adversity without forgetting their mother's example.

The task of life thus fulfilled, she calmly waits for the sleep of death, and rising from the grave, may say – Behold, thou gavest me a talent – and here are five talents.[1]

I wish to sum up what I have said in a few words, for I here throw down my gauntlet, and deny the existence of sexual virtues, not excepting modesty. For man and woman, truth, if I understand the meaning of the word, must be the same; yet the fanciful female character, so prettily drawn by poets and novelists, demanding the sacrifice of truth and sincerity, virtue becomes a relative idea, having no other foundation than utility, and of that utility men pretend arbitrarily to judge, shaping it to their own convenience.

Women, I allow, may have different duties to fulfil; but they are *human* duties, and the principles that should regulate the discharge of them, I sturdily maintain, must be the same.

To become respectable, the exercise of their understanding is necessary, there is no other foundation for independence of character; I mean explicitly to say that they must only bow to the authority of reason, instead of being the *modest* slaves of opinion.

In the superior ranks of life how seldom do we meet with a man of superior abilities, or even common acquirements? The reason appears to me clear, the state they are born in was an unnatural one. The human character has ever been formed by the employments the individual, or class, pursues; and if the faculties are not sharpened by necessity, they must remain obtuse. The argument may fairly be extended to women; for, seldom occupied by serious business, the pursuit of pleasure gives that insignificancy to their character which renders the society of the *great* so insipid. The same want of firmness, produced by a similar cause, forces them both to fly from themselves to noisy pleasures, and artificial passions, till vanity takes place of every social affection, and the characteristics of humanity can scarcely be discerned. Such are the blessings of civil governments, as they are at present organized, that wealth and female softness equally tend to debase mankind, and are produced by the same cause; but allowing women to be rational creatures, they should be incited to acquire virtues which they may call their own, for how can a rational being be ennobled by any thing that is not obtained by its *own* exertions?

---

1    [Matthew 25: 14-30; Luke 19: 12-26; cf. *Original Stories*; *Works* 4: 422-23, 432-33.]

# CHAP. IV.

## OBSERVATIONS ON THE STATE OF
## DEGRADATION TO WHICH WOMAN IS REDUCED BY
## VARIOUS CAUSES.

THAT woman is naturally weak, or degraded by a concurrence of circumstances, is, I think, clear. But this position I shall simply contrast
with a conclusion, which I have frequently heard fall from sensible
men in favour of an aristocracy: that the mass of mankind cannot be
any thing, or the obsequious slaves, who patiently allow themselves to
be driven forward, would feel their own consequence, and spurn their
chains. Men, they further observe, submit every where to oppression,
when they have only to lift up their heads to throw off the yoke; yet,
instead of asserting their birthright, they quietly lick the dust, and say,
let us eat and drink, for to-morrow we die.[1] Women, I argue from
analogy, are degraded by the same propensity to enjoy the present
moment; and, at last, despise the freedom which they have not sufficient virtue to struggle to attain. But I must be more explicit.

   With respect to the culture of the heart, it is unanimously allowed
that sex is out of the question; but the line of subordination in the
mental powers is never to be passed over[2]. Only "absolute in loveliness,"[3] the portion of rationality granted to woman, is, indeed, very
scanty; for, denying her genius and judgment, it is scarcely possible to
divine what remains to characterize intellect.

   The stamen of immortality, if I may be allowed the phrase, is the

---

1   [Psalms 72: 9; Isaiah 22: 13; 1 Corinthians 15: 32.]
2   Into what inconsistencies do men fall when they argue without the compass of
    principles. Women, weak women, are compared with angels; yet, a superiour order
    of beings should be supposed to possess more intellect than man; or, in what does
    their superiority consist? In the same strain, to drop the sneer, they are allowed to
    possess more goodness of heart, piety, and benevolence. – I doubt the fact, though it
    be courteously brought forward, unless ignorance be allowed to be the mother of
    devotion; for I am firmly persuaded that, on an average, the proportion between
    virtue and knowledge, is more upon a par than is commonly granted.
3   [Milton, *Paradise Lost* 8.547.]

perfectibility of human reason; for, were man created perfect, or did a flood of knowledge break in upon him, when he arrived at maturity, that precluded error, I should doubt whether his existence would be continued after the dissolution of the body. But, in the present state of things, every difficulty in morals that escapes from human discussion, and equally baffles the investigation of profound thinking, and the lightning glance of genius, is an argument on which I build my belief of the immortality of the soul.[1] Reason is, consequentially, the simple power of improvement; or, more properly speaking, of discerning truth. Every individual is in this respect a world in itself. More or less may be conspicuous in one being than another; but the nature of reason must be the same in all, if it be an emanation of divinity, the tie that connects the creature with the Creator; for, can that soul be stamped with the heavenly image, that is not perfected by the exercise of its own reason?[2] Yet outwardly ornamented with elaborate care, and so adorned to delight man, "that with honour he may love[3]," the soul of woman is not allowed to have this distinction, and man, ever placed between her and reason, she is always represented as only created to see through a gross medium, and to take things on trust. But dismissing these fanciful theories, and considering woman as a whole, let it be what it will, instead of a part of man, the inquiry is whether she have reason or not. If she have, which, for a moment, I will take for granted, she was not created merely to be the solace of man, and the sexual should not destroy the human character.

Into this error men have, probably, been led by viewing education in a false light; not considering it as the first step to form a being advancing gradually towards perfection[4]; but only as a preparation for life. On this sensual error, for I must call it so, has the false system of female manners been reared, which robs the whole sex of its dignity, and classes the brown and fair with the smiling flowers that only

---

1   [Cf. Macaulay, *Letters* 349, 380, 395.]
2   "The brutes," says Lord Monboddo, "remain in the state in which nature has placed them, except in so far as their natural instinct is improved by the culture *we* bestow upon them." [James Burnett, Lord Monboddo (1714-99), *Of the Origin and Progress of Language* (1773-92) 1: 137; Wollstonecraft's italics.]
3   Vide Milton. [*Paradise Lost* 8.577.]
4   This word is not strictly just, but I cannot find a better. [Cf. Macaulay, *Letters* 201-2 (Appendix B.2).]

adorn the land. This has ever been the language of men, and the fear of departing from a supposed sexual character, has made even women of superiour sense adopt the same sentiments¹. Thus understanding, strictly speaking, has been denied to woman; and instinct, sublimated into wit and cunning, for the purposes of life, has been substituted in its stead.

The power of generalizing ideas, of drawing comprehensive conclusions from individual observations, is the only acquirement, for an immortal being, that really deserves the name of knowledge.² Merely to observe, without endeavouring to account for any thing, may (in a

---

1          "Pleasure's the portion of th' *inferior* kind;
              But glory, virtue, Heaven for *man* design'd."
After writing these lines, how could Mrs. Barbauld write the following ignoble comparison?
              "*To a Lady, with some painted flowers.*"

"Flowers to the fair: to you these flowers I bring,
And strive to greet you with an earlier spring.
*Flowers* S W E E T , *and gay, and* D E L I C A T E L I K E Y O U;
*Emblems of innocence, and beauty too.*
With flowers the Graces bind their yellow hair,
And flowery wreaths consenting lovers wear.
*Flowers, the sole luxury which nature knew,*
In Eden's pure and guiltless garden grew.
*To loftier forms are rougher tasks assign'd;*
*The sheltering oak resists the stormy wind,*
*The tougher yew repels invading foes,*
*And the tall pine for future navies grows;*
*But this soft family, to cares unknown,*
*Were born for pleasure and delight* A L O N E .
Gay without toil, and lovely without art,
*They spring to* C H E E R *the sense, and* G L A D *the heart.*
Nor blush, my fair, to own you copy these;
*Your* B E S T , *your* S W E E T E S T *empire is –* to P L E A S E ."

So the men tell us; but virtue, says reason, must be acquired by *rough* toils, and useful struggles with worldly *cares.* [Both quotations are from *Poems* (1792) by Anna Laetitia Barbauld (1743-1825). The first is "To Mrs. P[riestley], with some Drawings of Birds and Insects" 101-2; note that "man" includes women; "th' *inferior* kind" is birds and insects. The second is quoted in its entirety. In both, the italics and block capitals are Wollstonecraft's. Wollstonecraft included several excerpts from Barbauld in *The Female Reader.*]

2    [John Locke, *An Essay concerning Human Understanding* (1689), ed. Peter H. Nidditch (Oxford: Clarendon P, 1975) 159-60; 2.11.9-10.]

very incomplete manner) serve as the common sense of life; but where is the store laid up that is to clothe the soul when it leaves the body?

This power has not only been denied to women; but writers have insisted that it is inconsistent, with a few exceptions, with their sexual character. Let men prove this, and I shall grant that woman only exists for man. I must, however, previously remark, that the power of generalizing ideas, to any great extent, is not very common amongst men or women. But this exercise is the true cultivation of the understanding; and every thing conspires to render the cultivation of the understanding more difficult in the female than the male world.

I am naturally led by this assertion to the main subject of the present chapter, and shall now attempt to point out some of the causes that degrade the sex, and prevent women from generalizing their observations.

I shall not go back to the remote annals of antiquity to trace the history of woman;[1] it is sufficient to allow that she has always been either a slave, or a despot, and to remark, that each of these situations equally retards the progress of reason. The grand source of female folly and vice has ever appeared to me to arise from narrowness of mind; and the very constitution of civil governments has put almost insuperable obstacles in the way to prevent the cultivation of the female understanding: – yet virtue can be built on no other foundation! The same obstacles are thrown in the way of the rich, and the same consequences ensue.

Necessity has been proverbially termed the mother of invention – the aphorism may be extended to virtue. It is an acquirement, and an acquirement to which pleasure must be sacrificed – and who sacrifices pleasure when it is within the grasp, whose mind has not been opened and strengthened by adversity, or the pursuit of knowledge goaded on by necessity? – Happy is it when people have the cares of life to struggle with; for these struggles prevent their becoming a prey to enervating vices, merely from idleness! But, if from their birth men and women be placed in a torrid zone, with the meridian sun of pleasure darting directly upon them, how can they sufficiently brace their

---

1  [Cf. Macaulay, *Letters* 206 (Appendix B.2).]

minds to discharge the duties of life, or even to relish the affections that carry them out of themselves?

Pleasure is the business of woman's life, according to the present modification of society, and while it continues to be so, little can be expected from such weak beings. Inheriting, in a lineal descent from the first fair defect in nature,[1] the sovereignty of beauty, they have, to maintain their power, resigned the natural rights, which the exercise of reason might have procured them, and chosen rather to be short-lived queens than labour to obtain the sober pleasures that arise from equality. Exalted by their inferiority (this sounds like a contradiction), they constantly demand homage as women, though experience should teach them that the men who pride themselves upon paying this arbitrary insolent respect to the sex, with the most scrupulous exactness, are most inclined to tyrannize over, and despise, the very weakness they cherish. Often do they repeat Mr. Hume's sentiments; when, comparing the French and Athenian character, he alludes to women. "But what is more singular in this whimsical nation, say I to the Athenians, is, that a frolick of yours during the Saturnalia, when the slaves are served by their masters, is seriously continued by them through the whole year, and through the whole course of their lives; accompanied too with some circumstances, which still further augment the absurdity and ridicule. Your sport only elevates for a few days those whom fortune has thrown down, and whom she too, in sport, may really elevate for ever above you. But this nation gravely exalts those, whom nature has subjected to them, and whose inferiority and infirmities are absolutely incurable. The women, though without virtue, are their masters and sovereigns."[2]

Ah! why do women, I write with affectionate solicitude, condescend to receive a degree of attention and respect from strangers, different from that reciprocation of civility which the dictates of humanity and the politeness of civilization authorise between man and man? And, why do they not discover, when "in the noon of beau-

---

1  [Milton, *Paradise Lost* 10.891-92.]

2  [David Hume (1711-76), "A Dialogue" (1777), *Enquiries concerning Human Understanding and concerning the Principles of Morals*, ed. L.A. Selby-Bigge (Oxford: Oxford UP, 1975) 332. The Saturnalia was the feast of Saturn (in Greek, Kronos), celebrated in midwinter; it involved a temporary suspension of social distinctions.]

ty's power,"[1] that they are treated like queens only to be deluded by hollow respect, till they are led to resign, or not assume, their natural prerogatives? Confined then in cages like the feathered race, they have nothing to do but to plume themselves, and stalk with mock majesty from perch to perch. It is true they are provided with food and raiment, for which they neither toil nor spin;[2] but health, liberty, and virtue, are given in exchange. But, where, amongst mankind, has been found sufficient strength of mind to enable a being to resign these adventitious prerogatives; one who, rising with the calm dignity of reason above opinion, dared to be proud of the privileges inherent in man? And it is vain to expect it whilst hereditary power chokes the affections and nips reason in the bud.

The passions of men have thus placed women on thrones, and, till mankind become more reasonable, it is to be feared that women will avail themselves of the power which they attain with the least exertion, and which is the most indisputable. They will smile, – yes, they will smile, though told that—

> "In beauty's empire is no mean,
> And woman, either slave or queen,
> Is quickly scorn'd when not ador'd."[3]

But the adoration comes first, and the scorn is not anticipated.

Lewis the XIVth, in particular, spread factitious manners, and caught, in a specious way, the whole nation in his toils; for, establishing an artful chain of despotism, he made it the interest of the people at large, individually to respect his station and support his power. And women, whom he flattered by a puerile attention to the whole sex, obtained in his reign that prince-like distinction so fatal to reason and virtue.

A king is always a king – and a woman always a woman[4]: his

---

1 [Wollstonecraft quotes her review of Christoph Martin Wieland (1733-1813), *Henrietta of Gerstenfeld* (trans. 1787-88), *Works* 7: 20. The reference is probably to Wieland 2: 24.]

2 [Matthew 6: 28; Luke 12: 27-28.]

3 [Barbauld, "Song V" (1772) 16-18.]

4 And a wit, always a wit, might be added; for the vain fooleries of wits and beauties to obtain attention, and make conquests, are much upon a par.

authority and her sex, ever stand between them and rational converse.[1] With a lover, I grant, she should be so, and her sensibility will naturally lead her to endeavour to excite emotion, not to gratify her vanity, but her heart. This I do not allow to be coquetry, it is the artless impulse of nature, I only exclaim against the sexual desire of conquest when the heart is out of the question.

This desire is not confined to women; "I have endeavoured," says Lord Chesterfield, "to gain the hearts of twenty women, whose persons I would not have given a fig for."[2] The libertine, who, in a gust of passion, takes advantage of unsuspecting tenderness, is a saint when compared with this cold-hearted rascal; for I like to use significant words. Yet only taught to please, women are always on the watch to please, and with true heroic ardour endeavour to gain hearts merely to resign or spurn them, when the victory is decided, and conspicuous.

I must descend to the minutiae of the subject.

I lament that women are systematically degraded by receiving the trivial attentions, which men think it manly to pay to the sex, when, in fact, they are insultingly supporting their own superiority. It is not condescension to bow to an inferior. So ludicrous, in fact, do these ceremonies appear to me, that I scarcely am able to govern my muscles, when I see a man start with eager, and serious solicitude, to lift a handkerchief, or shut a door, when the *lady* could have done it herself, had she only moved a pace or two.

A wild wish has just flown from my heart to my head, and I will not stifle it though it may excite a horse-laugh. – I do earnestly wish to see the distinction of sex confounded in society, unless where love animates the behaviour. For this distinction is, I am firmly persuaded, the foundation of the weakness of character ascribed to woman; is the cause why the understanding is neglected, whilst accomplishments are acquired with sedulous care: and the same cause accounts for their

---

1   [On the degradation of kings, cf. Burke, *A Vindication of Natural Society* (1756), *Works* 1: 32, 60; Catharine Macaulay Graham, *Observations on the Reflections of the Right Hon. Edmund Burke, on the Revolution in France, in a Letter to the Right Hon. the Earl of Stanhope* (London: C. Dilly, 1790) 74; Price, *Discourse* 22-23 (Appendix A.3).]

2   [Paraphrased from Philip Dormer Stanhope, 4th Earl of Chesterfield (1694-1773), *Letters to his Son* (1774) no. 294 (16 November 1752). Wollstonecraft included an excerpt from Chesterfield in *The Female Reader*.]

preferring the graceful before the heroic virtues.

Mankind, including every description, wish to be loved and respected by *something*; and the common herd will always take the nearest road to the completion of their wishes. The respect paid to wealth and beauty is the most certain, and unequivocal; and, of course, will always attract the vulgar eye of common minds. Abilities and virtues are absolutely necessary to raise men from the middle rank of life into notice; and the natural consequence is notorious, the middle rank contains most virtue and abilities. Men have thus, in one station, at least an opportunity of exerting themselves with dignity, and of rising by the exertions which really improve a rational creature; but the whole female sex are, till their character is formed, in the same condition as the rich: for they are born, I now speak of a state of civilization, with certain sexual privileges, and whilst they are gratuitously granted them, few will ever think of works of supererogation, to obtain the esteem of a small number of superior people.

When do we hear of women who, starting out of obscurity, boldly claim respect on account of their great abilities or daring virtues? Where are they to be found? – "To be observed, to be attended to, to be taken notice of with sympathy, complacency, and approbation, are all the advantages which they seek."[1] – True! my male readers will probably exclaim; but let them, before they draw any conclusion, recollect that this was not written originally as descriptive of women, but of the rich. In Dr. Smith's Theory of Moral Sentiments, I have found a general character of people of rank and fortune, that, in my opinion, might with the greatest propriety be applied to the female sex. I refer the sagacious reader to the whole comparison; but must be allowed to quote a passage to enforce an argument that I mean to insist on, as the one most conclusive against a sexual character. For if, excepting warriors, no great men, of any denomination, have ever appeared amongst the nobility, may it not be fairly inferred that their local situation swallowed up the man, and produced a character similar to that of women, who are *localized*, if I may be allowed the word, by the rank they are placed in, by *courtesy?* Women, commonly called Ladies, are not to be contradicted in company, are not allowed to exert any man-

---

1  [Adapted from Adam Smith (1723–90), *The Theory of Moral Sentiments* (1759), ed. D.D. Raphael and A.L. Macfie (Oxford: Clarendon P, 1976) 50; 1.3.2.1.]

ual strength; and from them the negative virtues only are expected, when any virtues are expected, patience, docility, good-humour, and flexibility; virtues incompatible with any vigorous exertion of intellect. Besides, by living more with each other, and being seldom absolutely alone, they are more under the influence of sentiments than passions. Solitude and reflection are necessary to give to wishes the force of passions, and to enable the imagination to enlarge the object, and make it the most desirable. The same may be said of the rich; they do not sufficiently deal in general ideas, collected by impassioned thinking, or calm investigation, to acquire that strength of character on which great resolves are built. But hear what an acute observer says of the great.

"Do the great seem insensible of the easy price at which they may acquire the publick admiration; or do they seem to imagine that to them, as to other men, it must be the purchase either of sweat or of blood? By what important accomplishments is the young nobleman instructed to support the dignity of his rank, and to render himself worthy of that superiority over his fellow-citizens, to which the virtue of his ancestors had raised them? Is it by knowledge, by industry, by patience, by self-denial, or by virtue of any kind? As all his words, as all his motions are attended to, he learns an habitual regard to every circumstance of ordinary behaviour, and studies to perform all those small duties with the most exact propriety. As he is conscious how much he is observed, and how much mankind are disposed to favour all his inclinations, he acts, upon the most indifferent occasions, with that freedom and elevation which the thought of this naturally inspires. His air, his manner, his deportment, all mark that elegant and graceful sense of his own superiority, which those who are born to inferior station can hardly ever arrive at. These are the arts by which he proposes to make mankind more easily submit to his authority, and to govern their inclinations according to his own pleasure: and in this he is seldom disappointed. These arts, supported by rank and pre-eminence, are, upon ordinary occasions, sufficient to govern the world. Lewis XIV. during the greater part of his reign, was regarded, not only in France, but over all Europe, as the most perfect model of a great prince. But what were the talents and virtues by which he acquired this great reputation? Was it by the scrupulous and inflexible justice of all his undertakings, by the immense dangers and difficulties with which they were attended, or by the unwearied and unrelenting application with which he pursued them? Was it by his extensive knowledge, by his exquisite judgment, or by his heroic valour? It was by none of these qualities. But he was, first of all, the most powerful prince in Europe, and consequently held the highest rank among kings; and then, says his historian, 'he surpassed all his courtiers in the gracefulness of his shape, and the majestic beauty of his features. The sound of his voice, noble and affecting, gained those hearts which his presence intimidated. He had a step and a deportment which could suit only him and his rank, and which would have been ridiculous in any other person. The embarrassment which he occasioned to those who spoke to him, flattered that secret satisfaction with which he felt his own superiority.' These frivolous accomplishments, supported by his rank, and, no doubt too, by a degree of other talents and virtues, which seems, however, not to have been much above mediocrity, established this prince in the esteem of his own age, and have drawn, even from posterity, a good deal of respect for his memory. Compared with these, in his own times, and in his own presence, no other virtue, it seems, appeared to have any merit. Knowledge, industry, valour, and beneficence, trembled, were abashed, and lost all dignity before them."[1]

Woman also thus "in herself complete," by possessing all these *frivolous* accomplishments, so changes the nature of things

> ——————— "That what she wills to do or say
> Seems wisest, virtuousest, discreetest, best;
> All higher knowledge in *her presence* falls
> Degraded. Wisdom in discourse with her
> Loses discountenanc'd, and, like Folly, shows;
> Authority and Reason on her wait."———[2]

And all this is built on her loveliness!

---

1 [Smith, *Theory* 54; 1.3.2.4 (abridged). The "historian" is Voltaire (1694-1778); Smith translates from *Le Siècle de Louis XIV* (Berlin, 1751) chap. 25.]
2 [Milton, *Paradise Lost* 8.548-54; Wollstonecraft's italics.]

In the middle rank of life, to continue the comparison, men, in their youth, are prepared for professions, and marriage is not considered as the grand feature in their lives; whilst women, on the contrary, have no other scheme to sharpen their faculties. It is not business, extensive plans, or any of the excursive flights of ambition, that engross their attention; no, their thoughts are not employed in rearing such noble structures. To rise in the world, and have the liberty of running from pleasure to pleasure, they must marry advantageously, and to this object their time is sacrificed, and their persons often legally prostituted.[1] A man when he enters any profession has his eye steadily fixed on some future advantage (and the mind gains great strength by having all its efforts directed to one point), and, full of his business, pleasure is considered as mere relaxation; whilst women seek for pleasure as the main purpose of existence. In fact, from the education, which they receive from society, the love of pleasure may be said to govern them all; but does this prove that there is a sex in souls? It would be just as rational to declare that the courtiers in France, when a destructive system of despotism had formed their character, were not men, because liberty, virtue, and humanity, were sacrificed to pleasure and vanity. – Fatal passions, which have ever domineered over the *whole* race!

The same love of pleasure, fostered by the whole tendency of their education, gives a trifling turn to the conduct of women in most circumstances: for instance, they are ever anxious about secondary things; and on the watch for adventures, instead of being occupied by duties.

A man, when he undertakes a journey, has, in general, the end in view; a woman thinks more of the incidental occurrences, the strange things that may possibly occur on the road; the impression that she may make on her fellow-travellers; and, above all, she is anxiously intent on the care of the finery that she carries with her, which is more than ever a part of herself, when going to figure on a new scene; when, to use an apt French turn of expression, she is going to produce a sensation. – Can dignity of mind exist with such trivial cares?

---

1   [Daniel Defoe (1660-1731) uses the phrase "legal prostitution" in *Conjugal Lewdness; or, Matrimonial Whoredom* (1727).]

In short, women, in general, as well as the rich of both sexes, have acquired all the follies and vices of civilization, and missed the useful fruit. It is not necessary for me always to premise, that I speak of the condition of the whole sex, leaving exceptions out of the question. Their senses are inflamed, and their understandings neglected, consequently they become the prey of their senses, delicately termed sensibility, and are blown about by every momentary gust of feeling. Civilized women are, therefore, so weakened by false refinement, that, respecting morals, their condition is much below what it would be were they left in a state nearer to nature. Ever restless and anxious, their over exercised sensibility not only renders them uncomfortable themselves, but troublesome, to use a soft phrase, to others. All their thoughts turn on things calculated to excite emotion; and feeling, when they should reason, their conduct is unstable, and their opinions are wavering – not the wavering produced by deliberation or progressive views, but by contradictory emotions. By fits and starts they are warm in many pursuits; yet this warmth, never concentrated into perseverance, soon exhausts itself; exhaled by its own heat, or meeting with some other fleeting passion, to which reason has never given any specific gravity, neutrality ensues. Miserable, indeed, must be that being whose cultivation of mind has only tended to inflame its passions! A distinction should be made between inflaming and strengthening them. The passions thus pampered, whilst the judgment is left unformed, what can be expected to ensue? – Undoubtedly, a mixture of madness and folly!

This observation should not be confined to the *fair* sex; however, at present, I only mean to apply it to them.

Novels, music, poetry, and gallantry, all tend to make women the creatures of sensation, and their character is thus formed in the mould of folly during the time they are acquiring accomplishments, the only improvement they are excited, by their station in society, to acquire. This overstretched sensibility naturally relaxes the other powers of the mind, and prevents intellect from attaining that sovereignty which it ought to attain to render a rational creature useful to others, and content with its own station: for the exercise of the understanding, as life advances, is the only method pointed out by nature to calm the passions.

Satiety has a very different effect, and I have often been forcibly struck by an emphatical description of damnation: – when the spirit is represented as continually hovering with abortive eagerness round the defiled body, unable to enjoy any thing without the organs of sense. Yet, to their senses, are women made slaves, because it is by their sensibility that they obtain present power.

And will moralists pretend to assert, that this is the condition in which one half of the human race should be encouraged to remain with listless inactivity and stupid acquiescence? Kind instructors! what were we created for? To remain, it may be said, innocent; they mean in a state of childhood. – We might as well never have been born, unless it were necessary that we should be created to enable man to acquire the noble privilege of reason, the power of discerning good from evil, whilst we lie down in the dust from whence we were taken, never to rise again. –

It would be an endless task to trace the variety of meannesses, cares, and sorrows, into which women are plunged by the prevailing opinion, that they were created rather to feel than reason, and that all the power they obtain, must be obtained by their charms and weakness:

"Fine by defect, and amiably weak!"[1]

And, made by this amiable weakness entirely dependent, excepting what they gain by illicit sway, on man, not only for protection, but advice, is it surprising that, neglecting the duties that reason alone points out, and shrinking from trials calculated to strengthen their minds, they only exert themselves to give their defects a graceful covering, which may serve to heighten their charms in the eye of the voluptuary, though it sink them below the scale of moral excellence?

Fragile in every sense of the word, they are obliged to look up to man for every comfort. In the most trifling dangers they cling to their support, with parasitical tenacity, piteously demanding succour; and their *natural* protector extends his arm, or lifts up his voice, to guard the lovely trembler – from what? Perhaps the frown of an old cow, or

---

1  [Pope, "Of the Characters of Women" 44.]

the jump of a mouse; a rat, would be a serious danger. In the name of reason, and even common sense, what can save such beings from contempt; even though they be soft and fair?

These fears, when not affected, may produce some pretty attitudes; but they shew a degree of imbecility which degrades a rational creature in a way women are not aware of – for love and esteem are very distinct things.

I am fully persuaded that we should hear of none of these infantine airs, if girls were allowed to take sufficient exercise, and not confined in close rooms till their muscles are relaxed, and their powers of digestion destroyed. To carry the remark still further, if fear in girls, instead of being cherished, perhaps, created, were treated in the same manner as cowardice in boys, we should quickly see women with more dignified aspects. It is true, they could not then with equal propriety be termed the sweet flowers that smile in the walk of man; but they would be more respectable members of society, and discharge the important duties of life by the light of their own reason. "Educate women like men," says Rousseau, "and the more they resemble our sex the less power will they have over us."¹ This is the very point I aim at. I do not wish them to have power over men; but over themselves.

In the same strain have I heard men argue against instructing the poor; for many are the forms that aristocracy assumes. "Teach them to read and write," say they, "and you take them out of the station assigned them by nature." An eloquent Frenchman has answered them, I will borrow his sentiments. But they know not, when they make man a brute, that they may expect every instant to see him transformed into a ferocious beast.² Without knowledge there can be no morality!

Ignorance is a frail base for virtue! Yet, that it is the condition for which woman was organized, has been insisted upon by the writers who have most vehemently argued in favour of the superiority of man; a superiority not in degree, but essence; though, to soften the argument, they have laboured to prove, with chivalrous generosity, that

---

1  [Rousseau, *Emile* 363; the sentence ends, "and then men will truly be the masters."]
2  [Possibly Honoré Riqueti, comte de Mirabeau (1749–91), who said, in the Constituent Assembly in 1790, "You have loosed the bull – do you expect he will not use his horns?" (Hardt 458).]

the sexes ought not to be compared; man was made to reason, woman to feel: and that together, flesh and spirit, they make the most perfect whole, by blending happily reason and sensibility into one character.

And what is sensibility? "Quickness of sensation; quickness of perception; delicacy." Thus is it defined by Dr. Johnson;[1] and the definition gives me no other idea than of the most exquisitely polished instinct. I discern not a trace of the image of God in either sensation or matter. Refined seventy times seven,[2] they are still material; intellect dwells not there; nor will fire ever make lead gold!

I come round to my old argument; if woman be allowed to have an immortal soul, she must have, as the employment of life, an understanding to improve. And when, to render the present state more complete, though every thing proves it to be but a fraction of a mighty sum, she is incited by present gratification to forget her grand destination, nature is counteracted, or she was born only to procreate and rot. Or, granting brutes, of every description, a soul,[3] though not a reasonable one, the exercise of instinct and sensibility may be the step, which they are to take, in this life, towards the attainment of reason in the next; so that through all eternity they will lag behind man, who, why we cannot tell, had the power given him of attaining reason in his first mode of existence.

When I treat of the peculiar duties of women, as I should treat of the peculiar duties of a citizen or father, it will be found that I do not mean to insinuate that they should be taken out of their families, speaking of the majority. "He that hath wife and children," says Lord Bacon, "hath given hostages to fortune; for they are impediments to great enterprises, either of virtue or mischief. Certainly the best works, and of greatest merit for the public, have proceeded from the unmarried or childless men."[4] I say the same of women. But, the welfare of society is not built on extraordinary exertions; and were it more reasonably organized, there would be still less need of great abilities, or heroic virtues.

In the regulation of a family, in the education of children, under-

---

1  [In his *Dictionary* (1755).]
2  [Matthew 18: 22.]
3  [Cf. Macaulay, *Letters* 1–2, 356–57.]
4  [Bacon, Essay 8, "Of Marriage and Single Life."]

standing, in an unsophisticated sense, is particularly required: strength both of body and mind; yet the men who, by their writings, have most earnestly laboured to domesticate women, have endeavoured, by arguments dictated by a gross appetite, which satiety had rendered fastidious, to weaken their bodies and cramp their minds. But, if even by these sinister methods they really *persuaded* women, by working on their feelings, to stay at home, and fulfil the duties of a mother and mistress of a family, I should cautiously oppose opinions that led women to right conduct, by prevailing on them to make the discharge of such important duties the main business of life, though reason were insulted. Yet, and I appeal to experience, if by neglecting the understanding they be as much, nay, more detached from these domestic employments, than they could be by the most serious intellectual pursuit, though it may be observed, that the mass of mankind will never vigorously pursue an intellectual object[1], I may be allowed to infer that reason is absolutely necessary to enable a woman to perform any duty properly, and I must again repeat, that sensibility is not reason.

The comparison with the rich still occurs to me; for, when men neglect the duties of humanity, women will follow their example; a common stream hurries them both along with thoughtless celerity. Riches and honours prevent a man from enlarging his understanding, and enervate all his powers by reversing the order of nature, which has ever made true pleasure the reward of labour. Pleasure – enervating pleasure is, likewise, within women's reach without earning it. But, till hereditary possessions are spread abroad, how can we expect men to be proud of virtue? And, till they are, women will govern them by the most direct means, neglecting their dull domestic duties to catch the pleasure that sits lightly on the wing of time.

"The power of the woman," says some author, "is her sensibility;"[2] and men, not aware of the consequence, do all they can to make this power swallow up every other. Those who constantly employ their sensibility will have most: for example; poets, painters, and composers[3]. Yet, when the sensibility is thus increased at the expence of

---

1 The mass of mankind are rather the slaves of their appetites than of their passions.
2 [Possibly a paraphrase of Gregory, *Legacy* 27.]
3 Men of these descriptions pour it into their compositions, to amalgamate the gross materials; and, moulding them with passion, give to the inert body a soul; but, in woman's imagination, love alone concentrates these ethereal beams.

reason, and even the imagination, why do philosophical men complain of their fickleness? The sexual attention of man particularly acts on female sensibility, and this sympathy has been exercised from their youth up. A husband cannot long pay those attentions with the passion necessary to excite lively emotions, and the heart, accustomed to lively emotions, turns to a new lover, or pines in secret, the prey of virtue or prudence. I mean when the heart has really been rendered susceptible, and the taste formed; for I am apt to conclude, from what I have seen in fashionable life, that vanity is oftener fostered than sensibility by the mode of education, and the intercourse between the sexes, which I have reprobated; and that coquetry more frequently proceeds from vanity than from that inconstancy, which overstrained sensibility naturally produces.

Another argument that has had great weight with me, must, I think, have some force with every considerate benevolent heart. Girls who have been thus weakly educated, are often cruelly left by their parents without any provision; and, of course, are dependent on, not only the reason, but the bounty of their brothers. These brothers are, to view the fairest side of the question, good sort of men, and give as a favour, what children of the same parents had an equal right to. In this equivocal humiliating situation, a docile female may remain some time, with a tolerable degree of comfort. But, when the brother marries, a probable circumstance, from being considered as the mistress of the family, she is viewed with averted looks as an intruder, an unnecessary burden on the benevolence of the master of the house, and his new partner.

Who can recount the misery, which many unfortunate beings, whose minds and bodies are equally weak, suffer in such situations – unable to work, and ashamed to beg? The wife, a cold-hearted, narrow-minded, woman, and this is not an unfair supposition; for the present mode of education does not tend to enlarge the heart any more than the understanding, is jealous of the little kindness which her husband shews to his relations; and her sensibility not rising to humanity, she is displeased at seeing the property of *her* children lavished on an helpless sister.

These are matters of fact, which have come under my eye again and again. The consequence is obvious, the wife has recourse to cunning to undermine the habitual affection, which she is afraid openly to oppose; and neither tears nor caresses are spared till the spy is worked out of her home, and thrown on the world, unprepared for its difficulties; or sent, as a great effort of generosity, or from some regard to propriety, with a small stipend, and an uncultivated mind, into joy-less solitude.

These two women may be much upon a par, with respect to rea-son and humanity; and changing situations, might have acted just the same selfish part; but had they been differently educated, the case would also have been very different. The wife would not have had that sensibility, of which self is the centre, and reason might have taught her not to expect, and not even to be flattered by, the affection of her husband, if it led him to violate prior duties. She would wish not to love him merely because he loved her, but on account of his virtues; and the sister might have been able to struggle for herself instead of eating the bitter bread of dependence.

I am, indeed, persuaded that the heart, as well as the understand-ing, is opened by cultivation; and by, which may not appear so clear, strengthening the organs; I am not now talking of momentary flashes of sensibility, but of affections. And, perhaps, in the education of both sexes, the most difficult task is so to adjust instruction as not to nar-row the understanding, whilst the heart is warmed by the generous juices of spring, just raised by the electric fermentation of the season; nor to dry up the feelings by employing the mind in investigations remote from life.

With respect to women, when they receive a careful education, they are either made fine ladies, brimful of sensibility, and teeming with capricious fancies; or mere notable women. The latter are often friendly, honest creatures, and have a shrewd kind of good sense joined with worldly prudence, that often render them more useful members of society than the fine sentimental lady, though they pos-sess neither greatness of mind nor taste. The intellectual world is shut against them; take them out of their family or neighbourhood, and they stand still; the mind finding no employment, for literature affords a fund of amusement which they have never sought to relish, but fre-quently to despise. The sentiments and taste of more cultivated minds appear ridiculous, even in those whom chance and family connections have led them to love; but in mere acquaintance they think it all affectation.

A man of sense can only love such a woman on account of her sex, and respect her, because she is a trusty servant. He lets her, to preserve his own peace, scold the servants, and go to church in clothes made of the very best materials. A man of her own size of understanding would, probably, not agree so well with her; for he might wish to encroach on her prerogative, and manage some domestic concerns himself. Yet women, whose minds are not enlarged by cultivation, or the natural selfishness of sensibility expanded by reflection, are very unfit to manage a family; for, by an undue stretch of power, they are always tyrannizing to support a superiority that only rests on the arbitrary distinction of fortune. The evil is sometimes more serious, and domestics are deprived of innocent indulgences, and made to work beyond their strength, in order to enable the notable woman to keep a better table, and outshine her neighbours in finery and parade. If she attend to her children, it is, in general, to dress them in a costly manner – and, whether this attention arise from vanity or fondness, it is equally pernicious.

Besides, how many women of this description pass their days; or, at least, their evenings, discontentedly. Their husbands acknowledge that they are good managers, and chaste wives; but leave home to seek for more agreeable, may I be allowed to use a significant French word, *piquant* society; and the patient drudge, who fulfils her task, like a blind horse in a mill, is defrauded of her just reward; for the wages due to her are the caresses of her husband; and women who have so few resources in themselves, do not very patiently bear this privation of a natural right.

A fine lady, on the contrary, has been taught to look down with contempt on the vulgar employments of life; though she has only been incited to acquire accomplishments that rise a degree above sense; for even corporeal accomplishments cannot be acquired with any degree of precision unless the understanding has been strengthened by exercise. Without a foundation of principles taste is superficial, grace must arise from something deeper than imitation. The imagination, however, is heated, and the feelings rendered fastidious, if not sophisticated; or, a counterpoise of judgment is not acquired, when the heart still remains artless, though it becomes too tender.

These women are often amiable; and their hearts are really more sensible to general benevolence, more alive to the sentiments that civilize life, than the square-elbowed family drudge; but, wanting a due proportion of reflection and self-government, they only inspire love; and are the mistresses of their husbands, whilst they have any hold on their affections; and the platonic friends of his male acquaintance. These are the fair defects in nature;[1] the women who appear to be created not to enjoy the fellowship of man, but to save him from sinking into absolute brutality, by rubbing off the rough angles of his character; and by playful dalliance to give some dignity to the appetite that draws him to them. – Gracious Creator of the whole human race! hast thou created such a being as woman, who can trace thy wisdom in thy works, and feel that thou alone art by thy nature exalted above her, – for no better purpose? – Can she believe that she was only made to submit to man, her equal, a being, who, like her, was sent into the world to acquire virtue? – Can she consent to be occupied merely to please him; merely to adorn the earth, when her soul is capable of rising to thee? – And can she rest supinely dependent on man for reason, when she ought to mount with him the arduous steeps of knowledge? –

Yet, if love be the supreme good, let women be only educated to inspire it, and let every charm be polished to intoxicate the senses; but, if they be moral beings, let them have a chance to become intelligent; and let love to man be only a part of that glowing flame of universal love, which, after encircling humanity, mounts in grateful incense to God.

To fulfil domestic duties much resolution is necessary, and a serious kind of perseverance that requires a more firm support than emotions, however lively and true to nature. To give an example of order, the soul of virtue, some austerity of behaviour must be adopted, scarcely to be expected from a being who, from its infancy, has been made the weathercock of its own sensations. Whoever rationally means to be useful must have a plan of conduct; and, in the discharge of the simplest duty, we are often obliged to act contrary to the present impulse of tenderness or compassion. Severity is frequently the

---

1   [Milton, *Paradise Lost* 10.891-92.]

most certain, as well as the most sublime proof of affection; and the want of this power over the feelings, and of that lofty, dignified affection, which makes a person prefer the future good of the beloved object to a present gratification, is the reason why so many fond mothers spoil their children, and has made it questionable whether negligence or indulgence be most hurtful: but I am inclined to think, that the latter has done most harm.[1]

Mankind seem to agree that children should be left under the management of women during their childhood. Now, from all the observation that I have been able to make, women of sensibility are the most unfit for this task, because they will infallibly, carried away by their feelings, spoil a child's temper. The management of the temper, the first, and most important branch of education, requires the sober steady eye of reason; a plan of conduct equally distant from tyranny and indulgence: yet these are the extremes that people of sensibility alternately fall into; always shooting beyond the mark. I have followed this train of reasoning much further, till I have concluded, that a person of genius is the most improper person to be employed in education, public or private. Minds of this rare species see things too much in masses, and seldom, if ever, have a good temper. That habitual cheerfulness, termed good-humour, is, perhaps, as seldom united with great mental powers, as with strong feelings. And those people who follow, with interest and admiration, the flights of genius; or, with cooler approbation suck in the instruction which has been elaborately prepared for them by the profound thinker, ought not to be disgusted, if they find the former choleric, and the latter morose; because liveliness of fancy, and a tenacious comprehension of mind, are scarcely compatible with that pliant urbanity which leads a man, at least, to bend to the opinions and prejudices of others, instead of roughly confronting them.

But, treating of education or manners, minds of a superior class are not to be considered, they may be left to chance; it is the multitude, with moderate abilities, who call for instruction, and catch the colour of the atmosphere they breathe. This respectable concourse, I contend, men and women, should not have their sensations heightened in the hot-bed of luxurious indolence, at the expence of their under-

---

1    [Cf. Rousseau, *Emile* 86; Macaulay, *Letters* 97-103.]

standing; for, unless there be a ballast of understanding, they will never become either virtuous or free: an aristocracy, founded on property, or sterling talents, will ever sweep before it, the alternately timid, and ferocious, slaves of feeling.

Numberless are the arguments, to take another view of the subject, brought forward with a shew of reason, because supposed to be deduced from nature, that men have used morally and physically, to degrade the sex. I must notice a few.

The female understanding has often been spoken of with contempt, as arriving sooner at maturity than the male. I shall not answer this argument by alluding to the early proofs of reason, as well as genius, in Cowley, Milton, and Pope[1], but only appeal to experience to decide whether young men, who are early introduced into company (and examples now abound), do not acquire the same precocity. So notorious is this fact, that the bare mentioning of it must bring before people, who at all mix in the world, the idea of a number of swaggering apes of men, whose understandings are narrowed by being brought into the society of men when they ought to have been spinning a top or twirling a hoop.

It has also been asserted, by some naturalists, that men do not attain their full growth and strength till thirty; but that women arrive at maturity by twenty.[2] I apprehend that they reason on false ground, led astray by the male prejudice, which deems beauty the perfection of woman – mere beauty of features and complexion, the vulgar acceptation of the word, whilst male beauty is allowed to have some connection with the mind. Strength of body, and that character of countenance, which the French term a *physionomie*, women do not acquire before thirty, any more than men. The little artless tricks of children, it is true, are particularly pleasing and attractive; yet, when the pretty freshness of youth is worn off, these artless graces become studied airs, and disgust every person of taste. In the countenance of girls we only look for vivacity and bashful modesty; but, the spring-

1 Many other names might be added. [Abraham Cowley (1618-67) published *Poetical Blossoms* when he was only fifteen; John Milton (1608-74) composed verse in both English and Latin when he was sixteen; Alexander Pope (1688-1744) refers to his own poetic precocity in "An Epistle to Dr. Arbuthnot" (1735) 127-28.]
2 [Georges, comte de Buffon, *Natural History*, trans. William Smellie (Edinburgh, 1780) 2: 436.]

tide of life over, we look for soberer sense in the face, and for traces of passion, instead of the dimples of animal spirits; expecting to see individuality of character, the only fastener of the affections[1]. We then wish to converse, not to fondle; to give scope to our imaginations as well as to the sensations of our hearts.

At twenty the beauty of both sexes is equal; but the libertinism of man leads him to make the distinction, and superannuated coquettes are commonly of the same opinion; for, when they can no longer inspire love, they pay for the vigour and vivacity of youth. The French, who admit more of mind into their notions of beauty, give the preference to women of thirty. I mean to say that they allow women to be in their most perfect state, when vivacity gives place to reason, and to that majestic seriousness of character, which marks maturity; – or, the resting point. In youth, till twenty, the body shoots out, till thirty the solids are attaining a degree of density; and the flexible muscles, growing daily more rigid, give character to the countenance; that is, they trace the operations of the mind with the iron pen of fate, and tell us not only what powers are within, but how they have been employed.[2]

It is proper to observe, that animals who arrive slowly at maturity, are the longest lived, and of the noblest species. Men cannot, however, claim any natural superiority from the grandeur of longevity; for in this respect nature has not distinguished the male.

Polygamy is another physical degradation; and a plausible argument for a custom, that blasts every domestic virtue, is drawn from the well-attested fact, that in the countries where it is established, more females are born than males. This appears to be an indication of nature, and to nature, apparently reasonable speculations must yield. A further conclusion obviously presented itself; if polygamy be necessary, woman must be inferior to man, and made for him.

With respect to the formation of the fetus in the womb, we are very ignorant; but it appears to me probable, that an accidental physical cause may account for this phenomenon, and prove it not to be a law of nature. I have met with some pertinent observations on the subject in Forster's Account of the Isles of the South-Sea, that will

---

1  The strength of an affection is, generally, in the same proportion as the character of the species in the object beloved, is lost in that of the individual.

2  [Cf. *Original Stories*; *Works* 4: 390-91.]

explain my meaning. After observing that of the two sexes amongst animals, the most vigorous and hottest constitution always prevails, and produces its kind; he adds, – "If this be applied to the inhabitants of Africa, it is evident that the men there, accustomed to polygamy, are enervated by the use of so many women, and therefore less vigorous; the women, on the contrary, are of a hotter constitution, not only on account of their more irritable nerves, more sensible organization, and more lively fancy; but likewise because they are deprived in their matrimony of that share of physical love which, in a monogamous condition, would all be theirs; and thus, for the above reasons, the generality of children are born females."[1]

"In the greater part of Europe it has been proved by the most accurate lists of mortality, that the proportion of men to women is nearly equal, or, if any difference takes place, the males born are more numerous, in the proportion of 105 to 100."

The necessity of polygamy, therefore, does not appear; yet when a man seduces a woman, it should, I think, be termed a *left-handed* marriage, and the man should be *legally* obliged to maintain the woman and her children, unless adultery, a natural divorcement, abrogated the law. And this law should remain in force as long as the weakness of women caused the word seduction to be used as an excuse for their frailty and want of principle; nay, while they depend on man for a subsistence, instead of earning it by the exertion of their own hands or heads. But these women should not, in the full meaning of the relationship, be termed wives, or the very purpose of marriage would be subverted, and all those endearing charities that flow from personal fidelity, and give a sanctity to the tie, when neither love nor friendship unites the hearts, would melt into selfishness. The woman who is faithful to the father of her children demands respect, and should not be treated like a prostitute; though I readily grant that if it be necessary for a man and woman to live together in order to bring up their offspring, nature never intended that a man should have more than one wife.

---

1 [John Reinhold Forster (1729-98), *Observations Made during a Voyage round the World* (London, 1778) 425-26. Forster had circumnavigated the globe with Cook in the Resolution, in 1772-75. The second paragraph in quotation marks is not by Forster; it is unidentified.]

Still, highly as I respect marriage, as the foundation of almost every social virtue, I cannot avoid feeling the most lively compassion for those unfortunate females who are broken off from society, and by one error torn from all those affections and relationships that improve the heart and mind. It does not frequently even deserve the name of error; for many innocent girls become the dupes of a sincere, affectionate heart, and still more are, as it may emphatically be termed, *ruined* before they know the difference between virtue and vice: – and thus prepared by their education for infamy, they become infamous. Asylums and Magdalens are not the proper remedies for these abuses.[1] It is justice, not charity, that is wanting in the world!

A woman who has lost her honour, imagines that she cannot fall lower, and as for recovering her former station, it is impossible; no exertion can wash this stain away. Losing thus every spur, and having no other means of support, prostitution becomes her only refuge, and the character is quickly depraved by circumstances over which the poor wretch has little power, unless she possesses an uncommon portion of sense and loftiness of spirit. Necessity never makes prostitution the business of men's lives; though numberless are the women who are thus rendered systematically vicious. This, however, arises, in a great degree, from the state of idleness in which women are educated, who are always taught to look up to man for a maintenance, and to consider their persons as the proper return for his exertions to support them. Meretricious airs, and the whole science of wantonness, have then a more powerful stimulus than either appetite or vanity; and this remark gives force to the prevailing opinion, that with chastity all is lost that is respectable in woman. Her character depends on the observance of one virtue, though the only passion fostered in her heart – is love. Nay, the honour of a woman is not made even to depend on her will.

When Richardson[2] makes Clarissa tell Lovelace that he had robbed her of her honour, he must have had strange notions of hon-

---

1  [London's Magdalen Hospital, a reformatory for prostitutes, was founded in 1758. It was named after St. Mary Magdalene, the type of the redeemed harlot (Luke 7: 37-50, 8: 2).]

2  Dr. Young supports the same opinion, in his plays, when he talks of the misfortune that shunned the light of day. [Samuel Richardson (1689-1761), *Clarissa* (1747-48) Mr. Lovelace to John Belford, Esq. (Friday, June 16) Paper 8; since Clarissa is still in

our and virtue. For, miserable beyond all names of misery is the condition of a being, who could be degraded without its own consent! This excess of strictness I have heard vindicated as a salutary error. I shall answer in the words of Leibnitz – "Errors are often useful; but it is commonly to remedy other errors."[1]

Most of the evils of life arise from a desire of present enjoyment that outruns itself. The obedience required of women in the marriage state comes under this description; the mind, naturally weakened by depending on authority, never exerts its own powers, and the obedient wife is thus rendered a weak indolent mother. Or, supposing that this is not always the consequence, a future state of existence is scarcely taken into the reckoning when only negative virtues are cultivated. For, in treating of morals, particularly when women are alluded to, writers have too often considered virtue in a very limited sense, and made the foundation of it *solely* worldly utility; nay, a still more fragile base has been given to this stupendous fabric, and the wayward fluctuating feelings of men have been made the standard of virtue. Yes, virtue as well as religion, has been subjected to the decisions of taste.

It would almost provoke a smile of contempt, if the vain absurdities of man did not strike us on all sides, to observe, how eager men are to degrade the sex from whom they pretend to receive the chief pleasure of life; and I have frequently with full conviction retorted Pope's sarcasm on them;[2] or, to speak explicitly, it has appeared to me applicable to the whole human race. A love of pleasure or sway seems to divide mankind, and the husband who lords it in his little haram thinks only of his pleasure or his convenience. To such lengths, indeed, does an intemperate love of pleasure carry some prudent men, or worn out libertines, who marry to have a safe bed-fellow, that they seduce their own wives. – Hymen banishes modesty, and chaste love takes its flight.

Love, considered as an animal appetite, cannot long feed on itself

<hr>

shock after being raped by Lovelace, the note may not express her considered opinion. Edward Young (1683-1765), *Busiris, King of Egypt* (1719) 1.1.158; the "black . . . story" that "well might shun the day" actually concerns how Myris persuaded Busiris to kill her brother, the rightful king of Egypt, and then married murderer. Wollstonecraft included several excerpts from Young in *The Female Reader*.]

1  [Gottfried Wilhelm von Leibniz (1646-1716), *Theodicy* (1710), preface.]
2  [Pope, "Of the Characters of Women" 207-10.]

without expiring. And this extinction in its own flame, may be termed the violent death of love. But the wife who has thus been rendered licentious, will probably endeavour to fill the void left by the loss of her husband's attentions; for she cannot contentedly become merely an upper servant after having been treated like a goddess. She is still handsome, and, instead of transferring her fondness to her children, she only dreams of enjoying the sunshine of life. Besides, there are many husbands so devoid of sense and parental affection, that during the first effervescence of voluptuous fondness they refuse to let their wives suckle their children.[1] They are only to dress and live to please them: and love – even innocent love, soon sinks into lasciviousness when the exercise of a duty is sacrificed to its indulgence.

Personal attachment is a very happy foundation for friendship; yet, when even two virtuous young people marry, it would, perhaps, be happy if some circumstances checked their passion; if the recollection of some prior attachment, or disappointed affection, made it on one side, at least, rather a match founded on esteem. In that case they would look beyond the present moment, and try to render the whole of life respectable, by forming a plan to regulate a friendship which only death ought to dissolve.

Friendship is a serious affection; the most sublime of all affections, because it is founded on principle, and cemented by time. The very reverse may be said of love. In a great degree, love and friendship cannot subsist in the same bosom; even when inspired by different objects they weaken or destroy each other, and for the same object can only be felt in succession. The vain fears and fond jealousies, the winds which fan the flame of love, when judiciously or artfully tempered, are both incompatible with the tender confidence and sincere respect of friendship.

Love, such as the glowing pen of genius has traced, exists not on earth, or only resides in those exalted, fervid imaginations that have sketched such dangerous pictures. Dangerous, because they not only afford a plausible excuse, to the voluptuary who disguises sheer sensuality under a sentimental veil; but as they spread affectation, and take from the dignity of virtue. Virtue, as the very word imports, should

---

1    [At this time, it was still common for women of the upper classes to employ wetnurses. Cf. Rousseau's advocacy of breast-feeding, *Emile* 44-47.]

have an appearance of seriousness, if not of austerity; and to endeavour to trick her out in the garb of pleasure, because the epithet has
been used as another name for beauty, is to exalt her on a quicksand; a
most insidious attempt to hasten her fall by apparent respect. Virtue
and pleasure are not, in fact, so nearly allied in this life as some eloquent writers have laboured to prove.[1] Pleasure prepares the fading
wreath, and mixes the intoxicating cup; but the fruit which virtue
gives, is the recompence of toil: and, gradually seen as it ripens, only
affords calm satisfaction; nay, appearing to be the result of the natural
tendency of things, it is scarcely observed. Bread, the common food of
life, seldom thought of as a blessing, supports the constitution and
preserves health; still feasts delight the heart of man, though disease
and even death lurk in the cup or dainty that elevates the spirits or
tickles the palate. The lively heated imagination likewise, to apply the
comparison, draws the picture of love, as it draws every other picture,
with those glowing colours, which the daring hand will steal from the
rainbow that is directed by a mind, condemned in a world like this, to
prove its noble origin by panting after unattainable perfection; ever
pursuing what it acknowledges to be a fleeting dream. An imagination of this vigorous cast can give existence to insubstantial forms, and
stability to the shadowy reveries which the mind naturally falls into
when realities are found vapid. It can then depict love with celestial
charms, and dote on the grand ideal object – it can imagine a degree
of mutual affection that shall refine the soul, and not expire when it
has served as a "scale to heavenly;"[2] and, like devotion, make it absorb
every meaner affection and desire. In each others arms, as in a temple,
with its summit lost in the clouds, the world is to be shut out, and
every thought and wish, that do not nurture pure affection and permanent virtue. – Permanent virtue! alas! Rousseau, respectable vision-
ary! thy paradise would soon be violated by the entrance of some
unexpected guest. Like Milton's it would only contain angels, or men
sunk below the dignity of rational creatures. Happiness is not material, it cannot be seen or felt! Yet the eager pursuit of the good which
every one shapes to his own fancy, proclaims man the lord of this
lower world, and to be an intelligential creature, who is not to receive,

---

1  [Cf. Rousseau, *Emile* 282; and *Original Stories*; *Works* 4: 370.]
2  [Milton, *Paradise Lost* 8.591-92.]

but acquire happiness. They, therefore, who complain of the delusions of passion, do not recollect that they are exclaiming against a strong proof of the immortality of the soul.

But leaving superior minds to correct themselves, and pay dearly for their experience, it is necessary to observe, that it is not against strong, persevering passions; but romantic wavering feelings that I wish to guard the female heart by exercising the understanding: for these paradisiacal reveries are oftener the effect of idleness than of a lively fancy.

Women have seldom sufficient serious employment to silence their feelings; a round of little cares, or vain pursuits frittering away all strength of mind and organs, they become naturally only objects of sense. – In short, the whole tenour of female education (the education of society) tends to render the best disposed romantic and inconstant; and the remainder vain and mean. In the present state of society this evil can scarcely be remedied, I am afraid, in the slightest degree; should a more laudable ambition ever gain ground they may be brought nearer to nature and reason, and become more virtuous and useful as they grow more respectable.

But, I will venture to assert that their reason will never acquire sufficient strength to enable it to regulate their conduct, whilst the making an appearance in the world is the first wish of the majority of mankind. To this weak wish the natural affections, and the most useful virtues are sacrificed. Girls marry merely to *better themselves*, to borrow a significant vulgar phrase, and have such perfect power over their hearts as not to permit themselves to *fall in love* till a man with a superiour fortune offers. On this subject I mean to enlarge in a future chapter; it is only necessary to drop a hint at present, because women are so often degraded by suffering the selfish prudence of age to chill the ardour of youth.

From the same source flows an opinion that young girls ought to dedicate great part of their time to needle-work; yet, this employment contracts their faculties more than any other that could have been chosen for them, by confining their thoughts to their persons.[1] Men order their clothes to be made, and have done with the subject;

---

1  [Rousseau disapproves of needle-work, but only for men (*Emile* 199); Macaulay defends it for women (*Letters* 64-65).]

women make their own clothes, necessary or ornamental, and are continually talking about them; and their thoughts follow their hands. It is not indeed the making of necessaries that weakens the mind; but the frippery of dress. For when a woman in the lower rank of life makes her husband's and children's clothes, she does her duty, this is her part of the family business; but when women work only to dress better than they could otherwise afford, it is worse than sheer loss of time. To render the poor virtuous they must be employed, and women in the middle rank of life, did they not ape the fashions of the nobility, without catching their ease, might employ them, whilst they themselves managed their families, instructed their children, and exercised their own minds. Gardening, experimental philosophy,[1] and literature, would afford them subjects to think of and matter for conversation, that in some degree would exercise their understandings. The conversation of French women, who are not so rigidly nailed to their chairs to twist lappets, and knot ribands, is frequently superficial; but, I contend, that it is not half so insipid as that of those English women whose time is spent in making caps, bonnets, and the whole mischief of trimmings, not to mention shopping, bargain-hunting, &c. &c.: and it is the decent, prudent women, who are most degraded by these practices; for their motive is simply vanity. The wanton who exercises her taste to render her passion alluring, has something more in view.

These observations all branch out of a general one, which I have before made, and which cannot be too often insisted upon, for, speaking of men, women, or professions, it will be found that the employment of the thoughts shapes the character both generally and individually. The thoughts of women ever hover round their persons, and is it surprising that their persons are reckoned most valuable? Yet some degree of liberty of mind is necessary even to form the person; and this may be one reason why some gentle wives have so few attractions beside that of sex. Add to this, sedentary employments render the majority of women sickly – and false notions of female excellence make them proud of this delicacy, though it be another fetter, that by calling the attention continually to the body, cramps the activity of the mind.

---

1   [Natural science.]

Women of quality seldom do any of the manual part of their dress, consequently only their taste is exercised, and they acquire, by thinking less of the finery, when the business of their toilet is over, that ease, which seldom appears in the deportment of women, who dress merely for the sake of dressing. In fact, the observation with respect to the middle rank, the one in which talents thrive best, extends not to women; for those of the superior class, by catching, at least, a smattering of literature, and conversing more with men, on general topics, acquire more knowledge than the women who ape their fashions and faults without sharing their advantages. With respect to virtue, to use the word in a comprehensive sense, I have seen most in low life. Many poor women maintain their children by the sweat of their brow,[1] and keep together families that the vices of the fathers[2] would have scattered abroad; but gentlewomen are too indolent to be actively virtuous, and are softened rather than refined by civilization. Indeed, the good sense which I have met with, among the poor women who have had few advantages of education, and yet have acted heroically, strongly confirmed me in the opinion that trifling employments have rendered woman a trifler.[3] Man, taking her[4] body, the mind is left to rust; so that while physical love enervates man,[5] as being his favourite recreation, he will endeavour to enslave woman: − and, who can tell, how many generations may be necessary to give vigour to the virtue and talents of the freed posterity of abject slaves[6]?

In tracing the causes that, in my opinion, have degraded woman, I have confined my observations to such as universally act upon the

---

1    [Genesis 3: 19. Wollstonecraft transfers to "poor women" the curse placed on Adam, not on Eve.]

2    [Cf. Exodus 20: 5.]

3    [Macaulay, however, defends woman's right to be a trifler (*Letters* 65, 78-79).]

4    "I take her body," says Ranger. [When Ranger, a rakish character in *The Suspicious Husband* (1747) by Benjamin Hoadly (1706-57), delivers this line (1.1), he is actually reading William Congreve (1670-1729), "Song" 13-14.]

5    [Cf. Rousseau, *Emile* 232.]

6    "Supposing that women are voluntary slaves − slavery of any kind is unfavourable to human happiness and improvement." *Knox's Essays*. [Vicesimus Knox (1752-1821), Essay 5, "On the Fear of Appearing Singular," *Essays, Moral and Literary* (London, 1778) 21. Wollstonecraft misquotes Knox, who is not referring specifically to women.]

morals and manners of the whole sex, and to me it appears clear that they all spring from want of understanding. Whether this arise from a physical or accidental weakness of faculties, time alone can determine; for I shall not lay any great stress on the example of a few women[1] who, from having received a masculine education, have acquired courage and resolution; I only contend that the men who have been placed in similar situations, have acquired a similar character – I speak of bodies of men, and that men of genius and talents have started out of a class, in which women have never yet been placed.

---

1   Sappho, Eloisa, Mrs. Macaulay, the Empress of Russia, Madame d'Eon, &c. These, and many more, may be reckoned exceptions; and, are not all heroes, as well as heroines, exceptions to general rules? I wish to see women neither heroines nor brutes; but reasonable creatures. [Sappho (c. 600 B.C.) was a distinguished poet. Héloïse (c. 1101-64), secretly married to the philosopher Peter Abelard (1079-1142), was herself a scholar; their love letters inspired Pope's "Eloisa to Abelard" (1717) and Rousseau's *Julie; ou, La Nouvelle Héloïse*. Catharine Macaulay Graham (1731-91) was the author of an eight-volume *History of England* (1763-83) and other works including *Observations on the Reflections of the Right Honourable Edmund Burke on the Revolution in France* (1790) and *Letters on Education* (1790). Catherine II of Russia (1729-96) displayed her "courage and resolution" by deposing and murdering her husband; but she also introduced inoculation for smallpox and promoted religious toleration and the education of women. Charles de Beaumont, Chevalier d'Eon (1728-1810), a distinguished French diplomat, dressed as a woman for much of his life, and (in consequence of litigation over wagers about his sex) had been legally declared one in 1777 (See Gary Kates, *Monsieur d'Eon Is a Woman: A Tale of Political Intrigue and Sexual Masquerade* [New York: Basic Books, 1995].) Rousseau repeatedly accuses feminists of basing their arguments on exceptions (*Emile* 362, 364).]

# CHAP. V.

## ANIMADVERSIONS ON SOME OF THE WRITERS WHO HAVE RENDERED WOMEN OBJECTS OF PITY, BORDERING ON CONTEMPT.

THE opinions speciously supported, in some modern publications on the female character and education, which have given the tone to most of the observations made, in a more cursory manner, on the sex, remain now to be examined.

### SECT. I

I SHALL begin with Rousseau, and give a sketch of his character of woman, in his own words, interspersing comments and reflections. My comments, it is true, will all spring from a few simple principles, and might have been deduced from what I have already said; but the artificial structure has been raised with so much ingenuity, that it seems necessary to attack it in a more circumstantial manner, and make the application myself.

Sophia, says Rousseau, should be as perfect a woman as Emilius is a man, and to render her so, it is necessary to examine the character which nature has given to the sex.[1]

He then proceeds to prove that woman ought to be weak and passive, because she has less bodily strength than man; and hence infers, that she was formed to please and to be subject to him; and that it is her duty to render herself *agreeable* to her master – this being the grand end of her existence[2]. Still, however, to give a little mock dignity to lust, he insists that man should not exert his strength, but depend on the will of the woman, when he seeks for pleasure with her.

---

1  [Rousseau, *Emile* 357.]
2  I have already inserted the passage, page 99 [161-62].

"Hence we deduce a third consequence from the different constitutions of the sexes; which is, that the strongest should be master in appearance, and be dependent in fact on the weakest; and that not from any frivolous practice of gallantry or vanity of protectorship, but from an invariable law of nature, which, furnishing woman with a greater facility to excite desires than she has given man to satisfy them, makes the latter dependent on the good pleasure of the former, and compels him to endeavour to please in his turn, *in order to obtain her consent that he should be strongest*[1]. On these occasions, the most delightful circumstance a man finds in his victory is, to doubt whether it was the woman's weakness that yielded to his superior strength, or whether her inclinations spoke in his favour: the females are also generally artful enough to leave this matter in doubt. The understanding of women answers in this respect perfectly to their constitution: so far from being ashamed of their weakness, they glory in it; their tender muscles make no resistance; they affect to be incapable of lifting the smallest burthens, and would blush to be thought robust and strong. To what purpose is all this? Not merely for the sake of appearing delicate, but through an artful precaution: it is thus they provide an excuse beforehand, and a right to be feeble when they think it expedient."[2]

I have quoted this passage, lest my readers should suspect that I warped the author's reasoning to support my own arguments. I have already asserted that in educating women these fundamental principles lead to a system of cunning and lasciviousness.

Supposing woman to have been formed only to please, and be subject to man, the conclusion is just, she ought to sacrifice every other consideration to render herself agreeable to him: and let this brutal desire of self-preservation be the grand spring of all her actions, when it is proved to be the iron bed of fate, to fit which her character should be stretched or contracted, regardless of all moral or physical distinctions.[3] But, if, as I think, may be demonstrated, the purposes, of even this life, viewing the whole, be subverted by practical rules built

---

1  What nonsense!
2  [Rousseau, *Emile* 359-60; Wollstonecraft's italics.]
3  [An allusion to the bed of Procrustes, which fit all his guests: if they were too short, he stretched them on the rack; if they were too tall, he cut off their extremities.]

upon this ignoble base, I may be allowed to doubt whether woman were created for man: and, though the cry of irreligion, or even atheism, be raised against me, I will simply declare, that were an angel from heaven to tell me that Moses's beautiful, poetical cosmogony, and the account of the fall of man, were literally true, I could not believe what my reason told me was derogatory to the character of the Supreme Being: and, having no fear of the devil before mine eyes, I venture to call this a suggestion of reason, instead of resting my weakness on the broad shoulders of the first seducer of my frail sex.

"It being once demonstrated," continues Rousseau, "that man and woman are not, nor ought to be, constituted alike in temperament and character, it follows of course that they should not be educated in the same manner. In pursuing the directions of nature, they ought indeed to act in concert, but they should not be engaged in the same employments: the end of their pursuits should be the same, but the means they should take to accomplish them, and of consequence their tastes and inclinations, should be different."[1]

\* \* \*

"Whether I consider the peculiar destination of the sex, observe their inclinations, or remark their duties, all things equally concur to point out the peculiar method of education best adapted to them. Woman and man were made for each other; but their mutual dependence is not the same. The men depend on the women only on account of their desires; the women on the men both on account of their desires and their necessities: we could subsist better without them than they without us."[2]

\* \* \*

"For this reason, the education of the women should be always relative to the men. To please, to be useful to us, to make us love and esteem them, to educate us when young, and take care of us when grown up, to advise, to console us, to render our lives easy and agree-

1 [Rousseau, *Emile* 363.]
2 [Rousseau, *Emile* 364.]

able: these are the duties of women at all times, and what they should be taught in their infancy. So long as we fail to recur to this principle, we run wide of the mark, and all the precepts which are given them contribute neither to their happiness nor our own."[1]

* * *

"Girls are from their earliest infancy fond of dress. Not content with being pretty, they are desirous of being thought so; we see, by all their little airs, that this thought engages their attention; and they are hardly capable of understanding what is said to them, before they are to be governed by talking to them of what people will think of their behaviour. The same motive, however, indiscreetly made use of with boys, has not the same effect: provided they are let pursue their amusements at pleasure, they care very little what people think of them. Time and pains are necessary to subject boys to this motive.

"Whencesoever girls derive this first lesson, it is a very good one. As the body is born, in a manner, before the soul, our first concern should be to cultivate the former; this order is common to both sexes, but the object of that cultivation is different. In the one sex it is the developement of corporeal powers; in the other, that of personal charms: not that either the quality of strength or beauty ought to be confined exclusively to one sex; but only that the order of the cultivation of both is in that respect reversed. Women certainly require as much strength as to enable them to move and act gracefully, and men as much address as to qualify them to act with ease."[2]

* * *

"Children of both sexes have a great many amusements in common; and so they ought; have they not also many such when they are grown up? Each sex has also its peculiar taste to distinguish in this particular. Boys love sports of noise and activity; to beat the drum, to whip the top, and to drag about their little carts: girls, on the other hand, are fonder of things of show and ornament; such as mirrors,

---

1  [Rousseau, *Emile* 365.]
2  [Rousseau, *Emile* 365-66.]

trinkets, and dolls: the doll is the peculiar amusement of the females; from whence we see their taste plainly adapted to their destination. The physical part of the art of pleasing lies in dress; and this is all which children are capacitated to cultivate of that art."[1]

\* \* \*

"Here then we see a primary propensity firmly established, which you need only to pursue and regulate. The little creature will doubtless be very desirous to know how to dress up her doll, to make its sleeve-knots, its flounces, its head-dress, &c. she is obliged to have so much recourse to the people about her, for their assistance in these articles, that it would be much more agreeable to her to owe them all to her own industry. Hence we have a good reason for the first lessons that are usually taught these young females: in which we do not appear to be setting them a task, but obliging them, by instructing them in what is immediately useful to themselves. And, in fact, almost all of them learn with reluctance to read and write; but very readily apply themselves to the use of their needles. They imagine themselves already grown up, and think with pleasure that such qualifications will enable them to decorate themselves."[2]

This is certainly only an education of the body;[3] but Rousseau is not the only man who has indirectly said that merely the person of a *young* woman, without any mind, unless animal spirits come under that description, is very pleasing. To render it weak, and what some may call beautiful, the understanding is neglected, and girls forced to sit still, play with dolls and listen to foolish conversations; – the effect of habit is insisted upon as an undoubted indication of nature. I know it was Rousseau's opinion that the first years of youth should be employed to form the body, though in educating Emilius he deviates from this plan; yet, the difference between strengthening the body, on which strength of mind in a great measure depends, and only giving it an easy motion, is very wide.

Rousseau's observations, it is proper to remark, were made in a

---

1  [Rousseau, *Emile* 367.]
2  [Rousseau, *Emile* 367-68.]
3  [Cf. Rousseau, *Emile* 94, 126, 132.]

country where the art of pleasing was refined only to extract the grossness of vice.[1] He did not go back to nature, or his ruling appetite disturbed the operations of reason, else he would not have drawn these crude inferences.

In France boys and girls, particularly the latter, are only educated to please, to manage their persons, and regulate their exterior behaviour; and their minds are corrupted, at a very early age, by the worldly and pious cautions they receive to guard them against immodesty. I speak of past times. The very confessions which mere children were obliged to make, and the questions asked by the holy men, I assert these facts on good authority, were sufficient to impress a sexual character; and the education of society was a school of coquetry and art. At the age of ten or eleven; nay, often much sooner, girls began to coquet, and talked, unreproved, of establishing themselves in the world by marriage.

In short, they were treated like women, almost from their very birth, and compliments were listened to instead of instruction. These, weakening the mind, Nature was supposed to have acted like a stepmother, when she formed this after-thought of creation.

Not allowing them understanding, however, it was but consistent to subject them to authority independent of reason; and to prepare them for this subjection, he gives the following advice:

"Girls ought to be active and diligent; nor is that all; they should also be early subjected to restraint. This misfortune, if it really be one, is inseparable from their sex; nor do they ever throw it off but to suffer more cruel evils. They must be subject, all their lives, to the most constant and severe restraint, which is that of decorum: it is, therefore, necessary to accustom them early to such confinement, that it may not afterwards cost them too dear; and to the suppression of their caprices, that they may the more readily submit to the will of others. If, indeed, they be fond of being always at work, they should be sometimes compelled to lay it aside. Dissipation, levity, and inconstancy, are faults that readily spring up from their first propensities, when corrupted or perverted by too much indulgence. To prevent this abuse, we should teach them, above all things, to lay a due restraint on themselves. The life of a modest woman is reduced, by

---

1 [Burke, *Reflections*; *Writings* 8: 127 (Appendix A.4.i).]

our absurd institutions, to a perpetual conflict with herself: not but it is just that this sex should partake of the sufferings which arise from those evils it hath caused us."[1]

And why is the life of a modest woman a perpetual conflict? I should answer, that this very system of education makes it so. Modesty, temperance, and self-denial, are the sober offspring of reason; but when sensibility is nurtured at the expence of the understanding, such weak beings must be restrained by arbitrary means, and be subjected to continual conflicts; but give their activity of mind a wider range, and nobler passions and motives will govern their appetites and sentiments.

"The common attachment and regard of a mother, nay, mere habit, will make her beloved by her children, if she do nothing to incur their hate. Even the constraint she lays them under, if well directed, will increase their affection, instead of lessening it; because a state of dependence being natural to the sex, they perceive themselves formed for obedience."[2]

This is begging the question; for servitude not only debases the individual, but its effects seem to be transmitted to posterity. Considering the length of time that women have been dependent, is it surprising that some of them hug their chains, and fawn like the spaniel? "These dogs," observes a naturalist, "at first kept their ears erect; but custom has superseded nature, and a token of fear is become a beauty."[3]

"For the same reason," adds Rousseau, "women have, or ought to have, but little liberty; they are apt to indulge themselves excessively in what is allowed them. Addicted in every thing to extremes, they are even more transported at their diversions than boys."[4]

The answer to this is very simple. Slaves and mobs have always indulged themselves in the same excesses, when once they broke loose from authority.[5] – The bent bow recoils with violence, when

---

1    [Rousseau, *Emile* 369.]
2    [Rousseau, *Emile* 369-70.]
3    [William Smellie (1740-95), *The Philosophy of Natural History* (1790) 1: 462. Wollstonecraft reviewed it (*Works* 7: 293-300).]
4    [Rousseau, *Emile* 370.]
5    [Possibly a reference to the revolution in St. Domingue (Haiti), which broke out in August 1791 and was marked by atrocities on both sides.]

the hand is suddenly relaxed that forcibly held it; and sensibility, the play-thing of outward circumstances, must be subjected to authority, or moderated by reason.

"There results," he continues, "from this habitual restraint a tractableness which women have occasion for during their whole lives, as they constantly remain either under subjection to the men, or to the opinions of mankind; and are never permitted to set themselves above those opinions. The first and most important qualification in a woman is good-nature or sweetness of temper: formed to obey a being so imperfect as man, often full of vices, and always full of faults, she ought to learn betimes even to suffer injustice, and to bear the insults of a husband without complaint; it is not for his sake, but her own, that she should be of a mild disposition. The perverseness and ill-nature of the women only serve to aggravate their own misfortunes, and the misconduct of their husbands; they might plainly perceive that such are not the arms by which they gain the superiority."[1]

Formed to live with such an imperfect being as man, they ought to learn from the exercise of their faculties the necessity of forbearance; but all the sacred rights of humanity are violated by insisting on blind obedience; or, the most sacred rights belong *only* to man.

The being who patiently endures injustice, and silently bears insults, will soon become unjust, or unable to discern right from wrong. Besides, I deny the fact, this is not the true way to form or meliorate the temper; for, as a sex, men have better tempers than women, because they are occupied by pursuits that interest the head as well as the heart; and the steadiness of the head gives a healthy temperature to the heart. People of sensibility have seldom good tempers. The formation of the temper is the cool work of reason, when, as life advances, she mixes with happy art, jarring elements. I never knew a weak or ignorant person who had a good temper, though that constitutional good humour, and that docility, which fear stamps on the behaviour, often obtains the name. I say behaviour, for genuine meekness never reached the heart or mind, unless as the effect of reflection; and that simple restraint produces a number of peccant humours in domestic life, many sensible men will allow, who find some of these gentle irritable creatures, very troublesome companions.

---

1   [Rousseau, *Emile* 370.]

"Each sex," he further argues, "should preserve its peculiar tone and manner; a meek husband may make a wife impertinent; but mildness of disposition on the woman's side will always bring a man back to reason, at least if he be not absolutely a brute, and will sooner or later triumph over him."[1] Perhaps the mildness of reason might sometimes have this effect; but abject fear always inspires contempt; and tears are only eloquent when they flow down fair cheeks.

Of what materials can that heart be composed, which can melt when insulted, and instead of revolting at injustice, kiss the rod? Is it unfair to infer that her virtue is built on narrow views and selfishness, who can caress a man, with true feminine softness, the very moment when he treats her tyrannically? Nature never dictated such insincerity; – and, though prudence of this sort be termed a virtue, morality becomes vague when any part is supposed to rest on falsehood. These are mere expedients, and expedients are only useful for the moment.

Let the husband beware of trusting too implicitly to this servile obedience; for if his wife can with winning sweetness caress him when angry, and when she ought to be angry, unless contempt had stifled a natural effervescence, she may do the same after parting with a lover. These are all preparations for adultery; or, should the fear of the world, or of hell, restrain her desire of pleasing other men, when she can no longer please her husband, what substitute can be found by a being who was only formed, by nature and art, to please man? what can make her amends for this privation, or where is she to seek for a fresh employment? where find sufficient strength of mind to determine to begin the search, when her habits are fixed, and vanity has long ruled her chaotic mind?

But this partial moralist recommends cunning systematically and plausibly.

"Daughters should be always submissive; their mothers, however, should not be inexorable. To make a young person tractable, she ought not to be made unhappy, to make her modest she ought not to be rendered stupid. On the contrary, I should not be displeased at her being permitted to use some art, not to elude punishment in case of disobedience, but to exempt herself from the necessity of obeying. It is not necessary to make her dependence burdensome, but only to let

---

1 [Rousseau, *Emile* 370.]

her feel it. Subtilty is a talent natural to the sex; and, as I am persuaded, all our natural inclinations are right and good in themselves, I am of opinion this should be cultivated as well as the others: it is requisite for us only to prevent its abuse."[1]

"Whatever is, is right,"[2] he then proceeds triumphantly to infer. Granted; – yet, perhaps, no aphorism ever contained a more paradoxical assertion. It is a solemn truth with respect to God. He, reverentially I speak, sees the whole at once, and saw its just proportions in the womb of time; but man, who can only inspect disjointed parts, finds many things wrong; and it is a part of the system, and therefore right, that he should endeavour to alter what appears to him to be so, even while he bows to the Wisdom of his Creator, and respects the darkness he labours to disperse.

The inference that follows is just, supposing the principle to be sound. "The superiority of address, peculiar to the female sex, is a very equitable indemnification for their inferiority in point of strength: without this, woman would not be the companion of man; but his slave: it is by her superiour art and ingenuity that she preserves her equality, and governs him while she affects to obey. Woman has every thing against her, as well our faults, as her own timidity and weakness; she has nothing in her favour, but her subtilty and her beauty. Is it not very reasonable, therefore, she should cultivate both?"[3] Greatness of mind can never dwell with cunning, or address; for I shall not boggle about words, when their direct signification is insincerity and falsehood, but content myself with observing, that if any class of mankind be so created that it must necessarily be educated by rules not strictly deducible from truth, virtue is an affair of convention. How could Rousseau dare to assert, after giving this advice, that in the grand end of existence the object of both sexes should be the same, when he well knew that the mind, formed by its pursuits, is expanded by great views swallowing up little ones, or that it becomes itself little?

Men have superiour strength of body; but were it not for mistaken notions of beauty, women would acquire sufficient to enable them to

---

1   [Rousseau, *Emile* 370.]
2   [Rousseau, *Emile* 371; Kenrick's translation incorporates Pope, *An Essay on Man* 1.294.]
3   [Rousseau, *Emile* 371.]

earn their own subsistence, the true definition of independence; and to bear those bodily inconveniencies and exertions that are requisite to strengthen the mind.

Let us then, by being allowed to take the same exercise as boys, not only during infancy, but youth, arrive at perfection of body, that we may know how far the natural superiority of man extends. For what reason or virtue can be expected from a creature when the seed-time of life is neglected? None – did not the winds of heaven casually scatter many useful seeds in the fallow ground.

"Beauty cannot be acquired by dress, and coquetry is an art not so early and speedily attained. While girls are yet young, however, they are in a capacity to study agreeable gesture, a pleasing modulation of voice, an easy carriage and behaviour; as well as to take the advantage of gracefully adapting their looks and attitudes to time, place, and occasion. Their application, therefore, should not be solely confined to the arts of industry and the needle, when they come to display other talents, whose utility is already apparent."[1]

"For my part, I would have a young Englishwoman cultivate her agreeable talents, in order to please her future husband, with as much care and assiduity as a young Circassian cultivates her's, to fit her for the Haram of an Eastern bashaw."[2]

To render women completely insignificant, he adds – "The tongues of women are very voluble; they speak earlier, more readily, and more agreeably, than the men; they are accused also of speaking much more: but so it ought to be, and I should be very ready to convert this reproach into a compliment; their lips and eyes have the same activity, and for the same reason. A man speaks of what he knows, a woman of what pleases her; the one requires knowledge, the other taste; the principal object of a man's discourse should be what is useful, that of a woman's what is agreeable. There ought to be nothing in common between their different conversation but truth."

"We ought not, therefore, to restrain the prattle of girls, in the same manner as we should that of boys, with that severe question; *To what purpose are you talking?* but by another, which is no less difficult to

---

1 [Rousseau, *Emile* 373.]
2 [Rousseau, *Emile* 374 (Circassia, on the northeastern coast of the Black Sea, was proverbial for the beauty of its women). Cf. Macaulay, *Letters* 48-49, 61.]

answer, *How will your discourse be received?* In infancy, while they are as
yet incapable to discern good from evil, they ought to observe it, as a
law, never to say any thing disagreeable to those whom they are
speaking to: what will render the practice of this rule also the more
difficult, is, that it must ever be subordinate to the former, of never
speaking falsely or telling an untruth."[1] To govern the tongue in this
manner must require great address indeed; and it is too much practised both by men and women. – Out of the abundance of the heart
how few speak![2] So few, that I, who love simplicity, would gladly give
up politeness for a quarter of the virtue that has been sacrificed to an
equivocal quality which at best should only be the polish of virtue.

But, to complete the sketch. "It is easy to be conceived, that if male
children be not in a capacity to form any true notions of religion,
those ideas must be greatly above the conception of the females: it is
for this very reason, I would begin to speak to them the earlier on this
subject; for if we were to wait till they were in a capacity to discuss
methodically such profound questions, we should run a risk of never
speaking to them on this subject as long as they lived. Reason in
women is a practical reason, capacitating them artfully to discover the
means of attaining a known end, but which would never enable them
to discover that end itself. The social relations of the sexes are indeed
truly admirable: from their union there results a moral person, of
which woman may be termed the eyes, and man the hand, with this
dependence on each other, that it is from the man that the woman is
to learn what she is to see, and it is of the woman that man is to learn
what he ought to do. If woman could recur to the first principles of
things as well as man, and man was capacitated to enter into their
*minutiae* as well as woman, always independent of each other, they
would live in perpetual discord, and their union could not subsist. But
in the present harmony which naturally subsists between them, their
different faculties tend to one common end; it is difficult to say which
of them conduces the most to it: each follows the impulse of the
other; each is obedient, and both are masters."

"As the conduct of a woman is subservient to the public opinion,
her faith in matters of religion should, for that very reason, be subject

1    [Rousseau, *Emile* 376.]
2    [Cf. Matthew 12: 34. Wollstonecraft inverts the meaning of the original.]

to authority. *Every daughter ought to be of the same religion as her mother, and every wife to be of the same religion as her husband: for, though such religion should be false, that docility which induces the mother and daughter to submit to the order of nature, takes away, in the sight of God, the criminality of their error*[1]. As they are not in a capacity to judge for themselves, they ought to abide by the decision of their fathers and husbands as confidently as by that of the church."

"As authority ought to regulate the religion of the women, it is not so needful to explain to them the reasons for their belief, as to lay down precisely the tenets they are to believe: for the creed, which presents only obscure ideas to the mind, is the source of fanaticism; and that which presents absurdities, leads to infidelity."[2]

Absolute, uncontroverted authority, it seems, must subsist somewhere: but is not this a direct and exclusive appropriation of reason? The *rights* of humanity have been thus confined to the male line from Adam downwards. Rousseau would carry his male aristocracy still further, for he insinuates, that he should not blame those, who contend for leaving woman in a state of the most profound ignorance, if it were not necessary in order to preserve her chastity and justify the man's choice, in the eyes of the world, to give her a little knowledge of men, and the customs produced by human passions; else she might propagate at home without being rendered less voluptuous and innocent by the exercise of her understanding: excepting, indeed, during the first year of marriage, when she might employ it to dress like Sophia. "Her dress is extremely modest in appearance, and yet very coquettish in fact: she does not make a display of her charms, she conceals them; but in concealing them, she knows how to affect your imagination. Every one who sees her will say, There is a modest and discreet girl; but while you are near her, your eyes and affections wander all over her person, so that you cannot withdraw them; and you would conclude, that every part of her dress, simple as it seems, was only put in its proper order to be taken to pieces by the imagina-

---

1   What is to be the consequence, if the mother's and husband's opinion should *chance* not to agree? An ignorant person cannot be reasoned out of an error – and when *persuaded* to give up one prejudice for another the mind is unsettled. Indeed, the husband may not have any religion to teach her, though in such a situation she will be in great want of a support to her virtue, independent of worldly considerations.

2   [Rousseau, *Emile* 377-78; Wollstonecraft's italics.]

tion."[1] Is this modesty? Is this a preparation for immortality? Again. – What opinion are we to form of a system of education, when the author says of his heroine, "that with her, doing things well, is but a *secondary* concern; her principal concern is to do them *neatly.*"[2]

Secondary, in fact, are all her virtues and qualities, for, respecting religion, he makes her parents thus address her, accustomed to submission – "Your husband will instruct you in *good time.*"[3]

After thus cramping a woman's mind, if, in order to keep it fair, he have not made it quite a blank, he advises her to reflect, that a reflecting man may not yawn in her company, when he is tired of caressing her. – What has she to reflect about who must obey? and would it not be a refinement on cruelty only to open her mind to make the darkness and misery of her fate *visible?*[4] Yet, these are his sensible remarks; how consistent with what I have already been obliged to quote, to give a fair view of the subject, the reader may determine.

"They who pass their whole lives in working for their daily bread, have no ideas beyond their business or their interest, and all their understanding seems to lie in their fingers' ends. This ignorance is neither prejudicial to their integrity nor their morals; it is often of service to them. Sometimes, by means of reflection, we are led to compound with our duty, and we conclude by substituting a jargon of words, in the room of things. Our own conscience is the most enlightened philosopher. There is no need to be acquainted with Tully's offices,[5] to make a man of probity: and perhaps the most virtuous woman in the world, is the least acquainted with the definition of virtue. But it is no less true, that an improved understanding only can render society agreeable; and it is a melancholy thing for a father of a family, who is fond of home, to be obliged to be always wrapped up in himself, and to have nobody about him to whom he can impart his sentiments.

"Besides, how should a woman void of reflection be capable of educating her children? How should she discern what is proper for

1  [Rousseau, *Emile* 394; cf. 417.]
2  [Rousseau, *Emile* 395; Wollstonecraft's italics.]
3  [Rousseau, *Emile* 397; Wollstonecraft's italics.]
4  [Milton, *Paradise Lost* 1.63.]
5  [*De Officiis*, by Marcus Tullius Cicero (106-43 B.C.), deals with probity and virtue, among other subjects.]

them? How should she incline them to those virtues she is unacquainted with, or to that merit of which she has no idea? She can only sooth or chide them; render them insolent or timid; she will make them formal coxcombs, or ignorant blockheads; but will never make them sensible or amiable."[1] How indeed should she, when her husband is not always at hand to lend her his reason? – when they both together make but one moral being. A blind will, "eyes without hands," would go a very little way; and perchance his abstract reason, that should concentrate the scattered beams of her practical reason, may be employed in judging of the flavour of wine, descanting on the sauces most proper for turtle; or, more profoundly intent at a card-table, he may be generalizing his ideas as he bets away his fortune, leaving all the *minutiae* of education to his helpmate, or to chance.

But, granting that woman ought to be beautiful, innocent, and silly, to render her a more alluring and indulgent companion; – what is her understanding sacrificed for? And why is all this preparation necessary only, according to Rousseau's own account, to make her the mistress of her husband, a very short time? For no man ever insisted more on the transient nature of love. Thus speaks the philosopher. "Sensual pleasures are transient. The habitual state of the affections always loses by their gratification. The imagination, which decks the object of our desires, is lost in fruition. Excepting the Supreme Being, who is self-existent, there is nothing beautiful but what is ideal."[2]

But he returns to his unintelligible paradoxes again, when he thus addresses Sophia. "Emilius, in becoming your husband, is become your master; and claims your obedience. Such is the order of nature. When a man is married, however, to such a wife as Sophia, it is proper he should be directed by her: this is also agreeable to the order of nature: it is, therefore, to give you as much authority over his heart as his sex gives him over your person, that I have made you the arbiter of his pleasures. It may cost you, perhaps, some disagreeable self-denial; but you will be certain of maintaining your empire over him, if you can preserve it over yourself – what I have already observed, also, shows me, that this difficult attempt does not surpass your courage.

"Would you have your husband constantly at your feet? keep him

1   [Rousseau, *Emile* 408-9.]
2   [Rousseau, *Emile* 447.]

at some distance from your person. You will long maintain the authority in love, if you know but how to render your favours rare and valuable. It is thus you may employ even the arts of coquetry in the service of virtue, and those of love in that of reason."[1]

I shall close my extracts with a just description of a comfortable couple. "And yet you must not imagine, that even such management will always suffice. Whatever precaution be taken, enjoyment will, by degrees, take off the edge of passion. But when love hath lasted as long as possible, a pleasing habitude supplies its place, and the attachment of a mutual confidence succeeds to the transports of passion. Children often form a more agreeable and permanent connection between married people than even love itself. When you cease to be the mistress of Emilius, you will continue to be his wife and friend, you will be the mother of his children[2]."

Children, he truly observes, form a much more permanent connexion between married people than love. Beauty, he declares, will not be valued, or even seen after a couple have lived six months together; artificial graces and coquetry will likewise pall on the senses: why then does he say that a girl should be educated for her husband with the same care as for an eastern haram?

I now appeal from the reveries of fancy and refined licentiousness to the good sense of mankind, whether, if the object of education be to prepare women to become chaste wives and sensible mothers, the method so plausibly recommended in the foregoing sketch, be the one best calculated to produce those ends? Will it be allowed that the surest way to make a wife chaste, is to teach her to practise the wanton arts of a mistress, termed virtuous coquetry, by the sensualist who can no longer relish the artless charms of sincerity, or taste the pleasure arising from a tender intimacy, when confidence is unchecked by suspicion, and rendered interesting by sense?

The man who can be contented to live with a pretty, useful companion, without a mind, has lost in voluptuous gratifications a taste for more refined enjoyments; he has never felt the calm satisfaction, that refreshes the parched heart, like the silent dew of heaven, – of being beloved by one who could understand him. – In the society of

1    [Rousseau, *Emile* 478-79.]
2    Rousseau's Emilius. [479.]

his wife he is still alone, unless when the man is sunk in the brute. "The charm of life," says a grave philosophical reasoner, is "sympathy; nothing pleases us more than to observe in other men a fellow-feeling with all the emotions of our own breast."[1]

But, according to the tenour of reasoning, by which women are kept from the tree of knowledge, the important years of youth, the usefulness of age, and the rational hopes of futurity, are all to be sacrificed to render women an object of desire for a *short* time. Besides, how could Rousseau expect them to be virtuous and constant when reason is neither allowed to be the foundation of their virtue, nor truth the object of their inquiries?

But all Rousseau's errors in reasoning arose from sensibility, and sensibility to their charms women are very ready to forgive! When he should have reasoned he became impassioned, and reflection inflamed his imagination instead of enlightening his understanding. Even his virtues also led him farther astray; for, born with a warm constitution and lively fancy, nature carried him toward the other sex with such eager fondness, that he soon became lascivious. Had he given way to these desires, the fire would have extinguished itself in a natural manner; but virtue, and a romantic kind of delicacy, made him practise self-denial; yet, when fear, delicacy, or virtue, restrained him, he debauched his imagination, and reflecting on the sensations to which fancy gave force, he traced them in the most glowing colours, and sunk them deep into his soul.[2]

He then sought for solitude, not sleep[3] with the man of nature; or calmly investigate the causes of things under the shade where Sir Isaac Newton indulged contemplation, but merely to indulge his feelings. And so warmly has he painted, what he forcibly felt, that, interesting the heart and inflaming the imagination of his readers; in proportion to the strength of their fancy, they imagine that their understanding is convinced when they only sympathize with a poetic writer, who skilfully exhibits the objects of sense, most voluptuously shadowed or gracefully veiled – And thus making us feel whilst dreaming that we

---

1   [Smith, *Theory* 13; 1.1.2.1.]
2   [Rousseau, *Confessions* 398. He recommends the same practice for his pupil (*Emile* 329).]
3   [The first edition reads "not to sleep."]

reason, erroneous conclusions are left in the mind.

Why was Rousseau's life divided between ecstasy and misery? Can any other answer be given than this, that the effervescence of his imagination produced both; but, had his fancy been allowed to cool, it is possible that he might have acquired more strength of mind. Still, if the purpose of life be to educate the intellectual part of man, all with respect to him was right; yet, had not death led to a nobler scene of action, it is probable that he would have enjoyed more equal happiness on earth, and have felt the calm sensations of the man of nature instead of being prepared for another stage of existence by nourishing the passions which agitate the civilized man.

But peace to his manes! I war not with his ashes, but his opinions. I war only with the sensibility that led him to degrade woman by making her the slave of love.

> ———"Curs'd vassalage,
> First idoliz'd till love's hot fire be o'er,
> Then slaves to those who courted us before."
>
> *Dryden.*[1]

The pernicious tendency of those books, in which the writers insidiously degrade the sex whilst they are prostrate before their personal charms, cannot be too often or too severely exposed

Let us, my dear contemporaries, arise above such narrow prejudices! If wisdom be desirable on its own account, if virtue, to deserve the name, must be founded on knowledge; let us endeavour to strengthen our minds by reflection, till our heads become a balance for our hearts; let us not confine all our thoughts to the petty occurrences of the day, or our knowledge to an acquaintance with our lovers' or husbands' hearts; but let the practice of every duty be subordinate to the grand one of improving our minds, and preparing our affections for a more exalted state!

Beware then, my friends, of suffering the heart to be moved by every trivial incident: the reed is shaken by a breeze, and annually dies, but the oak stands firm, and for ages braves the storm!

---

1  [John Dryden (1631-1700), *The State of Innocence: and Fall of Man* (1677) 5.1.58-60. The speaker is Eve.]

Were we, indeed, only created to flutter our hour out and die –
why let us then indulge sensibility, and laugh at the severity of reason.
– Yet, alas! even then we should want strength of body and mind, and
life would be lost in feverish pleasures or wearisome languor.

But the system of education, which I earnestly wish to see exploded, seems to presuppose what ought never to be taken for granted,
that virtue shields us from the casualties of life; and that fortune, slip-
ping off her bandage,[1] will smile on a well-educated female, and bring
in her hand an Emilius or a Telemachus.[2] Whilst, on the contrary, the
reward which virtue promises to her votaries is confined, it seems
clear, to their own bosoms; and often must they contend with the
most vexatious worldly cares, and bear with the vices and humours of
relations for whom they can never feel a friendship.

There have been many women in the world who, instead of being
supported by the reason and virtue of their fathers and brothers, have
strengthened their own minds by struggling with their vices and follies; yet have never met with a hero, in the shape of a husband; who,
paying the debt that mankind owed them, might chance to bring
back their reason to its natural dependent state, and restore the
usurped prerogative, of rising above opinion, to man.

## SECT. II

DR. FORDYCE's sermons[3] have long made a part of a young
woman's library; nay, girls at school are allowed to read them; but I
should instantly dismiss them from my pupil's, if I wished to strength-
en her understanding, by leading her to form sound principles on a
broad basis; or, were I only anxious to cultivate her taste; though they
must be allowed to contain many sensible observations.

Dr. Fordyce may have had a very laudable end in view; but these
discourses are written in such an affected style, that were it only on

---

1 [Blindfold.]
2 [Telemachus is the hero of *The Adventures of Telemachus, Son of Ulysses* (1699), by
   François de Salignac de la Mothe-Fénelon (1651-1715). Rousseau's Sophie reads
   the book and falls in love with him (*Emile* 403-5, 414).]
3 [James Fordyce (1720-96), *Sermons to Young Women* (1765).]

that account, and had I nothing to object against his *mellifluous* precepts, I should not allow girls to peruse them, unless I designed to hunt every spark of nature out of their composition, melting every human quality into female meekness and artificial grace. I say artificial, for true grace arises from some kind of independence of mind.

Children, careless of pleasing, and only anxious to amuse themselves, are often very graceful; and the nobility who have mostly lived with inferiors, and always had the command of money, acquire a graceful ease of deportment, which should rather be termed habitual grace of body, than that superiour gracefulness which is truly the expression of the mind. This mental grace, not noticed by vulgar eyes, often flashes across a rough countenance, and irradiating every feature, shows simplicity and independence of mind. – It is then we read characters of immortality in the eye, and see the soul in every gesture, though when at rest, neither the face nor limbs may have much beauty to recommend them; or the behaviour, any thing peculiar to attract universal attention. The mass of mankind, however, look for more *tangible* beauty; yet simplicity is, in general, admired, when people do not consider what they admire; and can there be simplicity without sincerity? But, to have done with remarks that are in some measure desultory, though naturally excited by the subject –

In declamatory periods Dr. Fordyce spins out Rousseau's eloquence; and in most sentimental rant, details his opinions respecting the female character, and the behaviour which woman ought to assume to render her lovely.

He shall speak for himself, for thus he makes Nature address man. "Behold these smiling innocents, whom I have graced with my fairest gifts, and committed to your protection; behold them with love and respect; treat them with tenderness and honour. They are timid and want to be defended. They are frail; O do not take advantage of their weakness! Let their fears and blushes endear them. Let their confidence in you never be abused. – But is it possible, that any of you can be such barbarians, so supremely wicked, as to abuse it? Can you find in your hearts[1] to despoil the gentle, trusting creatures of their treasure, or do any thing to strip them of their native robe of virtue?

---

1  Can you? – Can you? would be the most emphatical comment, were it drawled out in a whining voice.

Curst be the impious hand that would dare to violate the unblem-
ished form of Chastity! Thou wretch! thou ruffian! forbear; nor venture to provoke heaven's fiercest vengeance."¹ I know not any
comment that can be made seriously on this curious passage, and I
could produce many similar ones; and some, so very sentimental, that
I have heard rational men use the word indecent, when they mentioned them with disgust.

Throughout there is a display of cold artificial feelings, and that
parade of sensibility which boys and girls should be taught to despise
as the sure mark of a little vain mind. Florid appeals are made to heav-
en, and to the *beauteous innocents*, the fairest images of heaven here
below, whilst sober sense is left far behind. – This is not the language
of the heart, nor will it ever reach it, though the ear may be tickled.

I shall be told, perhaps, that the public have been pleased with
these volumes. – True – and Hervey's Meditations² are still read,
though he equally sinned against sense and taste.

I particularly object to the lover-like phrases of pumped up passion, which are every where interspersed. If women be ever allowed
to walk without leading-strings, why must they be cajoled into virtue
by artful flattery and sexual compliments? – Speak to them the language of truth and soberness, and away with the lullaby strains of condescending endearment! Let them be taught to respect themselves as
rational creatures, and not led to have a passion for their own insipid
persons. It moves my gall to hear a preacher descanting on dress and
needle-work; and still more, to hear him address the *British fair, the
fairest of the fair*, as if they had only feelings.³

Even recommending piety he uses the following argument.
"Never, perhaps, does a fine woman strike more deeply, than when,
composed into pious recollection, and possessed with the noblest
considerations, she assumes, without knowing it, superiour dignity
and new graces; so that the beauties of holiness seem to radiate about
her, and the by-standers are almost induced to fancy her already worshipping amongst her kindred angels!"⁴ Why are women to be thus

---

1  [Fordyce, *Sermons* 63.]
2  [James Hervey (1714-58), *Meditations and Contemplations* (1745-47).]
3  [Fordyce, *Sermons* 30. In fact, Fordyce's use of the phrase is sarcastic.]
4  [Fordyce, *Sermons* 275-76.]

bred up with a desire of conquest? the very word, used in this sense, gives me a sickly qualm! Do religion and virtue offer no stronger motives, no brighter reward? Must they always be debased by being made to consider the sex of their companions? Must they be taught always to be pleasing? And when levelling their small artillery at the heart of man, is it necessary to tell them that a little sense is sufficient to render their attention *incredibly soothing?* "As a small degree of knowledge entertains in a woman, so from a woman, though for a different reason, a small expression of kindness delights, particularly if she have beauty!"[1] I should have supposed for the same reason.

Why are girls to be told that they resemble angels; but to sink them below women? Or, that a gentle innocent female is an object that comes nearer to the idea which we have formed of angels than any other. Yet they are told, at the same time, that they are only like angels when they are young and beautiful; consequently, it is their persons, not their virtues, that procure them this homage.

Idle empty words! What can such delusive flattery lead to, but vanity and folly? The lover, it is true, has a poetical licence to exalt his mistress; his reason is the bubble of his passion, and he does not utter a falsehood when he borrows the language of adoration. His imagination may raise the idol of his heart, unblamed, above humanity; and happy would it be for women, if they were only flattered by the men who loved them; I mean, who love the individual, not the sex; but should a grave preacher interlard his discourses with such fooleries?

In sermons or novels, however, voluptuousness is always true to its text. Men are allowed by moralists to cultivate, as Nature directs, different qualities, and assume the different characters, that the same passions, modified almost to infinity, give to each individual. A virtuous man may have a choleric or a sanguine constitution, be gay or grave, unreproved; be firm till he is almost overbearing, or, weakly submissive, have no will or opinion of his own; but all women are to be levelled, by meekness and docility, into one character of yielding softness and gentle compliance.

I will use the preacher's own words. "Let it be observed, that in your sex manly exercises are never graceful; that in them a tone and

---

1  [Fordyce, *Sermons* 324.]

figure, as well as an air and deportment, of the masculine kind, are always forbidding; and that men of sensibility desire in every woman soft features, and a flowing voice, a form, not robust, and demeanour delicate and gentle."[1]

Is not the following portrait – the portrait of a house slave? "I am astonished at the folly of many women, who are still reproaching their husbands for leaving them alone, for preferring this or that company to theirs, for treating them with this and the other mark of disregard or indifference; when, to speak the truth, they have themselves in a great measure to blame. Not that I would justify the men in any thing wrong on their part. But had you behaved to them with more *respectful observance*, and a more *equal tenderness; studying their humours, overlooking their mistakes, submitting to their opinions* in matters indifferent, passing by little instances of unevenness, caprice, or passion, giving *soft* answers to hasty words, complaining as seldom as possible, and making it your daily care to relieve their anxieties and prevent their wishes, to enliven the hour of dulness, and call up the ideas of felicity: had you pursued this conduct, I doubt not but you would have maintained and even increased their esteem, so far as to have secured every degree of influence that could conduce to their virtue, or your mutual satisfaction; and your house might at this day have been the abode of domestic bliss."[2] Such a woman ought to be an angel – or she is an ass – for I discern not a trace of the human character, neither reason nor passion in this domestic drudge, whose being is absorbed in that of a tyrant's.

Still Dr. Fordyce must have very little acquaintance with the human heart, if he really supposed that such conduct would bring back wandering love, instead of exciting contempt. No, beauty, gentleness, &c. &c. may gain a heart; but esteem, the only lasting affection, can alone be obtained by virtue supported by reason. It is respect for the understanding that keeps alive tenderness for the person.

As these volumes are so frequently put into the hands of young people, I have taken more notice of them than, strictly speaking, they deserve; but as they have contributed to vitiate the taste, and enervate the understanding of many of my fellow-creatures, I could not pass them silently over.

---

1    [Fordyce, *Sermons* 308.]
2    [Fordyce, *Sermons* 332; Wollstonecraft's italics.]

SUCH paternal solicitude pervades Dr. Gregory's *Legacy to his Daughters*, that I enter on the task of criticism with affectionate respect; but as this little volume has many attractions to recommend it to the notice of the most respectable part of my sex, I cannot silently pass over arguments that so speciously support opinions which, I think, have had the most baneful effect on the morals and manners of the female world.

His easy familiar style is particularly suited to the tenor of his advice, and the melancholy tenderness which his respect for the memory of a beloved wife, diffuses through the whole work, renders it very interesting; yet there is a degree of concise elegance conspicuous in many passages that disturbs this sympathy; and we pop on the author, when we only expected to meet the – father.

Besides, having two objects in view, he seldom adhered steadily to either; for wishing to make his daughters amiable, and fearing lest unhappiness should only be the consequence, of instilling sentiments that might draw them out of the track of common life without enabling them to act with consonant independence and dignity, he checks the natural flow of his thoughts, and neither advises one thing nor the other.

In the preface he tells them a mournful truth, "that they will hear, at least once in their lives, the genuine sentiments of a man who has no interest in deceiving them."[1]

Hapless woman! what can be expected from thee when the beings on whom thou art said naturally to depend for reason and support, have all an interest in deceiving thee! This is the root of the evil that has shed a corroding mildew on all thy virtues; and blighting in the bud thy opening faculties, has rendered thee the weak thing thou art! It is this separate interest – this insidious state of warfare, that undermines morality, and divides mankind!

If love have made some women wretched – how many more has the cold unmeaning intercourse of gallantry rendered vain and useless! yet this heartless attention to the sex is reckoned so manly, so

---

1  [Gregory, *Legacy* 6.]

polite that, till society is very differently organized, I fear, this vestige of gothic manners will not be done away by a more reasonable and affectionate mode of conduct. Besides, to strip it of its imaginary dignity, I must observe, that in the most uncivilized European states this lip-service prevails in a very great degree, accompanied with extreme dissoluteness of morals. In Portugal, the country that I particularly allude to, it takes place of the most serious moral obligations; for a man is seldom assassinated when in the company of a woman. The savage hand of rapine is unnerved by this chivalrous spirit; and, if the stroke of vengeance cannot be stayed – the lady is entreated to pardon the rudeness and depart in peace, though sprinkled, perhaps, with her husband's or brother's blood.[1]

I shall pass over his strictures on religion, because I mean to discuss that subject in a separate chapter.

The remarks relative to behaviour, though many of them very sensible, I entirely disapprove of, because it appears to me to be beginning, as it were, at the wrong end. A cultivated understanding, and an affectionate heart, will never want starched rules of decorum – something more substantial than seemliness will be the result; and, without understanding the behaviour here recommended, would be rank affectation. Decorum, indeed, is the one thing needful![2] – decorum is to supplant nature, and banish all simplicity and variety of character out of the female world. Yet what good end can all this superficial counsel produce? It is, however, much easier to point out this or that mode of behaviour, than to set the reason to work; but, when the mind has been stored with useful knowledge, and strengthened by being employed, the regulation of the behaviour may safely be left to its guidance.

Why, for instance, should the following caution be given when art of every kind must contaminate the mind; and why entangle the grand motives of action, which reason and religion equally combine to enforce, with pitiful worldly shifts and slight of hand tricks to gain the applause of gaping tasteless fools? "Be even cautious in displaying your good sense[3]. It will be thought you assume a superiority over the

1   [Arthur William Costigan [James Ferrier], *Sketches of Society and Manners in Portugal* (London, 1787) 1: 400-3. Wollstonecraft reviewed it (*Works* 7: 29-32).]
2   [Cf. Luke 10: 42.]
3   Let women once acquire good sense – and if it deserve the name, it will teach them; or, of what use will it be? how to employ it.

rest of the company – But if you happen to have any learning, keep it a profound secret, especially from the men who generally look with a jealous and malignant eye on a woman of great parts, and a cultivated understanding."[1] If men of real merit, as he afterwards observes, be superior to this meanness, where is the necessity that the behaviour of the whole sex should be modulated to please fools, or men, who having little claim to respect as individuals, choose to keep close in their phalanx. Men, indeed, who insist on their common superiority, having only this sexual superiority, are certainly very excusable.

There would be no end to rules for behaviour, if it be proper always to adopt the tone of the company; for thus, for ever varying the key, a *flat* would often pass for a *natural* note.

Surely it would have been wiser to have advised women to improve themselves till they rose above the fumes of vanity; and then to let the public opinion come round – for where are rules of accommodation to stop? The narrow path of truth and virtue inclines neither to the right nor left[2] – it is a straightforward business, and they who are earnestly pursuing their road, may bound over many decorous prejudices, without leaving modesty behind. Make the heart clean,[3] and give the head employment, and I will venture to predict that there will be nothing offensive in the behaviour.

The air of fashion, which many young people are so eager to attain, always strikes me like the studied attitudes of some modern pictures, copied with tasteless servility after the antiques; – the soul is left out, and none of the parts are tied together by what may properly be termed character. This varnish of fashion, which seldom sticks very close to sense, may dazzle the weak; but leave nature to itself, and it will seldom disgust the wise. Besides, when a woman has sufficient sense not to pretend to any thing which she does not understand in some degree, there is no need of determining to hide her talents under a bushel.[4] Let things take their natural course, and all will be well.

It is this system of dissimulation, throughout the volume, that I

---

1   [Gregory, *Legacy* 31-32.]
2   [Cf. Matthew 7: 14.]
3   [Cf. Psalms 51.10.]
4   [Wollstonecraft combines the parables of the candle (Matthew 5: 15, Mark 4: 21, Luke 11: 33) and of the talents (Matthew 25: 14-30).]

despise. Women are always to *seem* to be this and that – yet virtue might apostrophize them, in the words of Hamlet – Seems! I know not seems! – Have that within that passeth show! – [1]

Still the same tone occurs; for in another place, after recommending, without sufficiently discriminating delicacy, he adds, "The men will complain of your reserve. They will assure you that a franker behaviour would make you more amiable. But, trust me, they are not sincere when they tell you so. – I acknowledge that on some occasions it might render you more agreeable as companions, but it would make you less amiable as women: an important distinction, which many of your sex are not aware of."[2] –

This desire of being always women, is the very consciousness that degrades the sex. Excepting with a lover, I must repeat with emphasis, a former observation, – it would be well if they were only agreeable or rational companions. – But in this respect his advice is even inconsistent with a passage which I mean to quote with the most marked approbation.

"The sentiment, that a woman may allow all innocent freedoms, provided her virtue is secure, is both grossly indelicate and dangerous, and has proved fatal to many of your sex."[3] With this opinion I perfectly coincide. A man, or a woman, of any feeling, must always wish to convince a beloved object that it is the caresses of the individual, not the sex, that are received and returned with pleasure; and, that the heart, rather than the senses, is moved. Without this natural delicacy, love becomes a selfish personal gratification that soon degrades the character.

I carry this sentiment still further. Affection, when love is out of the question, authorises many personal endearments, that naturally flowing from an innocent heart, give life to the behaviour; but the personal intercourse of appetite, gallantry, or vanity, is despicable. When a man squeezes the hand of a pretty woman, handing her to a carriage, whom he has never seen before, she will consider such an impertinent freedom in the light of an insult, if she have any true delicacy, instead of being flattered by this unmeaning homage to beauty.

---

1  [Shakespeare, *Hamlet* 1.2.76, 85.]
2  [Gregory, *Legacy* 36-37.]
3  [Gregory, *Legacy* 44.]

These are the privileges of friendship, or the momentary homage which the heart pays to virtue, when it flashes suddenly on the notice – mere animal spirits have no claim to the kindnesses of affection!

Wishing to feed the affections with what is now the food of vanity, I would fain persuade my sex to act from simpler principles. Let them merit love, and they will obtain it, though they may never be told that – "The power of a fine woman over the hearts of men, of men of the finest parts, is even beyond what she conceives."[1]

I have already noticed the narrow cautions with respect to duplicity, female softness, delicacy of constitution;[2] for these are the changes which he rings round without ceasing – in a more decorous manner, it is true, than Rousseau; but it all comes home to the same point, and whoever is at the trouble to analyze these sentiments, will find the first principles not quite so delicate as the superstructure.

The subject of amusements is treated in too cursory a manner; but with the same spirit.

When I treat of friendship, love, and marriage, it will be found that we materially differ in opinion; I shall not then forestall what I have to observe on these important subjects; but confine my remarks to the general tenor of them, to that cautious family prudence, to those confined views of partial unenlightened affection, which exclude pleasure and improvement, by vainly wishing to ward off sorrow and error – and by thus guarding the heart and mind, destroy also all their energy. – It is far better to be often deceived than never to trust; to be disappointed in love than never to love; to lose a husband's fondness than forfeit his esteem.

Happy would it be for the world, and for individuals, of course, if all this unavailing solicitude to attain worldly happiness, on a confined plan, were turned into an anxious desire to improve the understanding. – "Wisdom is the principal thing: *therefore* get wisdom; and with all thy gettings get understanding." – "How long, ye simple ones, will ye love simplicity, and hate knowledge?"[3] Saith Wisdom to the daughters of men! –

---

1   [Gregory, *Legacy* 42.]
2   [Gregory, *Legacy* 50–51.]
3   [Proverbs 4: 7, 1: 22.]

I DO not mean to allude to all the writers who have written on the subject of female manners – it would, in fact, be only beating over the old ground, for they have, in general, written in the same strain; but attacking the boasted prerogative of man – the prerogative that may emphatically be called the iron sceptre of tyranny, the original sin of tyrants, I declare against all power built on prejudices, however hoary.[1]

If the submission demanded be founded on justice – there is no appealing to a higher power – for God is Justice itself. Let us then, as children of the same parent, if not bastardized by being the younger born, reason together,[2] and learn to submit to the authority of reason – when her voice is distinctly heard. But, if it be proved, that this throne of prerogative only rests on a chaotic mass of prejudices, that have no inherent principle of order to keep them together, or on an elephant, tortoise, or even the mighty shoulders of a son of the earth,[3] they may escape, who dare to brave the consequence, without any breach of duty, without sinning against the order of things.

Whilst reason raises man above the brutal herd, and death is big with promises, they alone are subject to blind authority who have no reliance on their own strength. "They are free – who will be free[4]!" –

The being who can govern itself has nothing to fear in life; but if any thing be dearer than its own respect, the price must be paid to the last farthing. Virtue, like every thing valuable, must be loved for herself alone; or she will not take up her abode with us. She will not impart that peace, "which passeth understanding,"[5] when she is merely made the stilts of reputation; and respected, with pharisaical exactness,

---

1 [Burke, *Reflections*; *Writings* 8: 138; Appendix A.4.ii.]
2 [Isaiah 1: 18.]
3 [In the Indian cosmology, the earth was supported by three elephants, which stood on the back of a tortoise; in Greek mythology, the Titan Atlas was condemned to bear the weight of the heavens on his shoulders.]
4                  "He is the free man, whom the *truth* makes free!"

                                                  *Cowper.*

[William Cowper (1731-1800), *The Task* (1785) 5.733, quoting John 8: 32; Wollstonecraft's italics. Wollstonecraft included several excerpts from Cowper in *The Female Reader.*]
5 [Philippians 4: 7.]

because "honesty is the best policy."

That the plan of life which enables us to carry some knowledge and virtue into another world, is the one best calculated to ensure content in this, cannot be denied; yet few people act according to this principle, though it be universally allowed that it admits not of dispute. Present pleasure, or present power, carry before it these sober convictions; and it is for the day, not for life, that man bargains with happiness. How few! – how very few! have sufficient foresight, or resolution, to endure a small evil at the moment, to avoid a greater hereafter.

Woman in particular, whose virtue[1] is built on mutable prejudices, seldom attains to this greatness of mind; so that, becoming the slave of her own feelings, she is easily subjugated by those of others. Thus degraded, her reason, her misty reason! is employed rather to burnish than to snap her chains.

Indignantly have I heard women argue in the same track as men, and adopt the sentiments that brutalize them, with all the pertinacity of ignorance.

I must illustrate my assertion by a few examples. Mrs. Piozzi,[2] who often repeated by rote, what she did not understand, comes forward with Johnsonian periods.

"Seek not for happiness in singularity; and dread a refinement of wisdom as a deviation into folly." Thus she dogmatically addresses a new married man; and to elucidate this pompous exordium, she adds, "I said that the person of your lady would not grow more pleasing to you, but pray let her never suspect that it grows less so: that a woman will pardon an affront to her understanding much sooner than one to her person, is well known; nor will any of us contradict the assertion. All our attainments, all our arts, are employed to gain and keep the heart of man; and what mortification can exceed the disappointment, if the end be not obtained? There is no reproof however pointed, no punishment however severe, that a woman of spirit will not prefer to neglect; and if she can endure it without complaint, it only proves that she means to make herself amends by the attention of others for the

---

1 I mean to use a word that comprehends more than chastity the sexual virtue.
2 [Hester Lynch Thrale Piozzi (1741-1821), author of *Anecdotes of the Late Samuel Johnson* (1786).]

slights of her husband!"[1]

These are truly masculine sentiments. – "All our *arts* are employed to gain and keep the heart of man:" – and what is the inference? – if her person, and was there ever a person, though formed with Medicean symmetry,[2] that was not slighted? be neglected, she will make herself amends by endeavouring to please other men. Noble morality! But thus is the understanding of the whole sex affronted, and their virtue deprived of the common basis of virtue. A woman must know, that her person cannot be as pleasing to her husband as it was to her lover, and if she be offended with him for being a human creature, she may as well whine about the loss of his heart as about any other foolish thing. – And this very want of discernment or unreasonable anger, proves that he could not change his fondness for her person into affection for her virtues or respect for her understanding.

Whilst women avow, and act up to such opinions, their understandings, at least, deserve the contempt and obloquy that men, *who never* insult their persons, have pointedly levelled at the female mind. And it is the sentiments of these polite men, who do not wish to be encumbered with mind, that vain women thoughtlessly adopt. Yet they should know, that insulted reason alone can spread that *sacred* reserve about the person, which renders human affections, for human affections have always some base alloy, as permanent as is consistent with the grand end of existence – the attainment of virtue.

The Baroness de Stael speaks the same language as the lady just cited, with more enthusiasm. Her eulogium on Rousseau was accidentally put into my hands, and her sentiments, the sentiments of too many of my sex, may serve as the text for a few comments. "Though Rousseau," she observes, "has endeavoured to prevent women from interfering in public affairs, and acting a brilliant part in the theatre of politics; yet in speaking of them, how much has he done it to their satisfaction! If he wished to deprive them of some rights foreign to their sex, how has he for ever restored to them all those to which it has a claim! And in attempting to diminish their influence over the

---

1  [Piozzi, *Letters to and from the Late Samuel Johnson* (1788) 98–100; letter 72.]
2  [An allusion to the famous Greek statue, the Venus de' Medici, in the Uffizzi Gallery, Florence.]

deliberations of men, how sacredly has he established the empire they have over their happiness! In aiding them to descend from an usurped throne, he has firmly seated them upon that to which they were destined by nature; and though he be full of indignation against them when they endeavour to resemble men, yet when they come before him with all the *charms, weaknesses, virtues* and *errors*, of their sex, his respect for their *persons* amounts almost to adoration." True! – For never was there a sensualist who paid more fervent adoration at the shrine of beauty. So devout, indeed, was his respect for the person, that excepting the virtue of chastity, for obvious reasons, he only wished to see it embellished by charms, weaknesses, and errors. He was afraid lest the austerity of reason should disturb the soft playfulness of love. The master wished to have a meretricious slave to fondle, entirely dependent on his reason and bounty; he did not want a companion, whom he should be compelled to esteem, or a friend to whom he could confide the care of his children's education, should death deprive them of their father, before he had fulfilled the sacred task. He denies woman reason, shuts her out from knowledge, and turns her aside from truth; yet his pardon is granted, because "he admits the passion of love." It would require some ingenuity to shew why women were to be under such an obligation to him for thus admitting love; when it is clear that he admits it only for the relaxation of men, and to perpetuate the species; but he talked with passion, and that powerful spell worked on the sensibility of a young encomiast. "What signifies it," pursues this rhapsodist, "to women, that his reason disputes with them the empire, when his heart is devotedly theirs."[1] It is not empire, – but equality, that they should contend for. Yet, if they only wished to lengthen out their sway, they should not entirely trust to their persons, for though beauty may gain a heart, it cannot keep it, even while the beauty is in full bloom, unless the mind lend, at least, some graces.

When women are once sufficiently enlightened to discover their real interest, on a grand scale, they will, I am persuaded, be very ready to resign all the prerogatives of love, that are not mutual, speaking of

---

1   [Anne-Louise-Germaine, baronne de Staël (1766–1817), *Letters on the Works and Characters of J. J. Rousseau* (1788; trans. 1789) 15–16. Wollstonecraft reviewed it (*Works* 7: 136–37).]

them as lasting prerogatives, for the calm satisfaction of friendship, and the tender confidence of habitual esteem. Before marriage they will not assume any insolent airs, or afterwards abjectly submit; but endeavouring to act like reasonable creatures, in both situations, they will not be tumbled from a throne to a stool.

Madame Genlis has written several entertaining books for children; and her Letters on Education[1] afford many useful hints, that sensible parents will certainly avail themselves of; but her views are narrow, and her prejudices as unreasonable as strong.

I shall pass over her vehement argument in favour of the eternity of future punishments,[2] because I blush to think that a human being should ever argue vehemently in such a cause, and only make a few remarks on her absurd manner of making the parental authority supplant reason. For every where does she inculcate not only *blind* submission to parents; but to the opinion of the world[3].

She tells a story of a young man engaged by his father's express desire to a girl of fortune. Before the marriage could take place, she is deprived of her fortune, and thrown friendless on the world. The father practises the most infamous arts to separate his son from her, and when the son detects his villany, and following the dictates of honour marries the girl, nothing but misery ensues, because forsooth he married *without* his father's consent.[4] On what ground can religion or morality rest when justice is thus set at defiance? With the same view she represents an accomplished young woman, as ready to marry any body that her *mamma* pleased to recommend; and, as actually marrying the young man of her own choice, without feeling any

---

1  [Stéphanie-Félicité Ducrest de St. Aubin, comtesse de Genlis (1746-1830), *Adèle et Théodore, ou lettres sur l'education* (1782). Wollstonecraft reviewed translations of several of her works (*Works* 7: 82, 118, 413-14) and included her in *The Female Reader*.]
2  [Genlis, *Adelaide and Theodore* (trans. 1783) 1: 183, 225.]
3  A person is not to act in this or that way, though convinced they are right in so doing, because some equivocal circumstances may lead the world to *suspect* that they acted from different motives. – This is sacrificing the substance for a shadow. Let people but watch their own hearts, and act rightly, as far as they can judge, and they may patiently wait till the opinion of the world comes round. It is best to be directed by a simple motive – for justice has too often been sacrificed to propriety; – another word for convenience.
4  [Genlis, *Tales of the Castle*, trans. Thomas Holcroft (1785) chap. 3, "Theophilus and Olympia."]

emotions of passion, because that a well educated girl had not time to be in love.[1] Is it possible to have much respect for a system of education that thus insults reason and nature?

Many similar opinions occur in her writings, mixed with sentiments that do honour to her head and heart. Yet so much superstition is mixed with her religion, and so much worldly wisdom with her morality, that I should not let a young person read her works, unless I could afterwards converse on the subjects, and point out the contradictions.

Mrs. Chapone's Letters[2] are written with such good sense, and unaffected humility, and contain so many useful observations, that I only mention them to pay the worthy writer this tribute of respect. I cannot, it is true, always coincide in opinion with her; but I always respect her.

The very word respect brings Mrs. Macaulay to my remembrance. The woman of the greatest abilities, undoubtedly, that this country has ever produced. – And yet this woman has been suffered to die without sufficient respect being paid to her memory.[3]

Posterity, however, will be more just; and remember that Catharine Macaulay was an example of intellectual acquirements supposed to be incompatible with the weakness of her sex. In her style of writing, indeed, no sex appears, for it is like the sense it conveys, strong and clear.

I will not call hers a masculine understanding, because I admit not of such an arrogant assumption of reason; but I contend that it was a sound one, and that her judgment, the matured fruit of profound thinking, was a proof that a woman can acquire judgment, in the full extent of the word. Possessing more penetration than sagacity, more understanding than fancy, she writes with sober energy and argumentative closeness; yet sympathy and benevolence give an interest to her sentiments, and that vital heat to arguments, which forces the reader to weigh them[4].

---

1  [Genlis, *Adelaide and Theodore* 3: 237-38.]

2  [Hester Mulso Chapone (1727-1801), *Letters on the Improvement of the Mind: Addressed to a Lady* (1773). Wollstonecraft included excerpts from it in *The Female Reader*.]

3  [Macaulay died on 22 June 1791. Her reputation had suffered from her marriage, at the age of 47, to William Graham, 21.]

4  Coinciding in opinion with Mrs. Macaulay relative to many branches of education, I refer to her valuable work, instead of quoting her sentiments to support my own.

When I first thought of writing these strictures I anticipated Mrs. Macaulay's approbation, with a little of that sanguine ardour, which it has been the business of my life to depress; but soon heard with the sickly qualm of disappointed hope; and the still seriousness of regret – that she was no more!

## SECT. V.

TAKING a view of the different works which have been written on education, Lord Chesterfield's Letters must not be silently passed over. Not that I mean to analyze his unmanly, immoral system, or even to cull any of the useful, shrewd remarks which occur in his epistles – No, I only mean to make a few reflections on the avowed tendency of them – the art of acquiring an early knowledge of the world. An art, I will venture to assert, that preys secretly, like the worm in the bud,[1] on the expanding powers, and turns to poison the generous juices which should mount with vigour in the youthful frame, inspiring warm affections and great resolves[2].

For every thing, saith the wise man, there is a season;[3] – and who would look for the fruits of autumn during the genial months of spring? But this is mere declamation, and I mean to reason with those worldly-wise instructors, who, instead of cultivating the judgment, instill prejudices, and render hard the heart that gradual experience would only have cooled. An early acquaintance with human infirmities; or, what is termed knowledge of the world, is the surest way, in my opinion, to contract the heart and damp the natural youthful ardour which produces not only great talents, but great virtues. For the vain attempt to bring forth the fruit of experience, before the sapling has thrown out its leaves, only exhausts its strength, and prevents its assuming a natural form; just as the form and strength of sub-

---

1 [Cf. Shakespeare, *Twelfth Night* 2.4.110.]

2 That children ought to be constantly guarded against the vices and follies of the world, appears, to me, a very mistaken opinion; for in the course of my experience, and my eyes have looked abroad, I never knew a youth educated in this manner, who had early imbibed these chilling suspicions, and repeated by rote the hesitating *if* of age, that did not prove a selfish character.

3 [Ecclesiastes 3: 1.]

siding metals are injured when the attraction of cohesion is disturbed.

Tell me, ye who have studied the human mind, is it not a strange way to fix principles by showing young people that they are seldom stable? And how can they be fortified by habits when they are proved to be fallacious by example? Why is the ardour of youth thus to be damped, and the luxuriancy of fancy cut to the quick? This dry caution may, it is true, guard a character from worldly mischances; but will infallibly preclude excellence in either virtue or knowledge[1]. The stumbling-block thrown across every path by suspicion, will prevent any vigorous exertions of genius or benevolence, and life will be stripped of its most alluring charm long before its calm evening, when man should retire to contemplation for comfort and support.

A young man who has been bred up with domestic friends, and led to store his mind with as much speculative knowledge as can be acquired by reading and the natural reflections which youthful ebullitions of animal spirits and instinctive feelings inspire, will enter the world with warm and erroneous expectations. But this appears to be the course of nature; and in morals, as well as in works of taste, we should be observant of her sacred indications, and not presume to lead when we ought obsequiously to follow.

In the world few people act from principle; present feelings, and early habits, are the grand springs: but how would the former be deadened, and the latter rendered iron corroding fetters, if the world were shewn to young people just as it is; when no knowledge of mankind or their own hearts, slowly obtained by experience, rendered them forbearing? Their fellow creatures would not then be viewed as frail beings; like themselves, condemned to struggle with human infirmities, and sometimes displaying the light, and sometimes the dark side of their character; extorting alternate feelings of love and disgust; but guarded against as beasts of prey, till every enlarged social feeling, in a word, – humanity, was eradicated.

In life, on the contrary, as we gradually discover the imperfections of our nature, we discover virtues, and various circumstances attach us to our fellow creatures, when we mix with them, and view the same objects, that are never thought of in acquiring a hasty unnatural

---

1    I have already observed that an early knowledge of the world, obtained in a natural way, by mixing in the world, has the same effect: instancing officers and women.

knowledge of the world. We see a folly swell into a vice, by almost imperceptible degrees, and pity while we blame; but, if the hideous monster burst suddenly on our sight, fear and disgust rendering us more severe than man ought to be, might lead us with blind zeal to usurp the character of omnipotence, and denounce damnation on our fellow mortals, forgetting that we cannot read the heart, and that we have seeds of the same vices lurking in our own.

I have already remarked that we expect more from instruction, than mere instruction can produce: for, instead of preparing young people to encounter the evils of life with dignity, and to acquire wisdom and virtue by the exercise of their own faculties, precepts are heaped upon precepts, and blind obedience required, when conviction should be brought home to reason.

Suppose, for instance, that a young person in the first ardour of friendship deifies the beloved object – what harm can arise from this mistaken enthusiastic attachment? Perhaps it is necessary for virtue first to appear in a human form to impress youthful hearts; the ideal model, which a more matured and exalted mind looks up to, and shapes for itself, would elude their sight. He who loves not his brother whom he hath seen, how can he love God? asked the wisest of men.[1]

It is natural for youth to adorn the first object of its affection with every good quality, and the emulation produced by ignorance, or, to speak with more propriety, by inexperience, brings forward the mind capable of forming such an affection, and when, in the lapse of time, perfection is found not to be within the reach of mortals, virtue, abstractedly, is thought beautiful, and wisdom sublime. Admiration then gives place to friendship, properly so called, because it is cemented by esteem; and the being walks alone only dependent on heaven for that emulous panting after perfection which ever glows in a noble mind. But this knowledge a man must gain by the exertion of his own faculties; and this is surely the blessed fruit of disappointed hope! for He who delighteth to diffuse happiness and shew mercy to the weak creatures, who are learning to know him, never implanted a good propensity to be a tormenting ignis fatuus.[2]

---

1 [1 John 4: 20.]
2 [A will-of-the-wisp, here used as a symbol of a misleading guide.]

Our trees are now allowed to spread with wild luxuriance, nor do we expect by force to combine the majestic marks of time with youthful graces; but wait patiently till they have struck deep their root, and braved many a storm. – Is the mind then, which, in proportion to its dignity, advances more slowly towards perfection, to be treated with less respect? To argue from analogy, every thing around us is in a progressive state; and when an unwelcome knowledge of life produces almost a satiety of life, and we discover by the natural course of things that all that is done under the sun is vanity,[1] we are drawing near the awful close of the drama. The days of activity and hope are over, and the opportunities which the first stage of existence has afforded of advancing in the scale of intelligence, must soon be summed up. – A knowledge at this period of the futility of life, or earlier, if obtained by experience, is very useful, because it is natural; but when a frail being is shewn the follies and vices of man, that he may be taught prudently to guard against the common casualties of life by sacrificing his heart – surely it is not speaking harshly to call it the wisdom of this world, contrasted with the nobler fruit of piety and experience.

I will venture a paradox, and deliver my opinion without reserve; if men were only born to form a circle of life and death, it would be wise to take every step that foresight could suggest to render life happy. Moderation in every pursuit would then be supreme wisdom; and the prudent voluptuary might enjoy a degree of content, though he neither cultivated his understanding nor kept his heart pure. Prudence, supposing we were mortal, would be true wisdom, or, to be more explicit, would procure the greatest portion of happiness, considering the whole of life, but knowledge beyond the conveniences of life would be a curse.

Why should we injure our health by close study? The exalted pleasure which intellectual pursuits afford would scarcely be equivalent to the hours of languor that follow; especially, if it be necessary to take into the reckoning the doubts and disappointments that cloud our researches. Vanity and vexation close every inquiry: for the cause which we particularly wished to discover flies like the horizon before

---

1    [Ecclesiastes 1: 2, 9, 14. Cf. Macaulay, *Letters* 76-77.]

us as we advance. The ignorant, on the contrary, resemble children, and suppose, that if they could walk straight forward they should at last arrive where the earth and clouds meet. Yet, disappointed as we are in our researches, the mind gains strength by the exercise, sufficient, perhaps, to comprehend the answers which, in another step of existence, it may receive to the anxious questions it asked, when the understanding with feeble wing was fluttering round the visible effects to dive into the hidden cause.

The passions also, the winds of life, would be useless, if not injurious, did the substance which composes our thinking being, after we have thought in vain, only become the support of vegetable life, and invigorate a cabbage, or blush in a rose. The appetites would answer every earthly purpose, and produce more moderate and permanent happiness. But the powers of the soul that are of little use here, and, probably, disturb our animal enjoyments, even while conscious dignity makes us glory in possessing them, prove that life is merely an education, a state of infancy, to which the only hopes worth cherishing should not be sacrificed. I mean, therefore, to infer, that we ought to have a precise idea of what we wish to attain by education, for the immortality of the soul is contradicted by the actions of many people who firmly profess the belief.

If you mean to secure ease and prosperity on earth as the first consideration, and leave futurity to provide for itself; you act prudently in giving your child an early insight into the weaknesses of his nature. You may not, it is true, make an Inkle of him;[1] but do not imagine that he will stick to more than the letter of the law, who has very early imbibed a mean opinion of human nature; nor will he think it necessary to rise much above the common standard. He may avoid gross vices, because honesty is the best policy; but he will never aim at attaining great virtues. The example of writers and artists will illustrate this remark.

I must therefore venture to doubt whether what has been thought

---

1 [The story of Inkle had been told by Richard Steele in *The Spectator* 11 (13 March 1711), by a number of poets, and, recently, by George Colman the Younger in *Inkle and Yarico: An Opera* (1787); Wollstonecraft included Steele's version in *The Female Reader.* Yarico is a Native maiden who rescues Inkle, an English merchant. In return, he sells her into slavery. The fact that she is pregnant with his child only induces him to raise her price.]

an axiom in morals may not have been a dogmatical assertion made by men who have coolly seen mankind through the medium of books, and say, in direct contradiction to them, that the regulation of the passions is not, always, wisdom. – On the contrary, it should seem, that one reason why men have superiour judgment, and more fortitude than women, is undoubtedly this, that they give a freer scope to the grand passions, and by more frequently going astray enlarge their minds. If then by the exercise of their own[1] reason they fix on some stable principle, they have probably to thank the force of their passions, nourished by *false* views of life, and permitted to overleap the boundary that secures content. But if, in the dawn of life, we could soberly survey the scenes before as in perspective, and see every thing in its true colours, how could the passions gain sufficient strength to unfold the faculties?

Let me now as from an eminence survey the world stripped of all its false delusive charms. The clear atmosphere enables me to see each object in its true point of view, while my heart is still. I am calm as the prospect in a morning when the mists, slowly dispersing, silently unveil the beauties of nature, refreshed by rest.

In what light will the world now appear? – I rub my eyes and think, perchance, that I am just awaking from a lively dream.

I see the sons and daughters of men pursuing shadows, and anxiously wasting their powers to feed passions which have no adequate object – if the very excess of these blind impulses, pampered by that lying, yet constantly trusted guide, the imagination, did not, by preparing them for some other state, render short-sighted mortals wiser without their own concurrence; or, what comes to the same thing, when they were pursuing some imaginary present good.[2]

After viewing objects in this light, it would not be very fanciful to imagine that this world was a stage[3] on which a pantomime is daily performed for the amusement of superiour beings.[4] How would they be diverted to see the ambitious man consuming himself by running

---

1 "I find that all is but lip-wisdom which wants experience," says Sidney. [Sir Philip Sidney (1554-86), *The Countess of Pembroke's Arcadia (The New Arcadia)* (1590), ed. Victor Skretkowicz (Oxford: Clarendon P, 1987) 106.]
2 [Cf. Macaulay, *Letters* 384.]
3 [Cf. Shakespeare, *As You Like It* 2.7.139.]
4 [This fancy was indulged in by Soame Jenyns, in *A Free Enquiry into the Nature and*

after a phantom, and, "pursuing the bubble fame in the cannon's mouth"[1] that was to blow him to nothing: for when consciousness is lost, it matters not whether we mount in a whirlwind or descend in rain. And should they compassionately invigorate his sight and shew him the thorny path which led to eminence, that like a quicksand sinks as he ascends, disappointing his hopes when almost within his grasp, would he not leave to others the honour of amusing them, and labour to secure the present moment, though from the constitution of his nature he would not find it very easy to catch the flying stream? Such slaves are we to hope and fear!

But, vain as the ambitious man's pursuits would be, he is often striving for something more substantial than fame – that indeed would be the veriest meteor, the wildest fire that could lure a man to ruin. – What! renounce the most trifling gratification to be applauded when he should be no more! Wherefore this struggle, whether man be mortal or immortal, if that noble passion did not really raise the being above his fellows? –

And love! What diverting scenes would it produce – Pantaloon's tricks must yield to more egregious folly.[2] To see a mortal adorn an object with imaginary charms, and then fall down and worship the idol which he had himself set up – how ridiculous! But what serious consequences ensue to rob man of that portion of happiness, which the Deity by calling him into existence has (or, on what can his attributes rest?) indubitably promised: would not all the purposes of life have been much better fulfilled if he had only felt what has been termed physical love? And, would not the sight of the object, not seen through the medium of the imagination, soon reduce the passion to an appetite, if reflection, the noble distinction of man, did not give it force, and make it an instrument to raise him above this earthy dross, by teaching him to love the centre of all perfection; whose wisdom appears clearer and clearer in the works of nature, in proportion as reason is illuminated and exalted by contemplation, and by acquiring

---

    *Origin of Evil*, famously and savagely reviewed by Samuel Johnson (1709-84) in *The Literary Magazine; or, Universal Review* (May, June, July 1757).]

1  [Shakespeare, *As You Like It* 2.7.152-53.]

2  [Pantaloon is a character in the Italian commedia dell' arte and in the English pantomimes based on it.]

that love of order which the struggles of passion produce?

The habit of reflection, and the knowledge attained by fostering any passion, might be shewn to be equally useful, though the object be proved equally fallacious; for they would all appear in the same light, if they were not magnified by the governing passion implanted in us by the Author of all good, to call forth and strengthen the faculties of each individual, and enable it to attain all the experience that an infant can obtain, who does certain things, it cannot tell why.

I descend from my height, and mixing with my fellow-creatures, feel myself hurried along the common stream; ambition, love, hope, and fear, exert their wonted power, though we be convinced by reason that their present and most attractive promises are only lying dreams; but had the cold hand of circumspection damped each generous feeling before it had left any permanent character, or fixed some habit, what could be expected, but selfish prudence and reason just rising above instinct? Who that has read Dean Swift's disgusting description of the Yahoos, and insipid one of Houyhnhnm[1] with a philosophical eye, can avoid seeing the futility of degrading the passions, or making man rest in contentment?

The youth should *act*; for had he the experience of a grey head he would be fitter for death than life, though his virtues, rather residing in his head than his heart, could produce nothing great, and his understanding, prepared for this world, would not, by its noble flights, prove that it had a title to a better.

Besides, it is not possible to give a young person a just view of life; he must have struggled with his own passions before he can estimate the force of the temptation which betrayed his brother into vice. Those who are entering life, and those who are departing, see the world from such very different points of view, that they can seldom think alike, unless the unfledged reason of the former never attempted a solitary flight.

When we hear of some daring crime – it comes full on us in the deepest shade of turpitude, and raises indignation; but the eye that gradually saw the darkness thicken, must observe it with more compassionate forbearance. The world cannot be seen by an unmoved spectator, we must mix in the throng, and feel as men feel before we

---

1   [In *Gulliver's Travels* (1726), Part 4.]

can judge of their feelings. If we mean, in short, to live in the world to grow wiser and better, and not merely to enjoy the good things of life, we must attain a knowledge of others at the same time that we become acquainted with ourselves – knowledge acquired any other way only hardens the heart and perplexes the understanding.

I may be told, that the knowledge thus acquired, is sometimes purchased at too dear a rate. I can only answer that I very much doubt whether any knowledge can be attained without labour and sorrow; and those who wish to spare their children both, should not complain, if they are neither wise nor virtuous. They only aimed at making them prudent; and prudence, early in life, is but the cautious craft of ignorant self-love.

I have observed that young people, to whose education particular attention has been paid, have, in general, been very superficial and conceited, and far from pleasing in any respect, because they had neither the unsuspecting warmth of youth, nor the cool depth of age. I cannot help imputing this unnatural appearance principally to that hasty premature instruction, which leads them presumptuously to repeat all the crude notions they have taken upon trust, so that the careful education which they received, makes them all their lives the slaves of prejudices.

Mental as well as bodily exertion is, at first, irksome; so much so, that the many would fain let others both work and think for them. An observation which I have often made will illustrate my meaning. When in a circle of strangers, or acquaintances, a person of moderate abilities asserts an opinion with heat, I will venture to affirm, for I have traced this fact home, very often, that it is a prejudice. These echoes have a high respect for the understanding of some relation or friend, and without fully comprehending the opinions, which they are so eager to retail, they maintain them with a degree of obstinacy, that would surprise even the person who concocted them.

I know that a kind of fashion now prevails of respecting prejudices; and when any one dares to face them, though actuated by humanity and armed by reason, he is superciliously asked whether his ancestors were fools. No, I should reply; opinions, at first, of every description, were all, probably, considered, and therefore were founded on some reason; yet not unfrequently, of course, it was rather a local expedient than a fundamental principle, that would be reasonable at all times. But, moss-covered opinions assume the disproportioned form of prejudices, when they are indolently adopted only because age has given them a venerable aspect, though the reason on which they were built ceases to be a reason, or cannot be traced. Why are we to love prejudices, merely because they are prejudices[1]? A prejudice is a fond obstinate persuasion for which we can give no reason; for the moment a reason can be given for an opinion, it ceases to be a prejudice, though it may be an error in judgment: and are we then advised to cherish opinions only to set reason at defiance? This mode of arguing, if arguing it may be called, reminds me of what is vulgarly termed a woman's reason. For women sometimes declare that they love, or believe, certain things, *because* they love, or believe them.

It is impossible to converse with people to any purpose, who only use affirmatives and negatives. Before you can bring them to a point, to start fairly from, you must go back to the simple principles that were antecedent to the prejudices broached by power; and it is ten to one but you are stopped by the philosophical assertion, that certain principles are as practically false as they are abstractly true[2]. Nay, it may be inferred, that reason has whispered some doubts, for it generally happens that people assert their opinions with the greatest heat when they begin to waver; striving to drive out their own doubts by convincing their opponent, they grow angry when those gnawing doubts are thrown back to prey on themselves.

The fact is, that men expect from education, what education cannot give. A sagacious parent or tutor may strengthen the body and sharpen the instruments by which the child is to gather knowledge; but the honey must be the reward of the individual's own industry. It is almost as absurd to attempt to make a youth wise by the experience of another, as to expect the body to grow strong by the exercise which is only talked of, or seen[3]. Many of those children whose conduct has been most narrowly watched, become the weakest men,

---

1   Vide Mr. Burke. [*Reflections; Writings* 8: 138 (Appendix A.4.ii).]
2   "Convince a man against his will,
    He's of the same opinion still."
    [Butler, *Hudibras* 3.3.547-48. Cf. Burke, *Reflections; Writings* 8: 112.]
3   "One sees nothing when one is content to contemplate only; it is necessary to act oneself to be able to see how others act." *Rousseau.* [*Julie; ou, La Nouvelle Héloïse*, part

because their instructors only instill certain notions into their minds, that have no other foundation than their authority; and if they be loved or respected, the mind is cramped in its exertions and wavering in its advances. The business of education in this case, is only to conduct the shooting tendrils to a proper pole; yet after laying precept upon precept, without allowing a child to acquire judgment itself, parents expect them to act in the same manner by this borrowed fallacious light, as if they had illuminated it themselves; and be, when they enter life, what their parents are at the close. They do not consider that the tree, and even the human body, does not strengthen its fibres till it has reached its full growth.

There appears to be something analogous in the mind. The senses and the imagination give a form to the character, during childhood and youth; and the understanding, as life advances, gives firmness to the first fair purposes of sensibility – till virtue, arising rather from the clear conviction of reason than the impulse of the heart, morality is made to rest on a rock against which the storms of passion vainly beat.

I hope I shall not be misunderstood when I say, that religion will not have this condensing energy, unless it be founded on reason. If it be merely the refuge of weakness or wild fanaticism, and not a governing principle of conduct, drawn from self-knowledge, and a rational opinion respecting the attributes of God, what can it be expected to produce? The religion which consists in warming the affections, and exalting the imagination, is only the poetical part, and may afford the individual pleasure without rendering it a more moral being. It may be a substitute for worldly pursuits; yet narrow, instead of enlarging the heart: but virtue must be loved as in itself sublime and excellent, and not for the advantages it procures or the evils it averts, if any great degree of excellence be expected. Men will not become moral when they only build airy castles in a future world to compensate for the disappointments which they meet with in this; if they turn their thoughts from relative duties to religious reveries.

Most prospects in life are marred by the shuffling worldly wisdom

---

2, letter 17. Macaulay, however, argues that we do profit from the exertions of others (*Letters* 11-12).]

of men, who, forgetting that they cannot serve God and mammon,[1] endeavour to blend contradictory things. — If you wish to make your son rich, pursue one course — if you are only anxious to make him virtuous, you must take another; but do not imagine that you can bound from one road to the other without losing your way[2].

---

1   [Matthew 6: 24; Luke 16: 13.]
2   See an excellent essay on this subject by Mrs. Barbauld, in *Miscellaneous Pieces in Prose*. ["Against Inconsistency in our Expectations" (1773).]

# CHAP. VI.

## THE EFFECT WHICH AN EARLY ASSOCIATION OF IDEAS HAS UPON THE CHARACTER.

EDUCATED in the enervating style recommended by the writers on whom I have been animadverting; and not having a chance, from their subordinate state in society, to recover their lost ground, is it surprising that women every where appear a defect in nature? Is it surprising, when we consider what a determinate effect an early association of ideas has on the character, that they neglect their understandings, and turn all their attention to their persons?

The great advantages which naturally result from storing the mind with knowledge, are obvious from the following considerations. The association of our ideas is either habitual or instantaneous; and the latter mode seems rather to depend on the original temperature of the mind than on the will. When the ideas, and matters of fact, are once taken in, they lie by for use, till some fortuitous circumstance makes the information dart into the mind with illustrative force, that has been received at very different periods of our lives. Like the lightning's flash are many recollections; one idea assimilating and explaining another, with astonishing rapidity. I do not now allude to that quick perception of truth, which is so intuitive that it baffles research, and makes us at a loss to determine whether it is reminiscence or ratiocination, lost sight of in its celerity, that opens the dark cloud. Over those instantaneous associations we have little power; for when the mind is once enlarged by excursive flights, or profound reflection, the raw materials will, in some degree, arrange themselves. The understanding, it is true, may keep us from going out of drawing¹ when we group our thoughts, or transcribe from the imagination the warm sketches of fancy; but the animal spirits, the individual character, give

---

1    [Out of perspective.]

the colouring. Over this subtile electric fluid[1], how little power do we possess, and over it how little power can reason obtain! These fine intractable spirits appear to be the essence of genius, and beaming in its eagle eye, produce in the most eminent degree the happy energy of associating thoughts that surprise, delight, and instruct. These are the glowing minds that concentrate pictures for their fellow-creatures; forcing them to view with interest the objects reflected from the impassioned imagination, which they passed over in nature.

I must be allowed to explain myself. The generality of people cannot see or feel poetically, they want fancy, and therefore fly from solitude in search of sensible objects; but when an author lends them his eyes they can see as he saw, and be amused by images they could not select, though lying before them.

Education thus only supplies the man of genius with knowledge to give variety and contrast to his associations; but there is an habitual association of ideas, that grows "with our growth,"[2] which has a great effect on the moral character of mankind; and by which a turn is given to the mind that commonly remains throughout life. So ductile is the understanding, and yet so stubborn, that the associations which depend on adventitious circumstances, during the period that the body takes to arrive at maturity, can seldom be disentangled by reason. One idea calls up another, its old associate, and memory, faithful to the first impressions, particularly when the intellectual powers are not employed to cool our sensations, retraces them with mechanical exactness.

This habitual slavery, to first impressions, has a more baneful effect on the female than the male character, because business and other dry employments of the understanding, tend to deaden the feelings and break associations that do violence to reason. But females, who are

---

1   I have sometimes, when inclined to laugh at materialists, asked whether, as the most powerful effects in nature are apparently produced by fluids, the magnetic, &c. the passions might not be fine volatile fluids that embraced humanity, keeping the more refractory elementary parts together—or whether they were simply a liquid fire that pervaded the more sluggish materials, giving them life and heat? [Contemporary scientists believed that electricity and magnetism were "subtle" that is, very thin, fluids. In the life sciences, vitalists believed that life itself was such a fluid, the materialist position Wollstonecraft is mocking here.]

2   [Pope, *An Essay on Man* 2.136.]

made women of when they are mere children, and brought back to childhood when they ought to leave the go-cart for ever, have not sufficient strength of mind to efface the superinductions of art that have smothered nature.

Every thing that they see or hear serves to fix impressions, call forth emotions, and associate ideas, that give a sexual character to the mind. False notions of beauty and delicacy stop the growth of their limbs and produce a sickly soreness, rather than delicacy of organs; and thus weakened by being employed in unfolding instead of examining the first associations, forced on them by every surrounding object, how can they attain the vigour necessary to enable them to throw off their factitious character? – where find strength to recur to reason and rise superiour to a system of oppression, that blasts the fair promises of spring? This cruel association of ideas, which every thing conspires to twist into all their habits of thinking, or, to speak with more precision, of feeling, receives new force when they begin to act a little for themselves; for they then perceive that it is only through their address to excite emotions in men, that pleasure and power are to be obtained. Besides, the books professedly written for their instruction, which make the first impression on their minds, all inculcate the same opinions. Educated then in worse than Egyptian bondage,[1] it is unreasonable, as well as cruel, to upbraid them with faults that can scarcely be avoided, unless a degree of native vigour be supposed, that falls to the lot of very few amongst mankind.

For instance, the severest sarcasms have been levelled against the sex, and they have been ridiculed for repeating "a set of phrases learnt by rote,"[2] when nothing could be more natural, considering the education they receive, and that their "highest praise is to obey, unargued" – the will of man.[3] If they be not allowed to have reason sufficient to govern their own conduct – why, all they learn – must be learned by rote! And when all their ingenuity is called forth to adjust their dress, "a passion for a scarlet coat,"[4] is so natural, that it never surprised me; and, allowing Pope's summary of their character to be

---

1    [See Exodus 1, 5: 5-19.]
2    [Swift, "The Furniture of a Woman's Mind" 1.]
3    [Milton, *Paradise Lost* 4.635-38.]
4    [Swift, "The Furniture of a Woman's Mind" 2.]

just, "that every woman is at heart a rake,"[1] why should they be bitterly censured for seeking a congenial mind, and preferring a rake to a man of sense?

Rakes know how to work on their sensibility, whilst the modest merit of reasonable men has, of course, less effect on their feelings, and they cannot reach the heart by the way of the understanding, because they have few sentiments in common.

It seems a little absurd to expect women to be more reasonable than men in their *likings*, and still to deny them the uncontrouled use of reason. When do men *fall-in-love* with sense? When do they, with their superiour powers and advantages, turn from the person to the mind? And how can they then expect women, who are only taught to observe behaviour, and acquire manners rather than morals, to despise what they have been all their lives labouring to attain? Where are they suddenly to find judgment enough to weigh patiently the sense of an awkward virtuous man, when his manners, of which they are made critical judges, are rebuffing, and his conversation cold and dull, because it does not consist of pretty repartees, or well turned compliments? In order to admire or esteem any thing for a continuance, we must, at least, have our curiosity excited by knowing, in some degree, what we admire; for we are unable to estimate the value of qualities and virtues above our comprehension. Such a respect, when it is felt, may be very sublime; and the confused consciousness of humility may render the dependent creature an interesting object, in some points of view; but human love must have grosser ingredients; and the person very naturally will come in for its share – and, an ample share it mostly has!

Love is, in a great degree, an arbitrary passion, and will reign, like some other stalking mischiefs, by its own authority, without deigning to reason; and it may also be easily distinguished from esteem, the foundation of friendship, because it is often excited by evanescent beauties and graces, though, to give an energy to the sentiment, something more solid must deepen their impression and set the imagination to work, to make the most fair – the first good.

Common passions are excited by common qualities. – Men look for beauty and the simper of good-humoured docility: women are

---

1   [Pope, "Of the Characters of Women" 216.]

captivated by easy manners; a gentleman-like man seldom fails to please them, and their thirsty ears eagerly drink the insinuating nothings of politeness, whilst they turn from the unintelligible sounds of the charmer – reason, charm he never so wisely. With respect to superficial accomplishments, the rake certainly has the advantage; and of these females can form an opinion, for it is their own ground. Rendered gay and giddy by the whole tenor of their lives, the very aspect of wisdom, or the severe graces of virtue, must have a lugubrious appearance to them; and produce a kind of restraint from which they and love, sportive child, naturally revolt. Without taste, excepting of the lighter kind, for taste is the offspring of judgment, how can they discover that true beauty and grace must arise from the play of the mind? and how can they be expected to relish in a lover what they do not, or very imperfectly, possess themselves? The sympathy that unites hearts, and invites to confidence, in them is so very faint, that it cannot take fire, and thus mount to passion. No, I repeat it, the love cherished by such minds, must have grosser fewel!

The inference is obvious; till women are led to exercise their understandings, they should not be satirized for their attachment to rakes; or even for being rakes at heart, when it appears to be the inevitable consequence of their education. They who live to please – must find their enjoyments, their happiness, in pleasure! It is a trite, yet true remark, that we never do any thing well, unless we love it for its own sake.

Supposing, however, for a moment, that women were, in some future revolution of time, to become, what I sincerely wish them to be, even love would acquire more serious dignity, and be purified in its own fires; and virtue giving true delicacy to their affections, they would turn with disgust from a rake. Reasoning then, as well as feeling, the only province of woman, at present, they might easily guard against exterior graces, and quickly learn to despise the sensibility that had been excited and hackneyed in the ways of women, whose trade was vice; and allurements, wanton airs. They would recollect that the flame, one must use appropriated expressions, which they wished to light up, had been exhausted by lust, and that the sated appetite, losing all relish for pure and simple pleasures, could only be roused by licentious arts or variety. What satisfaction could a woman of delicacy promise herself in a union with such a man, when the very artlessness of her affection might appear insipid? Thus does Dryden describe the situation,

> —————"Where love is duty, on the female side,
> On theirs mere sensual gust, and sought with surly pride."[1]

But one grand truth women have yet to learn, though much it imports them to act accordingly. In the choice of a husband, they should not be led astray by the qualities of a lover – for a lover the husband, even supposing him to be wise and virtuous, cannot long remain.

Were women more rationally educated, could they take a more comprehensive view of things, they would be contented to love but once in their lives; and after marriage calmly let passion subside into friendship – into that tender intimacy, which is the best refuge from care, yet is built on such pure, still affections, that idle jealousies would not be allowed to disturb the discharge of the sober duties of life, or to engross the thoughts that ought to be otherwise employed. This is a state in which many men live; but few, very few women. And the difference may easily be accounted for, without recurring to a sexual character. Men, for whom we are told women were made, have too much occupied the thoughts of women; and this association has so entangled love with all their motives of action; and, to harp a little on an old string, having been solely employed either to prepare themselves to excite love, or actually putting their lessons in practice, they cannot live without love. But, when a sense of duty, or fear of shame, obliges them to restrain this pampered desire of pleasing beyond certain lengths, too far for delicacy, it is true, though far from criminality, they obstinately determine to love, I speak of the passion, their husbands to the end of the chapter – and then acting the part which they foolishly exacted from their lovers, they become abject woers, and fond slaves.

---

1 [Dryden, *Fables Ancient and Modern; Translated into Verse* (1700), "Palamon and Arcite" 3.230–31.]

Men of wit and fancy are often rakes; and fancy is the food of love.[1] Such men will inspire passion. Half the sex, in its present infantine state, would pine for a Lovelace; a man so witty, so graceful, and so valiant: and can they *deserve* blame for acting according to principles so constantly inculcated? They want a lover, and protector; and behold him kneeling before them – bravery prostrate to beauty! The virtues of a husband are thus thrown by love into the back ground, and gay hopes, or lively emotions, banish reflection till the day of reckoning come; and come it surely will, to turn the sprightly lover into a surly suspicious tyrant, who contemptuously insults the very weakness he fostered. Or, supposing the rake reformed, he cannot quickly get rid of old habits. When a man of abilities is first carried away by his passions, it is necessary that sentiment and taste varnish the enormities of vice, and give a zest to brutal indulgences; but when the gloss of novelty is worn off, and pleasure palls upon the sense, lasciviousness becomes barefaced, and enjoyment only the desperate effort of weakness flying from reflection as from a legion of devils.[2] Oh! virtue, thou art not an empty name! All that life can give – thou givest!

If much comfort cannot be expected from the friendship of a reformed rake of superiour abilities, what is the consequence when he lacketh sense, as well as principles? Verily misery, in its most hideous shape. When the habits of weak people are consolidated by time, a reformation is barely possible; and actually makes the beings miserable who have not sufficient mind to be amused by innocent pleasure; like the tradesman who retires from the hurry of business, nature presents to them only a universal blank;[3] and the restless thoughts prey on the damped spirits[4]. Their reformation, as well as his retirement, actually makes them wretched because it deprives them of

---

1  [Cf. Shakespeare, *Twelfth Night* 1.1.1.]
2  [Mark 5: 9; Luke 8: 30.]
3  [Milton, *Paradise Lost* 3.48-49.]
4  I have frequently seen this exemplified in women whose beauty could no longer be repaired. They have retired from the noisy scenes of dissipation; but, unless they became methodists, the solitude of the select society of their family connections or acquaintance, has presented only a fearful void; consequently, nervous complaints, and all the vapourish train of idleness, rendered them quite as useless, and far more unhappy, than when they joined the giddy throng.

all employment, by quenching the hopes and fears that set in motion their sluggish minds.[1]

If such be the force of habit; if such be the bondage of folly, how carefully ought we to guard the mind from storing up vicious associations; and equally careful should we be to cultivate the understanding, to save the poor wight from the weak dependent state of even harmless ignorance. For it is the right use of reason alone which makes us independent of every thing – excepting the unclouded Reason – "Whose service is perfect freedom."[2]

---

1   [Cf. *Original Stories; Works* 4: 405.]
2   [*The Book of Common Prayer* (1549), "Morning Prayer, Second Collect, for Peace"; the original subject is God. Cf. Macaulay, *Letters* 422–23.]

# CHAP. VII.

## MODESTY.—COMPREHENSIVELY CONSIDERED, AND NOT AS A SEXUAL VIRTUE.

MODESTY! Sacred offspring of sensibility and reason! – true delicacy of mind! – may I unblamed presume to investigate thy nature,[1] and trace to its covert the mild charm, that mellowing each harsh feature of a character, renders what would otherwise only inspire cold admiration – lovely! – Thou that smoothest the wrinkles of wisdom, and softenest the tone of the sublimest virtues till they all melt into humanity; – thou that spreadest the ethereal cloud that, surrounding love, heightens every beauty, it half shades, breathing those coy sweets that steal into the heart, and charm the senses – modulate for me the language of persuasive reason, till I rouse my sex from the flowery bed, on which they supinely sleep life away!

In speaking of the association of our ideas, I have noticed two distinct modes; and in defining modesty, it appears to me equally proper to discriminate that purity of mind, which is the effect of chastity, from a simplicity of character that leads us to form a just opinion of ourselves, equally distant from vanity or presumption, though by no means incompatible with a lofty consciousness of our own dignity. Modesty, in the latter signification of the term, is, that soberness of mind which teaches a man not to think more highly of himself than he ought to think, and should be distinguished from humility, because humility is a kind of self-abasement.[2]

A modest man often conceives a great plan, and tenaciously adheres to it, conscious of his own strength, till success gives it a sanction that determines its character. Milton was not arrogant when he suffered a suggestion of judgment to escape him that proved a prophecy;[3] nor was General Washington when he accepted of the

---

1 [Cf. Milton, *Paradise Lost* 3.1–3.]
2 [Cf. Macaulay, *Letters* 216–17.]
3 [Milton, "Ad Patrem [To my Father]" (1638?) 101–10.]

command of the American forces.[1] The latter has always been characterized as a modest man; but had he been merely humble, he would probably have shrunk back irresolute, afraid of trusting to himself the direction of an enterprise, on which so much depended.

A modest man is steady, an humble man timid, and a vain one presumptuous: – this is the judgment, which the observation of many characters, has led me to form. Jesus Christ was modest, Moses was humble, and Peter vain.

Thus, discriminating modesty from humility in one case, I do not mean to confound it with bashfulness in the other. Bashfulness, in fact, is so distinct from modesty, that the most bashful lass, or raw country lout, often become the most impudent; for their bashfulness being merely the instinctive timidity of ignorance, custom soon changes it into assurance[2].

The shameless behaviour of the prostitutes, who infest the streets of this metropolis, raising alternate emotions of pity and disgust, may serve to illustrate this remark. They trample on virgin bashfulness with a sort of bravado, and glorying in their shame, become more audaciously lewd than men, however depraved, to whom this sexual quality has not been gratuitously granted, ever appear to be. But these poor ignorant wretches never had any modesty to lose, when they consigned themselves to infamy; for modesty is a virtue, not a quality. No, they were only bashful, shame-faced innocents; and losing their innocence, their shame-facedness was rudely brushed off; a virtue would have left some vestiges in the mind, had it been sacrificed to passion,

---

1   [George Washington (1732-99) was appointed commander-in-chief of the army of the United Colonies in 1775. In 1792, he was first President of the United States.]

2              "Such is the country-maiden's fright,
            When first a red-coat is in sight;
            Behind the door she hides her face;
            Next time at distance eyes the lace:
            She now can all his terrors stand,
            Nor from his squeeze withdraws her hand.
            She plays familiar in his arms,
            And ev'ry soldier hath his charms;
            From tent to tent she spreads her flame;
            For custom conquers fear and shame."
                                    Gay.
    [*Fables* (1727) 13, "The Tame Stag" 27-36. Wollstonecraft included one of Gay's fables in *The Female Reader.*]

to make us respect the grand ruin.

Purity of mind, or that genuine delicacy, which is the only virtuous support of chastity, is near akin to that refinement of humanity, which never resides in any but cultivated minds. It is something nobler than innocence, it is the delicacy of reflection, and not the coyness of ignorance. The reserve of reason, which, like habitual cleanliness, is seldom seen in any great degree, unless the soul is active, may easily be distinguished from rustic shyness or wanton skittishness; and, so far from being incompatible with knowledge, it is its fairest fruit. What a gross idea of modesty had the writer of the following remark! "The lady who asked the question whether women may be instructed in the modern system of botany, consistently with female delicacy? – was accused of ridiculous prudery: nevertheless, if she had proposed the question to me, I should certainly have answered – They cannot."[1] Thus is the fair book of knowledge[2] to be shut with an everlasting seal! On reading similar passages I have reverentially lifted up my eyes and heart to Him who liveth for ever and ever, and said, O my Father, hast Thou by the very constitution of her nature forbid Thy child to seek Thee in the fair forms of truth? And, can her soul be sullied by the knowledge that awfully calls her to Thee?

I have then philosophically pursued these reflections till I inferred that those women who have most improved their reason must have the most modesty – though a dignified sedateness of deportment may have succeeded the playful, bewitching bashfulness of youth[3].

And thus have I argued. To render chastity the virtue from which unsophisticated modesty will naturally flow, the attention should be called away from employments which only exercise the sensibility; and the heart made to beat time to humanity, rather than to throb with love. The woman who has dedicated a considerable portion of her time to pursuits purely intellectual, and whose affections have been exercised by humane plans of usefulness, must have more purity

---

1   [John Berkenhout (1730?-91), *A Volume of Letters to his Son at the University* (Cambridge, 1790) 307. Berkenhout's point is that the Linnaean system of botany, popularized in Erasmus Darwin's poem *The Loves of the Plants* (1789), classified plants according to their sexual organs.]

2   [Milton, *Paradise Lost* 3.47.]

3   Modesty, is the graceful calm virtue of maturity; bashfulness, the charm of vivacious youth.

of mind, as a natural consequence, than the ignorant beings whose time and thoughts have been occupied by gay pleasures or schemes to conquer hearts[1]. The regulation of the behaviour is not modesty, though those who study rules of decorum are, in general, termed modest women. Make the heart clean, let it expand and feel for all that is human, instead of being narrowed by selfish passions; and let the mind frequently contemplate subjects that exercise the understanding, without heating the imagination, and artless modesty will give the finishing touches to the picture.

She who can discern the dawn of immortality, in the streaks that shoot athwart the misty night of ignorance, promising a clearer day, will respect, as a sacred temple, the body that enshrines such an improvable soul. True love, likewise, spreads this kind of mysterious sanctity round the beloved object, making the lover most modest when in her presence[2]. So reserved is affection that, receiving or returning personal endearments, it wishes, not only to shun the human eye, as a kind of profanation; but to diffuse an encircling cloudy obscurity to shut out even the saucy sparkling sunbeams. Yet, that affection does not deserve the epithet of chaste, which does not receive a sublime gloom of tender melancholy, that allows the mind for a moment to stand still and enjoy the present satisfaction, when a consciousness of the Divine presence is felt – for this must ever be the food of joy!

As I have always been fond of tracing to its source in nature any prevailing custom, I have frequently thought that it was a sentiment of affection for whatever had touched the person of an absent or lost friend, which gave birth to that respect for relicks, so much abused by

---

1    I have conversed, as man with man, with medical men, on anatomical subjects; and compared the proportions of the human body with artists—yet such modesty did I meet with, that I was never reminded by word or look of my sex, of the absurd rules which make modesty a pharisaical cloak of weakness. And I am persuaded that in the pursuit of knowledge women would never be insulted by sensible men, and rarely by men of any description, if they did not by mock modesty remind them that they were women: actuated by the same spirit as the Portugueze ladies, who would think their charms insulted, if, when left alone with a man, he did not, at least, attempt to be grossly familiar with their persons. Men are not always men in the company of women, nor would women always remember that they are women, if they were allowed to acquire more understanding.

2    Male or female; for the world contains many modest men.

selfish priests. Devotion, or love, may be allowed to hallow the garments as well as the person; for the lover must want fancy who has not a sort of sacred respect for the glove or slipper of his mistress. He could not confound them with vulgar things of the same kind. This fine sentiment, perhaps, would not bear to be analyzed by the experimental philosopher – but of such stuff is human rapture made up! – A shadowy phantom glides before us, obscuring every other object; yet when the soft cloud is grasped, the form melts into common air, leaving a solitary void, or sweet perfume, stolen from the violet, that memory long holds dear. But, I have tripped unawares on fairy ground, feeling the balmy gale of spring stealing on me, though november frowns.

As a sex, women are more chaste than men, and as modesty is the effect of chastity, they may deserve to have this virtue ascribed to them in rather an appropriated sense; yet, I must be allowed to add an hesitating if: – for I doubt whether chastity will produce modesty, though it may propriety of conduct, when it is merely a respect for the opinion of the world[1], and when coquetry and the lovelorn tales of novelists employ the thoughts. Nay, from experience, and reason, I should be led to expect to meet with more modesty amongst men than women, simply because men exercise their understandings more than women.

But, with respect to propriety of behaviour, excepting one class of females, women have evidently the advantage. What can be more disgusting than that impudent dross of gallantry, thought so manly, which makes many men stare insultingly at every female they meet? Can it be termed respect for the sex? No, this loose behaviour shews such habitual depravity, such weakness of mind, that it is vain to expect much public or private virtue, till both men and women grow more modest – till men, curbing a sensual fondness for the sex, or an affectation of manly assurance, more properly speaking, impudence, treat each other with respect – unless appetite or passion give the tone, peculiar to it, to their behaviour. I mean even personal respect – the modest respect of humanity, and fellow-feeling – not the libidinous

---

1    The immodest behaviour of many married women, who are nevertheless faithful to their husbands' beds, will illustrate this remark.

mockery of gallantry, nor the insolent condescension of protectorship. To carry the observation still further, modesty must heartily disclaim, and refuse to dwell with that debauchery of mind, which leads a man coolly to bring forward, without a blush, indecent allusions, or obscene witticisms, in the presence of a fellow creature; women are now out of the question, for then it is brutality. Respect for man, as man, is the foundation of every noble sentiment. How much more modest is the libertine who obeys the call of appetite or fancy, than the lewd joker who sets the table in a roar!

This is one of the many instances in which the sexual distinction respecting modesty has proved fatal to virtue and happiness. It is, however, carried still further, and woman, weak woman! made by her education the slave of sensibility, is required, on the most trying occasions, to resist that sensibility. "Can any thing," says Knox, "be more absurd than keeping women in a state of ignorance, and yet so vehemently to insist on their resisting temptation?"[1] – Thus when virtue or honour make it proper to check a passion, the burden is thrown on the weaker shoulders, contrary to reason and true modesty, which, at least, should render the self-denial mutual, to say nothing of the generosity of bravery, supposed to be a manly virtue.

In the same strain runs Rousseau's and Dr. Gregory's advice respecting modesty, strangely miscalled! for they both desire a wife to leave it in doubt whether sensibility or weakness led her to her husband's arms. – The woman is immodest who can let the shadow of such a doubt remain in her husband's mind a moment.

But to state the subject in a different light. – The want of modesty, which I principally deplore as subversive of morality, arises from the state of warfare so strenuously supported by voluptuous men as the very essence of modesty, though, in fact, its bane; because it is a refinement on lust, that men fall into who have not sufficient virtue to relish the innocent pleasures of love. A man of delicacy carries his notions of modesty still further, for neither weakness nor sensibility will gratify him – he looks for affection.

Again; men boast of their triumphs over women, what do they boast of? Truly the creature of sensibility was surprised by her sensi-

---

1   [Knox, *Essays, Moral and Literary* (1782) 154.]

bility into folly – into vice[1]; and the dreadful reckoning falls heavily on her own weak head, when reason wakes. For where art thou to find comfort, forlorn and disconsolate one? He who ought to have directed thy reason, and supported thy weakness, has betrayed thee! In a dream of passion thou consented to wander through flowery lawns, and heedlessly stepping over the precipice to which thy guide, instead of guarding, lured thee, thou startest from thy dream[2] only to face a sneering, frowning world, and to find thyself alone in a waste, for he that triumphed in thy weakness is now pursuing new conquests; but for thee – there is no redemption on this side the grave! – And what resource hast thou in an enervated mind to raise a sinking heart?

But, if the sexes be really to live in a state of warfare, if nature have pointed it out, let them act nobly, or let pride whisper to them, that the victory is mean when they merely vanquish sensibility. The real conquest is that over affection not taken by surprise – when, like Heloisa, a woman gives up all the world, deliberately, for love. I do not now consider the wisdom or virtue of such a sacrifice, I only contend that it was a sacrifice to affection, and not merely to sensibility, though she had her share. – And I must be allowed to call her a modest woman, before I dismiss this part of the subject, by saying, that till men are more chaste women will be immodest. Where, indeed, could modest women find husbands from whom they would not continually turn with disgust? Modesty must be equally cultivated by both sexes, or it will ever remain a sickly hot-house plant, whilst the affectation of it, the fig leaf borrowed by wantonness, may give a zest to voluptuous enjoyments.

Men will probably still insist that woman ought to have more modesty than man; but it is not dispassionate reasoners who will most earnestly oppose my opinion. No, they are the men of fancy, the favourites of the sex, who outwardly respect and inwardly despise the weak creatures whom they thus sport with. They cannot submit to resign the highest sensual gratification, nor even to relish the epicurism of virtue – self-denial.

To take another view of the subject, confining my remarks to women.

---

1   The poor moth fluttering round a candle, burns its wings.
2   [Cf. Rousseau, *Emile* 319-20.]

The ridiculous falsities[1] which are told to children, from mistaken notions of modesty, tend very early to inflame their imaginations and set their little minds to work, respecting subjects, which nature never intended they should think of till the body arrived at some degree of maturity; then the passions naturally begin to take place of the senses, as instruments to unfold the understanding, and form the moral character.

In nurseries, and boarding-schools, I fear, girls are first spoiled; particularly in the latter. A number of girls sleep in the same room, and wash together. And, though I should be sorry to contaminate an innocent creature's mind by instilling false delicacy, or those indecent prudish notions, which early cautions respecting the other sex naturally engender, I should be very anxious to prevent their acquiring nasty, or immodest habits; and as many girls have learned very nasty tricks, from ignorant servants, the mixing them thus indiscriminately together, is very improper.[2]

To say the truth women are, in general, too familiar with each other, which leads to that gross degree of familiarity that so frequently renders the marriage state unhappy. Why in the name of decency are sisters, female intimates, or ladies and their waiting-women, to be so grossly familiar as to forget the respect which one human creature owes to another? That squeamish delicacy which shrinks from the most disgusting offices when affection[3] or humanity lead us to watch at a sick pillow, is despicable. But, why women in health should be more familiar with each other than men are, when they boast of their

---

1 Children very early see cats with their kittens, birds with their young ones, &c. Why then are they not to be told that their mothers carry and nourish them in the same way? As there would then be no appearance of mystery they would never think of the subject more. Truth may always be told to children, if it be told gravely; but it is the immodesty of affected modesty, that does all the mischief; and this smoke heats the imagination by vainly endeavouring to obscure certain objects. If, indeed, children could be kept entirely from improper company, we should never allude to any such subjects; but as this is impossible, it is best to tell them the truth, especially as such information, not interesting them, will make no impression on their imagination. [Cf. Rousseau, *Emile* 215-19.]

2 [Cf. Locke, *Some Thoughts concerning Education* 126-27; para. 68.]

3 Affection would rather make one choose to perform these offices, to spare the delicacy of a friend, by still keeping a veil over them, for the personal helplessness, produced by sickness, is of an humbling nature.

superior delicacy, is a solecism in manners which I could never solve.

In order to preserve health and beauty, I should earnestly recommend frequent ablutions, to dignify my advice that it may not offend the fastidious ear; and, by example, girls ought to be taught to wash and dress alone, without any distinction of rank; and if custom should make them require some little assistance, let them not require it till that part of the business is over which ought never to be done before a fellow-creature; because it is an insult to the majesty of human nature. Not on the score of modesty, but decency; for the care which some modest women take, making at the same time a display of that care, not to let their legs be seen, is as childish as immodest[1].

I could proceed still further, till I animadverted on some still more nasty customs, which men never fall into. Secrets are told – where silence ought to reign; and that regard to cleanliness, which some religious sects have, perhaps, carried too far, especially the Essenes,[2] amongst the Jews, by making that an insult to God which is only an insult to humanity, is violated in a beastly manner. How can *delicate* women obtrude on notice that part of the animal oeconomy, which is so very disgusting? And is it not very rational to conclude, that the women who have not been taught to respect the human nature of their own sex, in these particulars, will not long respect the mere difference of sex in their husbands? After their maidenish bashfulness is once lost, I, in fact, have generally observed, that women fall into old habits; and treat their husbands as they did their sisters or female acquaintance.

Besides, women from necessity, because their minds are not cultivated, have recourse very often to what I familiarly term bodily wit; and their intimacies are of the same kind. In short, with respect to both mind and body, they are too intimate. That decent personal reserve which is the foundation of dignity of character, must be kept up between woman and woman, or their minds will never gain strength or modesty.

On this account also, I object to many females being shut up

---

1    I remember to have met with a sentence, in a book of education, that made me smile. "It would be needless to caution you against putting your hand, by chance, under your neck-handkerchief; for a modest woman never did so!" [Unidentified.]

2    [A Jewish sect, c. 100 B.C. - A.D. 100, which practised ritual ablutions.]

together in nurseries, schools, or convents. I cannot recollect without indignation, the jokes and hoiden tricks, which knots of young women indulge themselves in, when in my youth accident threw me, an awkward rustic, in their way. They were almost on a par with the double meanings, which shake the convivial table when the glass has circulated freely. But, it is vain to attempt to keep the heart pure, unless the head is furnished with ideas, and set to work to compare them, in order to acquire judgment, by generalizing simple ones; and modesty, by making the understanding damp the sensibility.

It may be thought that I lay too great a stress on personal reserve; but it is ever the handmaid of modesty. So that were I to name the graces that ought to adorn beauty, I should instantly exclaim, cleanliness, neatness, and personal reserve. It is obvious, I suppose, that the reserve I mean, has nothing sexual in it, and that I think it *equally* necessary in both sexes. So necessary, indeed, is that reserve and cleanliness which indolent women too often neglect, that I will venture to affirm that when two or three women live in the same house, the one will be most respected by the male part of the family, who reside with them, leaving love entirely out of the question, who pays this kind of habitual respect to her person.

When domestic friends meet in a morning, there will naturally prevail an affectionate seriousness, especially, if each look forward to the discharge of daily duties; and it may be reckoned fanciful, but this sentiment has frequently risen spontaneously in my mind, I have been pleased after breathing the sweet-bracing morning air, to see the same kind of freshness in the countenances I particularly loved; I was glad to see them braced, as it were, for the day, and ready to run their course with the sun. The greetings of affection in the morning are by these means more respectful than the familiar tenderness which frequently prolongs the evening talk. Nay, I have often felt hurt, not to say disgusted, when a friend has appeared, whom I parted with full dressed the evening before, with her clothes huddled on, because she chose to indulge herself in bed till the last moment.

Domestic affection can only be kept alive by these neglected attentions; yet if men and women took half as much pains to dress habitually neat, as they do to ornament, or rather to disfigure, their persons, much would be done towards the attainment of purity of mind. But women only dress to gratify men of gallantry; for the lover is always best pleased with the simple garb that fits close to the shape. There is an impertinence in ornaments that rebuffs affection; because love always clings round the idea of home.

As a sex, women are habitually indolent; and every thing tends to make them so. I do not forget the spurts of activity which sensibility produces; but as these flights of feelings only increase the evil, they are not to be confounded with the slow, orderly walk of reason. So great in reality is their mental and bodily indolence, that till their body be strengthened and their understanding enlarged by active exertions, there is little reason to expect that modesty will take place of bashfulness. They may find it prudent to assume its semblance; but the fair veil will only be worn on gala days.

Perhaps, there is not a virtue that mixes so kindly with every other as modesty. – It is the pale moon-beam that renders more interesting every virtue it softens, giving mild grandeur to the contracted horizon. Nothing can be more beautiful than the poetical fiction, which makes Diana with her silver crescent, the goddess of chastity. I have sometimes thought, that wandering with sedate step in some lonely recess, a modest dame of antiquity must have felt a glow of conscious dignity when, after contemplating the soft shadowy landscape, she has invited with placid fervour the mild reflection of her sister's beams to turn to her chaste bosom.

A Christian has still nobler motives to incite her to preserve her chastity and acquire modesty, for her body has been called the Temple of the living God;[1] of that God who requires more than modesty of mien. His eye searcheth the heart;[2] and let her remember, that if she hope to find favour in the sight of purity itself, her chastity must be founded on modesty, and not on worldly prudence; or verily a good reputation will be her only reward; for that awful intercourse, that sacred communication, which virtue establishes between man and his Maker, must give rise to the wish of being pure as he is pure![3]

After the foregoing remarks, it is almost superfluous to add, that I consider all those feminine airs of maturity, which succeed bashful-

---

1  [1 Corinthians 3: 16-17, 6: 18-19; 2 Corinthians 6: 16.]
2  [1 Chronicles 28: 9; Jeremiah 17: 10.]
3  [Matthew 5: 48; 1 John 3: 3.]

ness, to which truth is sacrificed, to secure the heart of a husband, or rather to force him to be still a lover when nature would, had she not been interrupted in her operations, have made love give place to friendship, as immodest. The tenderness which a man will feel for the mother of his children is an excellent substitute for the ardour of unsatisfied passion; but to prolong that ardour it is indelicate, not to say immodest, for women to feign an unnatural coldness of constitution. Women as well as men ought to have the common appetites and passions of their nature, they are only brutal when unchecked by reason: but the obligation to check them is the duty of mankind, not a sexual duty. Nature, in these respects, may safely be left to herself; let women only acquire knowledge and humanity, and love will teach them modesty[1]. There is no need of falsehoods, disgusting as futile, for studied rules of behaviour only impose on shallow observers; a man of sense soon sees through, and despises the affectation.

The behaviour of young people, to each other, as men and women, is the last thing that should be thought of in education. In fact, behaviour in most circumstances is now so much thought of, that simplicity of character is rarely to be seen: yet, if men were only anxious to cultivate each virtue, and let it take root firmly in the mind, the grace resulting from it, its natural exteriour mark, would soon strip affectation of its flaunting plumes; because, fallacious as unstable, is the conduct that is not founded upon truth!

Would ye, O my sisters, really possess modesty, ye must remember that the possession of virtue, of any denomination, is incompatible with ignorance and vanity! ye must acquire that soberness of mind, which the exercise of duties, and the pursuit of knowledge, alone inspire, or ye will still remain in a doubtful dependent situation, and only be loved whilst ye are fair! The downcast eye, the rosy blush, the retiring grace, are all proper in their season; but modesty, being the child of reason, cannot long exist with the sensibility that is not tempered by reflection. Besides, when love, even innocent love, is the

---

1   The behaviour of many newly married women has often disgusted me. They seem anxious never to let their husbands forget the privilege of marriage; and to find no pleasure in his society unless he is acting the lover. Short, indeed, must be the reign of love, when the flame is thus constantly blown up, without its receiving any solid fewel!

whole employ of your lives, your hearts will be too soft to afford modesty that tranquil retreat, where she delights to dwell, in close union with humanity.

# CHAP. VIII.

## MORALITY UNDERMINED BY SEXUAL NOTIONS OF THE IMPORTANCE OF A GOOD REPUTATION.

I T has long since occurred to me that advice respecting behaviour, and all the various modes of preserving a good reputation, which have been so strenuously inculcated on the female world, were specious poisons, that incrusting morality eat away the substance. And, that this measuring of shadows produced a false calculation, because their length depends so much on the height of the sun, and other adventitious circumstances.

Whence arises the easy fallacious behaviour of a courtier? From his situation, undoubtedly: for standing in need of dependents, he is obliged to learn the art of denying without giving offence, and, of evasively feeding hope with the chameleon's food:[1] thus does politeness sport with truth, and eating away the sincerity and humanity natural to man, produce the fine gentleman.

Women likewise acquire, from a supposed necessity, an equally artificial mode of behaviour. Yet truth is not with impunity to be sported with, for the practised dissembler, at last, become the dupe of his own arts, loses that sagacity, which has been justly termed common sense; namely, a quick perception of common truths: which are constantly received as such by the unsophisticated mind, though it might not have had sufficient energy to discover them itself, when obscured by local prejudices. The greater number of people take their opinions on trust to avoid the trouble of exercising their own minds, and these indolent beings naturally adhere to the letter, rather than the spirit of a law, divine or human.[2] "Women," says some author, I cannot recollect who, "mind not what only heaven sees."[3] Why, indeed, should they? it is the eye of man that they have been taught to

---

1   [Traditionally, air; see Shakespeare, *Hamlet* 3.2.90-91.]
2   [Romans 2: 27; 2 Corinthians 3: 6.]
3   [Possibly Shakespeare, *Othello* 3.3.202-3.]

dread – and if they can lull their Argus[1] to sleep, they seldom think of heaven or themselves, because their reputation is safe; and it is reputation, not chastity and all its fair train, that they are employed to keep free from spot, not as a virtue, but to preserve their station in the world.

To prove the truth of this remark, I need only advert to the intrigues of married women, particularly in high life, and in countries where women are suitably married, according to their respective ranks, by their parents. If an innocent girl become a prey to love, she is degraded for ever, though her mind was not polluted by the arts which married women, under the convenient cloke of marriage, practise; nor has she violated any duty – but the duty of respecting herself. The married woman, on the contrary, breaks a most sacred engagement, and becomes a cruel mother when she is a false and faithless wife. If her husband have still an affection for her, the arts which she must practise to deceive him, will render her the most contemptible of human beings; and, at any rate, the contrivances necessary to preserve appearances, will keep her mind in that childish, or vicious, tumult, which destroys all its energy. Besides, in time, like those people who habitually take cordials to raise their spirits, she will want an intrigue to give life to her thoughts, having lost all relish for pleasures that are not highly seasoned by hope or fear.

Sometimes married women act still more audaciously; I will mention an instance.

A woman of quality, notorious for her gallantries, though as she still lived with her husband, nobody chose to place her in the class where she ought to have been placed, made a point of treating with the most insulting contempt a poor timid creature, abashed by a sense of her former weakness, whom a neighbouring gentleman had seduced and afterwards married. This woman had actually confounded virtue with reputation; and, I do believe, valued herself on the propriety of her behaviour before marriage, though when once settled to the satisfaction of her family, she and her lord were equally faithless, – so that the half alive heir to an immense estate came from heaven knows where!

---

1    [A giant with a hundred eyes, assigned by the jealous Hera to keep watch over Io to frustrate the lustful plans of Zeus. Hermes lulled him to sleep and killed him.]

To view this subject in another light.

I have known a number of women who, if they did not love their husbands, loved nobody else, give themselves entirely up to vanity and dissipation, neglecting every domestic duty; nay, even squandering away all the money which should have been saved for their helpless younger children, yet have plumed themselves on their unsullied reputation, as if the whole compass of their duty as wives and mothers was only to preserve it. Whilst other indolent women, neglecting every personal duty, have thought that they deserved their husbands' affection, because, forsooth, they acted in this respect with propriety.

Weak minds are always fond of resting in the ceremonials of duty, but morality offers much simpler motives; and it were to be wished that superficial moralists had said less respecting behaviour, and outward observances, for unless virtue, of any kind, be built on knowledge, it will only produce a kind of insipid decency. Respect for the opinion of the world, has, however, been termed the principal duty of woman in the most express words, for Rousseau declares, "that reputation is no less indispensable than chastity."[1] "A man," adds he, "secure in his own good conduct, depends only on himself, and may brave the public opinion: but a woman, in behaving well, performs but half her duty; as what is thought of her, is as important to her as what she really is. It follows hence, that the system of a woman's education should, in this respect, be directly contrary to that of ours. Opinion is the grave of virtue among the men; but its throne among women."[2] It is strictly logical to infer that the virtue that rests on opinion is merely worldly, and that it is the virtue of a being to whom reason has been denied. But, even with respect to the opinion of the world, I am convinced that this class of reasoners are mistaken.

This regard for reputation, independent of its being one of the natural rewards of virtue, however, took its rise from a cause that I have already deplored as the grand source of female depravity, the impossibility of regaining respectability by a return to virtue, though men preserve theirs during the indulgence of vice. It was natural for women then to endeavour to preserve what once lost – was lost for ever, till this care swallowing up every other care, reputation for

---

1    [Rousseau, *Emile* 361.]
2    [Rousseau, *Emile* 364–65.]

chastity, became the one thing needful[1] to the sex. But vain is the scrupulosity of ignorance, for neither religion nor virtue, when they reside in the heart, require such a puerile attention to mere ceremonies, because the behaviour must, upon the whole, be proper, when the motive is pure.

To support my opinion I can produce very respectable authority; and the authority of a cool reasoner ought to have weight to enforce consideration, though not to establish a sentiment. Speaking of the general laws of morality, Dr. Smith observes, – "That by some very extraordinary and unlucky circumstance, a good man may come to be suspected of a crime of which he was altogether incapable, and upon that account be most unjustly exposed for the remaining part of his life to the horror and aversion of mankind. By an accident of this kind he may be said to lose his all, notwithstanding his integrity and justice, in the same manner as a cautious man, notwithstanding his utmost circumspection, may be ruined by an earthquake or an inundation. Accidents of the first kind, however, are perhaps still more rare, and still more contrary to the common course of things than those of the second; and it still remains true, that the practice of truth, justice, and humanity, is a certain and almost infallible method of acquiring what those virtues chiefly aim at, the confidence and love of those we live with. A person may be easily misrepresented with regard to a particular action; but it is scarce possible that he should be so with regard to the general tenor of his conduct. An innocent man may be believed to have done wrong: this, however, will rarely happen. On the contrary, the established opinion of the innocence of his manners will often lead us to absolve him where he has really been in the fault, notwithstanding very strong presumptions."[2]

I perfectly coincide in opinion with this writer, for I verily believe that few of either sex were ever despised for certain vices without deserving to be despised. I speak not of the calumny of the moment, which hovers over a character, like one of the dense morning fogs of November, over this metropolis, till it gradually subsides before the common light of day, I only contend that the daily conduct of the majority prevails to stamp their character with the impression of

1   [Cf. Luke 10: 42.]
2   [Smith, *Theory* 167; 3.5.8.]

truth. Quietly does the clear light, shining day after day, refute the ignorant surmise, or malicious tale, which has thrown dirt on a pure character. A false light distorted, for a short time, its shadow – reputation; but it seldom fails to become just when the cloud is dispersed that produced the mistake in vision.

Many people, undoubtedly, in several respects obtain a better reputation than, strictly speaking, they deserve; for unremitting industry will mostly reach its goal in all races. They who only strive for this paltry prize, like the Pharisees, who prayed at the corners of streets, to be seen of men, verily obtain the reward they seek;[1] for the heart of man cannot be read by man! Still the fair fame that is naturally reflected by good actions, when the man is only employed to direct his steps aright,[2] regardless of the lookers-on, is, in general, not only more true, but more sure.

There are, it is true, trials when the good man must appeal to God from the injustice of man; and amidst the whining candour or hissings of envy, erect a pavilion in his own mind to retire to till the rumour be overpast; nay, the darts of undeserved censure may pierce an innocent tender bosom through with many sorrows; but these are all exceptions to general rules. And it is according to common laws that human behaviour ought to be regulated. The eccentric orbit of the comet never influences astronomical calculations respecting the invariable order established in the motion of the principal bodies of the solar system.

I will then venture to affirm, that after a man is arrived at maturity, the general outline of his character in the world is just, allowing for the before-mentioned exceptions to the rule. I do not say that a prudent, worldly-wise man, with only negative virtues and qualities, may not sometimes obtain a smoother reputation than a wiser or a better man. So far from it, that I am apt to conclude from experience, that where the virtue of two people is nearly equal, the most negative character will be liked best by the world at large, whilst the other may have more friends in private life. But the hills and dales, clouds and sunshine, conspicuous in the virtues of great men, set off each other; and though they afford envious weakness a fairer mark to shoot at, the

---

1   [Matthew 6: 5.]
2   [Cf. Proverbs 16: 9; Jeremiah 10: 23.]

real character will still work its way to light, though bespattered by weak affection, or ingenious malice[1].

With respect to that anxiety to preserve a reputation hardly earned, which leads sagacious people to analyze it, I shall not make the obvious comment; but I am afraid that morality is very insidiously undermined, in the female world, by the attention being turned to the shew instead of the substance. A simple thing is thus made strangely complicated; nay, sometimes virtue and its shadow are set at variance. We should never, perhaps, have heard of Lucretia, had she died to preserve her chastity instead of her reputation.[2] If we really deserve our own good opinion we shall commonly be respected in the world; but if we pant after higher improvement and higher attainments, it is not sufficient to view ourselves as we suppose that we are viewed by others, though this has been ingeniously argued, as the foundation of our moral sentiments[3]. Because each by-stander may have his own prejudices, beside the prejudices of his age or country. We should rather endeavour to view ourselves as we suppose that Being views us who seeth each thought ripen into action, and whose judgment never swerves from the eternal rule of right.[4] Righteous are all his judgments – just as merciful![5]

The humble mind that seeketh to find favour in His sight, and calmly examines its conduct when only His presence is felt, will seldom form a very erroneous opinion of its own virtues. During the still hour of self-collection the angry brow of offended justice will be fearfully deprecated, or the tie which draws man to the Deity will be recognized in the pure sentiment of reverential adoration, that swells the heart without exciting any tumultuous emotions. In these solemn moments man discovers the germ of those vices, which like the Java tree shed a pestiferous vapour around[6] – death is in the shade! and he

---

1   I allude to various biographical writings, but particularly to Boswell's Life of Johnson. [This had just been published, in 1791.]
2   [Lucretia (d. c. 510 BC) was raped by Sextus Tarquinius, son of the king of Rome. After making her husband, father, and cousin swear to avenge her, she stabbed herself. See Shakespeare, *The Rape of Lucrece*.]
3   Smith. [*Theory* 128-32; 3.2.31-33.]
4   [Cf. Macaulay, *Letters* 381.]
5   [Psalms 19: 9, 119: 75.]
6   [The Upas. For a vivid account of this mythical plant, see Darwin, *The Loves of the Plants* 106-7n., 167-68.]

perceives them without abhorrence, because he feels himself drawn by some cord of love to all his fellow-creatures, for whose follies he is anxious to find every extenuation in their nature – in himself. If I, he may thus argue, who exercise my own mind, and have been refined by tribulation, find the serpent's egg in some fold of my heart, and crush it with difficulty,[1] shall not I pity those who have stamped with less vigour, or who have heedlessly nurtured the insidious reptile till it poisoned the vital stream it sucked? Can I, conscious of my secret sins, throw off my fellow-creatures, and calmly see them drop into the chasm of perdition, that yawns to receive them. – No! no! The agonized heart will cry with suffocating impatience – I too am a man! and have vices, hid, perhaps, from human eye, that bend me to the dust before God, and loudly tell me, when all is mute, that we are formed of the same earth, and breathe the same element. Humanity thus rises naturally out of humility, and twists the cords of love that in various convolutions entangle the heart.

This sympathy extends still further, till a man well pleased observes force in arguments that do not carry conviction to his own bosom, and he gladly places in the fairest light, to himself, the shews of reason that have led others astray, rejoiced to find some reason in all the errors of man; though before convinced that he who rules the day makes his sun to shine on all. Yet, shaking hands thus as it were with corruption, one foot on earth, the other with bold stride mounts to heaven, and claims kindred with superiour natures. Virtues, unobserved by man, drop their balmy fragrance at this cool hour, and the thirsty land, refreshed by the pure streams of comfort that suddenly gush out, is crowned with smiling verdure; this is the living green on which that eye may look with complacency that is too pure to behold iniquity!

But my spirits flag; and I must silently indulge the reverie these reflections lead to, unable to describe the sentiments, that have calmed my soul, when watching the rising sun, a soft shower drizzling through the leaves of neighbouring trees, seemed to fall on my languid, yet tranquil spirits, to cool the heart that had been heated by the passions which reason laboured to tame.

---

1    [Shakespeare, *Julius Caesar* 2.1.32–34.]

The leading principles which run through all my disquisitions, would render it unnecessary to enlarge on this subject, if a constant attention to keep the varnish of the character fresh, and in good condition, were not often inculcated as the sum total of female duty; if rules to regulate the behaviour, and to preserve the reputation, did not too frequently supersede moral obligations. But, with respect to reputation, the attention is confined to a single virtue – chastity. If the honour of a woman, as it is absurdly called, be safe, she may neglect every social duty; nay, ruin her family by gaming and extravagance; yet still present a shameless front – for truly she is an honourable woman![1]

Mrs. Macaulay has justly observed, that "there is but one fault which a woman of honour may not commit with impunity." She then justly and humanely adds – "This has given rise to the trite and foolish observation, that the first fault against chastity in woman has a radical power to deprave the character. But no such frail beings come out of the hands of nature. The human mind is built of nobler materials than to be easily corrupted; and with all their disadvantages of situation and education, women seldom become entirely abandoned till they are thrown into a state of desperation, by the venomous rancour of their own sex."[2]

But, in proportion as this regard for the reputation of chastity is prized by women, it is despised by men: and the two extremes are equally destructive to morality.

Men are certainly more under the influence of their appetites than women; and their appetites are more depraved by unbridled indulgence and the fastidious contrivances of satiety. Luxury has introduced a refinement in eating, that destroys the constitution; and, a degree of gluttony which is so beastly, that a perception of seemliness of behaviour must be worn out before one being could eat immoderately in the presence of another, and afterwards complain of the oppression that his intemperance naturally produced. Some women, particularly French women, have also lost a sense of decency in this respect; for they will talk very calmly of an indigestion. It were to be wished that idleness was not allowed to generate, on the rank soil of

---

1   [Shakespeare, *Julius Caesar* 3.2.81-99.]
2   [Macaulay, *Letters* 210, 212 (Appendix B.2).]

wealth, those swarms of summer insects[1] that feed on putrefaction, we should not then be disgusted by the sight of such brutal excesses.

There is one rule relative to behaviour that, I think, ought to regulate every other; and it is simply to cherish such an habitual respect for mankind as may prevent us from disgusting a fellow-creature for the sake of a present indulgence. The shameful indolence of many married women, and others a little advanced in life, frequently leads them to sin against delicacy. For, though convinced that the person is the band of union between the sexes, yet, how often do they from sheer indolence, or, to enjoy some trifling indulgence, disgust?

The depravity of the appetite which brings the sexes together, has had a still more fatal effect. Nature must ever be the standard of taste, the gauge of appetite – yet how grossly is nature insulted by the voluptuary. Leaving the refinements of love out of the question; nature, by making the gratification of an appetite, in this respect, as well as every other, a natural and imperious law to preserve the species, exalts the appetite, and mixes a little mind and affection with a sensual gust. The feelings of a parent mingling with an instinct merely animal, give it dignity; and the man and woman often meeting on account of the child, a mutual interest and affection is excited by the exercise of a common sympathy. Women then having necessarily some duty to fulfil, more noble than to adorn their persons, would not contentedly be the slaves of casual lust; which is now the situation of a very considerable number who are, literally speaking, standing dishes to which every glutton may have access.

I may be told that great as this enormity is, it only affects a devoted part of the sex – devoted for the salvation of the rest. But, false as every assertion might easily be proved, that recommends the sanctioning a small evil to produce a greater good;[2] the mischief does not stop here, for the moral character, and peace of mind, of the chaster part of the sex, is undermined by the conduct of the very women to whom they allow no refuge from guilt: whom they inexorably consign to the exercise of arts that lure their husbands from them, debauch their sons, and force them, let not modest women start, to assume, in some degree, the same character themselves. For I will venture to assert, that

---

1   [Cf. *Original Stories*; *Works* 4: 400, 444; and Burke, *Reflections*; *Writings* 8: 145.]
2   [Cf. Macaulay, *Letters* 359, 417, 480.]

all the causes of female weakness, as well as depravity, which I have already enlarged on, branch out of one grand cause – want of chastity in men.[1]

This intemperance, so prevalent, depraves the appetite to such a degree, that a wanton stimulus is necessary to rouse it; but the parental design of nature is forgotten, and the mere person, and that for a moment, alone engrosses the thoughts. So voluptuous, indeed, often grows the lustful prowler, that he refines on female softness. Something more soft than woman is then sought for; till, in Italy and Portugal, men attend the levees of equivocal beings, to sigh for more than female languor.

To satisfy this genus of men, women are made systematically voluptuous, and though they may not all carry their libertinism to the same height, yet this heartless intercourse with the sex, which they allow themselves, depraves both sexes, because the taste of men is vitiated; and women, of all classes, naturally square their behaviour to gratify the taste by which they obtain pleasure and power. Women becoming, consequently, weaker, in mind and body, than they ought to be, were one of the grand ends of their being taken into the account, that of bearing and nursing children, have not sufficient strength to discharge the first duty of a mother; and sacrificing to lasciviousness the parental affection, that ennobles instinct, either destroy the embryo in the womb, or cast it off when born. Nature in every thing demands respect, and those who violate her laws seldom violate them with impunity. The weak enervated women who particularly catch the attention of libertines, are unfit to be mothers, though they may conceive; so that the rich sensualist, who has rioted among women, spreading depravity and misery, when he wishes to perpetuate his name, receives from his wife only an half-formed being that inherits both its father's and mother's weakness.

Contrasting the humanity of the present age with the barbarism of antiquity, great stress has been laid on the savage custom of exposing the children whom their parents could not maintain; whilst the man of sensibility, who thus, perhaps, complains, by his promiscuous amours produces a most destructive barrenness and contagious flagitiousness of manners. Surely nature never intended that women, by

---

1  [Cf. Macaulay, *Letters* 220.]

satisfying an appetite, should frustrate the very purpose for which it was implanted?

I have before observed, that men ought to maintain the women whom they have seduced; this would be one means of reforming female manners, and stopping an abuse that has an equally fatal effect on population and morals. Another, no less obvious, would be to turn the attention of woman to the real virtue of chastity; for to little respect has that woman a claim, on the score of modesty, though her reputation may be white as the driven snow, who smiles on the libertine whilst she spurns the victims of his lawless appetites and their own folly.

Besides, she has a taint of the same folly, pure as she esteems herself, when she studiously adorns her person only to be seen by men, to excite respectful sighs, and all the idle homage of what is called innocent gallantry. Did women really respect virtue for its own sake, they would not seek for a compensation in vanity, for the self-denial which they are obliged to practise to preserve their reputation, nor would they associate with men who set reputation at defiance.

The two sexes mutually corrupt and improve each other.[1] This I believe to be an indisputable truth, extending it to every virtue. Chastity, modesty, public spirit, and all the noble train of virtues, on which social virtue and happiness are built, should be understood and cultivated by all mankind, or they will be cultivated to little effect. And, instead of furnishing the vicious or idle with a pretext for violating some sacred duty, by terming it a sexual one, it would be wiser to shew that nature has not made any difference, for that the unchaste man doubly defeats the purpose of nature, by rendering women barren, and destroying his own constitution, though he avoids the shame that pursues the crime in the other sex. These are the physical consequences, the moral are still more alarming; for virtue is only a nominal distinction when the duties of citizens, husbands, wives, fathers, mothers, and directors of families, become merely the selfish ties of convenience.

Why then do philosophers look for public spirit? Public spirit must be nurtured by private virtue,[2] or it will resemble the factitious

---

1   [Cf. Macaulay, *Letters* 216.]
2   [Another allusion to Mandeville, *The Fable of the Bees; or, Private Vices, Public Benefits*.]

sentiment which makes women careful to preserve their reputation, and men their honour. A sentiment that often exists unsupported by virtue, unsupported by that sublime morality which makes the habitual breach of one duty a breach of the whole moral law.

# CHAP. IX.

## OF THE PERNICIOUS EFFECTS WHICH ARISE FROM THE UNNATURAL DISTINCTIONS ESTABLISHED IN SOCIETY.

FROM the respect paid to property flow, as from a poisoned fountain, most of the evils and vices which render this world such a dreary scene to the contemplative mind. For it is in the most polished society that noisome reptiles and venomous serpents lurk under the rank herbage; and there is voluptuousness pampered by the still sultry air, which relaxes every good disposition before it ripens into virtue.

One class presses on another; for all are aiming to procure respect on account of their property: and property, once gained, will procure the respect due only to talents and virtue. Men neglect the duties incumbent on man, yet are treated like demi-gods; religion is also separated from morality by a ceremonial veil, yet men wonder that the world is almost, literally speaking, a den of sharpers or oppressors.

There is a homely proverb, which speaks a shrewd truth, that whoever the devil finds idle he will employ.[1] And what but habitual idleness can hereditary wealth and titles produce? For man is so constituted that he can only attain a proper use of his faculties by exercising them, and will not exercise them unless necessity, of some kind, first set the wheels in motion. Virtue likewise can only be acquired by the discharge of relative duties; but the importance of these sacred duties will scarcely be felt by the being who is cajoled out of his humanity by the flattery of sycophants. There must be more equality established in society, or morality will never gain ground, and this virtuous equality will not rest firmly even when founded on a rock,[2] if one half of mankind be chained to its bottom by fate, for they will be continually undermining it through ignorance or pride.

---

1   [Cf. Isaac Watts (1674-1748), *Divine Songs* (1720), "Song 20" 11-12.]
2   [Matthew 7: 24-25.]

It is vain to expect virtue from women till they are, in some degree, independent of men; nay, it is vain to expect that strength of natural affection, which would make them good wives and mothers. Whilst they are absolutely dependent on their husbands they will be cunning, mean, and selfish, and the men who can be gratified by the fawning fondness of spaniel-like affection, have not much delicacy, for love is not to be bought, in any sense of the words, its silken wings are instantly shrivelled up when any thing beside a return in kind is sought. Yet whilst wealth enervates men; and women live, as it were, by their personal charms, how can we expect them to discharge those ennobling duties which equally require exertion and self-denial. Hereditary property sophisticates the mind, and the unfortunate victims to it, if I may so express myself, swathed from their birth, seldom exert the locomotive faculty of body or mind; and, thus viewing every thing through one medium, and that a false one, they are unable to discern in what true merit and happiness consist. False, indeed, must be the light when the drapery of situation hides the man, and makes him stalk in masquerade, dragging from one scene of dissipation to another the nerveless limbs that hang with stupid listlessness, and rolling round the vacant eye which plainly tells us that there is no mind at home.

I mean, therefore, to infer that the society is not properly organized which does not compel men and women to discharge their respective duties, by making it the only way to acquire that countenance from their fellow-creatures, which every human being wishes some way to attain. The respect, consequently, which is paid to wealth and mere personal charms, is a true north-east blast, that blights the tender blossoms of affection and virtue. Nature has wisely attached affections to duties, to sweeten toil, and to give that vigour to the exertions of reason which only the heart can give. But, the affection which is put on merely because it is the appropriated insignia of a certain character, when its duties are not fulfilled, is one of the empty compliments which vice and folly are obliged to pay to virtue and the real nature of things.

To illustrate my opinion, I need only observe, that when a woman is admired for her beauty, and suffers herself to be so far intoxicated by the admiration she receives, as to neglect to discharge the indispensable duty of a mother, she sins against herself by neglecting to cultivate an affection that would equally tend to make her useful and happy. True happiness, I mean all the contentment, and virtuous satisfaction, that can be snatched in this imperfect state, must arise from well regulated affections; and an affection includes a duty. Men are not aware of the misery they cause, and the vicious weakness they cherish, by only inciting women to render themselves pleasing; they do not consider that they thus make natural and artificial duties clash, by sacrificing the comfort and respectability of a woman's life to voluptuous notions of beauty, when in nature they all harmonize.

Cold would be the heart of a husband, were he not rendered unnatural by early debauchery, who did not feel more delight at seeing his child suckled by its mother, than the most artful wanton tricks could ever raise; yet this natural way of cementing the matrimonial tie, and twisting esteem with fonder recollections, wealth leads women to spurn. To preserve their beauty, and wear the flowery crown of the day, which gives them a kind of right to reign for a short time over the sex, they neglect to stamp impressions on their husbands' hearts, that would be remembered with more tenderness when the snow on the head began to chill the bosom, than even their virgin charms. The maternal solicitude of a reasonable affectionate woman is very interesting, and the chastened dignity with which a mother returns the caresses that she and her child receive from a father who has been fulfilling the serious duties of his station, is not only a respectable, but a beautiful sight. So singular, indeed, are my feelings, and I have endeavoured not to catch factitious ones, that after having been fatigued with the sight of insipid grandeur and the slavish ceremonies that with cumberous pomp supplied the place of domestic affections, I have turned to some other scene to relieve my eye by resting it on the refreshing green every where scattered by nature. I have then viewed with pleasure a woman nursing her children, and discharging the duties of her station with, perhaps, merely a servant maid to take off her hands the servile part of the household business. I have seen her prepare herself and children, with only the luxury of cleanliness, to receive her husband, who returning weary home in the evening found smiling babes and a clean hearth. My heart has loitered in the midst of the group, and has even throbbed with sympathetic emotion, when the scraping of the well known foot has raised a pleasing tumult.

Whilst my benevolence has been gratified by contemplating this artless picture, I have thought that a couple of this description, equally necessary and independent of each other, because each fulfilled the respective duties of their station, possessed all that life could give. – Raised sufficiently above abject poverty not to be obliged to weigh the consequence of every farthing they spend, and having sufficient to prevent their attending to a frigid system of oeconomy, which narrows both heart and mind. I declare, so vulgar are my conceptions, that I know not what is wanted to render this the happiest as well as the most respectable situation in the world, but a taste for literature, to throw a little variety and interest into social converse, and some superfluous money to give to the needy and to buy books. For it is not pleasant when the heart is opened by compassion and the head active in arranging plans of usefulness, to have a prim urchin continually twitching back the elbow to prevent the hand from drawing out an almost empty purse, whispering at the same time some prudential maxim about the priority of justice.

Destructive, however, as riches and inherited honours are to the human character, women are more debased and cramped, if possible, by them, than men, because men may still, in some degree, unfold their faculties by becoming soldiers and statesmen.

As soldiers, I grant, they can now only gather, for the most part, vain glorious laurels, whilst they adjust to a hair the European balance, taking especial care that no bleak northern nook or sound[1] incline the beam. But the days of true heroism are over, when a citizen fought for his country like a Fabricius or a Washington, and then returned to his farm to let his virtuous fervour run in a more placid, but not a less salutary, stream.[2] No, our British heroes are oftener sent

---

1   [A reference to the Nootka Sound controversy, which nearly led to a war after Spain seized four British merchant ships in 1789, and which ended Spain's monopoly on trade and settlement on the west coast of North America. Wollstonecraft refers to Nootka Sound again in *Letters Written during a Short Residence in Sweden, Norway, and Denmark* (*Works* 6: 293).]

2   [Washington had returned to Mount Vernon after his victory over the British; he would do so again at the end of his presidency.]

from the gaming table than from the plow;[1] and their passions have been rather inflamed by hanging with dumb suspense on the turn of a die, than sublimated by panting after the adventurous march of virtue in the historic page.

The statesman, it is true, might with more propriety quit the Faro Bank, or card-table, to guide the helm, for he has still but to shuffle and trick. The whole system of British politics, if system it may courteously be called, consisting in multiplying dependents and contriving taxes which grind the poor to pamper the rich; thus a war, or any wild goose chace, is, as the vulgar use the phrase, a lucky turn-up of patronage for the minister, whose chief merit is the art of keeping himself in place. It is not necessary then that he should have bowels for the poor, so he can secure for his family the odd trick. Or should some shew of respect, for what is termed with ignorant ostentation an Englishman's birth-right, be expedient to bubble the gruff mastiff that he has to lead by the nose, he can make an empty shew, very safely, by giving his single voice, and suffering his light squadron to file off to the other side. And when a question of humanity is agitated he may dip a sop in the milk of human kindness,[2] to silence Cerberus,[3] and talk of the interest which his heart takes in an attempt to make the earth no longer cry for vengeance as it sucks in its children's blood, though his cold hand may at the very moment rivet their chains, by sanctioning the abominable traffick.[4] A minister is no longer a minister, than while he can carry a point, which he is determined to carry. — Yet it is not necessary that a minister should feel like a man, when a bold push might shake his seat.

But, to have done with these episodical observations, let me return to the more specious slavery which chains the very soul of woman, keeping her for ever under the bondage of ignorance.

---

1  [In 458 B.C., when Rome was under threat from the Aequi, the Senate appointed Cincinnatus commander-in-chief. Its representatives found him in his fields, ploughing. In sixteen days, he defeated the Aequi, rescued a consul, and was back on his farm.]
2  [Shakespeare, *Macbeth* 1.5.15.]
3  [In Greek mythology, the watch-dog of the underworld.]
4  [In April 1792, the House of Commons would pass a resolution calling for the "gradual abolition" of the slave trade, a benevolent gesture that did not actually commit the government to doing anything.]

The preposterous distinctions of rank, which render civilization a curse, by dividing the world between voluptuous tyrants, and cunning envious dependents, corrupt, almost equally, every class of people, because respectability is not attached to the discharge of the relative duties of life, but to the station, and when the duties are not fulfilled the affections cannot gain sufficient strength to fortify the virtue of which they are the natural reward. Still there are some loop-holes out of which a man may creep, and dare to think and act for himself; but for a woman it is an herculean task, because she has difficulties peculiar to her sex to overcome, which require almost super-human powers.

A truly benevolent legislator always endeavours to make it the interest of each individual to be virtuous; and thus private virtue becoming the cement of public happiness,[1] an orderly whole is consolidated by the tendency of all the parts towards a common centre. But, the private or public virtue of woman is very problematical; for Rousseau, and a numerous list of male writers, insist that she should all her life be subjected to a severe restraint, that of propriety. Why subject her to propriety – blind propriety, if she be capable of acting from a nobler spring, if she be an heir of immortality? Is sugar always to be produced by vital blood?[2] Is one half of the human species, like the poor African slaves, to be subject to prejudices that brutalize them, when principles would be a surer guard, only to sweeten the cup of man? Is not this indirectly to deny woman reason? for a gift is a mockery, if it be unfit for use.

Women are, in common with men, rendered weak and luxurious by the relaxing pleasures which wealth procures; but added to this they are made slaves to their persons, and must render them alluring that man may lend them his reason to guide their tottering steps aright. Or should they be ambitious, they must govern their tyrants by sinister tricks, for without rights there cannot be any incumbent duties. The laws respecting woman, which I mean to discuss in a future part, make an absurd unit of a man and his wife; and then, by

---

1   [Another allusion to Mandeville, *The Fable of the Bees; or, Private Vices, Public Benefits.*]
2   [A boycott of slave-produced sugar was one of the most successful aspects of the abolition campaign (and one in which women could play an active part): by 1792, between three and four hundred thousand consumers were taking part. See Appendix A.1.]

the easy transition of only considering him as responsible, she is reduced to a mere cypher.[1]

The being who discharges the duties of its station is independent; and, speaking of women at large, their first duty is to themselves as rational creatures, and the next, in point of importance, as citizens, is that, which includes so many, of a mother. The rank in life which dispenses with their fulfilling this duty, necessarily degrades them by making them mere dolls. Or, should they turn to something more important than merely fitting drapery upon a smooth block, their minds are only occupied by some soft platonic attachment; or, the actual management of an intrigue may keep their thoughts in motion; for when they neglect domestic duties, they have it not in their power to take the field and march and counter-march like soldiers, or wrangle in the senate to keep their faculties from rusting.

I know that, as a proof of the inferiority of the sex, Rousseau has exultingly exclaimed, How can they leave the nursery for the camp![2] – And the camp has by some moralists been termed the school of the most heroic virtues; though, I think, it would puzzle a keen casuist to prove the reasonableness of the greater number of wars that have dubbed heroes. I do not mean to consider this question critically; because, having frequently viewed these freaks of ambition as the first natural mode of civilization, when the ground must be torn up, and the woods cleared by fire and sword, I do not choose to call them pests; but surely the present system of war has little connection with virtue of any denomination, being rather the school of *finesse* and effeminacy, than of fortitude.

Yet, if defensive war, the only justifiable war,[3] in the present advanced state of society, where virtue can shew its face and ripen amidst the rigours which purify the air on the mountain's top, were alone to be adopted as just and glorious, the true heroism of antiquity might again animate female bosoms. – But fair and softly, gentle reader, male or female, do not alarm thyself, for though I have compared the character of a modern soldier with that of a civilized woman, I am

---

1  [Cf. William Blackstone (1723-80), *Commentaries on the Laws of England* (1765-69) 430; 1.15.]
2  [Rousseau, *Emile* 362.]
3  [Price, *Discourse* 29; Appendix A.3.]

not going to advise them to turn their distaff into a musket, though I sincerely wish to see the bayonet converted into a pruning-hook.[1] I only recreated an imagination, fatigued by contemplating the vices and follies which all proceed from a feculent stream of wealth that has muddied the pure rills of natural affection, by supposing that society will some time or other be so constituted, that man must necessarily fulfil the duties of a citizen, or be despised, and that while he was employed in any of the departments of civil life, his wife, also an active citizen, should be equally intent to manage her family, educate her children, and assist her neighbours.

But, to render her really virtuous and useful, she must not, if she discharge her civil duties, want, individually, the protection of civil laws; she must not be dependent on her husband's bounty for her subsistence during his life, or support after his death – for how can a being be generous who has nothing of its own? or, virtuous, who is not free? The wife, in the present state of things, who is faithful to her husband, and neither suckles nor educates her children, scarcely deserves the name of a wife, and has no right to that of a citizen. But take away natural rights, and duties become null.

Women then must be considered as only the wanton solace of men, when they become so weak in mind and body, that they cannot exert themselves, unless to pursue some frothy pleasure, or to invent some frivolous fashion. What can be a more melancholy sight to a thinking mind, than to look into the numerous carriages that drive helter-skelter about this metropolis in a morning full of pale-faced creatures who are flying from themselves. I have often wished, with Dr. Johnson,[2] to place some of them in a little shop with half a dozen children looking up to their languid countenances for support. I am much mistaken, if some latent vigour would not soon give health and spirit to their eyes, and some lines drawn by the exercise of reason on the blank cheeks, which before were only undulated by dimples, might restore lost dignity to the character, or rather enable it to attain the true dignity of its nature. Virtue is not to be acquired even by speculation, much less by the negative supineness that wealth natural-

---

1 [Isaiah 2: 4; cf. Price, *Discourse* 30, Appendix A.3.]
2 [Johnson, *The Rambler* 85 (8 January 1751), "The Mischiefs of Total Idleness." Wollstonecraft included several excerpts from Johnson in *The Female Reader*.]

ly generates.

Besides, when poverty is more disgraceful than even vice, is not morality cut to the quick? Still to avoid misconstruction, though I consider that women in the common walks of life are called to fulfil the duties of wives and mothers, by religion and reason, I cannot help lamenting that women of a superiour cast have not a road open by which they can pursue more extensive plans of usefulness and independence. I may excite laughter, by dropping an hint, which I mean to pursue, some future time, for I really think that women ought to have representatives, instead of being arbitrarily governed without having any direct share allowed them in the deliberations of government.[1]

But, as the whole system of representation is now, in this country, only a convenient handle for despotism, they need not complain, for they are as well represented as a numerous class of hard working mechanics, who pay for the support of royalty when they can scarcely stop their children's mouths with bread.[2] How are they represented whose very sweat supports the splendid stud of an heir apparent, or varnishes the chariot of some female favourite who looks down on shame? Taxes on the very necessaries of life, enable an endless tribe of idle princes and princesses to pass with stupid pomp before a gaping crowd, who almost worship the very parade which costs them so dear. This is mere gothic grandeur, something like the barbarous useless parade of having sentinels on horseback at Whitehall,[3] which I could never view without a mixture of contempt and indignation.

How strangely must the mind be sophisticated when this sort of state impresses it! But, till these monuments of folly are levelled by virtue, similar follies will leaven the whole mass. For the same character, in some degree, will prevail in the aggregate of society: and the refinements of luxury, or the vicious repinings of envious poverty, will equally banish virtue from society, considered as the characteristic of that society, or only allow it to appear as one of the stripes of the harlequin coat, worn by the civilized man.

In the superiour ranks of life, every duty is done by deputies, as if

---

1   [British women were not given the vote until 1928.]
2   [Cf. Macaulay, *Observations* 48-52; Price, *Discourse* 39-42 (Appendix A.3).]
3   [Whitehall is the location of the most important offices of the British government. The horse guards are still there.]

duties could ever be waved, and the vain pleasures which consequent idleness forces the rich to pursue, appear so enticing to the next rank, that the numerous scramblers for wealth sacrifice every thing to tread on their heels. The most sacred trusts are then considered as sinecures, because they were procured by interest, and only sought to enable a man to keep *good company*. Women, in particular, all want to be ladies. Which is simply to have nothing to do, but listlessly to go they scarcely care where, for they cannot tell what.

But what have women to do in society? I may be asked, but to loiter with easy grace; surely you would not condemn them all to suckle fools and chronicle small beer![1] No. Women might certainly study the art of healing, and be physicians as well as nurses. And midwifery, decency seems to allot to them, though I am afraid the word midwife, in our dictionaries, will soon give place to *accoucheur*, and one proof of the former delicacy of the sex be effaced from the language.

They might, also, study politics, and settle their benevolence on the broadest basis; for the reading of history will scarcely be more useful than the perusal of romances, if read as mere biography; if the character of the times, the political improvements, arts, &c. be not observed. In short, if it be not considered as the history of man; and not of particular men, who filled a niche in the temple of fame, and dropped into the black rolling stream of time, that silently sweeps all before it, into the shapeless void called – eternity. – For shape, can it be called, "that shape hath none?"[2]

Business of various kinds, they might likewise pursue, if they were educated in a more orderly manner, which might save many from common and legal prostitution. Women would not then marry for a support, as men accept of places under government, and neglect the implied duties; nor would an attempt to earn their own subsistence, a most laudable one! sink them almost to the level of those poor abandoned creatures who live by prostitution. For are not milliners and mantua-makers reckoned the next class? The few employments open to women, so far from being liberal, are menial; and when a superiour education enables them to take charge of the education of children as governesses, they are not treated like the tutors of sons, though even

---

1 [Shakespeare, *Othello* 2.1.159.]
2 [Milton, *Paradise Lost* 3.11-12, 2.667.]

clerical tutors are not always treated in a manner calculated to render them respectable in the eyes of their pupils, to say nothing of the private comfort of the individual. But as women educated like gentlewomen, are never designed for the humiliating situation which necessity sometimes forces them to fill; these situations are considered in the light of a degradation; and they know little of the human heart, who need to be told, that nothing so painfully sharpens sensibility as such a fall in life.

Some of these women might be restrained from marrying by a proper spirit or delicacy, and others may not have had it in their power to escape in this pitiful way from servitude; is not that government then very defective, and very unmindful of the happiness of one half of its members, that does not provide for honest, independent women, by encouraging them to fill respectable stations? But in order to render their private virtue a public benefit,[1] they must have a civil existence in the State, married or single; else we shall continually see some worthy woman, whose sensibility has been rendered painfully acute by undeserved contempt, droop like "the lily broken down by a plow-share."[2]

It is a melancholy truth; yet such is the blessed effect of civilization! the most respectable women are the most oppressed;[3] and, unless they have understandings far superiour to the common run of understandings, taking in both sexes, they must, from being treated like contemptible beings, become contemptible. How many women thus waste life away the prey of discontent, who might have practised as physicians, regulated a farm, managed a shop, and stood erect, supported by their own industry,[4] instead of hanging their heads surcharged with the dew of sensibility, that consumes the beauty to which it at first gave lustre;[5] nay, I doubt whether pity and love are so near akin as poets feign, for I have seldom seen much compassion excited by the helplessness of females, unless they were fair; then, per-

---

1   [Another allusion to Mandeville, *The Fable of the Bees; or, Private Vices, Public Benefits.*]
2   [Fénelon, *The Adventures of Telemachus*, trans. Isaac Littlebury (1699) 1: 152; cf. Robert Burns (1759-96), "To a Mountain-Daisy, On turning one down, with the Plough, in April—1786" 49-54.]
3   [An ironic echo of the opening sentences of Swift, "A Modest Proposal" (1729).]
4   [Cf. Thomas Gray, "Elegy Written in a Country Church-Yard" (1750) 53-60.]
5   [Cf. Shakespeare, Sonnet 73, line 12.]

haps, pity was the soft handmaid of love, or the harbinger of lust.

How much more respectable is the woman who earns her own bread by fulfilling any duty, than the most accomplished beauty! – beauty did I say? – so sensible am I of the beauty of moral loveliness, or the harmonious propriety that attunes the passions of a well-regulated mind, that I blush at making the comparison; yet I sigh to think how few women aim at attaining this respectability by withdrawing from the giddy whirl of pleasure, or the indolent calm that stupifies the good sort of women it sucks in.

Proud of their weakness, however, they must always be protected, guarded from care, and all the rough toils that dignify the mind. – If this be the fiat of fate, if they will make themselves insignificant and contemptible, sweetly to waste "life away," let them not expect to be valued when their beauty fades, for it is the fate of the fairest flowers to be admired and pulled to pieces by the careless hand that plucked them. In how many ways do I wish, from the purest benevolence, to impress this truth on my sex; yet I fear that they will not listen to a truth that dear bought experience has brought home to many an agitated bosom, nor willingly resign the privileges of rank and sex for the privileges of humanity, to which those have no claim who do not discharge its duties.

Those writers are particularly useful, in my opinion, who make man feel for man, independent of the station he fills, or the drapery of factitious sentiments. I then would fain convince reasonable men of the importance of some of my remarks; and prevail on them to weigh dispassionately the whole tenor of my observations. – I appeal to their understandings; and, as a fellow-creature, claim, in the name of my sex, some interest in their hearts. I entreat them to assist to emancipate their companion, to make her a *help meet* for them!

Would men but generously snap our chains, and be content with rational fellowship instead of slavish obedience, they would find us more observant daughters, more affectionate sisters, more faithful wives, more reasonable mothers – in a word, better citizens. We should then love them with true affection, because we should learn to respect ourselves; and the peace of mind of a worthy man would not be interrupted by the idle vanity of his wife, nor the babes sent to nestle in a strange bosom, having never found a home in their mother's.

# CHAP. X.

## PARENTAL AFFECTION.

PARENTAL affection is, perhaps, the blindest modification of perverse self-love; for we have not, like the French[1], two terms to distinguish the pursuit of a natural and reasonable desire, from the ignorant calculations of weakness. Parents often love their children in the most brutal manner, and sacrifice every relative duty to promote their advancement in the world. – To promote, such is the perversity of unprincipled prejudices, the future welfare of the very beings whose present existence they imbitter by the most despotic stretch of power. Power, in fact, is ever true to its vital principle, for in every shape it would reign without controul or inquiry. Its throne is built across a dark abyss, which no eye must dare to explore, lest the baseless fabric[2] should totter under investigation. Obedience, unconditional obedience, is the catch-word of tyrants of every description, and to render "assurance doubly sure,"[3] one kind of despotism supports another. Tyrants would have cause to tremble if reason were to become the rule of duty in any of the relations of life, for the light might spread till perfect day appeared. And when it did appear, how would men smile at the sight of the bugbears at which they started during the night of ignorance, or the twilight of timid inquiry.

Parental affection, indeed, in many minds, is but a pretext to tyrannize where it can be done with impunity, for only good and wise men are content with the respect that will bear discussion. Convinced that they have a right to what they insist on, they do not fear reason, or dread the sifting of subjects that recur to natural justice: because they firmly believe that the more enlightened the human mind

---

1   *L'amour propre. L'amour de soi même.* [Rousseau distinguishes between them in a note to the *Discourse on the Origin and Foundations of Inequality* (221-22), and in *Emile* (92, 213-14).]
2   [Shakespeare, *The Tempest* 4.1.151.]
3   [Shakespeare, *Macbeth* 4.1.83.]

becomes the deeper root will just and simple principles take. They do not rest in expedients, or grant that what is metaphysically true can be practically false;[1] but disdaining the shifts of the moment they calmly wait till time, sanctioning innovation, silences the hiss of selfishness or envy.

If the power of reflecting on the past, and darting the keen eye of contemplation into futurity, be the grand privilege of man, it must be granted that some people enjoy this prerogative in a very limited degree. Every thing new appears to them wrong;[2] and not able to distinguish the possible from the monstrous, they fear where no fear should find a place, running from the light of reason, as if it were a firebrand; yet the limits of the possible have never been defined to stop the sturdy innovator's hand.

Woman, however, a slave in every situation to prejudice, seldom exerts enlightened maternal affection; for she either neglects her children, or spoils them by improper indulgence. Besides, the affection of some women for their children is, as I have before termed it, frequently very brutish: for it eradicates every spark of humanity. Justice, truth, every thing is sacrificed by these Rebekah's, and for the sake of their *own* children they violate the most sacred duties, forgetting the common relationship that binds the whole family on earth together.[3] Yet, reason seems to say, that they who suffer one duty, or affection, to swallow up the rest, have not sufficient heart or mind to fulfil that one conscientiously. It then loses the venerable aspect of a duty, and assumes the fantastic form of a whim.

As the care of children in their infancy is one of the grand duties annexed to the female character by nature, this duty would afford many forcible arguments for strengthening the female understanding, if it were properly considered.

The formation of the mind must be begun very early, and the temper, in particular, requires the most judicious attention – an attention which women cannot pay who only love their children because they are their children, and seek no further for the foundation of their

---

1 [Burke, *Reflections*; *Writings* 8: 112.]
2 [Macaulay, *Letters* iii.]
3 [See Genesis 27, where Rebekah helps her favourite son, Jacob, trick his dying father, Isaac, to obtain his blessing.]

duty, than in the feelings of the moment. It is this want of reason in their affections which makes women so often run into extremes, and either be the most fond or most careless and unnatural mothers.

To be a good mother – a woman must have sense, and that independence of mind which few women possess who are taught to depend entirely on their husbands. Meek wives are, in general, foolish mothers; wanting their children to love them best, and take their part, in secret, against the father, who is held up as a scarecrow. When chastisement is necessary, though they have offended the mother, the father must inflict the punishment; he must be the judge in all disputes: but I shall more fully discuss this subject when I treat of private education, I now only mean to insist, that unless the understanding of woman be enlarged, and her character rendered more firm, by being allowed to govern her own conduct, she will never have sufficient sense or command of temper to manage her children properly. Her parental affection, indeed, scarcely deserves the name, when it does not lead her to suckle her children, because the discharge of this duty is equally calculated to inspire maternal and filial affection: and it is the indispensable duty of men and women to fulfil the duties which give birth to affections that are the surest preservatives against vice. Natural affection, as it is termed, I believe to be a very faint tie, affections must grow out of the habitual exercise of a mutual sympathy; and what sympathy does a mother exercise who sends her babe to a nurse, and only takes it from a nurse to send it to a school?

In the exercise of their maternal feelings providence has furnished women with a natural substitute for love, when the lover becomes only a friend, and mutual confidence takes place of overstrained admiration – a child then gently twists the relaxing cord, and a mutual care produces a new mutual sympathy. – But a child, though a pledge of affection, will not enliven it, if both father and mother be content to transfer the charge to hirelings; for they who do their duty by proxy should not murmur if they miss the reward of duty – parental affection produces filial duty.

# CHAP. XI.

## DUTY TO PARENTS.

THERE seems to be an indolent propensity in man to make prescription always take place of reason, and to place every duty on an arbitrary foundation. The rights of kings are deduced in a direct line from the King of kings; and that of parents from our first parent.

Why do we thus go back for principles that should always rest on the same base, and have the same weight to-day that they had a thousand years ago – and not a jot more? If parents discharge their duty they have a strong hold and sacred claim on the gratitude of their children; but few parents are willing to receive the respectful affection of their offspring on such terms. They demand blind obedience, because they do not merit a reasonable service: and to render these demands of weakness and ignorance more binding, a mysterious sanctity is spread round the most arbitrary principle; for what other name can be given to the blind duty of obeying vicious or weak beings merely because they obeyed a powerful instinct?

The simple definition of the reciprocal duty, which naturally subsists between parent and child, may be given in a few words: The parent who pays proper attention to helpless infancy has a right to require the same attention when the feebleness of age comes upon him.[1] But to subjugate a rational being to the mere will of another, after he is of age to answer to society for his own conduct, is a most cruel and undue stretch of power; and, perhaps, as injurious to morality as those religious systems which do not allow right and wrong to have any existence, but in the Divine will.

I never knew a parent who had paid more than common attention to his children, disregarded[2]; on the contrary, the early habit of relying almost implicitly on the opinion of a respected parent is not easily

---

1   [Cf. Macaulay, *Letters* 12.]
2   Dr. Johnson makes the same observation. [*The Rambler* 148 (17 August 1751), "The Cruelty of Parental Tyranny."]

shook, even when matured reason convinces the child that his father is not the wisest man in the world. This weakness, for a weakness it is, though the epithet amiable may be tacked to it, a reasonable man must steel himself against; for the absurd duty, too often inculcated, of obeying a parent only on account of his being a parent, shackles the mind, and prepares it for a slavish submission to any power but reason.

I distinguish between the natural and accidental duty due to parents.

The parent who sedulously endeavours to form the heart and enlarge the understanding of his child, has given that dignity to the discharge of a duty, common to the whole animal world, that only reason can give. This is the parental affection of humanity, and leaves instinctive natural affection far behind. Such a parent acquires all the rights of the most sacred friendship, and his advice, even when his child is advanced in life, demands serious consideration.

With respect to marriage, though after one and twenty a parent seems to have no right to withhold his consent on any account; yet twenty years of solicitude call for a return, and the son ought, at least, to promise not to marry for two or three years, should the object of his choice not entirely meet with the approbation of his first friend.

But, respect for parents is, generally speaking, a much more debasing principle; it is only a selfish respect for property. The father who is blindly obeyed, is obeyed from sheer weakness, or from motives that degrade the human character.

A great proportion of the misery that wanders, in hideous forms, around the world, is allowed to rise from the negligence of parents; and still these are the people who are most tenacious of what they term a natural right, though it be subversive of the birth-right of man, the right of acting according to the direction of his own reason.

I have already very frequently had occasion to observe, that vicious or indolent people are always eager to profit by enforcing arbitrary privileges; and, generally, in the same proportion as they neglect the discharge of the duties which alone render the privileges reasonable. This is at the bottom a dictate of common sense, or the instinct of self-defence, peculiar to ignorant weakness; resembling that instinct, which makes a fish muddy the water it swims in to elude its enemy, instead of boldly facing it in the clear stream.

From the clear stream of argument, indeed, the supporters of prescription, of every denomination, fly; and, taking refuge in the darkness, which, in the language of sublime poetry, has been supposed to surround the throne of Omnipotence,[1] they dare to demand that implicit respect which is only due to His unsearchable ways.[2] But, let me not be thought presumptuous, the darkness which hides our God from us, only respects speculative truths – it never obscures moral ones, they shine clearly, for God is light,[3] and never, by the constitution of our nature, requires the discharge of a duty, the reasonableness of which does not beam on us when we open our eyes.[4]

The indolent parent of high rank may, it is true, extort a shew of respect from his child, and females on the continent are particularly subject to the views of their families, who never think of consulting their inclination, or providing for the comfort of the poor victims of their pride. The consequence is notorious; these dutiful daughters become adulteresses, and neglect the education of their children, from whom they, in their turn, exact the same kind of obedience.

Females, it is true, in all countries, are too much under the dominion of their parents; and few parents think of addressing their children in the following manner, though it is in this reasonable way that Heaven seems to command the whole human race. It is your interest to obey me till you can judge for yourself; and the Almighty Father of all has implanted an affection in me to serve as a guard to you whilst your reason is unfolding; but when your mind arrives at maturity, you must only obey me, or rather respect my opinions, so far as they coincide with the light that is breaking in on your own mind.

A slavish bondage to parents cramps every faculty of the mind; and Mr. Locke very judiciously observes, that "if the mind be curbed and humbled too much in children; if their spirits be abased and broken much by too strict an hand over them; they lose all their vigour and industry."[5] This strict hand may in some degree account for the weakness of women; for girls, from various causes, are more kept down by

---

1    [Milton, *Paradise Lost* 3.380, 6.56-59.]
2    [Romans 11: 33.]
3    [1 John 1: 5; Milton, *Paradise Lost* 3.1-55.]
4    [Cf. Rousseau, *Emile* 308, 380-81.]
5    [Locke, *Some Thoughts concerning Education* 112; para. 46.2. Cf. Macaulay, *Letters* 98-99.]

their parents, in every sense of the word, than boys. The duty expected from them is, like all the duties arbitrarily imposed on women,
more from a sense of propriety, more out of respect for decorum, than
reason; and thus taught slavishly to submit to their parents, they are
prepared for the slavery of marriage. I may be told that a number of
women are not slaves in the marriage state. True, but they then
become tyrants; for it is not rational freedom, but a lawless kind of
power resembling the authority exercised by the favourites of
absolute monarchs, which they obtain by debasing means. I do not,
likewise, dream of insinuating that either boys or girls are always
slaves, I only insist that when they are obliged to submit to authority
blindly, their faculties are weakened, and their tempers rendered
imperious or abject. I also lament that parents, indolently availing
themselves of a supposed privilege, damp the first faint glimmering of
reason, rendering at the same time the duty, which they are so anxious
to enforce, an empty name; because they will not let it rest on the
only basis on which a duty can rest securely; for unless it be founded
on knowledge, it cannot gain sufficient strength to resist the squalls of
passion, or the silent sapping of self-love. But it is not the parents who
have given the surest proof of their affection for their children, or, to
speak more properly, who by fulfilling their duty, have allowed a natural parental affection to take root in their hearts, the child of exercised sympathy and reason, and not the over weening offspring of
selfish pride, who most vehemently insist on their children submitting
to their will merely because it is their will. On the contrary, the parent, who sets a good example, patiently lets that example work; and it
seldom fails to produce its natural effect – filial reverence.

Children cannot be taught too early to submit to reason, the true
definition of that necessity, which Rousseau insisted on, without
defining it; for to submit to reason is to submit to the nature of things,
and to that God, who formed them so, to promote our real interest.

Why should the minds of children be warped as they just begin to
expand, only to favour the indolence of parents, who insist on a privilege without being willing to pay the price fixed by nature? I have
before had occasion to observe, that a right always includes a duty, and
I think it may, likewise, fairly be inferred, that they forfeit the right,
who do not fulfil the duty.

It is easier, I grant, to command than reason; but it does not follow from hence that children cannot comprehend the reason why they are made to do certain things habitually: for, from a steady adherence to a few simple principles of conduct flows that salutary power which a judicious parent gradually gains over a child's mind. And this power becomes strong indeed, if tempered by an even display of affection brought home to the child's heart. For, I believe, as a general rule, it must be allowed that the affection which we inspire always resembles that we cultivate; so that natural affections, which have been supposed almost distinct from reason, may be found more nearly connected with judgment than is commonly allowed. Nay, as another proof of the necessity of cultivating the female understanding, it is but just to observe, that the affections seem to have a kind of animal capriciousness when they merely reside in the heart.

It is the irregular exercise of parental authority that first injures the mind, and to these irregularities girls are more subject than boys. The will of those who never allow their will to be disputed, unless they happen to be in a good humour, when they relax proportionally, is almost always unreasonable. To elude this arbitrary authority girls very early learn the lessons which they afterwards practise on their husbands; for I have frequently seen a little sharp-faced miss rule a whole family, excepting that now and then mamma's angry will burst out of some accidental cloud; – either her hair was ill dressed[1], or she had lost more money at cards, the night before, than she was willing to own to her husband; or some such moral cause of anger.

After observing sallies of this kind, I have been led into a melancholy train of reflection respecting females, concluding that when their first affection must lead them astray, or make their duties clash till they rest on mere whims and customs, little can be expected from them as they advance in life. How indeed can an instructor remedy this evil? for to teach them virtue on any solid principle is to teach them to despise their parents. Children cannot, ought not, to be taught to make allowance for the faults of their parents, because every

---

[1]  I myself heard a little girl once say to a servant, "My mamma has been scolding me finely this morning, because her hair was not dressed to please her." Though this remark was pert, it was just. And what respect could a girl acquire for such a parent without doing violence to reason?

such allowance weakens the force of reason in their minds, and makes them still more indulgent to their own. It is one of the most sublime virtues of maturity that leads us to be severe with respect to ourselves, and forbearing to others; but children should only be taught the simple virtues, for if they begin too early to make allowance for human passions and manners, they wear off the fine edge of the criterion by which they should regulate their own, and become unjust in the same proportion as they grow indulgent.

The affections of children, and weak people, are always selfish; they love their relatives, because they are beloved by them, and not on account of their virtues. Yet, till esteem and love are blended together in the first affection, and reason made the foundation of the first duty, morality will stumble at the threshold. But, till society is very differently constituted, parents, I fear, will still insist on being obeyed, because they will be obeyed, and constantly endeavour to settle that power on a Divine right which will not bear the investigation of reason.

# CHAP. XII.

## ON NATIONAL EDUCATION.

THE good effects resulting from attention to private education will ever be very confined, and the parent who really puts his own hand to the plow, will always, in some degree, be disappointed, till education becomes a grand national concern. A man cannot retire into a desert with his child, and if he did he could not bring himself back to child-hood, and become the proper friend and play-fellow of an infant or youth. And when children are confined to the society of men and women, they very soon acquire that kind of premature manhood which stops the growth of every vigorous power of mind or body. In order to open their faculties they should be excited to think for themselves; and this can only be done by mixing a number of children together, and making them jointly pursue the same objects.

A child very soon contracts a benumbing indolence of mind, which he has seldom sufficient vigour afterwards to shake off, when he only asks a question instead of seeking for information, and then relies implicitly on the answer he receives. With his equals in age this could never be the case, and the subjects of inquiry, though they might be influenced, would not be entirely under the direction of men, who frequently damp, if not destroy, abilities, by bringing them forward too hastily: and too hastily they will infallibly be brought forward, if the child be confined to the society of a man, however saga-cious that man may be.

Besides, in youth the seeds of every affection should be sown, and the respectful regard, which is felt for a parent, is very different from the social affections that are to constitute the happiness of life as it advances. Of these equality is the basis, and an intercourse of senti-ments unclogged by that observant seriousness which prevents disputa-tion, though it may not inforce submission. Let a child have ever such an affection for his parent, he will always languish to play and prattle with children; and the very respect he feels, for filial esteem always has a dash of fear mixed with it, will, if it do not teach him cunning, at least prevent him from pouring out the little secrets which first open the heart to friendship and confidence, gradually leading to more expansive benevolence. Added to this, he will never acquire that frank ingenuousness of behaviour, which young people can only attain by being frequently in society where they dare to speak what they think; neither afraid of being reproved for their presumption, nor laughed at for their folly.

Forcibly impressed by the reflections which the sight of schools, as they are at present conducted, naturally suggested, I have formerly delivered my opinion rather warmly in favour of a private education;[1] but further experience has led me to view the subject in a different light. I still, however, think schools, as they are now regulated, the hot-beds of vice and folly, and the knowledge of human nature, supposed to be attained there, merely cunning selfishness.

At school boys become gluttons and slovens, and, instead of cultivating domestic affections, very early rush into the libertinism which destroys the constitution before it is formed; hardening the heart as it weakens the understanding.

I should, in fact, be averse to boarding-schools, if it were for no other reason than the unsettled state of mind which the expectation of the vacations produce. On these the children's thoughts are fixed with eager anticipating hopes, for, at least, to speak with moderation, half of the time, and when they arrive they are spent in total dissipation and beastly indulgence.

But, on the contrary, when they are brought up at home, though they may pursue a plan of study in a more orderly manner than can be adopted when near a fourth part of the year is actually spent in idleness, and as much more in regret and anticipation; yet they there acquire too high an opinion of their own importance, from being allowed to tyrannize over servants, and from the anxiety expressed by most mothers, on the score of manners, who, eager to teach the accomplishments of a gentleman, stifle, in their birth, the virtues of a man. Thus brought into company when they ought to be seriously employed, and treated like men when they are still boys, they become

---

1   [In her review of Macaulay's *Letters on Education* (*Works* 7: 310-11); cf. Rousseau, *Emile* 48-50, 388.]

vain and effeminate.

The only way to avoid two extremes equally injurious to morality, would be to contrive some way of combining a public and private education. Thus to make men citizens two natural steps might be taken, which seem directly to lead to the desired point; for the domestic affections, that first open the heart to the various modifications of humanity, would be cultivated, whilst the children were nevertheless allowed to spend great part of their time, on terms of equality, with other children.

I still recollect, with pleasure, the country day school; where a boy trudged in the morning, wet or dry, carrying his books, and his dinner, if it were at a considerable distance; a servant did not then lead master by the hand, for, when he had once put on coat and breeches, he was allowed to shift for himself, and return alone in the evening to recount the feats of the day close at the parental knee. His father's house was his home, and was ever after fondly remembered; nay, I appeal to many superiour men, who were educated in this manner, whether the recollection of some shady lane where they conned their lesson; or, of some stile, where they sat making a kite, or mending a bat, has not endeared their country to them?

But, what boy ever recollected with pleasure the years he spent in close confinement, at an academy near London? unless, indeed, he should, by chance, remember the poor scare-crow of an usher,[1] whom he tormented; or, the tartman, from whom he caught a cake, to devour it with a cattish appetite of selfishness. At boarding-schools of every description, the relaxation of the junior boys is mischief; and of the senior, vice. Besides, in great schools, what can be more prejudicial to the moral character than the system of tyranny and abject slavery which is established amongst the boys, to say nothing of the slavery to forms, which makes religion worse than a farce? For what good can be expected from the youth who receives the sacrament of the Lord's supper, to avoid forfeiting half a guinea, which he probably afterwards spends in some sensual manner? Half the employment of the youths is to elude the necessity of attending public worship; and well they may, for such a constant repetition of the same thing must be a very irksome restraint on their natural vivacity. As these ceremonies have the

---

1  [An assistant teacher, as opposed to the master or proprietor of the school.]

most fatal effect on their morals, and as a ritual performed by the lips, when the heart and mind are far away, is not now stored up by our church as a bank to draw on for the fees of the poor souls in purgatory, why should they not be abolished?

But the fear of innovation, in this country, extends to every thing. – This is only a covert fear, the apprehensive timidity of indolent slugs, who guard, by sliming it over, the snug place, which they consider in the light of an hereditary estate; and eat, drink, and enjoy themselves, instead of fulfilling the duties, excepting a few empty forms, for which it was endowed.[1] These are the people who most strenuously insist on the will of the founder being observed, crying out against all reformation, as if it were a violation of justice. I am now alluding particularly to the relicks of popery retained in our colleges, when the protestant members seem to be such sticklers for the established church; but their zeal never makes them lose sight of the spoil of ignorance, which rapacious priests of superstitious memory have scraped together. No, wise in their generation,[2] they venerate the prescriptive right of possession, as a strong hold, and still let the sluggish bell tinkle to prayers, as during the days when the elevation of the host was supposed to atone for the sins of the people, lest one reformation should lead to another, and the spirit kill the letter.[3] These Romish customs have the most baneful effect on the morals of our clergy; for the idle vermin who two or three times a day perform in the most slovenly manner a service which they think useless, but call their duty, soon lose a sense of duty. At college, forced to attend or evade public worship, they acquire an habitual contempt for the very service, the performance of which is to enable them to live in idleness. It is mumbled over as an affair of business, as a stupid boy repeats his task, and frequently the college cant escapes from the preacher the moment after he has left the pulpit, and even whilst he is eating the dinner which he earned in such a dishonest manner.

Nothing, indeed, can be more irreverent than the cathedral service as it is now performed in this country, neither does it contain a set of weaker men than those who are the slaves of this childish routine. A

---

1  [Cf. Macaulay, *Letters* 273.]
2  [Luke 16: 8.]
3  [An ironic allusion to 2 Corinthians 3: 6.]

disgusting skeleton of the former state is still exhibited; but all the solemnity that interested the imagination, if it did not purify the heart, is stripped off. The performance of high mass on the continent must impress every mind, where a spark of fancy glows, with that awful melancholy, that sublime tenderness, so near akin to devotion. I do not say that these devotional feelings are of more use, in a moral sense, than any other emotion of taste; but I contend that the theatrical pomp which gratifies our senses, is to be preferred to the cold parade that insults the understanding without reaching the heart.

Amongst remarks on national education, such observations cannot be misplaced, especially as the supporters of these establishments, degenerated into puerilities, affect to be the champions of religion. – Religion, pure source of comfort in this vale of tears! how has thy clear stream been muddied by the dabblers, who have presumptuously endeavoured to confine in one narrow channel, the living waters that ever flow towards God – the sublime ocean of existence! What would life be without that peace which the love of God, when built on humanity, alone can impart? Every earthly affection turns back, at intervals, to prey upon the heart that feeds it; and the purest effusions of benevolence, often rudely damped by man, must mount as a free-will offering to Him who gave them birth, whose bright image they faintly reflect.

In public schools, however, religion, confounded with irksome ceremonies and unreasonable restraints, assumes the most ungracious aspect: not the sober austere one that commands respect whilst it inspires fear; but a ludicrous cast, that serves to point a pun. For, in fact, most of the good stories and smart things which enliven the spirits that have been concentrated at whist, are manufactured out of the incidents to which the very men labour to give a droll turn who countenance the abuse to live on the spoil.

There is not, perhaps, in the kingdom, a more dogmatical, or luxurious set of men, than the pedantic tyrants who reside in colleges and preside at public schools. The vacations are equally injurious to the morals of the masters and pupils, and the intercourse, which the former keep up with the nobility, introduces the same vanity and extravagance into their families, which banish domestic duties and comforts from the lordly mansion, whose state is awkwardly aped. The boys, who live at a great expence with the masters and assistants, are never domesticated, though placed there for that purpose; for, after a silent dinner, they swallow a hasty glass of wine, and retire to plan some mischievous trick, or to ridicule the person or manners of the very people they have just been cringing to, and whom they ought to consider as the representatives of their parents.

Can it then be a matter of surprise that boys become selfish and vicious who are thus shut out from social converse? or that a mitre often graces the brow of one of these diligent pastors?

The desire of living in the same style, as the rank just above them, infects each individual and every class of people, and meanness is the concomitant of this ignoble ambition; but those professions are most debasing whose ladder is patronage; yet, out of one of these professions the tutors of youth are, in general, chosen. But, can they be expected to inspire independent sentiments, whose conduct must be regulated by the cautious prudence that is ever on the watch for preferment?

So far, however, from thinking of the morals of boys, I have heard several masters of schools argue, that they only undertook to teach Latin and Greek; and that they had fulfilled their duty, by sending some good scholars to college.

A few good scholars, I grant, may have been formed by emulation and discipline; but, to bring forward these clever boys, the health and morals of a number have been sacrificed. The sons of our gentry and wealthy commoners are mostly educated at these seminaries, and will any one pretend to assert that the majority, making every allowance, come under the description of tolerable scholars?

It is not for the benefit of society that a few brilliant men should be brought forward at the expence of the multitude. It is true, that great men seem to start up, as great revolutions occur, at proper intervals, to restore order, and to blow aside the clouds that thicken over the face of truth; but let more reason and virtue prevail in society, and these strong winds would not be necessary. Public education, of every denomination, should be directed to form citizens; but if you wish to make good citizens, you must first exercise the affections of a son and a brother. This is the only way to expand the heart; for public affections, as well as public virtues, must ever grow out of the private character,[1] or they are merely meteors that shoot athwart a dark sky, and disappear as they are gazed at and admired.

Few, I believe, have had much affection for mankind, who did not first love their parents, their brothers, sisters, and even the domestic brutes, whom they first played with. The exercise of youthful sympathies forms the moral temperature; and it is the recollection of these first affections and pursuits that gives life to those that are afterwards more under the direction of reason. In youth, the fondest friendships are formed, the genial juices mounting at the same time, kindly mix; or, rather the heart, tempered for the reception of friendship, is accustomed to seek for pleasure in something more noble than the churlish gratification of appetite.

In order then to inspire a love of home and domestic pleasures, children ought to be educated at home, for riotous holidays only make them fond of home for their own sakes. Yet, the vacations, which do not foster domestic affections, continually disturb the course of study, and render any plan of improvement abortive which includes temperance; still, were they abolished, children would be entirely separated from their parents, and I question whether they would become better citizens by sacrificing the preparatory affections, by destroying the force of relationships that render the marriage state as necessary as respectable. But, if a private education produce self-importance, or insulate a man in his family, the evil is only shifted, not remedied.

This train of reasoning brings me back to a subject, on which I mean to dwell, the necessity of establishing proper day-schools.

But, these should be national establishments, for whilst schoolmasters are dependent on the caprice of parents, little exertion can be expected from them, more than is necessary to please ignorant people. Indeed, the necessity of a master's giving the parents some sample of the boy's abilities, which during the vacation is shewn to every visitor[2], is productive of more mischief than would at first be supposed. For it is seldom done entirely, to speak with moderation, by the child itself; thus the master countenances falsehood, or winds the poor

---

1 [Another allusion to Mandeville, *The Fable of the Bees; or, Private Vices, Public Benefits*.]

2 I now particularly allude to the numerous academies in and about London, and to the behaviour of the trading part of this great city.

machine up to some extraordinary exertion, that injures the wheels, and stops the progress of gradual improvement. The memory is loaded with unintelligible words, to make a shew of, without the understanding's acquiring any distinct ideas: but only that education deserves emphatically to be termed cultivation of mind, which teaches young people how to begin to think. The imagination should not be allowed to debauch the understanding before it gained strength, or vanity will become the forerunner of vice: for every way of exhibiting the acquirements of a child is injurious to its moral character.

How much time is lost in teaching them to recite what they do not understand? whilst, seated on benches, all in their best array, the mammas listen with astonishment to the parrot-like prattle, uttered in solemn cadences, with all the pomp of ignorance and folly.[1] Such exhibitions only serve to strike the spreading fibres of vanity through the whole mind; for they neither teach children to speak fluently, nor behave gracefully. So far from it, that these frivolous pursuits might comprehensively be termed the study of affectation; for we now rarely see a simple, bashful boy, though few people of taste were ever disgusted by that awkward sheepishness so natural to the age, which schools and an early introduction into society, have changed into impudence and apish grimace.

Yet, how can these things be remedied whilst school-masters depend entirely on parents for a subsistence; and, when so many rival schools hang out their lures, to catch the attention of vain fathers and mothers, whose parental affection only leads them to wish that their children should outshine those of their neighbours?

Without great good luck, a sensible, conscientious man, would starve before he could raise a school, if he disdained to bubble weak parents by practising the secret tricks of the craft.

In the best regulated schools, however, where swarms are not crammed together, many bad habits must be acquired; but, at common schools, the body, heart, and understanding, are equally stunted, for parents are often only in quest of the cheapest school, and the master could not live, if he did not take a much greater number than he could manage himself; nor will the scanty pittance, allowed for each child, permit him to hire ushers sufficient to assist in the dis-

---

1    [Cf. Rousseau, *Emile* 107; Macaulay, *Letters* 56-57.]

charge of the mechanical part of the business. Besides, whatever appearance the house and garden may make, the children do not enjoy the comfort of either, for they are continually reminded by irksome restrictions that they are not at home, and the state-rooms, garden, &c. must be kept in order for the recreation of the parents; who, of a Sunday, visit the school, and are impressed by the very parade that renders the situation of their children uncomfortable.

With what disgust have I heard sensible women, for girls are more restrained and cowed than boys, speak of the wearisome confinement, which they endured at school. Not allowed, perhaps, to step out of one broad walk in a superb garden, and obliged to pace with steady deportment stupidly backwards and forwards, holding up their heads and turning out their toes, with shoulders braced back, instead of bounding, as nature directs to complete her own design, in the various attitudes so conducive to health[1]. The pure animal spirits, which make both mind and body shoot out, and unfold the tender blossoms of hope, are turned sour, and vented in vain wishes or pert repinings, that contract the faculties and spoil the temper; else they mount to the brain, and sharpening the understanding before it gains proportionable strength, produce that pitiful cunning which disgracefully characterizes the female mind – and I fear will ever characterize it whilst women remain the slaves of power!

The little respect paid to chastity in the male world is, I am persuaded, the grand source of many of the physical and moral evils that torment mankind, as well as of the vices and follies that degrade and destroy women; yet at school, boys infallibly lose that decent bashfulness, which might have ripened into modesty, at home.

And what nasty indecent tricks do they not also learn from each

---

1   I remember a circumstance that once came under my own observation, and raised my indignation. I went to visit a little boy at a school where young children were prepared for a larger one. The master took me into the school-room, &c. but whilst I walked down a broad gravel walk, I could not help observing that the grass grew very luxuriantly on each side of me. I immediately asked the child some questions, and found that the poor boys were not allowed to stir off the walk, and that the master sometimes permitted sheep to be turned in to crop the untrodden grass. The tyrant of this domain used to sit by a window that overlooked the prison yard, and one nook turning from it, where the unfortunate babes could sport freely, he enclosed, and planted it with potatoes. The wife likewise was equally anxious to keep the children in order, lest they should dirty or tear their clothes.

other, when a number of them pig together in the same bedchamber, not to speak of the vices, which render the body weak, whilst they effectually prevent the acquisition of any delicacy of mind.[1] The little attention paid to the cultivation of modesty, amongst men, produces great depravity in all the relationships of society; for, not only love – love that ought to purify the heart, and first call forth all the youthful powers, to prepare the man to discharge the benevolent duties of life, is sacrificed to premature lust; but, all the social affections are deadened by the selfish gratifications, which very early pollute the mind, and dry up the generous juices of the heart. In what an unnatural manner is innocence often violated; and what serious consequences ensue to render private vices a public pest.[2] Besides, an habit of personal order, which has more effect on the moral character, than is, in general, supposed, can only be acquired at home, where that respectable reserve is kept up which checks the familiarity, that sinking into beastliness, undermines the affection it insults.

I have already animadverted on the bad habits which females acquire when they are shut up together; and, I think, that the observation may fairly be extended to the other sex, till the natural inference is drawn which I have had in view throughout – that to improve both sexes they ought, not only in private families, but in public schools, to be educated together.[3] If marriage be the cement of society, mankind should all be educated after the same model, or the intercourse of the sexes will never deserve the name of fellowship, nor will women ever fulfil the peculiar duties of their sex, till they become enlightened citizens, till they become free by being enabled to earn their own subsistence, independent of men; in the same manner, I mean, to prevent misconstruction, as one man is independent of another. Nay, marriage will never be held sacred till women, by being brought up with men, are prepared to be their companions rather than their mistresses; for the mean doublings of cunning will ever render them contemptible, whilst oppression renders them timid. So convinced am I of this truth, that I will venture to predict that virtue will never prevail in society till the virtues of both sexes are founded on reason; and, till

---

1  [Cf. Rousseau's warning against masturbation (*Emile* 334).]
2  [Another allusion to Mandeville, *The Fable of the Bees; or, Private Vices, Public Benefits*.]
3  [Cf. Macaulay, *Letters* 46-47, 50, 142.]

the affections common to both are allowed to gain their due strength by the discharge of mutual duties.

Were boys and girls permitted to pursue the same studies together, those graceful decencies might early be inculcated which produce modesty without those sexual distinctions that taint the mind. Lessons of politeness, and that formulary of decorum, which treads on the heels of falsehood, would be rendered useless by habitual propriety of behaviour. Not, indeed, put on for visitors like the courtly robe of politeness, but the sober effect of cleanliness of mind. Would not this simple elegance of sincerity be a chaste homage paid to domestic affections, far surpassing the meretricious compliments that shine with false lustre in the heartless intercourse of fashionable life? But, till more understanding preponderates in society, there will ever be a want of heart and taste, and the harlot's *rouge* will supply the place of that celestial suffusion which only virtuous affections can give to the face. Gallantry, and what is called love, may subsist without simplicity of character; but the main pillars of friendship, are respect and con-fidence – esteem is never founded on it cannot tell what!

A taste for the fine arts requires great cultivation; but not more than a taste for the virtuous affections; and both suppose that enlarge-ment of mind which opens so many sources of mental pleasure. Why do people hurry to noisy scenes, and crowded circles? I should answer, because they want activity of mind, because they have not cherished the virtues of the heart. They only, therefore, see and feel in the gross, and continually pine after variety, finding every thing that is simple insipid.

This argument may be carried further than philosophers are aware of, for if nature destined woman, in particular, for the discharge of domestic duties, she made her susceptible of the attached affections in a great degree. Now women are notoriously fond of pleasure; and, naturally must be so according to my definition, because they cannot enter into the minutiae of domestic taste; lacking judgment, the foun-dation of all taste. For the understanding, in spite of sensual cavillers, reserves to itself the privilege of conveying pure joy to the heart.

With what a languid yawn have I seen an admirable poem thrown down, that a man of true taste returns to, again and again with rap-ture; and, whilst melody has almost suspended respiration, a lady has asked me where I bought my gown. I have seen also an eye glanced coldly over a most exquisite picture, rest, sparkling with pleasure, on a caricature rudely sketched; and whilst some terrific feature in nature has spread a sublime stillness through my soul, I have been desired to observe the pretty tricks of a lap-dog, that my perverse fate forced me to travel with. Is it surprising that such a tasteless being should rather caress this dog than her children? Or, that she should prefer the rant of flattery to the simple accents of sincerity?

To illustrate this remark I must be allowed to observe, that men of the first genius, and most cultivated minds, have appeared to have the highest relish for the simple beauties of nature; and they must have forcibly felt, what they have so well described, the charm which natural affections, and unsophisticated feelings spread round the human character. It is this power of looking into the heart, and responsively vibrating with each emotion, that enables the poet to personify each passion, and the painter to sketch with a pencil of fire.

True taste is ever the work of the understanding employed in observing natural effects; and till women have more understanding, it is vain to expect them to possess domestic taste. Their lively senses will ever be at work to harden their hearts, and the emotions struck out of them will continue to be vivid and transitory, unless a proper education store their mind with knowledge.

It is the want of domestic taste, and not the acquirement of knowledge, that takes women out of their families, and tears the smiling babe from the breast that ought to afford it nourishment. Women have been allowed to remain in ignorance, and slavish dependence, many, very many years, and still we hear of nothing but their fondness of pleasure and sway, their preference of rakes and soldiers, their childish attachment to toys, and the vanity that makes them value accomplishments more than virtues.

History brings forward a fearful catalogue of the crimes which their cunning has produced, when the weak slaves have had sufficient address to over-reach their masters. In France, and in how many other countries, have men been the luxurious despots, and women the crafty ministers? – Does this prove that ignorance and dependence domesticate them? Is not their folly the by-word of the libertines, who relax in their society; and do not men of sense continually lament that an immoderate fondness for dress and dissipation carries the mother of a family for ever from home? Their hearts have not been debauched by knowledge, or their minds led astray by scientific pursuits; yet, they do not fulfil the peculiar duties which as women they are called upon by nature to fulfil. On the contrary, the state of warfare which subsists between the sexes, makes them employ those wiles, that often frustrate the more open designs of force.

When, therefore, I call women slaves, I mean in a political and civil sense; for, indirectly they obtain too much power, and are debased by their exertions to obtain illicit sway.

Let an enlightened nation[1] then try what effect reason would have to bring them back to nature, and their duty; and allowing them to share the advantages of education and government with man, see whether they will become better, as they grow wiser and become free. They cannot be injured by the experiment; for it is not in the power of man to render them more insignificant than they are at present.

To render this practicable, day schools, for particular ages, should be established by government, in which boys and girls might be educated together. The school for the younger children, from five to nine years of age, ought to be absolutely free and open to all classes[2]. A sufficient number of masters should also be chosen by a select committee, in each parish, to whom any complaint of negligence, &c. might be made, if signed by six of the children's parents.

Ushers would then be unnecessary; for I believe experience will ever prove that this kind of subordinate authority is particularly injurious to the morals of youth. What, indeed, can tend to deprave the character more than outward submission and inward contempt? Yet how can boys be expected to treat an usher with respect, when the master seems to consider him in the light of a servant, and almost to countenance the ridicule which becomes the chief amusement of the boys during the play hours?

But nothing of this kind could occur in an elementary day-school,

---

1 France.
2 Treating this part of the subject, I have borrowed some hints from a very sensible pamphlet, written by the late bishop of Autun on Public Education. [Cf. Talleyrand, *Rapport* 26-27.]

where boys and girls, the rich and poor, should meet together. And to prevent any of the distinctions of vanity, they should be dressed alike, and all obliged to submit to the same discipline, or leave the school. The school-room ought to be surrounded by a large piece of ground, in which the children might be usefully exercised, for at this age they should not be confined to any sedentary employment for more than an hour at a time. But these relaxations might all be rendered a part of elementary education, for many things improve and amuse the senses, when introduced as a kind of show, to the principles of which, dryly laid down, children would turn a deaf ear. For instance, botany, mechanics, and astronomy. Reading, writing, arithmetic, natural history, and some simple experiments in natural philosophy, might fill up the day; but these pursuits should never encroach on gymnastic plays in the open air. The elements of religion, history, the history of man, and politics, might also be taught by conversations, in the socratic form.

After the age of nine, girls and boys, intended for domestic employments, or mechanical trades, ought to be removed to other schools, and receive instruction, in some measure appropriated to the destination of each individual, the two sexes being still together in the morning; but in the afternoon, the girls should attend a school, where plain-work, mantua-making, millinery, &c. would be their employment.

The young people of superior abilities, or fortune, might now be taught, in another school, the dead and living languages, the elements of science, and continue the study of history and politics, on a more extensive scale, which would not exclude polite literature.

Girls and boys still together? I hear some readers ask: yes. And I should not fear any other consequence than that some early attachment might take place; which, whilst it had the best effect on the moral character of the young people, might not perfectly agree with the views of the parents, for it will be a long time, I fear, before the world will be so far enlightened that parents, only anxious to render their children virtuous, shall allow them to choose companions for life themselves.

Besides, this would be a sure way to promote early marriages, and from early marriages the most salutary physical and moral effects naturally flow. What a different character does a married citizen assume from the selfish coxcomb, who lives, but for himself, and who is often afraid to marry lest he should not be able to live in a certain style. Great emergencies excepted, which would rarely occur in a society of which equality was the basis, a man can only be prepared to discharge the duties of public life, by the habitual practice of those inferiour ones which form the man.[1]

In this plan of education the constitution of boys would not be ruined by the early debaucheries, which now make men so selfish, or girls rendered weak and vain, by indolence, and frivolous pursuits. But, I presuppose, that such a degree of equality should be established between the sexes as would shut out gallantry and coquetry, yet allow friendship and love to temper the heart for the discharge of higher duties.

These would be schools of morality – and the happiness of man, allowed to flow from the pure springs of duty and affection, what advances might not the human mind make? Society can only be happy and free in proportion as it is virtuous; but the present distinctions, established in society, corrode all private, and blast all public virtue.[2]

I have already inveighed against the custom of confining girls to their needle, and shutting them out from all political and civil employments; for by thus narrowing their minds they are rendered unfit to fulfil the peculiar duties which nature has assigned them.

Only employed about the little incidents of the day, they necessarily grow up cunning. My very soul has often sickened at observing the sly tricks practised by women to gain some foolish thing on which their silly hearts were set. Not allowed to dispose of money, or call any thing their own, they learn to turn the market penny; or, should a husband offend, by staying from home, or give rise to some emotions of jealousy – a new gown, or any pretty bawble, smooths Juno's angry brow.

But these *littlenesses* would not degrade their character, if women were led to respect themselves, if political and moral subjects were opened to them; and, I will venture to affirm, that this is the only way

---

1  [Cf. Rousseau's disapproval of early marriages (*Emile* 448).]
2  [Another allusion to Mandeville, *The Fable of the Bees; or, Private Vices, Public Benefits*.]

to make them properly attentive to their domestic duties. – An active mind embraces the whole circle of its duties, and finds time enough for all. It is not, I assert, a bold attempt to emulate masculine virtues; it is not the enchantment of literary pursuits, or the steady investigation of scientific subjects, that leads women astray from duty.[1] No, it is indolence and vanity – the love of pleasure and the love of sway,[2] that will reign paramount in an empty mind. I say empty emphatically, because the education which women now receive scarcely deserves the name. For the little knowledge that they are led to acquire, during the important years of youth, is merely relative to accomplishments; and accomplishments without a bottom, for unless the understanding be cultivated, superficial and monotonous is every grace. Like the charms of a made up face, they only strike the senses in a crowd; but at home, wanting mind, they want variety. The consequence is obvious; in gay scenes of dissipation we meet the artificial mind and face, for those who fly from solitude dread, next to solitude, the domestic circle; not having it in their power to amuse or interest, they feel their own insignificance, or find nothing to amuse or interest themselves.

Besides, what can be more indelicate than a girl's *coming out* in the fashionable world? Which, in other words, is to bring to market a marriageable miss, whose person is taken from one public place to another, richly caparisoned. Yet, mixing in the giddy circle under restraint, these butterflies long to flutter at large, for the first affection of their souls is their own persons, to which their attention has been called with the most sedulous care whilst they were preparing for the period that decides their fate for life. Instead of pursuing this idle routine, sighing for tasteless shew, and heartless state, with what dignity would the youths of both sexes form attachments in the schools that I have cursorily pointed out; in which, as life advanced, dancing, music, and drawing, might be admitted as relaxations, for at these schools young people of fortune ought to remain, more or less, till they were of age. Those, who were designed for particular professions, might attend, three or four mornings in the week, the schools appropriated for their immediate instruction.

I only drop these observations at present, as hints; rather, indeed, as

1  [Cf. Macaulay, *Letters* 202 (Appendix B.2).]
2  [Pope, "Of the Characters of Women" 210.]

an outline of the plan I mean, than a digested one; but I must add, that I highly approve of one regulation mentioned in the pamphlet[1] already alluded to, that of making the children and youths independent of the masters respecting punishments. They should be tried by their peers, which would be an admirable method of fixing sound principles of justice in the mind, and might have the happiest effect on the temper, which is very early soured or irritated by tyranny, till it becomes peevishly cunning, or ferociously overbearing.

My imagination darts forward with benevolent fervour to greet these amiable and respectable groups, in spite of the sneering of cold hearts, who are at liberty to utter, with frigid self-importance, the damning epithet – romantic; the force of which I shall endeavour to blunt by repeating the words of an eloquent moralist. – "I know not whether the allusions of a truly humane heart, whose zeal renders every thing easy, be not preferable to that rough and repulsing reason, which always finds an indifference for the public good, the first obstacle to whatever would promote it."[2]

I know that libertines will also exclaim, that woman would be unsexed by acquiring strength of body and mind, and that beauty, soft bewitching beauty! would no longer adorn the daughters of men. I am of a very different opinion, for I think that, on the contrary, we should then see dignified beauty, and true grace; to produce which, many powerful physical and moral causes would concur. – Not relaxed beauty, it is true, or the graces of helplessness; but such as appears to make us respect the human body as a majestic pile fit to receive a noble inhabitant, in the relics of antiquity.

I do not forget the popular opinion that the Grecian statues were not modelled after nature. I mean, not according to the proportions of a particular man; but that beautiful limbs and features were selected from various bodies to form an harmonious whole. This might, in some degree, be true. The fine ideal picture of an exalted imagination might be superiour to the materials which the statuary found in nature, and thus it might with propriety be termed rather the model of mankind than of a man. It was not, however, the mechanical selection of limbs and features; but the ebullition of an heated fancy that

---

1    The Bishop of Autun's. [Talleyrand, *Rapport* 106–8.]
2    [Unidentified.]

burst forth, and the fine senses and enlarged understanding of the artist selected the solid matter, which he drew into this glowing focus.

I observed that it was not mechanical, because a whole was produced – a model of that grand simplicity, of those concurring energies, which arrest our attention and command our reverence. For only insipid lifeless beauty is produced by a servile copy of even beautiful nature. Yet, independent of these observations, I believe that the human form must have been far more beautiful than it is at present, because extreme indolence, barbarous ligatures, and many causes, which forcibly act on it, in our luxurious state of society, did not retard its expansion, or render it deformed.[1] Exercise and cleanliness appear to be not only the surest means of preserving health, but of promoting beauty, the physical causes only considered; yet, this is not sufficient, moral ones must concur, or beauty will be merely of that rustic kind which blooms on the innocent, wholesome, countenances of some country people, whose minds have not been exercised. To render the person perfect, physical and moral beauty ought to be attained at the same time; each lending and receiving force by the combination. Judgment must reside on the brow, affection and fancy beam in the eye, and humanity curve the cheek, or vain is the sparkling of the finest eye or the elegantly turned finish of the fairest features: whilst in every motion that displays the active limbs and well-knit joints, grace and modesty should appear. But this fair assemblage is not to be brought together by chance; it is the reward of exertions calculated to support each other; for judgment can only be acquired by reflection, affection by the discharge of duties, and humanity by the exercise of compassion to every living creature.

Humanity to animals should be particularly inculcated as a part of national education, for it is not at present one of our national virtues.[2] Tenderness for their humble dumb domestics, amongst the lower class, is oftener to be found in a savage than a civilized state. For civilization prevents that intercourse which creates affection in the rude hut, or mud hovel, and leads uncultivated minds who are only depraved by the refinements which prevail in the society, where they are trodden under foot by the rich, to domineer over them to revenge

1    [Cf. Rousseau, Emile 366-67.]
2    [Cf. Macaulay, Letters 121-22, 189-97, 268-69, 277-78.]

the insults that they are obliged to bear from their superiours.

This habitual cruelty is first caught at school, where it is one of the rare sports of the boys to torment the miserable brutes that fall in their way. The transition, as they grow up, from barbarity to brutes to domestic tyranny over wives, children, and servants, is very easy. Justice, or even benevolence, will not be a powerful spring of action unless it extend to the whole creation; nay, I believe that it may be delivered as an axiom, that those who can see pain, unmoved, will soon learn to inflict it.

The vulgar are swayed by present feelings, and the habits which they have accidentally acquired; but on partial feelings much dependence cannot be placed, though they be just; for, when they are not invigorated by reflection, custom weakens them, till they are scarcely perceptible. The sympathies of our nature are strengthened by pondering cogitations, and deadened by thoughtless use. Macbeth's heart smote him more for one murder, the first, than for a hundred subsequent ones, which were necessary to back it.[1] But, when I used the epithet vulgar, I did not mean to confine my remark to the poor, for partial humanity, founded on present sensations, or whim, is quite as conspicuous, if not more so, amongst the rich.

The lady who sheds tears for the bird starved in a snare, and execrates the devils in the shape of men, who goad to madness the poor ox, or whip the patient ass, tottering under a burden above its strength, will, nevertheless, keep her coachman and horses whole hours waiting for her, when the sharp frost bites, or the rain beats against the well-closed windows which do not admit a breath of air to tell her how roughly the wind blows without. And she who takes her dogs to bed, and nurses them with a parade of sensibility, when sick, will suffer her babes to grow up crooked in a nursery. This illustration of my argument is drawn from a matter of fact. The woman whom I allude to was handsome, reckoned very handsome, by those who do not miss the mind when the face is plump and fair; but her understanding had not been led from female duties by literature, nor her innocence debauched by knowledge. No, she was quite feminine, according to the masculine acceptation of the word; and, so far from

---

1   [Macbeth's first murder, of course, was a regicide. Cf. Burke, *Reflections*; *Writings* 8: 128 (Appendix A.4.i).]

loving these spoiled brutes that filled the place which her children ought to have occupied, she only lisped out a pretty mixture of French and English nonsense, to please the men who flocked round her. The wife, mother, and human creature, were all swallowed up by the factitious character which an improper education and the selfish vanity of beauty had produced.

I do not like to make a distinction without a difference, and I own that I have been as much disgusted by the fine lady who took her lapdog to her bosom instead of her child; as by the ferocity of a man, who, beating his horse, declared, that he knew as well when he did wrong, as a Christian.[1]

This brood of folly shews how mistaken they are who, if they allow women to leave their harams, do not cultivate their understandings, in order to plant virtues in their hearts. For had they sense, they might acquire that domestic taste which would lead them to love with reasonable subordination their whole family, from their husband to the house-dog; nor would they ever insult humanity in the person of the most menial servant by paying more attention to the comfort of a brute, than to that of a fellow-creature.

My observations on national education are obviously hints; but I principally wish to enforce the necessity of educating the sexes together to perfect both, and of making children sleep at home that they may learn to love home; yet to make private support, instead of smothering, public affections, they should be sent to school to mix with a number of equals, for only by the jostlings of equality can we form a just opinion of ourselves.

To render mankind more virtuous, and happier of course, both sexes must act from the same principle; but how can that be expected when only one is allowed to see the reasonableness of it? To render also the social compact truly equitable, and in order to spread those enlightening principles, which alone can meliorate the fate of man, women must be allowed to found their virtue on knowledge, which is scarcely possible unless they be educated by the same pursuits as men. For they are now made so inferiour by ignorance and low desires, as not to deserve to be ranked with them; or, by the serpentine wrigglings of cunning they mount the tree of knowledge, and

---

1   [Possibly Wollstonecraft's father: see Godwin 207.]

only acquire sufficient to lead men astray.

It is plain from the history of all nations, that women cannot be confined to merely domestic pursuits, for they will not fulfil family duties, unless their minds take a wider range, and whilst they are kept in ignorance they become in the same proportion the slaves of pleasure as they are the slaves of man. Nor can they be shut out of great enterprises, though the narrowness of their minds often make them mar, what they are unable to comprehend.

The libertinism, and even the virtues of superiour men, will always give women, of some description, great power over them; and these weak women, under the influence of childish passions and selfish vanity, will throw a false light over the objects which the very men view with their eyes, who ought to enlighten their judgment. Men of fancy, and those sanguine characters who mostly hold the helm of human affairs, in general, relax in the society of women; and surely I need not cite to the most superficial reader of history the numerous examples of vice and oppression which the private intrigues of female favourites have produced; not to dwell on the mischief that naturally arises from the blundering interposition of well-meaning folly. For in the transactions of business it is much better to have to deal with a knave than a fool, because a knave adheres to some plan; and any plan of reason may be seen through much sooner than a sudden flight of folly. The power which vile and foolish women have had over wise men, who possessed sensibility, is notorious; I shall only mention one instance.

Whoever drew a more exalted female character than Rousseau?[1] though in the lump he constantly endeavoured to degrade the sex. And why was he thus anxious? Truly to justify to himself the affection which weakness and virtue had made him cherish for that fool Theresa.[2] He could not raise her to the common level of her sex; and therefore he laboured to bring woman down to her's. He found her a convenient humble companion, and pride made him determine to find some superiour virtues in the being whom he chose to live with; but did not her conduct during his life, and after his death, clearly

---

1 [In the heroine of *Julie; ou, La Nouvelle Héloïse*.]
2 [Thérèse Le Vasseur (1721-1801), his uneducated lover. For her simplicity, see *Confessions* 311; for her angelic heart, 330.]

shew how grossly he was mistaken who called her a celestial innocent. Nay, in the bitterness of his heart, he himself laments, that when his bodily infirmities made him no longer treat her like a woman, she ceased to have an affection for him. And it was very natural that she should, for having so few sentiments in common, when the sexual tie was broken, what was to hold her?[1] To hold her affection whose sensibility was confined to one sex, nay, to one man, it requires sense to turn sensibility into the broad channel of humanity; many women have not mind enough to have an affection for a woman, or a friendship for a man. But the sexual weakness that makes woman depend on man for a subsistence, produces a kind of cattish affection which leads a wife to purr about her husband as she would about any man who fed and caressed her.

Men are, however, often gratified by this kind of fondness, which is confined in a beastly manner to themselves; but should they ever become more virtuous, they will wish to converse at their fire-side with a friend, after they cease to play with a mistress.

Besides, understanding is necessary to give variety and interest to sensual enjoyments, for low, indeed, in the intellectual scale, is the mind that can continue to love when neither virtue nor sense give a human appearance to an animal appetite. But sense will always preponderate; and if women be not, in general, brought more on a level with men, some superiour women, like the Greek courtezans, will assemble the men of abilities around them, and draw from their families many citizens, who would have stayed at home had their wives had more sense, or the graces which result from the exercise of the understanding and fancy, the legitimate parents of taste. A woman of talents, if she be not absolutely ugly, will always obtain great power, raised by the weakness of her sex; and in proportion as men acquire virtue and delicacy, by the exertion of reason, they will look for both in women, but they can only acquire them in the same way that men do.

In France or Italy, have the women confined themselves to domestic life? Though they have not hitherto had a political existence, yet, have they not illicitly had great sway? corrupting themselves and the men with whose passions they played. In short, in whatever light I

---

[1]   [For the change in her feelings when Rousseau stopped sleeping with her, see *Confessions* 548-49; for their lack of common interests, 392.]

view the subject, reason and experience convince me that the only method of leading women to fulfil their peculiar duties, is to free them from all restraint by allowing them to participate the inherent rights of mankind.

Make them free, and they will quickly become wise and virtuous, as men become more so; for the improvement must be mutual, or the injustice which one half of the human race are obliged to submit to, retorting on their oppressors, the virtue of man will be worm-eaten by the insect whom he keeps under his feet.[1]

Let men take their choice, man and woman were made for each other, though not to become one being; and if they will not improve women, they will deprave them!

I speak of the improvement and emancipation of the whole sex, for I know that the behaviour of a few women, who, by accident, or following a strong bent of nature, have acquired a portion of knowledge superiour to that of the rest of their sex, has often been overbearing; but there have been instances of women who, attaining knowledge, have not discarded modesty, nor have they always pedantically appeared to despise the ignorance which they laboured to disperse in their own minds. The exclamations then which any advice respecting female learning, commonly produces, especially from pretty women, often arise from envy. When they chance to see that even the lustre of their eyes, and the flippant sportiveness of refined coquetry will not always secure them attention, during a whole evening, should a woman of a more cultivated understanding endeavour to give a rational turn to the conversation, the common source of consolation is, that such women seldom get husbands. What arts have I not seen silly women use to interrupt by *flirtation*, a very significant word to describe such a manoeuvre, a rational conversation which made the men forget that they were pretty women.

But, allowing what is very natural to man, that the possession of rare abilities is really calculated to excite over-weening pride, disgusting in both men and women – in what a state of inferiority must the female faculties have rusted when such a small portion of knowledge as those women attained, who have sneeringly been termed learned women, could be singular? – Sufficiently so to puff up the possessor,

---

1 [Cf. Macaulay, *Letters* 216.]

and excite envy in her contemporaries, and some of the other sex. Nay, has not a little rationality exposed many women to the severest censure? I advert to well known facts, for I have frequently heard women ridiculed, and every little weakness exposed, only because they adopted the advice of some medical men, and deviated from the beaten track in their mode of treating their infants. I have actually heard this barbarous aversion to innovation carried still further, and a sensible woman stigmatized as an unnatural mother, who has thus been wisely solicitous to preserve the health of her children, when in the midst of her care she has lost one by some of the casualties of infancy, which no prudence can ward off. Her acquaintance have observed, that this was the consequence of new-fangled notions – the new-fangled notions of ease and cleanliness. And those who pretending to experience, though they have long adhered to prejudices that have, according to the opinion of the most sagacious physicians, thinned the human race, almost rejoiced at the disaster that gave a kind of sanction to prescription.

Indeed, if it were only on this account, the national education of women is of the utmost consequence, for what a number of human sacrifices are made to that moloch prejudice![1] And in how many ways are children destroyed by the lasciviousness of man? The want of natural affection, in many women, who are drawn from their duty by the admiration of men, and the ignorance of others, render the infancy of man a much more perilous state than that of brutes; yet men are unwilling to place women in situations proper to enable them to acquire sufficient understanding to know how even to nurse their babes.

So forcibly does this truth strike me, that I would rest the whole tendency of my reasoning upon it, for whatever tends to incapacitate the maternal character, takes woman out of her sphere.

But it is vain to expect the present race of weak mothers either to take that reasonable care of a child's body, which is necessary to lay the foundation of a good constitution, supposing that it do not suffer for the sins of its fathers;[2] or, to manage its temper so judiciously that

---

1  [Milton, *Paradise Lost* 1.392-93. See Appendix A.4.ii.]
2  [Cf. Exodus 20: 5, 34: 7; Numbers 14: 18; Deuteronomy 5: 9. Cf. Macaulay, *Letters* 14.]

the child will not have, as it grows up, to throw off all that its mother, its first instructor, directly or indirectly taught; and unless the mind have uncommon vigour, womanish follies will stick to the character throughout life. The weakness of the mother will be visited on the children! And whilst women are educated to rely on their husbands for judgment, this must ever be the consequence, for there is no improving an understanding by halves, nor can any being act wisely from imitation, because in every circumstance of life there is a kind of individuality, which requires an exertion of judgment to modify general rules. The being who can think justly in one track, will soon extend its intellectual empire; and she who has sufficient judgment to manage her children, will not submit, right or wrong, to her husband, or patiently to the social laws which make a nonentity of a wife.

In public schools women, to guard against the errors of ignorance, should be taught the elements of anatomy and medicine, not only to enable them to take proper care of their own health, but to make them rational nurses of their infants, parents, and husbands; for the bills of mortality are swelled by the blunders of self-willed old women, who give nostrums of their own without knowing any thing of the human frame. It is likewise proper only in a domestic view, to make women acquainted with the anatomy of the mind, by allowing the sexes to associate together in every pursuit; and by leading them to observe the progress of the human understanding in the improvement of the sciences and arts; never forgetting the science of morality, or the study of the political history of mankind.

A man has been termed a microcosm; and every family might also be called a state. States, it is true, have mostly been governed by arts that disgrace the character of man; and the want of a just constitution, and equal laws, have so perplexed the notions of the worldly wise, that they more than question the reasonableness of contending for the rights of humanity. Thus morality, polluted in the national reservoir, sends off streams of vice to corrupt the constituent parts of the body politic; but should more noble, or rather, more just principles regulate the laws, which ought to be the government of society, and not those who execute them, duty might become the rule of private conduct.

Besides, by the exercise of their bodies and minds women would acquire that mental activity so necessary in the maternal character, united with the fortitude that distinguishes steadiness of conduct from the obstinate perverseness of weakness. For it is dangerous to advise the indolent to be steady, because they instantly become rigorous, and to save themselves trouble, punish with severity faults that the patient fortitude of reason might have prevented.

But fortitude presupposes strength of mind; and is strength of mind to be acquired by indolent acquiescence? by asking advice instead of exerting the judgment? by obeying through fear, instead of practising the forbearance, which we all stand in need of ourselves? – The conclusion which I wish to draw, is obvious; make women rational creatures, and free citizens, and they will quickly become good wives, and mothers; that is – if men do not neglect the duties of husbands and fathers.

Discussing the advantages which a public and private education combined, as I have sketched, might rationally be expected to produce, I have dwelt most on such as are particularly relative to the female world, because I think the female world oppressed; yet the gangrene, which the vices engendered by oppression have produced, is not confined to the morbid part, but pervades society at large: so that when I wish to see my sex become more like moral agents, my heart bounds with the anticipation of the general diffusion of that sublime contentment which only morality can diffuse.

# CHAP. XIII.

## SOME INSTANCES OF THE FOLLY WHICH THE IGNORANCE OF WOMEN GENERATES; WITH CONCLUDING REFLECTIONS ON THE MORAL IMPROVEMENT THAT A REVOLUTION IN FEMALE MANNERS MIGHT NATURALLY BE EXPECTED TO PRODUCE.

THERE are many follies, in some degree, peculiar to women: sins against reason of commission as well as of omission; but all flowing from ignorance or prejudice, I shall only point out such as appear to be particularly injurious to their moral character. And in animadverting on them, I wish especially to prove, that the weakness of mind and body, which men have endeavoured, impelled by various motives, to perpetuate, prevents their discharging the peculiar duty of their sex: for when weakness of body will not permit them to suckle their children, and weakness of mind makes them spoil their tempers – is woman in a natural state?

### SECT. I.

ONE glaring instance of the weakness which proceeds from ignorance, first claims attention, and calls for severe reproof.

In this metropolis a number of lurking leeches infamously gain a subsistence by practising on the credulity of women, pretending to cast nativities,[1] to use the technical phrase; and many females who, proud of their rank and fortune, look down on the vulgar with sovereign contempt, shew by this credulity, that the distinction is arbitrary, and that they have not sufficiently cultivated their minds to rise above vulgar prejudices. Women, because they have not been led to consider the knowledge of their duty as the one thing necessary to know, or, to

---

1   [Horoscopes.]

live in the present moment by the discharge of it, are very anxious to peep into futurity, to learn what they have to expect to render life interesting, and to break the vacuum of ignorance.

I must be allowed to expostulate seriously with the ladies who follow these idle inventions; for ladies, mistresses of families, are not ashamed to drive in their own carriages to the door of the cunning man[1]. And if any of them should peruse this work, I entreat them to answer to their own hearts the following questions, not forgetting that they are in the presence of God.

Do you believe that there is but one God, and that he is powerful, wise, and good?

Do you believe that all things were created by him, and that all beings are dependent on him?

Do you rely on his wisdom, so conspicuous in his works, and in your own frame, and are you convinced that he has ordered all things which do not come under the cognizance of your senses, in the same perfect harmony, to fulfil his designs?

Do you acknowledge that the power of looking into futurity, and seeing things that are not, as if they were, is an attribute of the Creator? And should he, by an impression on the minds of his creatures, think fit to impart to them some event hid in the shades of time yet unborn, to whom would the secret be revealed by immediate inspiration? The opinion of ages will answer this question – to reverend old men, to people distinguished for eminent piety.

The oracles of old were thus delivered by priests dedicated to the service of the God who was supposed to inspire them. The glare of worldly pomp which surrounded these impostors, and the respect paid to them by artful politicians, who knew how to avail themselves of this useful engine to bend the necks of the strong under the dominion of the cunning, spread a sacred mysterious veil of sanctity over their lies and abominations. Impressed by such solemn devotional parade, a Greek, or Roman lady might be excused, if she inquired of the oracle, when she was anxious to pry into futurity, or inquire

---

1  I once lived in the neighbourhood of one of these men, a *handsome* man, and saw with surprise and indignation, women, whose appearance and attendance bespoke that rank in which females are supposed to receive a superiour education, flock to his door.

about some dubious event: and her inquiries, however contrary to reason, could not be reckoned impious. – But, can the professors of Christianity ward off that imputation? Can a Christian suppose that the favourites of the most High, the highly favoured, would be obliged to lurk in disguise, and practise the most dishonest tricks to cheat silly women out of the money – which the poor cry for in vain?

Say not that such questions are an insult to common sense – for it is your own conduct, O ye foolish women! which throws an odium on your sex! And these reflections should make you shudder at your thoughtlessness, and irrational devotion. – For I do not suppose that all of you laid aside your religion, such as it is, when you entered those mysterious dwellings. Yet, as I have throughout supposed myself talking to ignorant women, for ignorant ye are in the most emphatical sense of the word, it would be absurd to reason with you on the egregious folly of desiring to know what the Supreme Wisdom has concealed.

Probably you would not understand me, were I to attempt to shew you that it would be absolutely inconsistent with the grand purpose of life, that of rendering human creatures wise and virtuous: and that, were it sanctioned by God, it would disturb the order established in creation; and if it be not sanctioned by God, do you expect to hear truth? Can events be foretold, events which have not yet assumed a body to become subject to mortal inspection, can they be foreseen by a vicious worldling, who pampers his appetites by preying on the foolish ones?

Perhaps, however, you devoutly believe in the devil, and imagine, to shift the question, that he may assist his votaries; but, if really respecting the power of such a being, an enemy to goodness and to God, can you go to church after having been under such an obligation to him?

From these delusions to those still more fashionable deceptions, practised by the whole tribe of magnetisers,[1] the transition is very natural. With respect to them, it is equally proper to ask women a few questions.

Do you know any thing of the construction of the human frame?

---

1  [Followers of Friedrich Mesmer (1733-1815), who claimed to be able to cure illnesses by "animal magnetism."]

If not, it is proper that you should be told what every child ought to know, that when its admirable oeconomy has been disturbed by intemperance or indolence, I speak not of violent disorders, but of chronical diseases, it must be brought into a healthy state again, by slow degrees, and if the functions of life have not been materially injured, regimen, another word for temperance, air, exercise, and a few medicines, prescribed by persons who have studied the human body, are the only human means, yet discovered, of recovering that inestimable blessing health, that will bear investigation.

Do you then believe that these magnetisers, who, by hocus pocus tricks, pretend to work a miracle, are delegated by God, or assisted by the solver of all these kind of difficulties — the devil?

Do they, when they put to flight, as it is said, disorders that have baffled the powers of medicine, work in conformity to the light of reason? or, do they effect these wonderful cures by supernatural aid?

By a communication, an adept may answer, with the world of spirits. A noble privilege, it must be allowed. Some of the ancients mention familiar daemons, who guarded them from danger by kindly intimating, we cannot guess in what manner, when any danger was nigh; or, pointed out what they ought to undertake.[1] Yet the men who laid claim to this privilege, out of the order of nature, insisted that it was the reward, or consequence, of superiour temperance and piety. But the present workers of wonders are not raised above their fellows by superiour temperance or sanctity. They do not cure for the love of God, but money. These are the priests of quackery, though it is true they have not the convenient expedient of selling masses for souls in purgatory, or churches where they can display crutches, and models of limbs made sound by a touch or a word.

I am not conversant with the technical terms, or initiated into the arcana, therefore, I may speak improperly; but it is clear that men who will not conform to the law of reason, and earn a subsistence in an honest way, by degrees, are very fortunate in becoming acquainted with such obliging spirits. We cannot, indeed, give them credit for either great sagacity or goodness, else they would have chosen more noble instruments, when they wished to shew themselves the benevolent friends of man.

---

1  [Socrates was attended by such a daemon: see *Apology* 40a-c; *Phaedrus* 242b-c.]

It is, however, little short of blasphemy to pretend to such powers!

From the whole tenour of the dispensations of Providence, it appears evident to sober reason, that certain vices produce certain effects; and can any one so grossly insult the wisdom of God, as to suppose that a miracle will be allowed to disturb his general laws, to restore to health the intemperate and vicious, merely to enable them to pursue the same course with impunity? Be whole, and sin no more, said Jesus.[1] And, are greater miracles to be performed by those who do not follow his footsteps, who healed the body to reach the mind?

The mentioning of the name of Christ, after such vile impostors, may displease some of my readers – I respect their warmth; but let them not forget that the followers of these delusions bear his name, and profess to be the disciples of him, who said, by their works we should know who were the children of God or the servants of sin.[2] I allow that it is easier to touch the body of a saint, or to be magnetised, than to restrain our appetites or govern our passions; but health of body or mind can only be recovered by these means, or we make the Supreme Judge partial and revengeful.

Is he a man that he should change, or punish out of resentment? He – the common father, wounds but to heal, says reason, and our irregularities producing certain consequences, we are forcibly shewn the nature of vice; that thus learning to know good from evil, by experience, we may hate one and love the other,[3] in proportion to the wisdom which we attain. The poison contains the antidote; and we either reform our evil habits and cease to sin against our own bodies, to use the forcible language of scripture, or a premature death, the punishment of sin, snaps the thread of life.

Here an awful stop is put to our inquiries. – But, why should I conceal my sentiments? Considering the attributes of God, I believe that whatever punishment may follow, will tend, like the anguish of disease, to shew the malignity of vice, for the purpose of reformation. Positive punishment appears so contrary to the nature of God, discoverable in all his works, and in our own reason, that I could sooner

---

1   [John 5: 14.]
2   [Matthew 7: 16; Romans 8: 16; Galatians 3: 26.]
3   [Cf. Matthew 6: 24; and *Original Stories*; *Works* 4: 438.]

believe that the Deity paid no attention to the conduct of men, than that he punished without the benevolent design of reforming.[1]

To suppose only that an all-wise and powerful Being, as good as he is great, should create a being foreseeing, that after fifty or sixty years of feverish existence, it would be plunged into never ending woe – is blasphemy. On what will the worm feed that is never to die?[2] On folly, on ignorance, say ye – I should blush indignantly at drawing the natural conclusion could I insert it, and wish to withdraw myself from the wing of my God! On such a supposition, I speak with reverence, he would be a consuming fire. We should wish, though vainly, to fly from his presence when fear absorbed love, and darkness involved all his counsels!

I know that many devout people boast of submitting to the Will of God blindly, as to an arbitrary sceptre or rod, on the same principle as the Indians worship the devil.[3] In other words, like people in the common concerns of life, they do homage to power, and cringe under the foot that can crush them. Rational religion, on the contrary, is a submission to the will of a being so perfectly wise, that all he wills must be directed by the proper motive – must be reasonable.

And, if thus we respect God, can we give credit to the mysterious insinuations, which insult his laws? can we believe, though it should stare us in the face, that he would work a miracle to authorize confusion by sanctioning an error? Yet we must either allow these impious conclusions, or treat with contempt every promise to restore health to a diseased body by supernatural means, or to foretell the incidents that can only be foreseen by God.

---

1 [Wollstonecraft borrows the phrase "positive punishment" from Macaulay (*Letters* 393, 474), who also believes that the sufferings of hell are temporary and reformatory (478, 502-3).]
2 [Isaiah 66: 24.]
3 [Cf. *Original Stories; Works* 4: 424; and Macaulay, *Letters* 380.]

ANOTHER instance of that feminine weakness of character, often produced by a confined education, is a romantic twist of the mind, which has been very properly termed *sentimental*.

Women subjected by ignorance to their sensations, and only taught to look for happiness in love, refine on sensual feelings, and adopt metaphysical notions respecting that passion, which lead them shamefully to neglect the duties of life, and frequently in the midst of these sublime refinements they plump into actual vice.

These are the women who are amused by the reveries of the stupid novelists, who, knowing little of human nature, work up stale tales, and describe meretricious scenes, all retailed in a sentimental jargon, which equally tend to corrupt the taste, and draw the heart aside from its daily duties.[1] I do not mention the understanding, because never having been exercised, its slumbering energies rest inactive, like the lurking particles of fire which are supposed universally to pervade matter.[2]

Females, in fact, denied all political privileges, and not allowed, as married women, excepting in criminal cases, a civil existence, have their attention naturally drawn from the interest of the whole community to that of the minute parts, though the private duty of any member of society must be very imperfectly performed when not connected with the general good. The mighty business of female life is to please, and restrained from entering into more important concerns by political and civil oppression, sentiments become events, and reflection deepens what it should, and would have effaced, if the understanding had been allowed to take a wider range.

But, confined to trifling employments, they naturally imbibe opinions which the only kind of reading calculated to interest an innocent frivolous mind, inspires. Unable to grasp any thing great, is it surprising that they find the reading of history a very dry task, and disquisitions addressed to the understanding intolerably tedious, and almost unintelligible? Thus are they necessarily dependent on the novelist for amusement. Yet, when I exclaim against novels, I mean when contrast-

---

1    [Cf. Macaulay on novel-reading, *Letters* 142-48.]
2    [Phlogiston.]

ed with those works which exercise the understanding and regulate the imagination. – For any kind of reading I think better than leaving a blank still a blank, because the mind must receive a degree of enlargement and obtain a little strength by a slight exertion of its thinking powers; besides, even the productions that are only addressed to the imagination, raise the reader a little above the gross gratification of appetites, to which the mind has not given a shade of delicacy.

This observation is the result of experience; for I have known several notable women, and one in particular, who was a very good woman – as good as such a narrow mind would allow her to be, who took care that her daughters (three in number) should never see a novel. As she was a woman of fortune and fashion, they had various masters to attend them, and a sort of menial governess to watch their footsteps. From their masters they learned how tables, chairs, &c. were called in French and Italian; but as the few books thrown in their way were far above their capacities, or devotional, they neither acquired ideas nor sentiments, and passed their time, when not compelled to repeat *words*, in dressing, quarrelling with each other, or conversing with their maids by stealth, till they were brought into company as marriageable.

Their mother, a widow, was busy in the mean time in keeping up her connections, as she termed a numerous acquaintance, lest her girls should want a proper introduction into the great world. And these young ladies, with minds vulgar in every sense of the word, and spoiled tempers, entered life puffed up with notions of their own consequence, and looking down with contempt on those who could not vie with them in dress and parade.

With respect to love, nature, or their nurses, had taken care to teach them the physical meaning of the word; and, as they had few topics of conversation, and fewer refinements of sentiment, they expressed their gross wishes not in very delicate phrases, when they spoke freely, talking of matrimony.

Could these girls have been injured by the perusal of novels? I almost forgot a shade in the character of one of them; she affected a simplicity bordering on folly, and with a simper would utter the most immodest remarks and questions, the full meaning of which she had learned whilst secluded from the world, and afraid to speak in her mother's presence, who governed with a high hand: they were all educated, as she prided herself, in a most exemplary manner; and read their chapters and psalms before breakfast, never touching a silly novel.

This is only one instance; but I recollect many other women who, not led by degrees to proper studies, and not permitted to choose for themselves, have indeed been overgrown children; or have obtained, by mixing in the world, a little of what is termed common sense: that is, a distinct manner of seeing common occurrences, as they stand detached: but what deserves the name of intellect, the power of gaining general or abstract ideas, or even intermediate ones, was out of the question. Their minds were quiescent, and when they were not roused by sensible objects and employments of that kind, they were low-spirited, would cry, or go to sleep.

When, therefore, I advise my sex not to read such flimsy works, it is to induce them to read something superiour; for I coincide in opinion with a sagacious man, who, having a daughter and niece under his care, pursued a very different plan with each.

The niece, who had considerable abilities, had, before she was left to his guardianship, been indulged in desultory reading. Her he endeavoured to lead, and did lead to history and moral essays; but his daughter, whom a fond weak mother had indulged, and who consequently was averse to every thing like application, he allowed to read novels: and used to justify his conduct by saying, that if she ever attained a relish for reading them, he should have some foundation to work upon; and that erroneous opinions were better than none at all.

In fact the female mind has been so totally neglected, that knowledge was only to be acquired from this muddy source, till from reading novels some women of superiour talents learned to despise them.

The best method, I believe, that can be adopted to correct a fondness for novels is to ridicule them: not indiscriminately, for then it would have little effect; but, if a judicious person, with some turn for humour, would read several to a young girl, and point out both by tones, and apt comparisons with pathetic incidents and heroic characters in history, how foolishly and ridiculously they caricatured human nature, just opinions might be substituted instead of romantic sentiments.

In one respect, however, the majority of both sexes resemble, and equally shew a want of taste and modesty. Ignorant women, forced to be chaste to preserve their reputation, allow their imagination to revel in the unnatural and meretricious scenes sketched by the novel writers of the day, slighting as insipid the sober dignity, and matron graces of history[1], whilst men carry the same vitiated taste into life, and fly for amusement to the wanton, from the unsophisticated charms of virtue, and the grave respectability of sense.

Besides, the reading of novels makes women, and particularly ladies of fashion, very fond of using strong expressions and superlatives in conversation; and, though the dissipated artificial life which they lead prevents their cherishing any strong legitimate passion, the language of passion in affected tones slips for ever from their glib tongues, and every trifle produces those phosphoric bursts which only mimick in the dark the flame of passion.


SECT. III.


IGNORANCE and the mistaken cunning that nature sharpens in weak heads as a principle of self-preservation, render women very fond of dress, and produce all the vanity which such a fondness may naturally be expected to generate, to the exclusion of emulation and magnanimity.

I agree with Rousseau that the physical part of the art of pleasing consists in ornaments, and for that very reason I should guard girls against the contagious fondness for dress so common to weak women, that they may not rest in the physical part. Yet, weak are the women who imagine that they can long please without the aid of the mind, or, in other words, without the moral art of pleasing. But the moral art, if it be not a profanation to use the word art, when alluding to the grace which is an effect of virtue, and not the motive of action, is never to be found with ignorance; the sportiveness of innocence, so pleasing to refined libertines of both sexes, is widely different in its

---

1  I am not now alluding to that superiority of mind which leads to the creation of ideal beauty, when he, surveyed with a penetrating eye, appears a tragi comedy, in which little can be seen to satisfy the heart without the help of fancy. [The first edition reads "life," not "he."]

essence from this superiour gracefulness.

A strong inclination for external ornaments ever appears in barbarous states, only the men not the women adorn themselves; for where women are allowed to be so far on a level with men, society has advanced, at least, one step in civilization.

The attention to dress, therefore, which has been thought a sexual propensity, I think natural to mankind. But I ought to express myself with more precision. When the mind is not sufficiently opened to take pleasure in reflection, the body will be adorned with sedulous care; and ambition will appear in tattooing or painting it.

So far is this first inclination carried, that even the hellish yoke of slavery cannot stifle the savage desire of admiration which the black heroes inherit from both their parents, for all the hardly earned savings of a slave are commonly expended in a little tawdry finery. And I have seldom known a good male or female servant that was not particularly fond of dress. Their clothes were their riches; and, I argue from analogy, that the fondness for dress, so extravagant in females, arises from the same cause – want of cultivation of mind. When men meet they converse about business, politics, or literature; but, says Swift, "how naturally do women apply their hands to each others lappets and ruffles."[1] And very natural is it – for they have not any business to interest them, have not a taste for literature, and they find politics dry, because they have not acquired a love for mankind by turning their thoughts to the grand pursuits that exalt the human race, and promote general happiness.

Besides, various are the paths to power and fame which by accident or choice men pursue, and though they jostle against each other, for men of the same profession are seldom friends, yet there is a much greater number of their fellow-creatures with whom they never clash. But women are very differently situated with respect to each other – for they are all rivals.

Before marriage it is their business to please men; and after, with a few exceptions, they follow the same scent with all the persevering pertinacity of instinct. Even virtuous women never forget their sex in company, for they are for ever trying to make themselves *agreeable*. A female beauty, and a male wit, appear to be equally anxious to draw

---

1    ["A Letter to a Young Lady on her Marriage" (1723).]

the attention of the company to themselves; and the animosity of contemporary wits is proverbial.

Is it then surprising that when the sole ambition of woman centres in beauty, and interest gives vanity additional force, perpetual rivalships should ensue? They are all running the same race, and would rise above the virtue of mortals, if they did not view each other with a suspicious and even envious eye.

An immoderate fondness for dress, for pleasure, and for sway,[1] are the passions of savages; the passions that occupy those uncivilized beings who have not yet extended the dominion of the mind, or even learned to think with the energy necessary to concatenate that abstract train of thought which produces principles. And that women from their education and the present state of civilized life, are in the same condition, cannot, I think, be controverted. To laugh at them then, or satirize the follies of a being who is never to be allowed to act freely from the light of her own reason, is as absurd as cruel; for, that they who are taught blindly to obey authority, will endeavour cunningly to elude it, is most natural and certain.

Yet let it be proved that they ought to obey man implicitly, and I shall immediately agree that it is woman's duty to cultivate a fondness for dress, in order to please, and a propensity to cunning for her own preservation.

The virtues, however, which are supported by ignorance must ever be wavering – the house built on sand could not endure a storm.[2] It is almost unnecessary to draw the inference. – If women are to be made virtuous by authority, which is a contradiction in terms, let them be immured in seraglios and watched with a jealous eye. – Fear not that the iron will enter into their souls[3] – for the souls that can bear such treatment are made of yielding materials, just animated enough to give life to the body.

> "Matter too soft a lasting mark to bear,
> And best distinguish'd by black, brown, or fair."[4]

---

1  [Pope, "Of the Characters of Women" 210.]
2  [Matthew 7: 26-27.]
3  [*The Book of Common Prayer*, "The Psalter" 105: 18; cf. Laurence Sterne (1713-68), *A Sentimental Journey* (1768), "The Captive: Paris."]
4  [Pope, "Of the Characters of Women" 3-4.]

The most cruel wounds will of course soon heal, and they may still people the world, and dress to please man – all the purposes which certain celebrated writers have allowed that they were created to fulfil.

## SECT. IV.

WOMEN are supposed to possess more sensibility, and even humanity, than men, and their strong attachments and instantaneous emotions of compassion are given as proofs; but the clinging affection of ignorance has seldom any thing noble in it, and may mostly be resolved into selfishness, as well as the affection of children and brutes. I have known many weak women whose sensibility was entirely engrossed by their husbands; and as for their humanity, it was very faint indeed, or rather it was only a transient emotion of compassion. Humanity does not consist "in a squeamish ear," says an eminent orator. "It belongs to the mind as well as the nerves."[1]

But this kind of exclusive affection, though it degrades the individual, should not be brought forward as a proof of the inferiority of the sex, because it is the natural consequence of confined views: for even women of superior sense, having their attention turned to little employments, and private plans, rarely rise to heroism, unless when spurred on by love! and love, as an heroic passion, like genius, appears but once in an age. I therefore agree with the moralist who asserts, "that women have seldom so much generosity as men;"[2] and that their narrow affections, to which justice and humanity are often sacrificed, render the sex apparently inferior, especially, as they are commonly inspired by men; but I contend that the heart would expand as the understanding gained strength, if women were not depressed from their cradles.

I know that a little sensibility, and great weakness, will produce a strong sexual attachment, and that reason must cement friendship; consequently, I allow that more friendship is to be found in the male than the female world, and that men have a higher sense of justice.

---

1   [Unidentified.]
2   [Smith, *Theory* 190; 4.2.10.]

The exclusive affections of women seem indeed to resemble Cato's most unjust love for his country. He wished to crush Carthage, not to save Rome, but to promote its vain-glory;[1] and, in general, it is to similar principles that humanity is sacrificed, for genuine duties support each other.

Besides, how can women be just or generous, when they are the slaves of injustice?


### SECT. V.

As the rearing of children, that is, the laying a foundation of sound health both of body and mind in the rising generation, has justly been insisted on as the peculiar destination of woman, the ignorance that incapacitates them must be contrary to the order of things. And I contend that their minds can take in much more, and ought to do so, or they will never become sensible mothers. Many men attend to the breeding of horses, and overlook the management of the stable, who would, strange want of sense and feeling! think themselves degraded by paying any attention to the nursery; yet, how many children are absolutely murdered by the ignorance of women! But when they escape, and are destroyed neither by unnatural negligence nor blind fondness, how few are managed properly with respect to the infant mind! So that to break the spirit, allowed to become vicious at home, a child is sent to school; and the methods taken there, which must be taken to keep a number of children in order, scatter the seeds of almost every vice in the soil thus forcibly torn up.

I have sometimes compared the struggles of these poor children, who ought never to have felt restraint, nor would, had they been always held in with an even hand, to the despairing plunges of a spirited filly, which I have seen breaking on a strand: its feet sinking deeper and deeper in the sand every time it endeavoured to throw its rider, till at last it sullenly submitted.

I have always found horses, animals I am attached to, very tractable when treated with humanity and steadiness, so that I doubt whether

---

1   [Marcus Porcius Cato the Elder (234-149 B.C.) is best remembered for his implacable hatred of Carthage. Cf. Smith, *Theory* 228; 6.2.2.3]

the violent methods taken to break them, do not essentially injure them; I am, however, certain that a child should never be thus forcibly tamed after it has injudiciously been allowed to run wild; for every violation of justice and reason, in the treatment of children, weakens their reason. And, so early do they catch a character, that the base of the moral character, experience leads me to infer, is fixed before their seventh year, the period during which women are allowed the sole management of children. Afterwards it too often happens that half the business of education is to correct, and very imperfectly is it done, if done hastily, the faults, which they would never have acquired if their mothers had had more understanding.

One striking instance of the folly of women must not be omitted. – The manner in which they treat servants in the presence of children, permitting them to suppose that they ought to wait on them, and bear their humours. A child should always be made to receive assistance from a man or woman as a favour; and, as the first lesson of independence, they should practically be taught, by the example of their mother, not to require that personal attendance, which it is an insult to humanity to require, when in health; and instead of being led to assume airs of consequence, a sense of their own weakness should first make them feel the natural equality of man. Yet, how frequently have I indignantly heard servants imperiously called to put children to bed, and sent away again and again, because master or miss hung about mamma, to stay a little longer. Thus made slavishly to attend the little idol, all those most disgusting humours were exhibited which characterize a spoiled child.

In short, speaking of the majority of mothers, they leave their children entirely to the care of servants; or, because they are their children, treat them as if they were little demi-gods, though I have always observed, that the women who thus idolize their children, seldom shew common humanity to servants, or feel the least tenderness for any children but their own.

It is, however, these exclusive affections, and an individual manner of seeing things, produced by ignorance, which keep women for ever at a stand, with respect to improvement, and make many of them dedicate their lives to their children only to weaken their bodies and spoil their tempers, frustrating also any plan of education that a more rational father may adopt; for unless a mother concur, the father who restrains will ever be considered as a tyrant.

But, fulfilling the duties of a mother, a woman with a sound constitution, may still keep her person scrupulously neat, and assist to maintain her family, if necessary, or by reading and conversations with both sexes, indiscriminately, improve her mind. For nature has so wisely ordered things, that did women suckle their children, they would preserve their own health, and there would be such an interval between the birth of each child, that we should seldom see a houseful of babes. And did they pursue a plan of conduct, and not waste their time in following the fashionable vagaries of dress, the management of their household and children need not shut them out from literature, or prevent their attaching themselves to a science, with that steady eye which strengthens the mind, or practising one of the fine arts that cultivate the taste.

But, visiting to display finery, card-playing, and balls, not to mention the idle bustle of morning trifling, draw women from their duty to render them insignificant, to render them pleasing, according to the present acceptation of the word, to every man, but their husband. For a round of pleasures in which the affections are not exercised, cannot be said to improve the understanding, though it be erroneously called seeing the world; yet the heart is rendered cold and averse to duty, by such a senseless intercourse, which becomes necessary from habit even when it has ceased to amuse.

But, we shall not see women affectionate till more equality be established in society, till ranks are confounded and women freed, neither shall we see that dignified domestic happiness, the simple grandeur of which cannot be relished by ignorant or vitiated minds; nor will the important task of education ever be properly begun till the person of a woman is no longer preferred to her mind. For it would be as wise to expect corn from tares, or figs from thistles,[1] as that a foolish ignorant woman should be a good mother.

---

1    [Matthew 7: 16, 13: 24-30; Luke 6: 44.]

IT is not necessary to inform the sagacious reader, now I enter on my concluding reflections, that the discussion of this subject merely consists in opening a few simple principles, and clearing away the rubbish which obscured them. But, as all readers are not sagacious, I must be allowed to add some explanatory remarks to bring the subject home to reason – to that sluggish reason, which supinely takes opinions on trust, and obstinately supports them to spare itself the labour of thinking.

Moralists have unanimously agreed, that unless virtue be nursed by liberty, it will never attain due strength – and what they say of man I extend to mankind, insisting that in all cases morals must be fixed on immutable principles; and, that the being cannot be termed rational or virtuous, who obeys any authority, but that of reason.

To render women truly useful members of society, I argue that they should be led, by having their understandings cultivated on a large scale, to acquire a rational affection for their country, founded on knowledge, because it is obvious that we are little interested about what we do not understand. And to render this general knowledge of due importance, I have endeavoured to shew that private duties are never properly fulfilled unless the understanding enlarges the heart; and that public virtue is only an aggregate of private.[1] But, the distinctions established in society undermine both, by beating out the solid gold of virtue, till it becomes only the tinsel-covering of vice; for whilst wealth renders a man more respectable than virtue, wealth will be sought before virtue; and, whilst women's persons are caressed, when a childish simper shews an absence of mind – the mind will lie fallow. Yet, true voluptuousness must proceed from the mind – for what can equal the sensations produced by mutual affection, supported by mutual respect? What are the cold, or feverish caresses of appetite, but sin embracing death,[2] compared with the modest overflowings of a pure heart and exalted imagination? Yes, let me tell the libertine of fancy when he despises understanding in woman – that

---

1    [Another allusion to Mandeville, *The Fable of the Bees: or Private Vices, Public Benefits.*]

2    [Milton, *Paradise Lost* 2.790-809. In the original, Death rapes his mother, Sin.]

the mind, which he disregards, gives life to the – enthusiastic affection from which rapture, short-lived as it is, alone can flow! And, that, without virtue, a sexual attachment must expire, like a tallow candle in the socket, creating intolerable disgust. To prove this, I need only observe, that men who have wasted great part of their lives with women, and with whom they have sought for pleasure with eager thirst, entertain the meanest opinion of the sex. – Virtue, true refiner of joy! – if foolish men were to fright thee from earth, in order to give loose to all their appetites without a check – some sensual wight of taste would scale the heavens to invite thee back, to give a zest to pleasure!

That women at present are by ignorance rendered foolish or vicious, is, I think, not to be disputed; and, that the most salutary effects tending to improve mankind might be expected from a REVO-LUTION in female manners, appears, at least, with a face of probability, to rise out of the observation. For as marriage has been termed the parent of those endearing charities which draw man from the brutal herd, the corrupting intercourse that wealth, idleness, and folly, produce between the sexes, is more universally injurious to morality than all the other vices of mankind collectively considered. To adulterous lust the most sacred duties are sacrificed, because before marriage, men, by a promiscuous intimacy with women, learned to consider love as a selfish gratification – learned to separate it not only from esteem, but from the affection merely built on habit, which mixes a little humanity with it. Justice and friendship are also set at defiance, and that purity of taste is vitiated which would naturally lead a man to relish an artless display of affection rather than affected airs. But that noble simplicity of affection, which dares to appear unadorned, has few attractions for the libertine, though it be the charm, which by cementing the matrimonial tie, secures to the pledges of a warmer passion the necessary parental attention; for children will never be properly educated till friendship subsists between parents. Virtue flies from a house divided against itself – and a whole legion of devils take up their residence there.[1]

The affection of husbands and wives cannot be pure when they have so few sentiments in common, and when so little confidence is

---

1  [Matthew 12: 25; Mark 3: 25, 5: 9; Luke 8: 30, 11: 17.]

established at home, as must be the case when their pursuits are so different. That intimacy from which tenderness should flow, will not, cannot subsist between the vicious.

Contending, therefore, that the sexual distinction which men have so warmly insisted upon, is arbitrary, I have dwelt on an observation, that several sensible men, with whom I have conversed on the subject, allowed to be well founded; and it is simply this, that the little chastity to be found amongst men, and consequent disregard of modesty, tend to degrade both sexes; and further, that the modesty of women, characterized as such, will often be only the artful veil of wantonness instead of being the natural reflection of purity, till modesty be universally respected.

From the tyranny of man, I firmly believe, the greater number of female follies proceed; and the cunning, which I allow makes at present a part of their character, I likewise have repeatedly endeavoured to prove, is produced by oppression.

Were not dissenters, for instance, a class of people, with strict truth, characterized as cunning? And may I not lay some stress on this fact to prove, that when any power but reason curbs the free spirit of man, dissimulation is practised, and the various shifts of art are naturally called forth? Great attention to decorum, which was carried to a degree of scrupulosity, and all that puerile bustle about trifles and consequential solemnity, which Butler's caricature of a dissenter, brings before the imagination, shaped their persons as well as their minds in the mould of prim littleness.[1] I speak collectively, for I know how many ornaments to human nature have been enrolled amongst sectaries; yet, I assert, that the same narrow prejudice for their sect, which women have for their families, prevailed in the dissenting part of the community, however worthy in other respects; and also that the same timid prudence, or headstrong efforts, often disgraced the exertions of both. Oppression thus formed many of the features of their character perfectly to coincide with that of the oppressed half of mankind; for is it not notorious that dissenters were, like women, fond of deliberating together, and asking advice of each other, till by a

---

1 [Possibly a reference to the protagonist of Butler's *Hudibras*; more probably, to "An Hypocritical Nonconformist," *Characters*, ed. Charles W. Daves (Cleveland: Case Western Reserve UP, 1970) 45-55.]

complication of little contrivances, some little end was brought about? A similar attention to preserve their reputation was conspicuous in the dissenting and female world, and was produced by a similar cause.

Asserting the rights which women in common with men ought to contend for, I have not attempted to extenuate their faults; but to prove them to be the natural consequence of their education and station in society. If so, it is reasonable to suppose that they will change their character, and correct their vices and follies, when they are allowed to be free in a physical, moral, and civil sense[1].

Let woman share the rights and she will emulate the virtues of man; for she must grow more perfect when emancipated, or justify the authority that chains such a weak being to her duty. – If the latter, it will be expedient to open a fresh trade with Russia for whips; a present which a father should always make to his son-in-law on his wedding day, that a husband may keep his whole family in order by the same means; and without any violation of justice reign, wielding this sceptre, sole master of his house, because he is the only being in it who has reason: – the divine, indefeasible earthly sovereignty breathed into man by the Master of the universe. Allowing this position, women have not any inherent rights to claim; and, by the same rule, their duties vanish, for rights and duties are inseparable.

Be just then, O ye men of understanding! and mark not more severely what women do amiss, than the vicious tricks of the horse or the ass for whom ye provide provender – and allow her the privileges of ignorance, to whom ye deny the rights of reason, or ye will be worse than Egyptian task-masters,[2] expecting virtue where nature has not given understanding!

END OF THE FIRST VOLUME.

---

1  I had further enlarged on the advantages which might reasonably be expected to result from an improvement in female manners, towards the general reformation of society; but it appeared to me that such reflections would more properly close the last volume.

2  [See Exodus 5: 6-19.]

# Appendix A: The Revolutionary Moment

### 1. *The Life of Olaudah Equiano, or Gustavus Vassa the African. Written by Himself* (1789).

While I was thus employed by my master, I was often a witness to cruelties of every kind, which were exercised on my unhappy fellow slaves. I used frequently to have different cargoes of new negroes in my care for sale; and it was almost a constant practice with our clerks, and other whites, to commit violent depredations on the chastity of the female slaves; and these I was, though with reluctance, obliged to submit to at all times, being unable to help them. When we have had some of these slaves on board my master's vessels, to carry them to other islands, or to America, I have known our mates to commit these acts most shamefully, to the disgrace, not of Christians only, but of men. I have even known them gratify their brutal passion with females not ten years old; and these abominations, some of them practiced to such scandalous excess, that one of our captains discharged the mate and others on that account. And yet in Montserrat I have seen a negro man staked to the ground, and cut most shockingly, and then his ears cut off bit by bit, because he had been connected with a white woman, who was a common prostitute. As if it were no crime in the whites to rob an innocent African girl of her virtue; but most heinous in a black man only to gratify a passion of nature, where the temptation was offered by one of a different color, though the most abandoned woman of her species.

One Mr. D—— told me that he had sold 41,000 negroes, and that he once cut off a negro man's leg for running away. – I asked him if the man had died in the operation, how he, as a Christian, could answer for the horrid act before God? and he told me, answering was a thing of another world, what he thought and did were policy. I told him that the Christian doctrine taught us to do unto others as we would that others should do unto us. He then said that his scheme had the desired effect – it cured that man and some others of running away.

Another negro man was half hanged, and then burnt, for attempting to poison a cruel overseer. Thus, by repeated cruelties, are the wretched first urged to despair, and then murdered, because they still retain so much of human nature about them as to wish to put an end to their misery, and retaliate on their tyrants! These overseers are indeed for the most part persons of the worst character of any denomination of men in the West Indies. Unfortunately, many humane gentlemen, but not residing on their estates, are obliged to leave the management of them in the hands of these human butchers, who cut and mangle the slaves in a shocking manner on the most trifling occasions, and altogether treat them in every respect like brutes. They pay no regard to the situation of pregnant women, nor the least attention to the lodging of the field negroes. Their huts, which ought to be well covered, and the place dry where they take their little repose, are often open sheds, built in damp places; so that when the poor creatures return tired from the toils of the field, they contract many disorders, from being exposed to the damp air in this uncomfortable state, while they are heated, and their pores are open. This neglect certainly conspires with many others to cause a decrease in the births as well as in the lives of the grown negroes. I can quote many instances of gentlemen who reside on their estates in the West Indies, and then the scene is quite changed; the negroes are treated with lenity and proper care, by which their lives are prolonged, and their masters profited. To the honor of humanity, I knew several gentlemen who managed their estates in this manner, and they found that benevolence was their true interest. And, among many I could mention in several of the islands, I knew one in Montserrat[1] whose slaves looked remarkably well, and never needed any fresh supplies of negroes; and there are many other estates, especially in Barbadoes, which, from such judicious treatment, need no fresh stock of negroes at any time. I have the honor of knowing a most worthy and humane gentleman, who is a native of Barbadoes, and has estates there.[2] This gentleman has written a treatise on the usage of his own slaves. He allows them two hours of refreshment at mid-day, and many other indulgencies and comforts, particularly in their lodging; and, besides

---

1   Mr. Dubury, and many others, Montserrat.
2   Sir Phillip Gibbes, Baronet, Barbadoes. [(1730–1815), author of *Instructions for the Treatment of Negroes* (1786).]

this, he raises more provisions on his estate than they can destroy; so that by these attentions he saves the lives of his negroes, and keeps them healthy, and as happy as the condition of slavery can admit. I myself, as shall appear in the sequel, managed an estate, where, by those attentions, the negroes were uncommonly cheerful and healthy, and did more work by half than by the common mode of treatment they usually do. For want, therefore, of such care and attention to the poor negroes, and otherwise oppressed as they are, it is no wonder that the decrease should require 20,000 new negroes annually, to fill up the vacant places of the dead.

Even in Barbadoes, notwithstanding those humane exceptions which I have mentioned, and others I am acquainted with, which justly make it quoted as a place where slaves meet with the best treatment, and need fewest recruits of any in the West Indies, yet this island requires 1,000 negroes annually to keep up the original stock, which is only 80,000. So that the whole term of a negro's life may be said to be there but sixteen years![1] And yet the climate here in every respect is the same as that from which they are taken, except in being more wholesome. Do the British colonies decrease in this manner? And yet what prodigious difference is there between an English and West India climate?

While I was in Montserrat I knew a negro man, named Emanuel Sankey, who endeavored to escape from his miserable bondage, by concealing himself on board of a London ship, but fate did not favor the poor oppressed man; for, being discovered when the vessel was under sail, he was delivered up again to his master. This *Christian master* immediately pinned the wretch down to the ground at each wrist and ancle and then took some sticks of sealing wax, and lighted them, and dropped it all over his back. There was another master who was noted for cruelty; and I believe he had not a slave but what had been cut, and had pieces fairly taken out of the flesh. And after they had been punished thus, he used to make them get into a long wooden box or case he had for that purpose, in which he shut them up during pleasure. It was just about the height and breadth of a man; and the poor wretches had no room, when in the case, to move.

---

1   Benezet's Account of Guinea, p. 16. [Anthony Benezet (1713-84), *Some Historical Account of Guinea, with an Inquiry into the Rise and Progress of the Slave-Trade* (1772).]

It was very common in several of the islands, particularly in St. Kitt's, for the slaves to be branded with the initial letters of their master's name; and a load of heavy iron hooks hung about their necks. Indeed, on the most trifling occasions, they were loaded with chains; and often instruments of torture were added. The iron muzzle, thumb-screws, &c., are so well known, as not to need a description, and were sometimes applied for the slightest faults. I have seen a negro beaten till some of his bones were broken, for only letting a pot boil over.[1] Is it surprising that usage like this should drive the poor creatures to despair, and make them seek a refuge in death from those evils which render their lives intolerable? – while,

> "With shudd'ring horror pale, and eyes aghast,
> They view their lamentable lot, and find
> No rest!"[2]

This they frequently do. A negro man, on board a vessel of my master, while I belonged to her, having been put in irons for some trifling misdemeanor, and kept in that state for some days, being weary of life, took an opportunity of jumping overboard into the sea; however, he was picked up without being drowned. Another, whose life was also a burden to him, resolved to starve himself to death, and refused to eat any victuals. This procured him a severe flogging; and he also, on the first occasion which offered, jumped overboard at Charleston, but was saved.

Nor is there any greater regard shown to the little property, than there is to the persons and lives of the negroes. I have already related an instance or two of particular oppression out of many which I have

---

1 [The version in *The Classic Slave Narratives* (1987), ed. Henry Louis Gates, Jr., adds the following details: "It is not uncommon, after a flogging, to make slaves go on their knees and thank their owners, and pray, or rather say, 'God bless you.' I have often asked many of the men slaves (who used to go several miles to their wives, and late in the night, after having been wearied with a hard day's labour) why they went so far for wives, and did not take them of their own master's negro-women, and particularly those who lived together as household slaves. Their answers have ever been— 'Because when the master or mistress choose to punish the women, they make the husbands flog their own wives, and that we could not bear to do'" (77).]

2 [Milton, *Paradise Lost* 2.616-18.]

witnessed; but the following is frequent in all the islands. The wretched field slaves, after toiling all the day for an unfeeling owner, who gives them but little victuals, steal sometimes a few moments from rest or refreshment to gather some small portion of grass, according as their time will admit. This they commonly tie up in a parcel; either a bit's worth (sixpence) or half a bit's worth, and bring it to town, or to the market, to sell. Nothing is more common than for the white people on this occasion to take the grass from them without paying for it; and not only so, but too often also, to my knowledge, our clerks, and many others, at the same time have committed acts of violence on the poor, wretched, and helpless females; whom I have seen for hours stand crying to no purpose, and get no redress or pay of any kind. Is not this one common and crying sin enough to bring down God's judgment on the islands? He tells us the oppressor and the oppressed are both in his hands; and if these are not the poor, the broken-hearted, the blind, the captive, the bruised, which our Saviour speaks of, who are they? One of these depredators once, in St. Eustatia, came on board of our vessel, and bought some fowls and pigs of me; and a whole day after his departure with the things, he returned again and wanted his money back. I refused to give it, and, not seeing my captain on board, he began the common pranks with me; and swore he would even break open my chest and take my money. I therefore expected, as my captain was absent, that he would be as good as his word. And was just proceeding to strike me, when fortunately a British seaman on board, whose heart had not been debauched by a West India climate, interposed and prevented him. But had the cruel man struck me I certainly should have defended myself at the hazard of my life; for what is life to a man thus oppressed? He went away, however, swearing, and threatened that whenever he caught me on shore, he would shoot me, and pay for me afterwards.

The small account in which the life of a negro is held in the West Indies, is so universally known, that it might seem impertinent to quote the following extract, if some people had not been hardy enough of late to assert that negroes are on the same footing in that respect as Europeans. By the 329th Act, page 125, of the Assembly of Barbadoes, it is enacted "That if any negro, or other slave, under punishment by his master, or his order, for running away, or any other crime or misdemeanor towards his said master, unfortunately shall suffer in life or member, no person whatsoever shall be liable to a fine; but if any person shall, out of wantonness, or only of bloody-mindedness, or cruel intention, wilfully kill a negro, or other slave, of his own, he shall pay into the public treasury fifteen pounds sterling." And it is the same in most, if not all of the West India islands. Is not this one of the many acts of the islands which call loudly for redress? And do not the assembly which enacted it deserve the appellation of savages and brutes, rather than of Christians and men? It is an act at once unmerciful, unjust, and unwise; which for cruelty would disgrace an assembly of those who are called barbarians; and for its injustice and insanity would shock the morality and common sense of a Samaide or Hottentot.

Shocking as this and many other acts of the bloody West India code at first view appear, how is the iniquity of it heightened when we consider to whom it may be extended! Mr. James Tobin,[1] a zealous laborer in the vineyard of slavery, gives an account of a French planter of his acquaintance, in the island of Martinico, who showed him many mulattoes working in the field like beasts of burden; and he told Mr. Tobin these were all the produce of his own loins! And I myself have known similar instances. Pray, reader, are these sons and daughters of the French planter less his children by being the progeny of black women? And what must be the virtue of those legislators, and the feelings of those fathers, who estimate the lives of their sons, however begotten, at no more than fifteen pounds; though they should be murdered, as the act says, out of wantonness and bloody-mindedness! But is not the slave trade entirely at war with the heart of man? And surely that which is begun by breaking down the barriers of virtue, involves in its continuance destruction to every principle, and buries all sentiment in ruin!

I have often seen slaves, particularly those who were meagre, in different islands, put into scales and weighed, and then sold from three pence to six pence or nine pence a pound. My master, however, whose humanity was shocked at this mode, used to sell such by the

---

1    [Tobin, a prominent Nevis planter and author of *Cursory Remarks*, would give evidence in favour of the slave trade before the House of Commons in 1790.]

lump. And at or after a sale, it was not uncommon to see negroes taken from their wives, wives taken from their husbands, and children from their parents, and sent off to other islands, and wherever else their merciless lords choose; and probably never more during life see each other! Oftentimes my heart has bled at these partings, when the friends of the departed have been at the water side, and with sighs and tears, have kept their eyes fixed on the vessel, till it went out of sight.

A poor Creole negro, I knew well, who, after having been often thus transported from island to island, at last resided in Montserrat. This man used to tell me many melancholy tales of himself. Generally, after he had done working for his master, he used to employ his few leisure moments to go a fishing. When he had caught any fish, his master would frequently take them from him without paying him; and at other times some other white people would serve him in the same manner. One day he said to me, very movingly, "Sometimes when a white man take away my fish, I go to my maser, and he get me my right; and when my maser by strength take away my fishes, what me must do? I can't go to any body to be righted; then," said the poor man, looking up above, "I must look up to God Mighty, in the top, for right." This artless tale moved me much, and I could not help feeling the just cause Moses had in redressing his brother against the Egyptian.[1] I exhorted the man to look up still to the God on the top, since there was no redress below. Though I little thought then that I myself should more than once experience such imposition, and need the same exhortation hereafter, in my own transactions in the islands, and that even this poor man and I should some time after suffer together in the same manner, as shall be related hereafter.

Nor was such usage as this confined to particular places or individuals; for, in all the different islands in which I have been, (and I have visited no less than fifteen,) the treatment of slaves was nearly the same; so nearly, indeed, that the history of an island, or even a plantation, with a few such exceptions as I have mentioned, might serve for a history of the whole. Such a tendency has the slave trade to debauch men's minds, and harden them to every feeling of humanity! For I will not suppose that the dealers in slaves are born worse than other men – No; such is the fatality of this mistaken avarice, that it corrupts

---

1   [Exodus 2: 11-12.]

the milk of human kindness[1] and turns it into gall. And, had the pursuits of those men been different, they might have been as generous, as tender-hearted and just, as they are unfeeling, rapacious, and cruel. Surely this traffic cannot be good, which spreads like a pestilence, and taints what it touches! Which violates that first natural right of mankind, equality and independency, and gives one man a dominion over his fellows which God could never intend! For it raises the owner to a state as far above man as it depresses the slave below it; and, with all the presumption of human pride, sets a distinction between them, immeasurable in extent, and endless in duration! Yet how mistaken is the avarice even of the planters. Are slaves more useful by being thus humbled to the condition of brutes, than they would be if suffered to enjoy the privileges of men? The freedom which diffuses health and prosperity throughout Britain answers you – No. When you make men slaves, you deprive them of half their virtue, you set them, in your own conduct, an example of fraud, rapine, and cruelty, and compel them to live with you in a state of war; and yet you complain that they are not honest or faithful! You stupify them with stripes, and think it necessary to keep them in a state of ignorance. And yet you assert that they are incapable of learning; that their minds are such a barren soil or moor, that culture would be lost on them; and that they come from a climate, where nature, though prodigal of her bounties in a degree unknown to yourselves, has left man alone scant and unfinished, and incapable of enjoying the treasures she has poured out for him! An assertion at once impious and absurd. Why do you use those instruments of torture? Are they fit to be applied by one rational being to another? And are ye not struck with shame and mortification, to see the partakers of your nature reduced so low? But, above all, are there no dangers attending this mode of treatment? Are you not hourly in dread of an insurrection? Nor would it be surprising; for when

> "————No peace is given
> To us enslav'd, but custody severe,
> And stripes and arbitrary punishment
> Inflicted – What peace can we return?

---

1   [Shakespeare, *Macbeth* 1.5.15.]

But to our power, hostility and hate;
Untam'd reluctance, and revenge, tho' slow.
Yet ever plotting how the conqueror least
May reap his conquest, and may least rejoice
In doing what we most in suffering feel."[1]

But by changing your conduct, and treating your slaves as men, every cause of fear would be banished. They would be faithful, honest, intelligent, and vigorous; and peace, prosperity, and happiness would attend you. [115-27]

## 2. Declaration Of The Rights Of Men And Of Citizens, By The National Assembly Of France (1789)

THE Representatives of the people of FRANCE formed into a National Assembly, considering that ignorance, neglect, or contempt of human rights, are the sole causes of public misfortunes and corruptions of government, have resolved to set forth in a solemn declaration, these natural, imprescriptible, and unalienable rights: that this declaration being constantly present to the minds of the members of the body social, they may be ever kept attentive to their rights and their duties: That the acts of the legislative and executive powers of government being capable of being every moment compared with the end of political institutions, may be more respected: and also, that the future claims of the citizens, being directed by simple and incontestible principles, may always tend to the maintenance of the Constitution, and the general happiness.

For these reasons, the NATIONAL ASSEMBLY doth recognize and declare, in the presence of the Supreme Being and with the hope of his blessing and favour, the following *sacred* rights of men and of citizens.

I. Men were born and always continue free, and equal in respect of their rights. Civil distinctions, therefore, can be founded only on public utility.

II. The end of all political associations is the preservation of the natural and imprescriptible rights of man; and these rights are liberty,

---

1   [Milton, *Paradise Lost* 2.332-40.]

property, security, and resistance of oppression.

III. The nation is essentially the source of all sovereignty; nor can any individual, or any body of men be entitled to any authority which is not expressly derived from it.

IV. Political liberty consists in the power of doing whatever does not injure another. The exercise of the natural rights of every man, has no other limits than those which are necessary to secure to every *other* man the free exercise of the same rights; and these limits are determinable only by the law.

V. The law ought to prohibit only actions hurtful to society. What is not prohibited by the law should not be hindered; nor should any one be compelled to that which the law does not require.

VI. The law is an expression of the will of the community. All citizens have a right to concur, either personally or by their representatives, in its formation. It should be the same to all, whether it protects or punishes; and all being equal in its sight, are equally eligible to all honours, places, and employments, according to their different abilities, without any other distinction than that created by their virtues and talents.

VII. No man should be accused, arrested, or held in confinement, except in cases determined by the law, and according to the forms which it has prescribed. All who promote, solicit, execute, or cause to be executed arbitrary orders, ought to be punished: and every citizen called upon or apprehended by virtue of the law, ought immediately to obey, and renders himself culpable by resistance.

VIII. The law ought to impose no other penalties than such as are absolutely and evidently necessary; and no one ought to be punished but in virtue of a law promulgated before the offense, and legally applied.

IX. Every man being presumed innocent till he has been convicted, whenever his detention becomes indispensible, all rigour to him, more than is necessary to secure his person, ought to be provided against by the law.

X. No man ought to be molested on account of his opinions, not even on account of his *religious* opinions, provided his avowal of them does not disturb the public order established by the law.

XI. The unrestrained communication of thoughts and opinions

being one of the most precious rights of man, every citizen may speak, write, and publish freely, provided he is responsible for the abuse of this liberty in cases determined by the law.

XII. A public force being necessary to give security to the rights of men and of citizens, that force is instituted for the benefit of the community, and not for the particular benefit of the persons with whom it is entrusted.

XIII. A common contribution being necessary for the support of the public force, and for defraying the other expences of government, it ought to be divided equally among the members of the community, according to their abilities.

XIV. Every citizen has a right, either by himself or his representative, to a free voice in determining the necessity of public contributions, the appropriation of them, and their amount, mode of assessment, and duration.

XV. Every community has a right to demand of all its agents an account of their conduct.

XVI. Every community in which a separation of powers and a security of rights is not provided for, wants a constitution.

XVII. The right to property being inviolable and sacred, no one ought to be deprived of it, except in cases of evident public necessity legally ascertained, and on condition of a previous just indemnity. [Price, Appendix 5-8]

### 3. Richard Price, *A Discourse on the Love of our Country* (1789).

PSALM cxxii. 2d, and following verses.
*Our feet shall stand within thy gates, O Jerusalem, whither the tribes go up; the tribes of the Lord unto the testimony of Israel. To give thanks to the name of the Lord, for there sit the thrones of judgment; the throne of the House of David. Pray for the peace of* JERUSALEM *.. They shall prosper that love thee. Peace be within thy walls, and prosperity within thy palaces. For my brethren and companions sake I will now say peace be within thee. Because of the House of the Lord our God, I will seek thy good.*

IN these words the Psalmist expresses, in strong and beautiful language, his love of his country, and the reasons on which he founded it; and my present design is, to take occasion from them to explain the duty we owe to our country, and the nature, foundation, and proper expressions of that love to it which we ought to cultivate.

I reckon this a subject particularly suitable to the services of this day, and to the Anniversary of our deliverance at the Revolution from the dangers of popery and arbitrary power; and should I, on such an occasion, be led to touch more on political subjects than would at any other time be proper in the pulpit, you will, I doubt not, excuse me.

The love of our country has in all times been a subject of warm commendations; and it is certainly a noble passion; but, like all other passions, it requires regulation and direction. There are mistakes and prejudices by which, in this instance, we are in particular danger of being misled.——I will briefly mention some of these to you, and observe,

First, That by our country is meant, in this case, not the soil or the spot of earth on which we happen to have been born; not the forests and fields, but that community of which we are members; or that body of companions and friends and kindred who are associated with us under the same constitution of government, protected by the same laws, and bound together by the same civil polity.

Secondly, It is proper to observe, that even in this sense of our country, that love of it which is our duty, does not imply any conviction of the superior value of it to other countries, or any particular preference of its laws and constitution of government. Were this implied, the love of their country would be the duty of only a very small part of mankind; for there are few countries that enjoy the advantage of laws and governments which deserve to be preferred. To found, therefore, this duty on such a preference, would be to found it on error and delusion. It is, however, a common delusion. There is the same partiality in countries, to themselves, that there is in individuals. All our attachments should be accompanied, as far as possible, with right opinions.——We are too apt to confine wisdom and virtue within the circle of our own acquaintance and party. Our friends, our country, and in short every thing related to us, we are disposed to overvalue. A wise man will guard himself against this delusion. He will study to think of all things as they are, and not suffer any partial affections to blind his understanding. In other families there may be as much worth as in our own. In other circles of friends there may be as much wisdom; and in other countries as much of all that deserves esteem; but, notwithstanding this, our obligation to love our own families, friends, and country, and to seek, in the first place, their good, will remain the same.

Thirdly, It is proper I should desire you particularly to distinguish between the love of our country and that spirit of rivalship and ambition which has been common among nations.——What has the love of their country hitherto been among mankind? What has it been but a love of domination; a desire of conquest, and a thirst for grandeur and glory, by extending territory, and enslaving surrounding countries? What has it been but a blind and narrow principle, producing in every country a contempt of other countries, and forming men into combinations and factions against their common rights and liberties? This is the principle that has been too often cried up as a virtue of the first rank: a principle of the same kind with that which governs clans of *Indians* or tribes of *Arabs*, and leads them out to plunder and massacre. As most of the evils which have taken place in private life, and among individuals, have been occasioned by the desire of private interest overcoming the public affections; so most of the evils which have taken place among bodies of men have been occasioned by the desire of their own interest overcoming the principle of universal benevolence: and leading them to attack one another's territories, to encroach on one another's rights, and to endeavour to build their own advancement on the degradation of all within the reach of their power——What was the love of their country among the *Jews*, but a wretched partiality to themselves, and a proud contempt of all other nations? What was the love of their country among the old *Romans?* We have heard much of it; but I cannot hesitate in saying that, however great it appeared in some of its exertions, it was in general no better than a principle holding together a band of robbers in their attempts to crush all liberty but their own. What is now the love of his country in a *Spaniard,* a *Turk,* or a *Russian?* Can it be considered as any thing better than a passion for slavery, or a blind attachment to a spot where he enjoys no rights, and is disposed of as if he was a beast?

Let us learn by such reflexions to correct and purify this passion, and to make it a just and rational principle of action.

It is very remarkable that the founder of our religion has not once mentioned this duty, or given us any recommendation of it; and this has, by unbelievers, been made an objection to Christianity. What I have said will entirely remove this objection. Certain it is, that, by inculcating on men an attachment to their country, Christianity would, at the time it was propagated, have done unspeakably more harm than good. Among the *Jews*, it would have been an excitement to war and insurrections; for they were then in eager expectation of becoming soon (as the favourite people of Heaven) the lords and conquerors of the earth, under the triumphant reign of the *Messiah*. Among the *Romans*, likewise, this principle had, as I have just observed, exceeded its just bounds, and rendered them enemies to the peace and happiness of mankind. By inculcating it, therefore, Christianity would have confirmed both Jews and Gentiles in one of the most pernicious faults. Our Lord and his Apostles have done better. They have recommended that UNIVERSAL BENEVOLENCE which is an unspeakably nobler principle than any partial affections. They have laid such stress on loving all men, even our enemies, and made an ardent and extensive charity so essential a part of virtue, that the religion they have preached may, by way of distinction from all other religions, be called the Religion of Benevolence. Nothing can be more friendly to the general rights of mankind; and were it duly regarded and practised, every man would consider every other man as his brother, and all the animosity that now takes place among contending nations would be abolished. If you want any proof of this, think of our Saviour's parable of the good Samaritan.[1] The *Jews* and *Samaritans* were two rival nations that entertained a hatred of one another the most inveterate. The design of this parable was to shew to a *Jew*, that even a *Samaritan*, and consequently all men of all nations and religions, were included in the precept, THOU SHALT LOVE THY NEIGHBOUR AS THY SELF.

But I am digressing from what I had chiefly in view; which was, after noticing that love of our country which is false and spurious, to explain the nature and effects of that which is just and reasonable. With this view I must desire you to recollect that we are so constituted that our affections are more drawn to some among mankind than

1  [Luke 10: 30-37.]

to others, in proportion to their degrees of nearness to us, and our power of being useful to them. It is obvious that this is a circumstance in the constitution of our natures which proves the wisdom and goodness of our Maker; for had our affections been determined alike to all our fellow-creatures, human life would have been a scene of embarrassment and distraction. Our regards, according to the order of nature, begin with ourselves; and every man is charged primarily with the care of himself. Next come our families, and benefactors, and friends; and after them our country. We can do little for the interest of mankind at large. To this interest, however, all other interests are subordinate. The noblest principle in our nature is the regard to general justice, and that good-will which embraces all the world.——I have already observed this; but it cannot be too often repeated. Though our immediate attention must be employed in promoting our own interest and that of our nearest connexions; yet we must remember, that a narrower interest ought always to give way to a more extensive interest. In pursuing particularly the interest of our country, we ought to carry our views beyond it. We should love it ardently, but not exclusively. We ought to seek its good, by all the means that our different circumstances and abilities will allow; but at the same time we ought to consider ourselves as citizens of the world, and take care to maintain a just regard to the rights of other countries.

The enquiry by what means (subject to this limitation) we may best promote the interest of our country is very important; and all that remains of this discourse shall be employed in answering it, and in exhorting you to manifest your love to your country, by the means I shall mention.

The chief blessings of human nature are the three following:——
TRUTH—VIRTUE—and LIBERTY.——These are, therefore, the blessings in the possession of which the interest of our country lies, and to the attainment of which our love of it ought to direct our endeavours. By the diffusion of KNOWLEDGE it must be distinguished from a country of *Barbarians:* by the practice of religious VIRTUE, it must be distinguished from a country of *gamblers, Atheists,* and *libertines:* and by the possession of LIBERTY, it must be distinguished from a country of *slaves.*——I will dwell for a few moments on each of these heads:

Our first concern, as lovers of our country, must be to *enlighten* it. – Why are the nations of the world so patient under despotism? – Why do they crouch to tyrants, and submit to be treated as if they were a herd of cattle? Is it not because they are kept in darkness, and want knowledge? Enlighten them and you will elevate them. Shew them they are *men*, and they will act like *men*. Give them just ideas of civil government, and let them know that it is an expedient for gaining protection against injury and defending their rights[1], and it will be impossible for them to submit to governments which, like most of those now in the world, are usurpations on the rights of men, and little better than contrivances for enabling the *few* to oppress the *many*. Convince them that the Deity is a righteous and benevolent as well as omnipotent being, who regards with equal eye all his creatures, and connects his favour with nothing but an honest desire to know and do his will; and that zeal for mystical doctrines which has led men to hate and harass one another will be exterminated. Set religion before them as a rational service, consisting not in any rites and ceremonies, but in worshipping God with a pure heart and practising righteousness from the fear of his displeasure and the apprehension of a future righteous judgment, and that gloomy and cruel superstition will be abolished which has hitherto gone under the name of religion, and to the support of which civil government has been perverted.——Ignorance is the parent of bigotry, intolerance, persecution and slavery. Inform and instruct mankind; and these evils will be excluded.—— Happy is the person who, himself raised above vulgar errors, is conscious of having aimed at giving mankind this instruction. Happy is the Scholar or Philosopher who at the close of life can reflect that he has made this use of his learning and abilities: but happier far must he be, if at the same time he has reason to believe he has been successful, and actually contributed, by his instructions, to disseminate among his fellow-creatures just notions of themselves, of their rights, of religion, and the nature and end of civil government. Such were *Milton, Locke, Sidney, Hoadly,* &c. in this country; such were *Montesquieu, Marmontel, Turgot,* &c. in France.[2] They sowed a seed which has since taken root,

---

1    See the Declaration of Rights by the National Assembly of *France*, in the Appendix. [A.2.]

2    [ John Milton (1608-1674) wrote *Areopagitica* (1644), *The Tenure of Kings and Magis-*

and is now growing up to a glorious harvest. To the information they conveyed by their writings we owe those revolutions in which every friend to mankind is now exulting.——What an encouragement is this to us all in our endeavours to enlighten the world? Every degree of illumination which we can communicate must do the greatest good. It helps to prepare the minds of men for the recovery of their rights, and hastens the overthrow of priestcraft and tyranny.——In short, we may, in this instance, learn our duty from the conduct of the oppressors of the world. They know that light is hostile to them, and therefore they labour to keep men in the dark. With this intention they have appointed licensers of the press; and, in Popish countries, prohibited the reading of the Bible. Remove the darkness in which they envelope the world, and their usurpations will be exposed, their power will be subverted, and the world emancipated.

The next great blessing of human nature which I have mentioned is V I R T U E. This ought to follow knowledge, and to be directed by it. Virtue without knowledge makes enthusiasts; and knowledge without virtue makes devils; but both united elevates to the top of human dignity and perfection.——We must, therefore, if we would serve our country, make both these the objects of our zeal. We must discourage vice in all its forms; and our endeavours to enlighten must have ultimately in view a reformation of manners and virtuous practice.

I must add here, that in the practice of virtue I include the discharge of the public duties of religion. By neglecting these we may injure our country essentially. But it is melancholy to observe that it is a common neglect among us; and in a great measure owing to a cause which is not likely to be soon removed: I mean, the defects (may I not say, the absurdities?) in our established codes of faith and worship. In

---

*trates* (1649), *Pro Populo Anglicano Defensio* (1651), and other political works. John Locke (1632-1704), wrote *Letters concerning Toleration* (1689-92) and *Two Treatises of Government* (1690). Algernon Sidney (1622-1683) fought on the Parliamentary side in the Civil War and was later executed for allegedly conspiring to assassinate Charles II; his *Discourses concerning Government* was published in 1698. Benjamin Hoadly (1676-1761) wrote *The Measures of Submission to the Civil Magistrate Considered* (1706), *The Original and Institution of Civil Government Discussed* (1710), and *The Common Rights of Subjects Defended* (1718). Charles-Louis, baron de Montesquieu (1689-1755) wrote *L'Esprit des lois* (1748). Jean-François Marmontel (1723-1799) wrote the philosophical romances *Bélisaire* (1767) and *Les Incas* (1777). Anne-Robert-Jacques Turgot (1727-1781) wrote *Lettres sur la tolérance* (1753).]

foreign countries, the higher ranks of men, not distinguishing between the religion they see established and the Christian religion, are generally driven to irreligion and infidelity. The like evil is produced by the like cause in this country; and if no reformation of our established formularies can be brought about, it must be expected that religion will go on to lose its credit, and that little of it will be left except among the lower orders of people, many of whom, while their superiors give up all religion, are sinking into a barbarism in religion lately revived by Methodism, and mistaking, as the world has generally done, the service acceptable to God for a system of faith souring the temper, and a service of forms supplanting morality.

I hope you will not mistake what I am now saying, or consider it as the effect of my prejudices as a Dissenter from the established church. The complaint I am making, is the complaint of many of the wisest and best men in the established church itself, who have been long urging the necessity of a revisal of its Liturgy and Articles[1]. These were framed above two centuries ago, when Christendom was just emerging from the ignorance and barbarity of the dark ages. They remain now much the same they were then; and, therefore, cannot be properly adapted to the good sense and liberality of the present times. – This imperfection, however, in our public forms of worship, affords no excuse to any person for neglecting public worship. All communities will have some religion; and it is of infinite consequence that they should be led to that which, by enforcing the obligations of virtue and putting men upon loving instead of damning one another, is most favourable to the interest of society.

If there is a Governor of the world, who directs all events, he ought to be invoked and worshipped; and those who dislike that mode of worship which is prescribed by public authority, ought (if they can find no worship *out* of the church which they approve) to set up a separate worship for themselves; and by doing this, and giving an example of a rational and manly worship, men of weight, from their

---

1   See a pamphlet ascribed to a great name, and which would dignify any name, entitled, *Hints, &c. submitted to the serious Attention of the Clergy, Nobility, and Gentry, newly assembled. By a Layman, a Friend to the true Principles of the Constitution in Church and State, and to Civil and Religious Liberty.* The Third Edition, corrected; and printed for *White* and *Debrett,* 1789.

rank or literature, may do the greatest service to society and the world. They may bear a testimony against that application of civil power to the support of particular modes of faith, which obstructs human improvement, and perpetuates error; and they may hold out an instruction which will discountenance superstition, and at the same time recommend religion, by making it appear to be (what it certainly is when rightly understood) the strongest incentive to all that is generous and worthy, and consequently the best friend to public order and happiness.

LIBERTY is the next great blessing which I have mentioned as the object of patriotic zeal. It is inseparable from knowledge and virtue, and together with them completes the glory of a community. An enlightened and virtuous country must be a free country. It cannot suffer invasions of its rights, or bend to tyrants.——I need not, on this occasion, take any pains to shew you how great a blessing liberty is. The smallest attention to the history of past ages, and the present state of mankind, will make you sensible of its importance. Look round the world, and you will find almost every country, respectable or contemptible, happy or miserable, a fruitful field or a frightful waste, according as it possesses or wants this blessing. Think of *Greece*, formerly the seat of arts and science, and the most distinguished spot under heaven; but now, having lost liberty, a vile and wretched spot, a region of darkness, poverty, and barbarity.——Such reflexions must convince you that, if you love your country, you cannot be zealous enough in promoting the cause of liberty in it. But it will come in my way to say more to this purpose presently.

The observations I have made include our whole duty to our country; for by endeavouring to liberalize and enlighten it, to discourage vice and to promote virtue in it, and to assert and support its liberties, we shall endeavour to do all that is necessary to make it great and happy.——But it is proper that, on this occasion, I should be more explicit, and exemplify our duty to our country by observing farther, that it requires us to obey its laws, and to respect its magistrates.

Civil government (as I have before observed) is an institution of human prudence for guarding our persons, our property, and our good name, against invasion; and for securing to the members of a community that liberty to which all have an equal right, as far as they do not, by any overt act, use it to injure the liberty of others. Civil laws are regulations agreed upon by the community for gaining these ends[1]; and civil magistrates are officers appointed by the community for executing these laws. Obedience, therefore, to the laws and to magistrates, are necessary expressions of our regard to the community; and without this obedience the ends of government cannot be obtained, or a community avoid falling into a state of anarchy that will destroy those rights and subvert that liberty, which government is instituted to protect.

I wish it was in my power to give you a just account of the importance of this observation. It shews the ground on which the duty of obeying civil governors stands, and that there are two extremes in this case which ought to be avoided.——These extremes are adulation and servility on one hand; and a proud and licentious contempt on the other. The former is the extreme to which mankind in general have been most prone; for it has oftener happened that men have been too passive than too unruly; and the rebellion of Kings against their people has been more common, and done more mischief, than the rebellion of people against their Kings.

Adulation is always odious, and when offered to men in power it corrupts *them*, by giving them improper ideas of their situation; and it debases those who offer it, by manifesting an abjectness founded on improper ideas of *themselves*. I have lately observed in this kingdom too near approaches to this abjectness. In our late addresses to the King, on his recovery from the severe illness with which God has been pleased to afflict him, we have appeared more like a herd crawling at the feet of a master, than like enlightened and manly citizens rejoicing with a beloved sovereign, but at the same time conscious that he derives all his consequence from themselves. But, perhaps, these servilities in the language of our late addresses should be pardoned, as only *forms* of civility and expressions of an overflow of good-nature. They have, however, a dangerous tendency. The potentates of this world are sufficiently apt to consider themselves as possessed of an inherent superiority, which gives them a right to govern,

---

1   See Articles III. and VI. of the Declaration of Rights, by the National Assembly of France, in the Appendix. [A.2.]

and makes mankind *their own*; and this infatuation is almost every where fostered in them by the creeping sycophants about them, and the language of flattery which they are continually hearing.

Civil governors are properly the servants of the public; and a King is no more than the first servant of the public, created by it, maintained by it, and responsible to it: and all the homage paid him, is due to him on no other account than his relation to the public. His sacredness is the sacredness of the community. His authority is the authority of the community; and the term MAJESTY, which it is usual to apply to him, is by no means *his own* majesty, but the MAJESTY OF THE PEOPLE. For this reason, whatever he may be in his private capacity; and though, in respect of personal qualities, not equal to, or even far below many among ourselves—For this reason, I say, (that is, as representing the community and its first magistrate), he is entitled to our reverence and obedience. The words MOST EXCELLENT MAJESTY are rightly applied to him; and there is a respect which it would be criminal to withhold from him.

You cannot be too attentive to this observation. The improvement of the world depends on the attention to it: nor will mankind be ever as virtuous and happy, as they are capable of being, till the attention to it becomes universal and efficacious. If we forget it, we shall be in danger of an idolatry as gross and stupid as that of the ancient heathens, who, after fabricating blocks of wood or stone, fell down and worshiped them.——The disposition in mankind to this kind of idolatry is indeed a very mortifying subject of reflexion.——In TURKEY millions of human beings adore a silly mortal, and are ready to throw themselves at his feet, and to submit their lives to his discretion.——In RUSSIA, the common people are only a STOCK on the lands of grandees, or appendages to their estates, which, like the fixtures in a house, are bought and sold with the estates. In SPAIN, in GERMANY, and under most of the governments of the world, mankind are in a similar state of humiliation. Who, that has a just sense of the dignity of his nature, can avoid execrating such a debasement of it?

Had I been to address the King on a late occasion, I should have been inclined to do it in a style very different from that of most of the addressers, and to use some such language as the following:—— "I rejoice, Sir, in your recovery. I thank God for his goodness to you. I honour you not only as my King, but as almost the only lawful King in the world, because the only one who owes his crown to the choice of his people. May you enjoy all possible happiness. May God shew you the folly of those effusions of adulation which you are now receiving, and guard you against their effects. May you be led to such a just sense of the nature of your situation, and endowed with such wisdom, as shall render your restoration to the government of these kingdoms a blessing to it, and engage you to consider yourself as more properly the *Servant* than the *Sovereign* of your people."

But I must not forget the opposite extreme to that now taken notice of; that is, a disdainful pride, derived from a consciousness of equality, or, perhaps, superiority, in respect of all that gives true dignity, to men in power, and producing a contempt of them, and a disposition to treat them with rudeness and insult. It is a trite observation, that extremes generally beget one another. This is particularly true in the present case. Persons justly informed on the subject of government, when they see men dazzled by looking up to high stations, and observe loyalty carried to a length that implies ignorance and servility: such persons, in such circumstances, are in danger of spurning at all public authority, and throwing off that respectful demeanor to persons invested with it which the order of society requires. There is undoubtedly a particular deference and homage due to civil magistrates, on account of their stations and offices; nor can that man be either truly wise or truly virtuous, who despises governments, and wantonly *speaks evil of his rulers*; or who does not, by all the means in his power, endeavour to strengthen their hands, and to give weight to their exertions in the discharge of their duty.——*Fear God*, says St. Peter. *Love the brotherhood. Honour all men. Honour the King.*[1]—— *You must needs*, says St. Paul, *be subject to rulers, not only for wrath* (that is, from the fear of suffering the penalties annexed to the breach of the laws), *but for conscience sake. For rulers are ministers of God, and revengers for executing wrath on all that do evil.*[2]

Another expression of our love to our country is defending it against enemies. These enemies are of two sorts, internal and external;

---

1   [1 Peter 2: 17.]
2   [Romans 13: 4-5.]

or domestic and foreign. The former are the most dangerous, and they have generally been the most successful. I have just observed, that there is a submission due to the executive officers of government, which is our duty; but you must not forget what I have also observed, that it must not be a blind and slavish submission. Men in power (unless better disposed than is common) are always endeavouring to extend their power. They hate the doctrine, that it is a TRUST derived from the people, and not a *right* vested in themselves. For this reason, the tendency of every government is to despotism; and in this the best constituted governments must end, if the people are not vigilant, ready to take alarms, and determined to resist abuses as soon as they begin. This vigilance, therefore, it is our duty to maintain. Whenever it is withdrawn, and a people cease to reason about their rights and to be awake to encroachments, they are in danger of being enslaved, and their *servants* will soon become their *masters*.

I need not say how much it is our duty to defend our country against foreign enemies. When a country is attacked in any of its rights by another country, or when any attempts are made by ambitious foreign powers to injure it, a war in its defence becomes necessary: and, in such circumstances, to die for our country is meritorious and noble. These *defensive* wars are, in my opinion, the only just wars. *Offensive* wars are always unlawful; and to seek the aggrandizement of our country by them, that is, by attacking other countries, in order to extend dominion, or to gratify avarice, is wicked and detestable. Such, however, have been most of the wars which have taken place in the world; but the time is, I hope, coming, when a conviction will prevail, of the folly[1] as well as the iniquity of wars; and when the nations of the earth, happy under just governments, and no longer in danger from the passions of Kings, will find out better ways of settling their

---

1   See a striking representation of the folly of wars, in the last sections of Mr. *Necker's* Treatise on the *Administration of the Finances of* FRANCE. There is reason to believe that the sentiments on this subject in that treatise, are now the prevailing sentiments in the court and legislature of FRANCE; and, consequently, that one of the happy effects of the revolution in that country may be, if not our own fault, such a harmony between the two first kingdoms in the world, strengthened by a common participation in the blessings of liberty, as shall not only prevent their engaging in any future wars with one another, but dispose them to unite in preventing wars every where, and in making the world free and happy. [Jacques Necker (1732-1804), *De l'administration des finances de France* (1784).]

disputes; and beat (as Isaiah prophecies) *their swords into plowshares, and their spears into pruning-hooks. . . .*[1] [1-30]

But the most important instance of the imperfect state in which the Revolution left our constitution, is the INEQUALITY OF OUR REPRESENTATION. I think, indeed, this defect in our constitution so gross and so palpable, as to make it excellent chiefly in form and theory. You should remember that a representation in the legislature of a kingdom is the *basis* of constitutional liberty in it, and of all legitimate government; and that without it a government is nothing but an usurpation[2]. When the representation is fair and equal, and at the same time vested with such powers as our House of Commons possesses, a kingdom may be said to govern itself, and consequently to possess true liberty. When the representation is partial, a kingdom possesses liberty only partially; and if extremely partial, it only gives a *semblance* of liberty; but if not only extremely partial, but corruptly chosen, and under corrupt influence after being chosen, it becomes a *nuisance*, and produces the worst of all forms of government – a government by corruption – a government carried on and supported by spreading venality and profligacy through a kingdom. May heaven preserve this kingdom from a calamity so dreadful! It is the point of depravity to which abuses under such a government as ours naturally tend, and the last stage of national unhappiness. We are, at present, I hope, at a great distance from it. But it cannot be pretended that there are no advances towards it, or that there is no reason for apprehension and alarm.

The inadequateness of our representation has been long a subject of complaint. This is, in truth, our fundamental grievance; and I do not think that any thing is much more our duty, as men who love their country, and are grateful for the Revolution, than to unite our zeal in endeavouring to get it redressed. At the time of the American war, associations were formed for this purpose in LONDON, and other parts of the kingdom; and our present Minister[3] himself has, since that war, directed to it an effort which made him a favourite with many of

---

1   [Isaiah 2: 4.]
2   Except in states so small as to admit of a Legislative Assembly, consisting of all the members of the state.
3   [William Pitt the Younger (1759-1806), prime minster 1783-1801, 1804-06.]

us. But all attention to it seems now lost, and the probability is, that this inattention will continue, and that nothing will be done towards gaining for us this essential blessing, till some great calamity again alarms our fears, or till some great abuse of power again provokes our resentment; or, perhaps, till the acquisition of a pure and equal representation by other countries (while we are mocked with the shadow[1]) kindles our shame.

Such is the conduct by which we ought to express our gratitude for the Revolution. – We should always bear in mind the principles that justify it. We should contribute all we can towards supplying what it left deficient; and shew ourselves anxious about transmitting the blessings obtained by it to our posterity, unimpaired and improved. – But, brethren, while we thus shew our patriotic zeal, let us take care not to disgrace the cause of patriotism, by any licentious, or immoral conduct.——Oh! how earnestly do I wish that all who profess zeal in this cause, were as distinguished by the purity of their morals, as some of them are by their abilities; and that I could make them sensible of the advantages they would derive from a virtuous character, and of the suspicions they incur and the loss of consequence they suffer by wanting it.——Oh! that I could see in men who oppose tyranny in the state, a disdain of the tyranny of low passions in themselves; or, at least, such a sense of shame, and regard to public order and decency as would induce them to *hide* their irregularities, and to avoid insulting the virtuous part of the community by an open exhibition of vice! – I cannot reconcile myself to the idea of an immoral patriot, or to that separation of private from public virtue, which some think to be possible. Is it to be expected that——— But I must forbear. I am afraid of applications, which many are too ready to make, and for which I should be sorry to give any just occasion. . . . [39-43]

You may reasonably expect that I should now close this address to you. But I cannot yet dismiss you. I must not conclude without recalling, particularly, to your recollection, a consideration to which I have more than once alluded, and which, probably, your thoughts have been all along anticipating: A consideration with which my mind is impressed more than I can express. I mean, the consideration of the

---

1  A representation chosen principally by the Treasury, and a few thousands of the dregs of the people, who are generally paid for their votes.

favourableness of the present times to all exertions in the cause of public liberty.

What an eventful period is this! I am thankful that I have lived to it; and I could almost say, *Lord, now lettest thou thy servant depart in peace, for mine eyes have seen thy salvation.*[1] I have lived to see a diffusion of knowledge, which has undermined superstition and error – I have lived to see the rights of men better understood than ever; and nations panting for liberty, which seemed to have lost the idea of it.———I have lived to see THIRTY MILLIONS of people, indignant and resolute, spurning at slavery, and demanding liberty with an irresistible voice; their king led in triumph, and an arbitrary monarch surrendering himself to his subjects.———After sharing in the benefits of one Revolution, I have been spared to be a witness to two other Revolutions, both glorious.———And now, methinks, I see the ardor for liberty catching and spreading; a general amendment beginning in human affairs; the dominion of kings changed for the dominion of laws, and the dominion of priests giving way to the dominion of reason and conscience.

Be encouraged, all ye friends of freedom, and writers in its defence! The times are auspicious. Your labours have not been in vain. Behold kingdoms, admonished by you, starting from sleep, breaking their fetters, and claiming justice from their oppressors! Behold, the light you have struck out, after setting AMERICA free, reflected to FRANCE, and there kindled into a blaze that lays despotism in ashes, and warms and illuminates EUROPE!

Tremble all ye oppressors of the world! Take warning all ye supporters of slavish governments, and slavish hierarchies! Call no more (absurdly and wickedly) REFORMATION, innovation. You cannot now hold the world in darkness. Struggle no longer against increasing light and liberality. Restore to mankind their rights; and consent to the correction of abuses, before they and you are destroyed together.

FINIS.

[48-51]

---

1    [Luke 2: 29-30.]

## 4. Edmund Burke, *Reflections on the Revolution in France* (1790; quoted by permission of Oxford University Press)

i. [6 October 1789: The End of the Age of Chivalry]

I find a preacher of the gospel prophaning the beautiful and prophetic ejaculation, commonly called "*nunc dimittis*," made on the first presentation of our Saviour in the Temple, and applying it, with an inhuman and unnatural rapture, to the most horrid, atrocious, and afflicting spectacle, that perhaps ever was exhibited to the pity and indignation of mankind. This "*leading in triumph*," a thing in its best form unmanly and irreligious, which fills our Preacher with such unhallowed transports, must shock, I believe, the moral taste of every well-born mind. Several English were the stupified and indignant spectators of that triumph. It was (unless we have been strangely deceived) a spectacle more resembling a procession of American savages, entering into Onondaga,[1] after some of their murders called victories, and leading into hovels hung round with scalps, their captives, overpowered with the scoffs and buffets of women as ferocious as themselves, much more than it resembled the triumphal pomp of a civilized martial nation; – if a civilized nation, or any men who had a sense of generosity, were capable of a personal triumph over the fallen and afflicted. . . .

History will record, that on the morning of the 6th of October 1789, the king and queen of France, after a day of confusion, alarm, dismay, and slaughter, lay down, under the pledged security of public faith, to indulge nature in a few hours of respite, and troubled melancholy repose. From this sleep the queen was first startled by the voice of the centinel at her door, who cried out to her, to save herself by flight – that this was the last proof of fidelity he could give – that they were upon him, and he was dead. Instantly he was cut down. A band of cruel ruffians and assassins, reeking with his blood, rushed into the chamber of the queen, and pierced with an hundred strokes of bayonets and poniards the bed, from whence this persecuted woman had but just time to fly almost naked, and through ways unknown to the murderers had escaped to seek refuge at the feet of a

---

1 [The Onondaga are one of the Six Nations.]

king and husband, not secure of his own life for a moment.

This king, to say no more of him, and this queen, and their infant children (who once would have been the pride and hope of a great and generous people) were then forced to abandon the sanctuary of the most splendid palace in the world, which they left swimming in blood, polluted by massacre, and strewed with scattered limbs and mutilated carcases. Thence they were conducted into the capital of their kingdom. Two had been selected from the unprovoked, unresisted, promiscuous slaughter, which was made of the gentlemen of birth and family who composed the king's body guard. These two gentlemen, with all the parade of an execution of justice, were cruelly and publickly dragged to the block, and beheaded in the great court of the palace. Their heads were stuck upon spears, and led the procession; whilst the royal captives who followed in the train were slowly moved along, amidst the horrid yells, and shrilling screams, and frantic dances, and infamous contumelies, and all the unutterable abominations of the furies of hell, in the abused shape of the vilest of women. After they had been made to taste, drop by drop, more than the bitterness of death, in the slow torture of a journey of twelve miles, protracted to six hours, they were, under a guard, composed of those very soldiers who had thus conducted them through this famous triumph, lodged in one of the old palaces of Paris, now converted into a Bastile for kings.[1]

Is this a triumph to be consecrated at altars? to be commemorated with grateful thanksgiving? to be offered to the divine humanity with fervent prayer and enthusiastick ejaculation? – These Theban and Thracian Orgies,[2] acted in France, and applauded only in the Old Jewry,[3] I assure you, kindle prophetic enthusiasm in the minds but of very few people in this kingdom; although a saint and apostle, who may have revelations of his own and who has so completely vanquished all the mean superstitions of the heart, may incline to think it pious and decorous to compare it with the entrance into the world of the Prince of Peace, proclaimed in an holy temple by a venerable sage, and not long before not worse announced by the voice of angels

1    [The Tuileries.]
2    [The ceremonies of the mystery cults of Dionysus and Artemis, respectively.]
3    [The chapel in which Price delivered the *Discourse*.]

to the quiet innocence of shepherds.

At first I was at a loss to account for this fit of unguarded transport. I knew, indeed, that the sufferings of monarchs make a delicious repast to some sort of palates. There were reflexions which might serve to keep this appetite within some bounds of temperance. But when I took one circumstance into my consideration, I was obliged to confess, that much allowance ought to be made for the Society, and that the temptation was too strong for common discretion; I mean the circumstance of the Io Paean[1] of the triumph, the animating cry which called "for *all* the BISHOPS to be hanged on the lamp-posts,"[2] might well have brought forth a burst of enthusiasm on the foreseen consequences of this happy day. I allow to so much enthusiasm some little deviation from prudence. I allow this prophet to break forth into hymns of joy and thanksgiving on an event which appears like the precursor of the Millenium, and the projected fifth monarchy,[3] in the destruction of all church establishments. There was, however (as in all human affairs there is) in the midst of this joy something to exercise the patience of these worthy gentlemen, and to try the long-suffering of their faith. The actual murder of the king and queen, and their child, was wanting to the other auspicious circumstances of this "*beautiful day*."[4] The actual murder of the bishops, though called for by so many holy ejaculations, was also wanting. A groupe of regicide and sacrilegious slaughter, was indeed boldly sketched, but it was only sketched. It unhappily was left unfinished, in this great history-piece of the massacre of innocents. What hardy pencil of a great master, from the school of the rights of men, will finish it, is to be seen hereafter. The age has not yet the compleat benefit of that diffusion of knowledge that has undermined superstition and error; and the king of France wants another object or two, to consign to oblivion, in consideration of all the good which is to arise from his own sufferings, and the patriotic crimes of an enlightened age.[5]

---

1  [A hymn of praise to Apollo.]
2  Tous les Eveques à la lanterne.
3  [The Fifth Monarchy Men, a seventeenth-century Puritan sect, believed that the monarchies of Assyria, Persia, Greece, and Rome would soon be followed by a fifth, ruled by Christ.]
4  [Allegedly the remark of Jean-Sylvain Bailly.]
5  [Footnote omitted.]

Although this work of our new light and knowledge, did not go to the length, that in all probability it was intended it should be carried; yet I must think, that such treatment of any human creatures must be shocking to any but those who are made for accomplishing Revolutions. But I cannot stop here. Influenced by the inborn feelings of my nature, and not being illuminated by a single ray of this new-sprung modern light, I confess to you, Sir, that the exalted rank of the persons suffering, and particularly the sex, the beauty, and the amiable qualities of the descendant of so many kings and emperors, with the tender age of royal infants, insensible only through infancy and innocence of the cruel outrages to which their parents were exposed, instead of being a subject of exultation, adds not a little to my sensibility on that most melancholy occasion.

I hear that the august person, who was the principal object of our preacher's triumph, though he supported himself, felt much on that shameful occasion. As a man, it became him to feel for his wife and his children, and the faithful guards of his person, that were massacred in cold blood about him; as a prince, it became him to feel for the strange and frightful transformation of his civilized subjects, and to be more grieved for them, than solicitous for himself. It derogates little from his fortitude, while it adds infinitely to the honour of his humanity. I am very sorry to say it, very sorry indeed, that such personages are in a situation in which it is not unbecoming in us to praise the virtues of the great.

I hear, and I rejoice to hear, that the great lady, the other object of the triumph, has borne that day (one is interested that beings made for suffering should suffer well) and that she bears all the succeeding days, that she bears the imprisonment of her husband, and her own captivity, and the exile of her friends, and the insulting adulation of addresses, and the whole weight of her accumulated wrongs, with a serene patience, in a manner suited to her rank and race, and becoming the offspring of a sovereign distinguished for her piety and her courage; that like her she has lofty sentiments; that she feels with the dignity of a Roman matron; that in the last extremity she will save herself from the last disgrace, and that if she must fall, she will fall by no ignoble hand.

It is now sixteen or seventeen years since I saw the queen of

France, then the dauphiness, at Versailles; and surely never lighted on this orb, which she hardly seemed to touch, a more delightful vision. I saw her just above the horizon, decorating and cheering the elevated sphere she just began to move in, – glittering like the morning-star, full of life, and splendor, and joy. Oh! what a revolution! and what an heart must I have, to contemplate without emotion that elevation and that fall! Little did I dream when she added titles of veneration to those of enthusiastic, distant, respectful love, that she should ever be obliged to carry the sharp antidote against disgrace concealed in that bosom; little did I dream that I should have lived to see such disasters fallen upon her in a nation of gallant men, in a nation of men of honour and of cavaliers. I thought ten thousand swords must have leaped from their scabbards to avenge even a look that threatened her with insult. – But the age of chivalry is gone. – That of sophisters, oeconomists, and calculators, has succeeded; and the glory of Europe is extinguished for ever. Never, never more, shall we behold that generous loyalty to rank and sex, that proud submission, that dignified obedience, that subordination of the heart, which kept alive, even in servitude itself, the spirit of an exalted freedom. The unbought grace of life, the cheap defence of nations, the nurse of manly sentiment and heroic enterprize is gone! It is gone, that sensibility of principle, that chastity of honour, which felt a stain like a wound, which inspired courage whilst it mitigated ferocity, which ennobled whatever it touched, and under which vice itself lost half its evil, by losing all its grossness.

This mixed system of opinion and sentiment had its origin in the antient chivalry; and the principle, though varied in its appearance by the varying state of human affairs, subsisted and influenced through a long succession of generations, even to the time we live in. If it should ever be totally extinguished, the loss I fear will be great. It is this which has given its character to modern Europe. It is this which has distinguished it under all its forms of government, and distinguished it to its advantage, from the states of Asia, and possibly from those states which flourished in the most brilliant periods of the antique world. It was this, which, without confounding ranks, had produced a noble equality, and handed it down through all the gradations of social life. It was this opinion which mitigated kings into companions, and raised private men to be fellows with kings. Without force, or opposition, it subdued the fierceness of pride and power; it obliged sovereigns to submit to the soft collar of social esteem, compelled stern authority to submit to elegance, and gave a domination vanquisher of laws, to be subdued by manners.

But now all is to be changed. All the pleasing illusions, which made power gentle, and obedience liberal, which harmonized the different shades of life, and which, by a bland assimilation, incorporated into politics the sentiments which beautify and soften private society, are to be dissolved by this new conquering empire of light and reason. All the decent drapery of life is to be rudely torn off. All the superadded ideas, furnished from the wardrobe of a moral imagination, which the heart owns, and the understanding ratifies, as necessary to cover the defects of our naked shivering nature, and to raise it to dignity in our own estimation, are to be exploded as a ridiculous, absurd, and antiquated fashion.

On this scheme of things, a king is but a man; a queen is but a woman; a woman is but an animal; and an animal not of the highest order. All homage paid to the sex in general as such, and without distinct views, is to be regarded as romance and folly. Regicide, and parricide, and sacrilege, are but fictions of superstition, corrupting jurisprudence by destroying its simplicity. The murder of a king, or a queen, or a bishop, or a father, are only common homicide; and if the people are by any chance, or in any way gainers by it, a sort of homicide much the most pardonable, and into which we ought not to make too severe a scrutiny.

On the scheme of this barbarous philosophy, which is the offspring of cold hearts and muddy understandings, and which is as void of solid wisdom, as it is destitute of all taste and elegance, laws are to be supported only by their own terrors, and by the concern, which each individual may find in them, from his own private speculations, or can spare to them from his own private interests. In the groves of *their* academy, at the end of every visto, you see nothing but the gallows. Nothing is left which engages the affections on the part of the commonwealth. On the principles of this mechanic philosophy, our institutions can never be embodied, if I may use the expression, in persons; so as to create in us love, veneration, admiration, or attachment. But that sort of reason which banishes the affections is incapable of filling their place. These public affections, combined with manners, are required sometimes as supplements, sometimes as correctives, always as aids to law. The precept given by a wise man, as well as a great critic, for the construction of poems, is equally true as to states. *Non satis est pulchra esse poemata, dulcia sunto.*[1] There ought to be a system of manners in every nation which a well-formed mind would be disposed to relish. To make us love our country, our country ought to be lovely. [8: 117-29]

ii. [In Defense of Prejudices]

You see, Sir, that in this enlightened age I am bold enough to confess, that we are generally men of untaught feelings; that instead of casting away all our old prejudices, we cherish them to a very considerable degree, and, to take more shame to ourselves, we cherish them because they are prejudices; and the longer they have lasted, and the more generally they have prevailed, the more we cherish them. We are afraid to put men to live and trade each on his own private stock of reason; because we suspect that this stock in each man is small, and that the individuals would be better to avail themselves of the general bank and capital of nations, and of ages. Many of our men of speculation, instead of exploding general prejudices, employ their sagacity to discover the latent wisdom which prevails in them. If they find what they seek, and they seldom fail, they think it more wise to continue the prejudice, with the reason involved, than to cast away the coat of prejudice, and to leave nothing but the naked reason; because prejudice, with its reason, has a motive to give action to that reason, and an affection which will give it permanence. Prejudice is of ready application in the emergency; it previously engages the mind in a steady course of wisdom and virtue, and does not leave the man hesitating in the moment of decision, sceptical, puzzled, and unresolved. Prejudice renders a man's virtue his habit; and not a series of unconnected acts. Through just prejudice, his duty becomes a part of his nature.

Your literary men, and your politicians, and so do the whole clan

---

1  ["It is not enough for poems to be beautiful; they must also be sweet": Horace, *De Arte Poetica* 99-100.]

of the enlightened among us, essentially differ in these points. They have no respect for the wisdom of others; but they pay it off by a very full measure of confidence in their own. With them it is a sufficient motive to destroy an old scheme of things, because it is an old one. As to the new, they are in no sort of fear with regard to the duration of a building run up in haste; because duration is no object to those who think little or nothing has been done before their time, and who place all their hopes in discovery. They conceive, very systematically, that all things which give perpetuity are mischievous, and therefore they are at inexpiable war with all establishments. They think that government may vary like modes of dress, and with as little ill effect. That there needs no principle of attachment, except a sense of present conveniency, to any constitution of the state. They always speak as if they were of opinion that there is a singular species of compact between them and their magistrates, which binds the magistrate, but which has nothing reciprocal in it, but that the majesty of the people has a right to dissolve it without any reason, but its will. Their attachment to their country itself, is only so far as it agrees with some of their fleeting projects; it begins and ends with that scheme of polity which falls in with their momentary opinion. [8: 138-39]

## 5. Olympe de Gouges, *The Rights of Woman* (1791)

### TO THE QUEEN.

MADAME,

BEING unused to the language one addresses to Kings, I shall not employ the flattery of Courtiers in presenting you with this singular production. My aim, Madame, is to speak to you frankly; I have not waited for the era of Liberty in order to express myself in this way: I revealed myself with the same energy in a time when the blindness of Despots punished such noble boldness.

When the whole Empire was accusing you and making you responsible for its calamities, in a time of trouble and tempest, I alone had the fortitude to take up your defense. I was never able to persuade myself that a Princess, raised in the bosom of dignities, had all the vices of vulgarity.

Yes, Madame, when I saw the sword raised against you, I threw my remarks between that sword and the victim; but today, when I see that the bribed mob of mutineers is watched closely, and that it is restrained by the fear of the laws, I shall say to you, Madame, what I would not have said then.

If foreigners carry the sword into France, you are no longer in my eyes that falsely accused Queen, that interesting Queen, but an implacable enemy of the French. Ah! Madame, reflect that you are a wife and mother; make use of all your influence for the return of the Princes.[1] This influence, so wisely bestowed, fortifies the crown of the father, preserves it to the son, and reconciles to you the love of the French. This worthy negotiation is the true duty of a Queen. Intrigue, conspiracy, bloodthirsty schemes would precipitate your fall, if one could believe you capable of such schemes.

May a more noble occupation, Madame, distinguish you, excite your ambition, and attract your attention. To give momentum to the flight of the Rights of Woman, and to hasten their success, is the sole prerogative of one whom chance has raised to a place of eminence. If you were less well educated, Madame, I could fear that your personal interests would outweigh those of your sex. You love glory: reflect, Madame, that the greatest crimes immortalize one like the greatest virtues; but what a difference in the annals of history! the one is forever taken as an example, and the other is the eternal execration of the human race.

It will never be made a crime for you to labour for the restoration of morals, to give to your sex all the firmness of which it is capable. This work is not the labour of a day, unfortunately for the new regime. This revolution will only come to pass when all women are struck with their miserable fate, and with the rights they have lost in society. Sustain such a splendid cause, Madame; defend this unhappy sex, and you will soon have for yourself one half of the kingdom, and at least a third of the other half.

There, Madame, those are the exploits by which you should distinguish yourself and use your influence. Believe me, Madame, our life is a very trifling thing, especially for a Queen, when that life is not

---

1   [The royal émigrés hostile to the Revolution included Louis Joseph, prince de Condé, Louis François, prince de Conti, and Louis-Stanislas-Xavier, comte de Provence, the brother of Louis XVI.]

adorned by the love of the people, and by the eternal charms of beneficence.

If it is true that Frenchmen are arming all the powers against their fatherland; why? for frivolous prerogatives, for chimeras. Believe me, Madame, if I judge of it by what I feel, the monarchical party will abolish itself of its own accord, it will abandon all the tyrants, and all hearts will rally around the fatherland to defend it.

There, Madame, those are my principles. In speaking to you of my fatherland, I lose sight of the aim of this dedication. It is thus that every good Citizen sacrifices his glory, his interests, when his only object is those of his country.

I am with the most profound respect,

MADAME,

Your very humble and very obedient servant,

DE GOUGES.

## THE RIGHTS OF WOMAN.

MAN, are you able to be just? It is a woman who asks you the question; you will not take that right, at least, away from her. Tell me: what has given you the sovereign power to oppress my sex? your strength? your talents? Observe the creator in his wisdom; survey nature in all its grandeur, to which you seem to want to compare yourself, and give me, if you dare, an example of this tyrannical power.[1] Go back to the animals, consult the elements, study the vegetables, cast a glance, finally, over all the modifications of organized matter; and submit to the evidence when I give you the means to; search, excavate and distinguish the sexes, if you can, in the government of nature. Everywhere you will find them mingled, everywhere they cooperate as a harmonious consort in this immortal masterpiece.

Man alone has dressed up this exception as a principle. Bizarre, blind, bloated with sciences and degenerated, in this age of enlightenment and wisdom, into the crassest ignorance, he wants to rule like a despot over a sex which has received all the intellectual faculties; he

---

1    From Paris to Peru, from Rome to Japan,
     The dumbest animal, in my view, is man.

pretends to rejoice in the revolution, and to claim his rights to equality, in order to say no more about it.

## DECLARATION OF THE RIGHTS OF WOMAN AND OF THE FEMALE CITIZEN,

*To be decreed by the National Assembly in its last sessions or in that of the next legislature.*

### PREAMBLE.

The mothers, daughters, sisters, representatives of the nation, demand to be formed into a national assembly. Considering that ignorance, neglect, or contempt of the rights of woman, are the sole causes of public misfortunes and the corruption of governments, have resolved to set forth in a solemn declaration, the natural, inalienable, and sacred rights of woman, that this declaration, being constantly present to all the members of the body social, may ever remind them of their rights and their duties, that the acts of the power of women, and those of the power of men, being capable of being every moment compared with the end of all political institutions, may be more respected, that the claims of the female citizens, founded hereafter on simple and incontestable principles, may always tend to the maintenance of the constitution and of good morals, and to the general happiness.

Accordingly, the sex that is as superior in beauty as in courage, in the sufferings of maternity, recognizes and declares, in the presence and under the auspices of the supreme Being, the following Rights of Woman and of the Female Citizen.

### FIRST ARTICLE.

Woman is born free and remains equal to man in rights. Social distinctions can only be founded on common utility.

### II.

The end of all political association is the preservation of the natural and imprescriptible rights of Woman and of Man: these rights are liberty, property, security, and above all resistance to oppression.

## III.

The principle of all sovereignty resides essentially in the Nation, which is nothing more than the union of Woman and Man: no body, no individual, can exercise an authority which does not emanate expressly from it.

## IV.

Liberty and justice consist in rendering to others all that belongs to them; thus the exercise of the natural rights of woman has no other limits than the perpetual tyranny that man opposes to it; these limits should be reformed by the laws of nature and of reason.

## V.

The laws of nature and of reason prohibit all actions hurtful to society: nothing that is not prohibited by these laws, wise and divine, may be hindered, nor may anyone be compelled to do what they do not enjoin.

## VI.

The Law should be the expression of the general will; all the Female and Male Citizens should concur personally, or by their representatives, in its formation; it should be the same for all: all the female and all the male citizens, being equal in its eyes, should be equally admissible to all honours, positions and public employments, according to their capacities, and without any other distinctions than those of their virtues and their talents.

## VII.

No woman is exempt; she is accused, arrested, and detained in cases determined by the Law. Women like men obey this rigorous Law.

## VIII.

The law should impose only those penalties which are strictly and evidently necessary, and no one can be punished except by virtue of a Law established and promulgated previously to the offense and legally applied to women.

## IX.

Whenever a woman is declared guilty, all rigour is exercised by the Law.

## X.

No-one should be molested for their opinions, even fundamental ones; woman has the right to mount the scaffold; she should equally have the right to mount the Tribune; provided that her actions do not disturb the public order established by the Law.

## XI.

The free communication of thoughts and opinions is one of the most precious rights of woman, since this liberty ensures that fathers acknowledge their children. Every Female Citizen may therefore say freely, I am the mother of a child who belongs to you, without a barbarous prejudice to force her to conceal the truth; provided she is held responsible for the abuse of this liberty in the cases determined by the Law.

## XII.

The good of the majority is necessary in order to secure the rights of woman and the female citizen; this security should be instituted for the advantage of all, and not for the particular good of those women to whom it is entrusted.

## XIII.

For the maintenance of the public force, and for the expenses of government, the contributions of woman and man are equal; she takes part in all the drudgery, in all the laborious tasks; she should therefore take the same part in the distribution of positions, of employments, of commissions, of honours and of business.

## XIV.

The Female and Male Citizens have the right to determine, by themselves or by their representatives, the necessity of public contributions. The Female Citizens cannot enjoy this right except by being allowed an equal share, not only in wealth, but also in public administration, and by being allowed to determine the amount, the basis, the collection and the duration of taxation.

## XV.

The mass of women, united for the purposes of taxation with that of men, has the right to demand of all its public agents an account of their administration.

## XVI.

Every society, in which the security of rights is not assured, and the separation of powers is not determined, has no constitution; the constitution is null and void, if the majority of the individuals who make up the Nation has not cooperated in drawing it up.

## XVII.

Property belongs to both sexes, individually or collectively; it is everyone's inviolable and sacred right; as it is a true patrimony of nature, no-one may be deprived of it, except when public necessity, legally ascertained, evidently demands it, and on condition of a previously established and just indemnity.

## POSTAMBLE.

Woman, arise; the tocsin of reason makes itself heard through the whole universe; know your rights. The mighty empire of nature is no longer surrounded with prejudices, fanaticism, superstition and lies. The torch of truth has dissipated the mists of stupidity and usurpation. While enslaved, man increased his strengths, he needed to have recourse to yours to break his chains. Having become free, he has become unjust towards his companion. O women! women, when will you stop being blind? What advantages have you received from the revolution? A more obvious contempt, a more conspicuous disdain. In the ages of corruption you reigned only over the weakness of men. Your empire is destroyed; then what remains to you? the conviction of the injustices of man. The claiming of your patrimony, founded on the wise decrees of nature: what would you have to fear from such a splendid enterprise? the *bon mot* of the Legislator of Cana?[1] Are you

---

1    [John 2: 4.]

afraid that our French Legislators, correctors of that morality which has long been hooked to the branches of politics, but which is no longer in season, will repeat to you: women, what have you to do with us? Everything, you would have to reply. If they should persist, in their weakness, in employing this irrelevancy, in contradiction to their principles, then courageously oppose the vain pretensions of superiority with the force of reason; rally beneath the standards of philosophy; display all the energy of your character, and you will soon see these arrogant men, not servile worshippers crawling at your feet, but proud to share the treasures of the Supreme Being with you. Whatever barriers may be opposed to you, it is in your power to emancipate yourselves; you have only to will it. Now let us change the subject to the frightful picture of what you have been in society, and since it is a question, at this point, of a national education, let us see if our wise Legislators will think soundly about the education of women.

Women have done more evil than good. Constraint and dissimulation have been their lot. What force has robbed from them, guile has restored to them; they have had recourse to all the resources of their charms, and the most irreproachable did not resist them. Poison, the sword, everything was obedient to them; they commanded crime as well as virtue. The French government, above all, has depended, for centuries, on the nocturnal administration of women; the cabinet had no secrets on account of their inquisitiveness; embassy, command, ministry, presidency, pontificate, [1]cardinalate; everything, finally, profane and sacred, which characterizes the stupidity of men, everything was obedient to the cupidity and ambition of this sex, in former times despicable and respected, and since the revolution respectable and despised.

In such an antithesis, what remarks do I not have to offer! I have only a moment to make them, but this moment will attract the attention of the remotest posterity. Under the old regime, all was vicious, all was culpable; but could not one notice the improvement of things even in the substance of vices? A woman needed only to be beautiful

---

1    M. de Bernis, of the making of Madame de Pompadour. [François-Joachim de Bernis (1717–94) was a protégé of Jeanne Antoinette, marquise de Pompadour (1721–64), mistress of Louis XV, but by 1758, when he was made cardinal, he had lost her favour. He was opposed to the Revolution.]

or amiable; when she possessed these two advantages, she saw a hundred fortunes at her feet. If she did not profit from them, she had a whimsical character, or an unusual philosophy, which led her to despise riches; then she was only considered perverse; the most immodest made herself respected with gold; the commerce in women was a species of business accepted in the highest class, which, henceforward, will have no more credit. If it still had it, the revolution would be lost, and we would always be corrupted in new ways; however, reason can deceive itself so that every other road to fortune is closed to the woman whom the man buys, like a slave on the coasts of Africa. The difference is great; it is known. The slave rules the master; but if the master gives her her freedom without compensation, and at an age when the slave has lost all her charms, what becomes of this unfortunate? The plaything of contempt, even the doors of beneficence are shut to her; she is poor and old, it is said; why didn't she know how to make her fortune? Other examples, even more pathetic, come to mind. A young person without experience, seduced by a man she loves, will leave her parents to follow him; the ingrate will discard her after a few years, and the more she has grown old with him, the more inhuman will be his inconstancy; if she has children, he will abandon her just the same. If he is rich, he will believe that he is exempt from sharing his fortune with his noble victims. If some obligation binds him to his duties, he will violate the force of it while hoping for everything from the laws. If he is married, every other obligation loses its rights. What laws remain to be made to tear up vice by the roots? That of the sharing of fortunes, and of public administration, between men and women. It is easily conceived that she who is born of a rich family, gains much from an equal sharing. But she who is born of a poor family, with merit and virtues, what is her lot? Poverty and shame. If she does not excel specifically in music or painting, she cannot be admitted to any public employment, although she would be entirely capable of it. I only want to give a glimpse of these things; I will go into them more deeply in the new edition of all my political works which I intend to give to the public in a few days, with notes.

I take up my text with regard to morals. Marriage is the grave of confidence and love. The married woman can with impunity give bastards to her husband, and give them the fortune which does not belong to them. The one who is not married has only a feeble right: the ancient and inhuman laws refuse her, and her children, the right to the name and the wealth of their father, and new laws have not been made on this subject. If attempting to give my sex a just and honourable firmness is considered at this moment like a paradox on my part, and like attempting the impossible, I leave to the men to come the glory of dealing with this subject; but, in the meantime, one can prepare for it by national education, by the restoration of morals and by conjugal agreements.

*Form of the Social Contract of Man and Woman.*
We N and N, moved by our own will, unite ourselves for the term of our life, and for the duration of our mutual inclinations, on the following conditions: We intend and wish to put our fortunes in common, reserving however for ourselves the right to divide them for the benefit of our children, and of those for whom we could have a particular inclination, recognizing mutually that our goods belong directly to our children, whatever bed they come from, and that all of them equally have the right to bear the name of the fathers and mothers who have acknowledged them, and we force ourselves to subscribe to the law that punishes the renunciation of one's own blood. We oblige ourselves equally, in the case of a separation, to divide our fortune, first deducting the portion of our children, as indicated by the law; and, in the case of a perfect union, the first to die would renounce half of his properties in favour of his children; and if one died without children, the survivor would inherit by right, unless the dying person had disposed of half of the common property in favour of whomever he deemed appropriate.

That is roughly the formula of the conjugal deed whose implementation I propose. On reading this singular document, I can see the Tartuffes,[1] the prudes, the clergy, and the whole infernal gang rise against me. But how it will offer to the wise the moral means to arrive at the perfection of a happy government! I am going to give the physical proof in a few words. The rich Epicurean without chil-

---

1   [From the title character of Molière's *Le Tartuffe* (1664), a satire on religious hypocrisy.]

dren thinks very well of going to his poor neighbour to increase his family. When there is a law that will authorize the poor man's wife to have the rich man adopt her children, the bonds of society will be strengthened, and morals made more pure. Perhaps this law will preserve the good of the community, and prevent the disorder which leads so many victims into the asylums of shame, of baseness, and of the degeneration of human principles, where nature has groaned for a long time. Let the detractors of sound philosophy cease, therefore, to cry out against primitive morals, or let them go lose themselves in the source of their citations.[1]

I would also like a law that would benefit widows and young women deceived by the false promises of a man to whom they were attached; I would like, I say, for this law to force an inconstant man to keep his engagements, or pay an indemnity in proportion to his fortune. I would also like this law to be rigorously enforced against women, at least against those who had the boldness to have recourse to a law which they themselves had infringed by their misconduct, if it were proved. I would like, at the same time, as I explained it in *The Primitive Happiness of Man*, in 1788,[2] for prostitutes to be placed in designated quarters. It is not the public women who contribute the most to the corruption of morals, it is the women of society. In reforming the latter, one changes the former. This chain of fraternal union will at first present disorder, but by its consequences, it will produce in the end a perfect harmony.

I offer an invincible means to raise up the souls of women; it is to unite them to all the activities of man: if man persists in finding this means impracticable, let him share his fortune with woman, not according to his whim, but by the wisdom of the laws. Prejudice will fall, morals will become pure, and nature will recover its rights. Add to this the marriage of priests; the King would be strengthened on his throne, and the French government could not be destroyed.

It was very necessary that I say a few words about the troubles that are caused, it is said, by the decree in favour of the men of colour, in

---

1   Abraham had some very legitimate children by Hagar, the handmaid of his wife. [Genesis 16.]

2   [*Le Bonheur primitif de l'homme* (Amsterdam, 1789).]

our islands.[1] It is there that nature shudders with horror; it is there that reason and humanity have not yet touched hardened souls; it is there above all that division and discord trouble the inhabitants. It is not difficult to find out the instigators of these incendiary agitations: there are some of them in the very bosom of the National Assembly: they are lighting in Europe the fire that should set America in a blaze. The Planters insist on reigning like despots over men whose fathers and brothers they are; and disregarding the rights of nature, they seek the source of their claim in the smallest tinge of their blood. These inhuman Planters say: our blood circulates in their veins, but we will spill it all, if necessary, to satisfy our greed, or our blind ambition. It is in these places, the closest to nature, that the father disowns the son; deaf to the cries of blood, he stifles all its charms; what can one hope from the resistance which is opposed to him? to constrain it with violence is to make it terrible; to leave it in its chains is to send every calamity on its way to America. A divine hand seems to pour out everywhere the prerogative of man, *liberty;* the law alone has the right to curb that liberty, if it degenerates into license; but it should be the same for all, it is the law above all which should confirm the National Assembly in its decree, dictated by prudence and justice. If only it could operate in the same way with regard to the state of France, and make itself as attentive to new abuses, as it has been to the old ones which become more frightful every day! My opinion would still be to reconcile the executive power with the legislative power, because it seems to me that the one is everything, that the other is nothing; from whence will begin, perhaps unfortunately, the fall of the French Empire. I consider these two powers like man and woman,[2] who should be united, but equal in strength and virtue, to make a good household.

---

It is true, indeed, that no individual can escape fate; I experienced

1   [The National Assembly addressed the situation in Saint-Domingue (Haiti) in an ineffectual decree on 8 March 1790. A Mulatto revolt was suppressed in October 1790; the great slave uprising began in August 1791.]

2   At the magic supper of M. de Merville, Ninon asked who was the mistress of Louis XVI? She was answered, it is the Nation, that mistress will corrupt the government if she assumes too much sway. [Unidentified; "XVI" may be a misprint for "XIV," since the celebrated beauty Ninon de Lenclos lived from 1620 to 1705.]

it today.

I had resolved and decided not to permit myself the smallest funny story in this production, but fate decided otherwise: here is the fact:

Thrift is not forbidden, especially in this time of poverty. I live in the country. This morning at eight o'clock I left Auteuil, & set out towards the road which leads from Paris to Versailles, where one often finds those famous little taverns where travellers gather together cheaply. No doubt an evil star had been following me since the morning. I arrive at the barrier, where I don't find even the pathetic aristocratic cab. I rest on the steps of this insolent edifice which shelters toll-collectors. Nine o'clock strikes, and I continue on my way: a vehicle presents itself to my sight, I take a place in it, & at a quarter past nine, according to two different watches, I arrive at the Pont-Royal. There I take the cab, and fly to my Printer's, in the rue Christine, because I can only go there very early: in correcting my proofs, there is always something left for me to do, if the pages are not very closely set and filled up. I stay about twenty minutes; and tired from walking, composition and printing, I decide to go take a bath in the Temple quarter, where I was going to have dinner. I arrive at a quarter to eleven by the bath clock; so I owed the coachman for an hour and a half; but, so as not to have an argument with him, I offer him 48 sous: he insists on more, as usual; he makes a scene. I still don't want to give him more than his due, because a just being prefers to be generous rather than duped. I threaten him with the law, he tells me that he laughs at it, and that I will pay him for two hours. We come to a commissioner of the peace, whom I have the generosity not to name, although the act of authority he allowed himself towards me deserves a formal denunciation. No doubt he did not know that the woman who was claiming justice was the woman author of so much beneficence and equity. Without taking my reasons into consideration, he pitilessly condemns me to pay the coachman what he asked. Knowing the law better than he does, I say to him, Monsieur, I refuse, and I beg you to bear in mind that you are not a beginner in your position. Then this man, or to be more precise, this madman, loses his temper, threatens me with Force if I do not pay instantly, or with staying all day at his office. I demand to be taken to the departmental tribunal or to the town hall, having a complaint to make about his act of authority. The grave magistrate, in a dusty frock-coat as disgusting as his conversation, said pleasantly to me: no doubt this affair will go before the National Assembly? That could well be, I say to him; & I was half furious about it and half laughing at the judgment of this modern Bride-Oison,[1] saying, so that's the kind of man who deserves to judge an enlightened people! That's all one sees. Similar adventures happen indiscriminately to good patriots, as to bad ones. There is nothing but an outcry against the disorders of the sections and the tribunals. Justice is not done; the law is disregarded, & the police are becoming God knows what. One entrusts one's effects to coachmen and then can't find them again; they change their numbers as the fancy takes them, and several persons, like me, have experienced considerable losses in their vehicles. Under the old regime, whatever its highway robbery was, one found the trail of one's losses, by calling the roll of the coachmen, and carefully examining numbers; in the end, one was safe. What do these justices of the peace do? what do these commissioners, these inspectors of the new regime, do? Nothing but stupidities and monopolies. The National Assembly should direct all its attention to this faction, which is setting the social order on fire.

P.S. This work had been composed for several days; it was still held up in the printing; and at the moment when M. Taleyrand, whose name will always be dear to posterity, had just given us his work on the principles of national education,[2] this production was already in press. I will be happy if I have coincided with the views of this orator! Nevertheless, I cannot prevent myself from stopping the press, giving free rein to the pure joy which my heart felt at the news that the king had just accepted the Constitution,[3] and that the national assembly – which I now worship, not excepting abbé Maury;[4] and la Fayette[5] is a god – had proclaimed, with a unanimous voice, a general amnesty.

---

1  [Brid'oison is a foolish magistrate in Le Mariage de Figaro (1784), by Beaumarchais.]
2  [See Appendix B.1.]
3  [Louis XVI accepted the constitution on 14 September 1791.]
4  [Jean Siffrein Maury (1746-1817), known as a defender of the clergy and nobility, went into exile in 1791.]
5  [Marie Joseph, marquis de Lafayette (1757-1834), moderate leader and hero of the early phase of the Revolution; he lost his popularity after the Massacre of the Champ de Mars (17 July 1791) and went into exile in 1792.]

Divine providence, grant that this public joy is not a false illusion! Send back to us, in a body, all our fugitives – if only I could soar, with an affectionate people, over their journey – and on that solemn day, we will all render homage to your power.

# Appendix B: The Education Debate

## 1. Talleyrand, *Rapport sur l'instruction publique* (1791)

### i. [The Five Principles of Education]

One of the most striking characteristics of man is *perfectibility*; and this characteristic, perceptible in the individual, is much more so in the species: for perhaps it is impossible to say of any particular man, that he has reached the utmost he is able to attain, and it will eternally be impossible to affirm it of the whole species, whose intellectual and moral riches increase without interruption, with all the products of the preceeding ages.

Men arrive on the earth with various abilities, which are at once the instruments of their well-being and the means to accomplish the destiny to which society calls them; but these abilities, initially inert, need time, and things, and men, in order to receive their full development, to acquire all their energy; but each individual enters life with a profound ignorance of what he can and should be one day; it is up to education to show him; it is up to it to strengthen, to add to his natural abilities all those to which society gives birth, and which time heaps up. It is the art, more or less perfected, of making the most of men, as much for themselves as for their fellows; of teaching them fully to enjoy their rights, to respect and easily to fulfil all their duties; in a word, to live happily and to live usefully; and thus to prepare the solution to perhaps the most difficult problem of societies, which consists in the best distribution of men.

Society should be considered as, in effect, a vast workshop. It is not enough that everyone works there; it is necessary that they all be in their places, without which there is opposition of forces, instead of the cooperation which multiplies them. Who does not know that a small number, arranged with intelligence, should do more and better than a greater number, endowed with the same means, but placed differently? The greatest of all economies, because it is the economy of men, consists, then, in putting them in their true position: now, it is incontestable that a good system of education is the first means of arriving there.

How is this system to be created? It will be, no doubt, after many reports, the work of time purified by experience; but it is essential to hasten its epoch. It is necessary then to point out its foundations, and to recognize the principles, of which it must be the gradual development.

Education may be considered as a product of society, as a source of benefits for society; as an equally prolific source of benefits for individuals.

And first, it is impossible to conceive of a body of men, a gathering of intelligent beings, without immediately perceiving means of education there. These means are born of the free communication of ideas, as also from the mutual influence of interests. It is then above all that it is true to say that men are pupils of everything that surrounds them: but these elements of education, so universally distributed, need to be brought together, combined, and directed, so that there arises from them an art, that is to say, a quick and easy means to bring to everyone, by certain paths, the portion of education that is necessary for him. The true system of education lies in a happy combination of these means.

From this first point of view, education requires the following principles.

1. It must be available to all: because it is one of the results, as well as one of the advantages, of association, one must conclude that it is a common good of the associates: no-one may be legitimately excluded from it; and he who has the least private property even seems to have an additional right to partake of this public property.

2. This principle is associated with another. If everyone has the right to receive the benefits of education, everyone conversely has the right to cooperate in propagating them: for it is from the cooperation and the competition of individual efforts that the greatest good will always be born. Trust alone should determine the choices for educational duties; but all the talents are called by right to contend for this prize of public esteem. All privilege is, by its nature, odious: a privilege in matters of education would be even more odious and absurd.

3. As for its object, education should be universal: for then it is truly a common good, in which everyone can appropriate the share

that suits him. The various knowledges which it encompasses may not appear to be equally useful; but there is not one of them which is truly not useful, which cannot become more so, and which consequently should be rejected or neglected. Moreover, there exists an eternal alliance among them, a mutual dependancy; for they all have, in the reason of man, a common meeting place, of such a sort that one is necessarily enriched and strengthened by another: from this it follows that, in a well-organized society, although no-one can succeed in knowing everything, it must nevertheless be possible to learn anything.

4. Education should be available to both sexes; that is very plain: since it is a common good, on what principle could one of the two be disinherited of it by Society, which protects the rights of all?

5. Finally it should be available to all ages. It is a common prejudice to see it as only an institution for youth. Education should preserve and perfect those it has already formed: moreover, it is a social and universal benefit; it should therefore naturally be extended to all ages, if all ages are capable of it: now, who does not see that there is no age at which the human faculties cannot be usefully exercised, at which man cannot be confirmed in happy habits, encouraged to do good, enlightened about the means to bring it about: and what are all these helps, if not emanations of the educational Power?

From these principles, which, strictly speaking, are only consequences of the first one, arise further consequences, already clearly indicated.

Because Education should be available to all, there must exist establishments that spread it in each part of the Empire, in proportion to its needs, to the number of its inhabitants, and to its relations in the political association.

Because everyone has the right to cooperate in spreading it, all exclusive privilege respecting Education must be abolished irrevocably.

Because it should be universal, Society must therefore encourage and facilitate all kinds of instruction, and at the same time especially patronize those whose present and immediate utility shall be most generally recognized and best suited to the constitution and to the national morals.

Because education should be available to each sex, schools must quickly be established, both for the one, and for the other; but principles of education must also be established for girls: for it is not the schools, but the principles that direct them, which must be regarded as the true propagators of education.

Finally, because it should be available to all ages, it is necessary not to think exclusively, as has been done to this day among us, of establishments for youth; it is also necessary to establish and to organize institutions of another order, which would be, for men of all ages, of all estates, and in the different circumstances of life, prolific sources of instruction and happiness. [7-11]

ii. [The Education of Women]

At the beginning of our work, we announced principles of education for women: these principles seemed to us very simple.

First of all, the questions relative to their education cannot be separated here from the investigation of their political rights; for in bringing them up, it is very necessary to know what they are destined for. If we acknowledge the same rights for them as for men, they must be given the same means to make use of them. If we think that their lot should be only domestic happiness and the duties of the inner life, they must be formed early to fulfill this destiny.

One half of the human race excluded by the other from all participation in government; persons native in fact and foreign in law in the land which nevertheless saw their birth; landowners without direct influence and without representation: those are political phenomena which, on abstract principles, it seems impossible to explain; but it is an order of ideas in which the question changes and can be resolved easily. The end of all institutions should be the happiness of the greatest number. Everything that deviates from this is an error; everything that leads towards it, a truth. If the exclusion from public office pronounced against women is a means for both sexes to increase the sum of their mutual happiness, then it is a law which all Societies have had to acknowledge and sanction.

Any other ambition would be an overthrow of the best destinies; and women would never have an interest in changing the assignment they have been given.

Now, it seems incontestable to us that the common happiness, especially that of women, requires that they do not aspire to the exercise of political rights and duties. On this point, we must seek for their interests in the wishes of nature. Is it not obvious that their delicate constitution, their peaceful inclinations, the numerous duties of maternity, constantly estrange them from vigorous practices, from painful duties, and call them to gentle occupations, to domestic cares? And how can one fail to see that the guardian principle of Societies, which established harmony in the division of powers, was expressed and as it were revealed by nature, when she thus distributed such obviously distinct duties to the two sexes? Let us be content with that, and not invoke principles irrelevant to the question. Do not make rivals out of the companions of our life: let a union which no interest, which no rivalry could break continue to exist in this world. Believe that the good of you all requires it.

Far from the tumult of affairs, ah! no doubt there remains for women a beautiful lot in life. The title of mother, the feeling that no-one flatters himself with having expressed, is a solitary joy from which public cares could detract: and to preserve for women that power of love which other passions weaken, is not this, above all, to think of the happiness of their life?

It is said that, on great occasions, women have strengthened the character of men; but then they were out of the race. If they had run after the same glory, they would have lost the right to bestow the garlands.

It was said, again, that some women had borne the sceptre with glory; but what are a small number of brilliant exceptions? Do they permit us to disturb the general plan of nature? Moreover, if there were a few women whom the chance of their education or their talents seemed to call to the existence of a man, they should sacrifice it for the happiness of the greater number, show themselves above their sex in judging it, in marking out its true place for it, and not demand that women be given over to the same studies as we are, sacrificing all of them to gain, perhaps, a few more men in a century.

Let us search no longer for the solution to a problem that is already adequately solved; let us bring up women, not to aspire to advantages which the Constitution denies them, but to know and appreciate those which it guarantees them: instead of making them scorn the share of happiness which Society reserves for them in exchange for the important services which it asks of them, let us teach them that it is the true standard of their duties and their rights. Let them find, not chimerical expectations, but real goods under the empire of liberty and equality; that, the less they concur in the formation of the law, the more they receive its protection and force; and above all that at the moment they renounce all political rights, they gain the certainty of seeing their civil rights confirmed and even increased.

Assured of such an existence by the system of the laws, they must be prepared for it by education; but let us develop their abilities without changing their nature; and let the apprenticeship of life be at once a school of happiness and of virtue for them.

Men are destined to live on the stage of the world. A public education suits them: it early places before their eyes all the scenes of life: only the proportions are different.

The paternal home is better for the education of women; they have less need to learn to deal with the interests of others, than to accustom themselves to a calm and secluded life. Destined to domestic cares, it is in the bosom of their family that they should receive their first lessons and their first examples. The fathers and mothers, informed of this sacred duty, will feel the extent of the obligations it imposes: the presence of a young girl purifies the spot where she lives, and innocence commands repentance or virtue from all that surrounds it. Let all your institutions tend to concentre the education of women in this domestic refuge: there is nothing which is better suited to modesty, and which develops sweeter habits.

But the providence of the law, after having recommended the most perfect institution, should still prepare resources for exceptions and remedies for misfortune. The Fatherland should also be a tender and vigilant mother. Before the abolition of the monastic vows, a multitude of religious houses, intended for this object, attracted a number of young persons of the sex towards a public education. This general direction was not good; for these establishments were not at all suitable for forming wives and mothers. But at least they offered a refuge to innocence, and it is indispensible to find a substitute for this benefit. We will not need to regret the loss of the education of the Convents; but we would rightly regret the loss of their impenetrable residences, if other houses, no less reassuring and better directed, did not make up for their abolition.

Each Department should therefore make it its business to establish a sufficient number of these houses, and to place in them schoolmistresses whose virtue would guarantee the public trust.

The women who will dedicate themselves to such delicate duties will not pronounce vows; but they will make Society promises which will be the more sacred as they are more free, and which will produce the same effect for the security of families.

In these houses the young persons should find all the resources necessary for their education, and especially an apprenticeship in the different trades which can ensure their livelihood.

Until the age of eight years they could, without inconvenience, attend the primary Schools, and there pick up the elements of knowledge which should be common to the two sexes; but before leaving their childhood, they should withdraw from them, and confine themselves in the paternal home, for which, it must not be forgotten, the houses of retreat are an imperfect replacement. Then it will be necessary to provide them with other aids to instruct them in the useful arts, and to give them the means to live independently, by the products of their labour.[1]

Thus, taking as a rule the terms of the Constitution, we shall recommend a domestic education for women, as the most suitable to train them in the virtues it is important for them to acquire. In the absence of this benefit, we shall ensure them secluded houses under the inspection of the Departments, and we shall facilitate their apprenticeship in trades which are suited to their sex. [117-22]

---

1   One can offer the Departments, as a model of this kind of establishment, a Memoir addressed to the National Assembly by an ingenious Artist (Mme Guyard) who, in this work, has known how to ennoble the arts by associating them with commerce, and applying them to the progress of industry.

## 2. Macaulay, *Letters on Education* (1790)

*Morals must be taught on immutable Principles.*

... In order to take from public sentiment a reproach which leaves a deep stain on the human character, and to correct many irregularities, and even enormities, which arise from incorrect systems of ethics, it ought to be the first care of education to teach virtue on immutable principles, and to avoid that confusion which must arise from confounding the laws and customs of society with those obligations which are founded on correct principles of equity. But as you have had patience to go through my whole plan of education, from infancy to manhood, it is but fair that I should attend to your objections, and examine whether my plan is founded on error, or on the principles of reason and truth. Know then, good Hortensia, that I have given similar rules for male and female education, on the following grounds of reasoning.

First, That there is but one rule of right for the conduct of all rational beings; consequently that true virtue in one sex must be equally so in the other, whenever a proper opportunity calls for its exertion; and, *vice versa*, what is vice in one sex, cannot have a different property when found in the other.

Secondly, That true wisdom, which is never found at variance with rectitude, is as useful to women as to men; because it is necessary to the highest degree of happiness, which can never exist with ignorance.

Lastly, That as on our first entrance into another world, our state of happiness may possibly depend on the degree of perfection we have attained in this, we cannot justly lessen, in one sex or the other, the means by which perfection, that is another word for wisdom, is acquired.

It would be paying you a bad compliment, Hortensia, were I to answer all the frivolous objections which prejudice has framed against the giving a learned education to women; for I know of no learning, worth having, that does not tend to free the mind from error, and enlarge our stock of useful knowledge. Thus much it may be proper to observe, that those hours which are spent in studious retirement by learned women, will not in all probability intrude so much on the time for useful avocation, as the wild and spreading dissipations of the present day; that levity and ignorance will always be found in opposition to what is useful and graceful in life; and that the contrary may be expected from a truly enlightened understanding. However, Hortensia, to throw some illustration on what I have advanced on this subject, it may be necessary to shew you, that all those vices and imperfections which have been generally regarded as inseparable from the female character, do not in any manner proceed from sexual causes, but are entirely the effects of situation and education. But these observations must be left to farther discussion.

LETTER XXII.

*No characteristic Difference in Sex.*

THE great difference that is observable in the characters of the sexes, Hortensia, as they display themselves in the scenes of social life, has given rise to much false speculation on the natural qualities of the female mind.—For though the doctrine of innate ideas, and innate affections, are in a great measure exploded by the learned, yet few persons reason so closely and so accurately on abstract subjects as, through a long chain of deductions, to bring forth a conclusion which in no respect militates with their premises.

It is a long time before the crowd give up opinions they have been taught to look upon with respect; and I know many persons who will follow you willingly through the course of your argument, till they perceive it tends to the overthrow of some fond prejudice; and then they will either sound a retreat, or begin a contest in which the contender for truth, though he cannot be overcome, is effectually silenced, from the mere weariness of answering positive assertions, reiterated without end. It is from such causes that the notion of a sexual difference in the human character has, with a very few exceptions, universally prevailed from the earliest times, and the pride of one sex, and the ignorance and vanity of the other, have helped to support an opinion which a close observation of Nature, and a more accurate way of reasoning, would disprove.

It must be confessed, that the virtues of the males among the human species, though mixed and blended with a variety of vices and errors, have displayed a bolder and a more consistent picture of excellence than female nature has hitherto done. It is on these reasons that, when we compliment the appearance of a more than ordinary energy in the female mind, we call it masculine; and hence it is, that Pope has elegantly said *a perfect woman's but a softer man.*[1] And if we take in the consideration, that there can be but one rule of moral excellence for beings made of the same materials, organized after the same manner, and subjected to similar laws of Nature, we must either agree with Mr. Pope, or we must reverse the proposition, and say, that *a perfect man is a woman formed after a coarser mold.* The difference that actually does subsist between the sexes, is too flattering for men to be willingly imputed to accident; for what accident occasions, wisdom might correct; and it is better, says Pride, to give up the advantages we might derive from the perfection of our fellow associates, than to own that Nature has been just in the equal distribution of her favours. These are the sentiments of the men; but mark how readily they are yielded to by the women; not from humility I assure you, but merely to preserve with character those fond vanities on which they set their hearts. No; suffer them to idolize their persons, to throw away their life in the pursuit of trifles, and to indulge in the gratification of the meaner passions, and they will heartily join in the sentence of their degradation.

Among the most strenuous asserters of a sexual difference in character, Rousseau is the most conspicuous, both on account of that warmth of sentiment which distinguishes all his writings, and the eloquence of his compositions: but never did enthusiasm and the love of paradox, those enemies to philosophical disquisition, appear in more strong opposition to plain sense than in Rousseau's definition of this difference. He sets out with a supposition, that Nature intended the subjection of the one sex to the other; that consequently there must be an inferiority of intellect in the subjected party; but as man is a very imperfect being, and apt to play the capricious tyrant, Nature, to bring things nearer to an equality, bestowed on the woman such attractive graces, and such an insinuating address, as to turn the bal-

---

1 [Pope, "Epistle II. To a Lady. Of the Characters of Women" 272.]

ance on the other scale. Thus Nature, in a giddy mood, recedes from her purposes, and subjects prerogative to an influence which must produce confusion and disorder in the system of human affairs. Rousseau saw this objection; and in order to obviate it, he has made up a moral person of the union of the two sexes, which, for contradiction and absurdity, outdoes every metaphysical riddle that was ever formed in the schools. In short, it is not reason, it is not wit; it is pride and sensuality that speak in Rousseau, and, in this instance, has lowered the man of genius to the licentious pedant.

But whatever might be the wise purpose intended by Providence in such a disposition of things, certain it is, that some degree of inferiority, in point of corporal strength, seems always to have existed between the two sexes; and this advantage, in the barbarous ages of mankind, was abused to such a degree, as to destroy all the natural rights of the female species, and reduce them to a state of abject slavery. What accidents have contributed in Europe to better their condition, would not be to my purpose to relate; for I do not intend to give you a history of women; I mean only to trace the sources of their peculiar foibles and vices; and these I firmly believe to originate in situation and education only: for so little did a wise and just Providence intend to make the condition of slavery an unalterable law of female nature, that in the same proportion as the male sex have consulted the interest of their own happiness, they have relaxed in their tyranny over women; and such is their use in the system of mundane creation, and such their natural influence over the male mind, that were these advantages properly exerted, they might carry every point of any importance to their honour and happiness. However, till that period arrives in which women will act wisely, we will amuse ourselves in talking of their follies.

The situation and education of women, Hortensia, is precisely that which must necessarily tend to corrupt and debilitate both the powers of mind and body. From a false notion of beauty and delicacy, their system of nerves is depraved before they come out of their nursery; and this kind of depravity has more influence over the mind, and consequently over morals, than is commonly apprehended. But it would be well if such causes only acted towards the debasement of the sex; their moral education is, if possible, more absurd than their physical.

The principles and nature of virtue, which is never properly explained to boys, is kept quite a mystery to girls. They are told indeed, that they must abstain from those vices which are contrary to their personal happiness, or they will be regarded as criminals, both by God and man; but all the higher parts of rectitude, every thing that ennobles our being, and that renders us both innoxious and useful, is either not taught, or is taught in such a manner as to leave no proper impression on the mind. This is so obvious a truth, that the defects of female education have ever been a fruitful topic of declamation for the moralist; but not one of this class of writers have laid down any judicious rules for amendment. Whilst we still retain the absurd notion of a sexual excellence, it will militate against the perfecting a plan of education for either sex. The judicious Addison animadverts on the absurdity of bringing a young lady up with no higher idea of the end of education than to make her agreeable to a husband, and confining the necessary excellence for this happy acquisition to the mere graces of person.[1]

Every parent and tutor may not express himself in the same manner as is marked out by Addison; yet certain it is, that the admiration of the other sex is held out to women as the highest honour they can attain; and whilst this is considered as their *summum bonum*, and the beauty of their persons the chief *desideratum* of men, Vanity, and its companion Envy, must taint, in their characters, every native and every acquired excellence. Nor can you, Hortensia, deny, that these qualities, when united to ignorance, are fully equal to the engendering and rivetting all those vices and foibles which are peculiar to the female sex; vices and foibles which have caused them to be considered, in ancient times, as beneath cultivation, and in modern days have subjected them to the censure and ridicule of writers of all descriptions, from the deep thinking philosopher to the man of ton and gallantry, who, by the bye, sometimes distinguishes himself by qualities which are not greatly superior to those he despises in women. Nor can I better illustrate the truth of this observation than by the following picture, to be found in the polite and gallant Chesterfield. "Women," says his Lordship, "are only children of a larger growth. They have an entertaining tattle, sometimes wit; but for solid reasoning, and good sense, I never in my life knew one that had it, or who

---

1   [Actually Steele, *Spectator* 66 (16 May 1711).]

acted or reasoned in consequence of it for four and twenty hours together. A man of sense only trifles with them, plays with them, humours and flatters them, as he does an engaging child; but he neither consults them, nor trusts them in serious matters."[1]

## LETTER XXIII
### *Coquettry.*

THOUGH the situation of women in modern Europe, Hortensia, when compared with that condition of abject slavery in which they have always been held in the east, may be considered as brilliant; yet if we withhold comparison, and take the matter in a positive sense, we shall have no great reason to boast of our privileges, or of the candour and indulgence of the men towards us. For with a total and absolute exclusion of every political right to the sex in general, married women, whose situation demand a particular indulgence, have hardly a civil right to save them from the grossest injuries; and though the gallantry of some of the European societies have necessarily produced indulgence, yet in others the faults of women are treated with a severity and rancour which militates against every principle of religion and common sense. Faults, my friend, I hear you say; you take the matter in too general a sense; you know there is but one fault which a woman of honour may not commit with impunity; let her only take care that she is not caught in a love intrigue, and she may lie, she may deceive, she may defame, she may ruin her own family with gaming, and the peace of twenty others with her coquettry, and yet preserve both her reputation and her peace. These are glorious privileges indeed, Hortensia; but whilst plays and novels are the favourite study of the fair, whilst the admiration of men continues to be set forth as the chief honour of woman, whilst power is only acquired by personal charms, whilst continual dissipation banishes the hour of reflection, Nature and flattery will too often prevail; and when this is the case, self preservation will suggest to conscious weakness those methods which are the most likely to conceal the ruinous trespass, however base and criminal they may be in their nature. The crimes that women have committed, both to conceal and to indulge their natural

---

1   [Chesterfield, *Letters to his Son* no. 294 (16 November 1752).]

failings, shock the feelings of moral sense; but indeed every love intrigue, though it does not terminate in such horrid catastrophes, must naturally tend to debase the female mind, from its violence to educational impressions, from the secrecy with which it must be conducted, and the debasing dependancy to which the intriguer, if she is a woman of reputation, is subjected. Lying, flattery, hypocrisy, bribery, and a long catalogue of the meanest of the human vices, must all be employed to preserve necessary appearances. Hence delicacy of sentiment gradually decreases; the warnings of virtue are no longer felt; the mind becomes corrupted, and lies open to every solicitation which appetite or passion presents. This must be the natural course of things in every being formed after the human plan; but it gives rise to the trite and foolish observation, that the first fault against chastity in woman has a radical power to deprave the character. But no such frail beings come out of the hands of Nature. The human mind is built of nobler materials than to be so easily corrupted; and with all the disadvantages of situation and education, women seldom become entirely abandoned till they are thrown into a state of desperation by the venomous rancour of their own sex.

The superiority of address peculiar to the female sex, says Rousseau, is a very equitable indemnification for their inferiority in point of strength. Without this, woman would not be the companion of man, but his slave; it is by her superior art and ingenuity that she preserves her equality, and governs him, whilst she affects to obey. Woman has every thing against her; as well our faults, as her own timidity and weakness. She has nothing in her favor but her subtlety and her beauty; is it not very reasonable therefore that she should cultivate both?

I am persuaded that Rousseau's understanding was too good to have led him into this error, had he not been blinded by his pride and his sensuality. The first was soothed by the opinion of superiority, lulled into acquiescence by cajolement; and the second was attracted by the idea of women playing off all the arts of coquettry to raise the passions of the sex. Indeed the author fully avows his sentiments, by acknowledging that he would have a young French woman cultivate her agreeable talents, in order to please her future husband, with as much care and assiduity as a young Circassian cultivates her's to fit her for the harem of an eastern bashaw.

These agreeable talents, as the author expresses it, are played off to great advantage by women all the courts of Europe; who, for the arts of female allurement, do not give place to the Circassian. But it is the practice of these very arts, directed to enthral the men, which act in a peculiar manner to corrupting the female mind. Envy, malice, jealousy, a cruel delight in inspiring sentiments which at first perhaps were never intended to be reciprocal, are lading features in the character of the coquet, whose aim is to subject the whole world to her own humour; but in this vain attempt she commonly sacrifices both her decency and her virtue.

By the intrigues of women, and their rage for personal power and importance, the whole world has been filled with violence and injury; and their levity and influence have proved so hostile to the existence or permanence of rational manners, that it fully justifies the keenness of Mr. Pope's satire on the sex.

But I hear my Hortensia say, whither will this fit of moral anger carry you? I expected an apology, instead of a libel, on women; according to your description of the sex, the philosopher has more reason to regret the indulgence, than what you have sometimes termed the injustice of the men; and to look with greater complacency on the surly manners of the ancient Greeks, and the selfishness of Asiatic luxury, than on the gallantry of modern Europe.

Though you have often heard me express myself with warmth in the vindication of female nature, Hortensia, yet I never was an apologist for the conduct of women. But I cannot think the surliness of the Greek manners, or the selfishness of Asiatic luxury, a proper remedy to apply to the evil. If we could inspect narrowly into the domestic concerns of ancient and modern Asia, I dare say we should perceive that the first springs of the vast machine of society were set a going by women; and as to the Greeks, though it might be supposed that the peculiarity of their manners would have rendered them indifferent to the sex, yet they were avowedly governed by them. They only transferred that confidence which they ought to have given their wives, to their courtezans, in the same manner as our English husbands do their tenderness and their complaisance. They will sacrifice a wife of fortune and family to resentment, or the love of change, provided she give them opportunity, and bear with much Christian patience to be supplanted by their footman in the person of their mistress.

No; as Rousseau observes, it was ordained by Providence that women should govern some way or another; and all that reformation can do, is to take power out of the hands of vice and folly, and place it where it will not be liable to be abused.

To do the sex justice, it must be confessed that history does not set forth more instances of positive power abused by women, than by men; and when the sex have been taught wisdom by education, they will be glad to give up indirect influence for rational privileges; and the precarious sovereignty of an hour enjoyed with the meanest and most infamous of the species, for those established rights which, independent of accidental circumstances, may afford protection to the whole sex. [200-15]

## Appendix C:

**HINTS.** [*Chiefly designed to have been incorporated in the Second Part of the* Vindication of the Rights of Woman.]

1.

INDOLENCE is the source of nervous complaints, and a whole host of cares. This devil might say that his name was legion.[1]

2.

It should be one of the employments of women of fortune, to visit hospitals, and superintend the conduct of inferiors.

3.

It is generally supposed, that the imagination of women is particularly active, and leads them astray. Why then do we seek by education only to exercise their imagination and feeling, till the understanding, grown rigid by disuse, is unable to exercise itself—and the superfluous nourishment the imagination and feeling have received, renders the former romantic, and the latter weak?

4.

Few men have risen to any great eminence in learning, who have not received something like a regular education. Why are women expected to surmount difficulties that men are not equal to?

5.

Nothing can be more absurd than the ridicule of the critic, that the heroine of his mock-tragedy was in love with the very man whom she ought least to have loved; he could not have given a better reason. How can passion gain strength any other way? In Otahcite,[2] love cannot be known, where the obstacles to irritate an indiscrimi-

---

1    [Mark 5: 9; Luke 8: 30.]
2    [Tahiti.]

nate appetite, and sublimate the simple sensations of desire till they mount to passion, are never known. There a man or woman cannot love the very person they ought not to have loved—nor does jealousy ever fan the flame.

### 6.

It has frequently been observed, that, when women have an object in view, they pursue it with more steadiness than men, particularly love. This is not a compliment. Passion pursues with more heat than reason, and with most ardour during the absence of reason.

### 7.

Men are more subject to the physical love than women. The confined education of women makes them more subject to jealousy.

### 8.

Simplicity seems, in general, the consequence of ignorance, as I have observed in the characters of women and sailors—the being confined to one track of impressions.

### 9.

I know of no other way of preserving the chastity of mankind, than that of rendering women rather objects of love than desire. The difference is great. Yet, while women are encouraged to ornament their persons at the expence of their minds, while indolence renders them helpless and lascivious (for what other name can be given to the common intercourse between the sexes?) they will be, generally speaking, only objects of desire; and, to such women, men cannot be constant. Men, accustomed only to have their senses moved, merely seek for a selfish gratification in the society of women, and their sexual instinct, being neither supported by the understanding nor the heart, must be excited by variety.

### 10.

We ought to respect old opinions; though prejudices, blindly adopted, lead to error, and preclude all exercise of the reason.

The emulation which often makes a boy mischievous, is a generous spur; and the old remark, that unlucky, turbulent boys, make the wisest and best men, is true, spite of Mr. Knox's arguments.[1] It has been observed, that the most adventurous horses, when tamed or domesticated, are the most mild and tractable.[2]

## 11.

The children who start up suddenly at twelve or fourteen, and fall into decays, in consequence, as it is termed, of outgrowing their strength, are in general, I believe, those children, who have been bred up with mistaken tenderness, and not allowed to sport and take exercise in the open air. This is analogous to plants: for it is found that they run up sickly, long stalks, when confined.

## 12.

Children should be taught to feel deference, not to practise submission.

## 13.

It is always a proof of false refinement, when a fastidious taste overpowers sympathy.

## 14.

Lust appears to be the most natural companion of wild ambition; and love of human praise, of that dominion erected by cunning.

## 15.

"Genius decays as judgment increases."[3] Of course, those who have the least genius, have the earliest appearance of wisdom.

---

1 [Vicesimus Knox, *Essays, Moral and Literary* (1782) 2, "On the Example of Henry V and the Opinion that a Profligate Youth is Likely to Terminate in a Wise Manhood."]

2 [Georges-Louis Leclerc, comte de Buffon, *Natural History*, trans. Smellie (1785) 2: 309.]

3 [Immanuel Kant (1724-1804), *The Critique of Judgement* (1790) 1.1.2.50, "The combination of taste and genius in products of fine art." See also Wollstonecraft's first novel, *Mary* (1788; *Works* 1: 37).]

## 16.

A knowledge of the fine arts, is seldom subservient to the promotion of either religion or virtue. Elegance is often indecency; witness our prints.

## 17.

There does not appear to be any evil in the world, but what is necessary. The doctrine of rewards and punishments, not considered as a means of reformation, appears to me an infamous libel on divine goodness.

## 18.

Whether virtue is founded on reason or revelation, virtue is wisdom, and vice is folly. Why are positive punishments?

## 19.

Few can walk alone. The staff of Christianity is the necessary support of human weakness. But an acquaintance with the nature of man and virtue, with just sentiments on the attributes, would be sufficient, without a voice from heaven, to lead some to virtue, but not the mob.

## 20.

I only expect the natural reward of virtue, whatever it may be. I rely not on a positive reward.

The justice of God can be vindicated by a belief in a future state—but a continuation of being vindicates it as clearly, as the positive system of rewards and punishments—by evil educing good for the individual, and not for an imaginary whole. The happiness of the whole must arise from the happiness of the constituent parts, or this world is not a state of trial, but a school.

## 21.

The vices acquired by Augustus to retain his power, must have tainted his soul, and prevented that increase of happiness a good man expects in the next stage of existence. This was a natural punishment.[1]

---

1  [Gaius Julius Caesar Octavianus (surnamed Augustus, 63 B.C.-A.D. 14) rose to

### 22.

The lover is ever most deeply enamoured, when it is with he knows not what—and the devotion of a mystic has a rude Gothic grandeur in it, which the respectful adoration of a philosopher will never reach. I may be thought fanciful; but it has continually occurred to me, that, though, I allow, reason in this world is the mother of wisdom—yet some flights of the imagination seem to reach what wisdom cannot teach—and, while they delude us here, afford a glorious hope, if not a foretaste, of what we may expect hereafter. He that created us, did not mean to mark us with ideal images of grandeur, the *baseless fabric of a vision*[1]—No—that perfection we follow with hopeless ardour when the whisperings of reason are heard, may be found, when not incompatible with our state, in the round of eternity. Perfection indeed must, even then, be a comparative idea—but the wisdom, the happiness of a superior state, has been supposed to be intuitive, and the happiest effusions of human genius have seemed like inspiration—the deductions of reason destroy sublimity.

### 23.

I am more and more convinced, that poetry is the first effervescence of the imagination, and the forerunner of civilization.

### 24.

When the Arabs had no trace of literature or science, they composed beautiful verses on the subjects of love and war. The flights of the imagination, and the laboured deductions of reason, appear almost incompatible.

### 25.

Poetry certainly flourishes most in the first rude state of society. The passions speak most eloquently, when they are not shackled by reason. The sublime expression, which has been so often quoted, [Genesis, ch. 1, ver. 3.] is perhaps a barbarous flight; or rather the grand conception of an uncultivated mind; for it is contrary to nature

---

power at the cost not only of civil war, but of some 2,300 assassinations. Cf. Rousseau, *Emile* 242-43.]

1  [Shakespeare, *The Tempest* 4.1.151.]

and experience, to suppose that this account is founded on facts—It is doubtless a sublime allegory. But a cultivated mind would not thus have described the creation—for, arguing from analogy, it appears that creation must have been a comprehensive plan, and that the Supreme Being always uses second causes, slowly and silently to fulfil his purpose. This is, in reality, a more sublime view of that power which wisdom supports: but it is not the sublimity that would strike the impassioned mind, in which the imagination took place of intellect. Tell a being, whose affections and passions have been more exercised than his reason, that God said, *Let there be light! and there was light*; and he would prostrate himself before the Being who could thus call things out of nothing, as if they were: but a man in whom reason had taken place of passion, would not adore, till wisdom was conspicuous as well as power, for his admiration must be founded on principle.

### 26.

Individuality is ever conspicuous in those enthusiastic flights of fancy, in which reason is left behind, without being lost sight of.

### 27.

The mind has been too often brought to the test of enquiries which only reach to matter—put into the crucible, though the magnetic and electric fluid escapes from the experimental philosopher.

### 28.

Mr. Kant has observed, that the understanding is sublime, the imagination beautiful[1]—yet it is evident, that poets, and men who undoubtedly possess the liveliest imagination, are most touched by the sublime, while men who have cold, enquiring minds, have not this exquisite feeling in any great degree, and indeed seem to lose it as they cultivate their reason.

### 29.

The Grecian buildings are graceful—they fill the mind with all those pleasing emotions, which elegance and beauty never fail to

---

1 [Kant, *Observations on the Feeling of the Beautiful and Sublime* (1764) 51; *The Critique of Judgement* (1790) 1.1.2, "Analytic of the Sublime."]

excite in a cultivated mind—utility and grace strike us in unison—the mind is satisfied—things appear just what they ought to be: a calm satisfaction is felt, but the imagination has nothing to do—no obscurity darkens the gloom—like reasonable content, we can say why we are pleased—and this kind of pleasure may be lasting, but it is never great.

## 30.

When we say that a person is an original, it is only to say in other words that he thinks. "The less a man has cultivated his rational faculties, the more powerful is the principle of imitation, over his actions, and his habits of thinking. Most women, of course, are more influenced by the behaviour, the fashions, and the opinions of those with whom they associate, than men." (Smellie.)[1]

When we read a book which supports our favourite opinions, how eagerly do we suck in the doctrines, and suffer our minds placidly to reflect the images which illustrate the tenets we have embraced? We indolently or quietly acquiesce in the conclusion, and our spirit animates and connects the various subjects. But, on the contrary, when we peruse a skilful writer, who does not coincide in opinion with us, how is the mind on the watch to detect fallacy? And this coolness often prevents our being carried away by a stream of eloquence, which the prejudiced mind terms declamation—a pomp of words.—We never allow ourselves to be warmed; and, after contending with the writer, are more confirmed in our own opinion, as much perhaps from a spirit of contradiction as from reason.—Such is the strength of man!

## 31.

It is the individual manner of seeing and feeling, pourtrayed by a strong imagination in bold images that have struck the senses, which creates all the charms of poetry. A great reader is always quoting the description of another's emotions; a strong imagination delights to paint its own. A writer of genius makes us feel; an inferior author reason.

---

1 [William Smellie, *The Philosophy of Natural History* (1790) 1: 469. Wollstonecraft reviewed it (*Works* 7: 293-300).]

## 32.

Some principle prior to self-love must have existed: the feeling which produced the pleasure, must have existed before the experience.

THE END

[Wollstonecraft, *Posthumous Works* 4: 177-95.]

# Appendix D: Contemporary Reviews

## 1. *A Vindication of the Rights of Men*

### i. *Analytical Review* 8 (1790): 416–19

PERHAPS no publication of this country has been purchased with greater avidity, or read with more eagerness than Mr. Burke's Reflections on the late Revolution in the Government of France. Possessing a high character as an orator, having taken an active part as a statesman, and moving in the more elevated ranks of society, the first intimation of his design excited the attention of the public in no common degree; but the accomplishment of it, while it highly gratified the wishes and the interests of some, at the same time aroused the detestation and abhorrence of others. When this Right Honourable Author first threw down the *gauntlet*, and entering the ground from whence Sir Robert Filmer[1] was forced so shamefully to retire, stood forth the champion of *hereditary right*, he undoubtedly expected to be opposed by all those men, who in a liberal and enlightened age, had ranged themselves on the side of liberty; but how deeply must it wound the feelings of a *chivalrous knight*, who owes the fealty of "proud submission and dignified obedience" to the fair sex, to perceive that two of the boldest of his adversaries are women! This writer, after premising that she does not think it necessary to apologize "with courtly insincerity" for her correspondence, and that "truth, in morals, has ever appeared to her to be the essence of the *sublime*," informs Mr. B. that she should not have engaged in the present contest had not his wit "burnished up some rusty, baneful opinions, and swelled the shallow current of ridicule, till it resembled the flow of reason, and presumed to be the test of truth."

The birth right of man, according to her short but authorised definition, "is such a degree of liberty, civil and religious, as is compatible with the liberty of every other individual with whom he is unit-

1  [Filmer (1588–1653), author of *Patriarcha* (1680), refuted by Locke in *Two Treatises of Government* (1690).]

ed in a social compact, and the continued existence of that compact." It is acknowledged, indeed, that "Liberty in this *simple, unsophisticated sense*, has never yet been fully established in any of the governments, hitherto formed throughout the world," and this is attributed to the "demon of property, which has ever been ready to encroach on the sacred rights of men."

Our author speaking of the "wild declamation" observable in Mr. B.'s letter, thinks that, if it contain any thing like "argument or first principles," the following is the result:—"that we are to reverence the rust of antiquity, and term the unnatural customs which ignorance or mistaken self-love have consolidated, the sage fruit of experience; nay, that if we do discover some errors, our *feelings* should lead us to excuse with blind love, or unprincipled filial affection, the venerable vestiges of ancient days;" but these, according to her opinion, "are Gothic notions of beauty."

After a variety of observations on his pertinacious attachment to ancient customs, and an assertion that the civilization of Europe has been prematurely stopped by "hereditary property and hereditary honours," the writer of the "Vindication" somewhat *jocularly* asserts, that had her antagonist happened to have been a JEW, he would have joined in the cry of "crucify him!" "crucify him!" With many others she is at a loss to conceive on what grounds he could defend American independence, and yet be the enemy of the rights of men? Or with what propriety he could feel for the sufferings of a king of France, and yet wish, with an indecent haste, to strip a king of England of his hereditary honours?

Like the Right Honourable writer so freely censured, his adversary makes many agreeable and interesting digressions from her subject. While alluding to the barbarous custom of impressing seamen, we meet with the following observations: [Quotes "it is only the property of the rich ... the family that depend on his industry for subsistence?" (44) and "I cannot avoid expressing my surprise ... there is no longer any apprehension of a war" (45).]

Treating of another grievance that as yet remains unsanctioned by the plea of *necessity*, we are told that: [Quotes "The game-laws are almost as oppressive ... his children's bread is given to dogs!" (47).] We heartily sympathise in the humanity and even the justice of these observations, and trust that the day is not far distant when that part of our code, which the liberal and elegant Blackstone terms "a bastard slip of the forest law,"[1] shall be no more!

We lament that the limits of our review, will not allow us to give more ample quotations from a pamphlet, which notwithstanding it may be "the effusions of the moment," yet evidently abounds with just sentiments, and lively and animated remarks, expressed in elegant and nervous language, and which may be read, with pleasure and improvement, when the controversy, which gave rise to them, is forgotten.

It is but justice, however, to add, that we never before heard that Mr. B. had a pension of fifteen hundred pounds *per annum*, on the Irish establishment, in the name of another person; and that we shall be very glad to have it in our power to contradict it if it be not true.

ii. *Critical Review* 70 (1790): 694-96[2]

Our author has called his reply to Mr. Burke a hasty one: it is indeed in many respects a hasty, and in none more so than in the incongruity of the title with the substance of the pamphlet. The rights of men occupy a very small part, and kings as well as the clergy, the law and the gospel, almost share this author's attention. The language is also so animated and rapid, that the author forgets at the end of a sentence the metaphor with which he began it. The work first speaks of the rights of men, but it is a violent attack on Mr. Burke, and a warm panegyric on Dr. Price.

"The birthright of man, he observes, is such a degree of liberty, civil and religious, as is compatible with the liberty of the other individuals, with whom he is united in social compact." We fear then that

---

1  [Sir William Blackstone, *Commentaries on the Laws of England* (1765-69) 4: 408-9.]

2  It has been observed in an old play, that minds have no sex; and in truth we did not discover this Defender of the Rights of *Man* to be a *Woman*. The second edition, however, which often reveals secrets, has attributed this pamphlet to Mrs. Woolstonecraft, and if she assumes the disguise of a man, she must not be surprised that she is not treated with the civility and respect that she would have received in her own person. As the article was written before we saw this second edition, we have prefered an acknowledgment of this kind to the necessary alterations. It would not have been sufficient to have corrected merely verbal errors: a Lady should have been addressed with more respect.

no one enjoys his birthright, for, in every social state, there must be laws, and laws imply subordination, and consequently restraint. Our author's state must be that of Shakspeare in his Desart Island, where of three inhabitants, one is a duke, and the two others viceroys.

In other parts of the reasoning he seems to assume as a position, that the national assembly have already established a constitution, where wisdom combines with liberty, to make every one free and happy. It is the point yet in dispute, and we think, if the author had pursued his enquiry, in one half only of the original publications that have fallen under our eyes, he would have thought that the dispute was far from being at an end. But, till it is settled, his opposition to Mr. Burke's arguments against innovations lose much of its force.

This gentleman, in the same enquiry, falls into another error: he looks at antiquity for our constitution, in the place where it does not occur, at the period when it was overlooked and neglected, the aera of the Plantagenets, the houses of York and Lancaster, and the Tudors. He would have found more to his purpose among the inhabitants of the Hercynian forest; but, as no traces of liberty occur, where he searches for them, he concludes that innovation cannot introduce greater evils than have been already felt. His illiberal personal attacks on Mr. Burke, and his warm defence of Dr. Price, for different reasons, we shall pass over. That Mr. Burke's book originated from envy of Dr. Price's popularity is an idle fancy not worthy of notice: Mr. Burke, we have already said, has to answer for various political errors, errors very inconsistent with the doctrines contained in this work; but as the sentiments in the Reflections are his latest, we must suppose that they are his *corrected* opinions.

The observations on the clergy, and on Mr. Burke's predilection for rank, engage this author's attention. On neither subject, as he has conducted it, can we agree with him, and some parts require to be a little more carefully digested to bring them into any form that "man may question." If there is any effect produced on minds by the successive cultivation of different ages, there will be some influence from successive generations of able patriots, judicious statesmen, or gallant officers. But it is useless to enlarge on various opinions, not sufficiently matured, or too nearly approaching to the levelling principles of the present times. If our author reviews his hasty work with cool deliberation, he will find something which he will perhaps choose to omit, and several passages that he would probably alter.

iii. *English Review* 17 (1791): 59-61

I T was to be supposed that Mr. Burke's extraordinary opinions would have produced a variety of answers, not only on account of their novelty, but because sentiments so subversive of the advantages to be derived from the improbability of man need only to be divested of their speciousness, in order to confute themselves. Miss Wollstonecraft has a claim to no inconsiderable praise for the strength and plainness of her language, the justness of her opinions, and the indignant scorn with which she treats a dazzling trifle, that for a moment bewilders the understanding, while it saps all the foundations of virtue, public spirit, and genuine benevolence. "I perceive," says she, "that you have a mortal antipathy to reason; that we are to reverence the rust of antiquity, and term the unnatural customs which ignorance and self-interest have consolidated the sage fruits of experience.—Yes, Sir, the strong have gained riches, the few have sacrificed the many to their vices, and to be able to pamper their appetites, and supinely exist without exercising mind or body, they have ceased to be men." Some of our readers will say, Mr. Burke is here too much repaid in his own coin; but should the expressions be thought too bold and general, it should be remembered they were penned under the impression made by perusing a book that no feeling mind could retire from without horror. Our author next examines Mr. Burke's opinions of the abstract rights of men, and shews that if we are only to regard customs and existing institutions as the plea for our rights, we must look for the origin of them in laws made by invaders for their mutual security, and for keeping their conquered vassals in a state of eternal ignorance and poverty. This is placed in such lively and strong colours, as must convince every mind, not previously petrified by a consciousness of his own security, and an indifference for the happiness of all others, or rather a dread lest he should lose any thing by a general participation. Nor are the arguments against the preference given to primogeniture less conspicuous or forceable: but, as we so fully transcribed Mr. Burke's dastardly attack on an amiable character, we consider it a duty to take particular notice of this lady's reply:

[Quotes "You have shewn, Sir, by your silence ... his unseemly transport—if such it must be deemed" (47-49).]

This is only a part of what is here offered in behalf of one whom Mr. Burke never thought proper to attack at a time when he first proposed his political opinions to the world, and on a subject that might be thought more important to this country—at a time when England was engaged in war with her colonies. But it is not a little remarkable Mr. Burke should never stumble on America in his whole book. Neither the similarity, as he might conceive, of the circumstances, the quantity of paper issued by Congress, nor the success with which they have struggled through so many difficulties, ever reminds him of the warmth with which he used to attack the then Chancellor of the Exchequer. It is true, indeed, no hierarchy was then overturned, no church was pillaged, no nobility was levelled. For, strange as the phenomenon may seem, America had arisen to a flourishing condition, which she now maintains, without bishops, nobility, or any vestiges of the age of chivalry. But to return to Miss Wollstonecraft.—Many ingenious remarks are to be met with in the rest of her letter; and where she keeps to her purpose in answering Mr. Burke, she does it with strength, clearness, and brevity, and as much politeness as his own unqualified language entitles him to. But Mr. Burke has perhaps taught her to digress a little too often, and sometimes a little too far from the main subject. These digressions are, however, ingenious and well managed, if not always apposite; and we scruple not to assert that her book will be read with pleasure by all such as wish to promote the true interests of society.

The language may be thought by some too bold and pointed for a female pen; but when women undertake to write on masculine subjects, and reason as Miss Wollstonecraft does, we wish their language to be free from all female *prettinesses*, and to express with energy and perspicuity, the ideas they mean to convey.

We have omitted one specific charge against Mr. Burke which it becomes his friends to confute if untrue—that he receives 1500*l.* per ann. on the Irish establishment, under a disguised name. Let us admire the obsequiousness of an university that could thus reward one of the silent plunderers of her country. But we have too high an opinion of the good sense of that oppressed kingdom to think this measure will ever meet with their general approbation.

iv. *General Magazine and Impartial Review* 4 (1791): 26-27

The title and subject of this lady's performance have furnished the prurient wags, who feed the public mind, by diurnal lucubrations, with many a clumsy jest, and many a pointless sarcasm. These jokes, low, lascivious, and poor as they are, may have helped to sell the pamphlet, which, to say the truth, is more witty than wise; for this good lady, in her zeal for what she conceives to be the Rights of Men, forgets those without which society could not exist. Her arguments, carried all the length to which the principle on which they are founded goes, would bring all to the most perfect equality, and, by establishing absolute democracy, annihilate every species of subordination, and introduce anarchy, in the room of order. We admire, notwithstanding, her eloquence, her pleasantries, and her spirit. She possesses no common command of language. Her attack is generally so managed as to expose or ridicule her antagonist, with considerable success. She is particularly happy in elucidating the importance, and ascertaining the province, of our rational powers. These, she distinguishes with a correct discrimination of the principles of morals, from all those feelings or sentiments which enter so much into human conduct, and from the predominancy of which, all the colouring extravagance, and follies of life, inevitably proceed. It is probable, however, that she pays too much court to this department in the human system. And no discovery we have yet made, in science, or ethics, or religion, gives us any reason to hope, that this earth of ours will ever be the habitation of human beings purely intellectual. But until this be the case, individuals of both sexes must remain the same peccable creatures they have always been. And all the philosophy of our modern materialists, who would reduce every religious prepossession, idea, or sentiment, to their own frigid and repulsive standard, will never be able to effect a society absolutely perfect or unexceptionable, while the members of which it is composed continue thus erroneous and imperfect. It is, indeed, the prerogative of reason, to aim at all the excellence our faculties can command; but reason is prostituted, when occupied in suggesting apologies for discontent. This *breath of the Almighty* is given, for opening our eyes, and pointing out the way to happiness, but not for clothing the fair face of things with sadness and melancholy.

v. *Gentleman's Magazine* 61.1 (1791): 151-54

THE *rights of men* asserted by a fair lady! The age of chivalry cannot be over, or the sexes have changed their ground. Miss Williams is half afraid of *shivering lances*; but Mrs. Wolstencraft enters the lists armed *cap-à-pie*;—as the ladies some years ago took the field at Warley Common. We should be sorry to raise a horse-laugh against a fair lady; but we were always taught to suppose that the *rights of women* were the proper theme of the female sex; and that, while the Romans governed the world, the women governed the Romans. We remember too the time when "Liberty and Property" were favourite toasts in Old England; but Mrs. W. has plainly told us, p. 8 [38], that "that *demon* of *property* has ever been at hand to encroach on the sacred rights of men, and to fence round, with awful pomp, laws that war with justice." Agreeably to this doctrine, one of our brother reviewers, on a passage on Mr. Burke's Reflections [The rights of men in government are their advantages], adds this comment:

"Till we met with this sentence, we could never discover, to our own satisfaction, the true ground on which the rich and powerful lord justifies his claim to so many, and so great rights, over the poor and weak commonner."

*Property* is an odious word; and "the poor consider the rich as their lawful prey" is a favourite maxim, and cannot be too often inculcated.

Mrs. W. may upbraid Mr. B. with "a mortal antipathy to *reason*," p. 9 [38]. We cannot for our lives find a shadow of reason in her declamation. No man is to enjoy six pennyworth of property more than another. The Scripture every where keeps up a distinction of rich and poor; but Mrs. W's millenium is to restore mankind to the level of the golden age. Poverty, in her eyes, whether occasioned by the vices of the rich, or the vices of the poor, is equally an object of pity. "A father may dissipate his property without his child having any right to complain," p. 22 [43], is a novel doctrine; and we cannot help thinking it far more dangerous than the unequal distribution of property. But the object is, that there be no property at all, rather than that one man should enjoy more than another. Laws contrary to reason are specious terms with those who can persuade themselves that all men's reason is equal; that every man, whether in a state of nature or of society, is a philosopher, or superior to self-interest and every selfish passion; and that "the enthusiastic flame in Greece and Rome consumed every sordid passion." For shame! Mrs. W. Do not you know, and does not every History of Greece and Rome teach us, that these popular governments were the slaves of every sordid passion? Will you assert, that the property and liberty of Englishmen are not sacred? and will you produce an instance when "the liberty of an honest mechanick—his all—is often sacrificed to secure the property of the rich?" p. 25 [44-45]. Prove to us how many families are ruined in the sporting countries; and whether, in all the boasted liberty of France, a liberty of saying or doing quite so much as you wish to have said or done, is permitted to the "poor men in their native dignity."

After a great deal of rant about Mr. Burke's conduct on the Regency Bill, a puerile objection to the title of *Our Sovereign Lord the King*, worthy of Dr. Price himself, an insolent reflection on his Majesty, "as harmless a character as Louis XVI. and the Queen of Great Britain, though her heart may not be enlarged by generosity," p. 60 [59], and some idle objections to the feeling language of romance and chivalry, we are gravely told, p. 74 [64-65], that *inbred* sentiments are not naturally virtuous; that *passion*, or *heroism*, is the child of reflection, the consequence of dwelling with intent contemplation on one object; that the appetites are the only perfect inbred powers our writer can discern; [quotes "and they like instincts ... Happiness, liter ally speaking, dwells not here" (65)], &c. &c. &c. Here is the grand secret. Millions of people, both of the *great* and *little* vulgar, are to be taught the truth, and the free exercise of their reason, whether they wish it or are capable of it or not, by our new philosophers; and, in order to induce them to be reasonable, virtuous, and happy, they are to be released from every subordination, to be indulged in murdering their superiors, except their fathers; because the necessary distinction of ranks in civil society has made them their superior; and every man advanced to rank does not owe his advancement to merit alone, but to inheritance, favour, or other causes; and, to complete the line, equalization of property, or rather no property at all, is to take place. Admit, for a moment, all these different equalizations could take place in this kingdom, by the most harmonious and cheerful concurrence of all parties, would the majority of the people be happier or honester than they are at present? Would they be more the servants of Reason than the slaves of Prejudice? Would they forget all notions of right and wrong in the rights of men, and all distinction of social dignity in the dignity of human nature? They must be born again, and created anew, by some superior power, before this desireable change could take place; and they must persuade all nations of the earth to become like them; or they must, like the Pietists of the last age, or the Quakers of the present, be forced to keep very bad company, and shine as lights in the midst of a crooked and perverse generation. The *people* of England collectively feel the fear which Mr. B. ascribes to them (*Reflections*, p. 128); whatever Mrs. W. or a few modern philosophers avowedly more selfish than the characters they asperse, affect to make the object of their fear. To promote the views of Mrs. W. and her party, the old round of abuse against electors and representatives, against establishments and the clergy, is run; and she forgets that the electors are as ready to sell their votes and interest as the representative is to bribe and buy them; and if the noble father makes a butt of his son's tutor, it is not the fault of the plan or conduct of education, but of the brutal derider. Such are the men who inspire a contempt for religion; such the nurses who communicate with their milk a contempt for the clergy (p. 93 [72]). But we hear Mrs. W. allow that "the rapacity of the *only* men *who exercised their reason*, the priests, secured such vast property to the church." Does REASON then, in any class of men, teach such lessons? Let us take care how we extend its empire over the bulk of bad men, and multiply the number of Barringtons, Tylers, &c. Tell us not this was Reason aided by Religion; and that Reason, aided by Morality, will act a whit better. Mrs. W. is proud to acknowledge, p. 94 [73], that civilization and the cultivation of the understanding naturally make a man religious. Is then Religion an adscititious property, not congenial with her so-much-vaunted reason? Can she find the smallest allusion to the *dignity of human nature*, in the whole Bible, which inculcates, that man should humble himself before his Creator, not set himself up even as a faint image of him? We will not follow Mrs. W. in all her wanderings after reason and *rational* affections, the only common nature or common relation among men. "Time may shew that this obscure throng, the National Assembly, knew more of the human heart, and of legislation, than the profligates of rank, emaciated by hereditary effeminacy" (p. 97 [74]). Appearances are at present rather against their knowledge and their practice. "It is not, perhaps, of very great consequence who were the founders of a state, savages, thieves, curates, or practitioners in the law." All have formed their societies or states in miniature; but we cannot help thinking, as far as our acquaintance with them goes, they are materially and fundamentally different. Both the National Assembly and the Thirteen Stripes applied proportionably, in turn, to the understanding and imagination when they met to settle the newly-acquired liberty on a solid foundation. Else whence the federation, cemented in a circle of the national guard; or the American republick, by the fantastical grand federal processions? See our vol. LVIII. pp. 748, 826, 925, 1018, 1177; proofs, if any were wanting, how much easier it is "to impress the senses, than to subjugate the passions."

Obliterating all traces of the government of their forefathers, and unacquainted with our constitution, or debasing instead of improving what they do know of it, the French reformers are groping blindfold in the chaos of their reason; and thus hold themselves out to the world, through the medium of a few puffing friends in England, as the models of legislation and right reason. Should the abolition of ranks and titles by poor men and philosophers, those disinterested minds, be hereafter rescinded, our author will console herself in the weakness of human nature. "The rich and weak find it pleasanter to enjoy than to think" (p. 133 [88]); so do nine-tenths of mankind.

Mrs. W. (p. 132 [88]) tells us, "the tenderest mothers are often the most unhappy wives; but can the good that accrues from the private distress that produces a sober dignity of mind, justify the inflictor?" This passage, together with what she says, or seems to say, about the ladies tormenting the negroes, and thence rants about Mr. B's *Essay on the Sublime and Beautiful*, are past our comprehension.

The rights of men, and the views of modern philosophers, are fully explained when we are told that [quotes "benevolence is a very ami-able specious quality ... cunning has ever been a substitute for force" (88)]. Happy is it that our modern philosophers speak so plain. We can the better guard against their designs; and they must find, in all instances, they are the instruments of their own defeat. Other plans having failed, they now try to inspire the poor of this country with jealousy and resentment against the rich, and throw every thing into confusion by this contrivance. Much as our author decries instinctive feelings, she appears transported by them beyond reason, when she represents the due subordination of the poor as absolute slavery, trem-bling at the frowns of a being whose heart is supplied by the same vital current (p. 146 [93]); when in the very next page she declares she has enjoyed the contrary scenes in England. To follow all her exagger-ated pleadings for the poor, we must encourage them in stealing land from the commons, and the next step is stealing fuel from the inclo-sures, and making themselves partakers of all their productions. Lon-don, and every seat of commerce and industry (we must not dare to say art and elegance), must be depopulated. Her picture of civilized misery must be wiped away every now and then by outrages of a day like the 6th of October.

In the extravagances of rhapsodical bombast there are some strong expressions, and in the enthusiasm of reason some sensible reasoning.

Perhaps the supreme Ruler of the universe, who has proposed two dispensations to the free choice and understanding of his moral sub-jects, during the six millenaries and a half that this world has already subsisted, finding how little they are disposed to improve by either, is now leaving the bewildered part of them to their own imagination, to follow strong delusions, and believe a lie, to prefer their own *reason* and *philosophy* to his revealed will, and to stand or fall by their own devices.

Religion has been made the unsuccessful engine of a discontented party. Humanity to the negroes was next engaged on their side, and how it will succeed will soon be seen. Their last shift is to poison and inflame the minds of the lower class of his Majesty's subjects to violate their subordination and obedience. Mrs. W, if she be a real and not a fictitious lady, is engaged in a service wherein their great leaders have run themselves aground. Malcontents, who have nothing to lose, may lend their names, and offer their hands, for any mischief. But reflecting minds will see through their stale and shameful tricks, and not involve themselves in the ruin of their country.—Why will not these devotees of reason give an example of the dispossession of the demon of Property, by dividing their property (if they have any) into aliquot parts between their children and the first beggars that present themselves to ask alms of them? Every experimental philosopher should first try the experiments on himself before he electrifies a whole kingdom.

## vi. *Monthly Review* ns 4 (1791): 95–97

That a person may have too many ideas, perhaps will not be readily admitted: but that he may mix those ideas too much together, and, in discussing a particular question, may produce too many for the subject, so as to perplex both the writer and the reader, is a case that frequently happens. The work before us in some degree exemplifies this observation. The author appears to have read and thought much: but she overloads her sentences with foreign ideas and a multiplicity of words. Her principal assertion often lies concealed among remote connections, dependencies, and allusions, and is sometimes involved in tropes and figures, which rather darken than illuminate. Every thing is so mixed and confused in the crowd, that it is difficult to distinguish an individual. Hence there is a want of perspicuity in this pamphlet: which contains, however, many very good and judicious remarks.

From the title-page, we expected this work would have been confined to an examination of Mr. Burke's political principles. This, however, occupies but a small part of the whole. The author discusses many points of a moral, and metyphysical, and some of a miscellaneous nature. She exposes, very properly, Mr. Burke's extravagant veneration for ancient customs, manners, precedents, and institutions; points out the absurd consequences into which it would lead him; contends against the existence of natural instincts and inbred sentiments, and shews the folly of exalting them above reason:—she proves that our constitution, civil and ecclesiastical, in the way in which it is administered, is far from being a model of perfection; vindicates Dr.

Price from the attack of Mr. Burke; justifies the national assembly of France for appropriating the ecclesiastical revenues to extricate the kingdom from its difficulties; brings forward several of Mr. Burke's inconsistencies; contrasts his present doctrines with his former conduct, and his pathetic lamentation over the king and queen of France, with his treatment of our own king and queen, on a late occasion:— she reprobates the notion that refinement of manners can atone for corruption of morals, and that vice loses half its evil by losing all its grossness; she illustrates, very forcibly, the mischievous and immoral effects that result from that vast inequality in rank, and in the distribution of property, that prevails so generally throughout the world: pleads the cause of the poor and oppressed of every class, not with that mistaken benevolence which only relieves their temporary wants, but with that true humanity which would make them permanently happy, by allowing them the free exercise of their faculties, by inspiring them with just sentiments of the end and intention of their creation, and by convincing them of the value and importance of a habit of virtuous industry; she inquires into the true ground of vindicating the justice of Providence in the permission, or production, of physical and moral evil: she makes some remarks on the incompatibility of the two faculties of imagination and judgment; and she indulges some conjectures concerning Mr. Burke's motives for writing his reflections. In page 20, she mentions a secret pension of 1500 l. *per ann.* on the Irish establishment, received in the name of another; which she says Mr. Burke will understand better than any of her readers.

The pamphlet is written with an air of eager warmth and positiveness, that some readers may imagine might as well have been omitted: but we think this defect is fully compensated by the ardent love of liberty, humanity, and virtue, which evidently actuates the heart, and directs the pen of the very ingenious author.

### 2. *A Vindication of the Rights of Woman*

i. *Analytical Review* 12 (1792): 241-49; 13 (1792): 481-89

... It is with some reluctance that for the present we take our leave of this singular, and, on the whole, excellent production. The subjects which it investigates, are of the utmost importance to human nature, and we should be wanting in our engagements, and in our duty, if we passed it over too slightly. This circumstance makes it necessary to defer the further analysis to a future Review, when we shall proceed to the remaining topics of this volume.

It might have been supposed that Mrs. W. had taken advantage of the popular topic of the "Rights of Man" in calling her work "A Vindication of the Rights of Woman," had she not already published a work, one of the first answers that appeared to Mr. Burke, under the title of, "A Vindication of the Rights of Man." But in reality the present work is an elaborate *treatise* of *female education*. The lesser wits will probably affect to make themselves merry at the title and apparent object of this publication; but we have no doubt if even her contemporaries should fail to do her justice, posterity will compensate the defect; and have no hesitation in declaring, that if the bulk of the great truths which this publication contains were reduced to practice, the nation would be better, wiser and happier, than it is upon the wretched, trifling, useless and absurd system of education which is now prevalent. [12: 248-49]

ii. *Critical Review* ns 4 (1792): 389-98; 5 (1792): 132-41

ONE of the strictest proofs in mathematical demonstrations, is the reducing the question to an absurdity; by allowing, for instance, that the proposition is not true, and then showing that this would lead to the most obvious inconsistencies. Miss Wollstonecraft has converted this method of proceeding with the same success: reasoning on the boasted principles of the Rights of Man, she finds they lead very clearly to the object of her work, a Vindication of the Rights of Woman; and, by the absurdity of many of her conclusions, shows, while we admit the reasoning, that the premises must be, in some respects, fallacious.

"Dismissing then those pretty feminine phrases, which the men condescendingly use to soften our slavish dependence, and despising that weak elegancy of mind, exquisite sensibility, and sweet docility of manners, supposed to be the sexual characteristics of the weaker vessel, I wish to shew that elegance is inferior to virtue, that the first object of laudable ambition is to obtain a character as a human being, regardless of the distinction of sex; and that secondary views should be brought to this simple touchstone."

This is the outline of her plan; but before she proceeds to show that this change would be suitable, useful, advantageous, it will be first necessary to prove that there is no sexual distinction of character; that the female mind is equally fitted for the more arduous mental operations; that women are equally able to pursue the toilsome road of minute, laborious, investigation; that their judgments are equally sound, their resolution equally strong. After this is done, the benefit derived must be considered; and, when all are strong, to whom must the weaker operations belong? The female Plato will find it unsuitable to "the dignity of her virtue" to dress the child, and descend to the disgusting offices of a nurse: the new Archimedes will measure the shirts by means of the altitude taken by a quadrant; and the young lady, instead of studying the softer and more amiable arts of pleasing, must contend with her lover for superiority of mind, for greater dignity of virtue; and before she condescends to become his wife, must prove herself his equal or superior.—It may be fancy, prejudice, or obstinacy, we contend not for a name, but we are infinitely better pleased with the present system; and, in truth, dear young lady, for by the appellation sometimes prefixed to your name we must suppose you to be young, endeavour to attain "the weak elegancy of mind," the "sweet docility of manners," "the exquisite sensibility," the former ornaments of your sex; we are certain you will be more pleasing, and we dare pronounce that you will be infinitely happier. Mental superiority is not an object worth contending for, if happiness be the aim. But, as this is the first female combatant in the new field of the Rights of Woman, if we smile only, we shall be accused of wishing to decline the contest; if we content ourselves with paying a compliment to her talents, it will be styled inconsistent with "true dignity," and as showing that we want to continue the "slavish dependence."—We must contend then with this new Atalanta; and who knows whether, in this modern instance, we may not gain two victories by the contest?[1] There is more than one batchelor in our corps; and, if we should *suc-*

---

1   [In the Greek myth, Atalanta promised to marry any man who could defeat her in a footrace; suitors who failed to do so were put to death.]

*ceed*, miss Wollstonecraft may take her choice.

This work is dedicated to M. Talleyrand-Perigord, late bishop of Autun, who, in his treatise on National Education, does not seem to be perfectly convinced that the rights of man extend to woman; yet in France the diffusion of knowledge, our author asserts, is greater than in any other European nation, on account of the more unreserved communication between the sexes, though what the ladies have gained in knowledge they seem confessedly to have lost in delicacy. The following passage we must transcribe, for we confess we do not fully understand it.

"Contending for the rights of woman, my main argument is built on this simple principle, that if she be not prepared by education to become the companion of man, she will stop the progress of knowledge, for truth must be common to all, or it will be inefficacious with respect to its influence on general practice. And how can woman be expected to co-operate unless she know why she ought to be virtuous! unless freedom strengthen her reason till she comprehend her duty, and see in what manner it is connected with her real good? If children are to be educated to understand the true principle of patriotism, their mother must be a patriot; and the love of mankind, from which an orderly train of virtues spring, can only be produced by considering the moral and civil interest of mankind; but the education and situation of woman, at present, shuts her out from such investigations.

"In this work I have produced many arguments, which to me were conclusive, to prove that the prevailing notion respecting a sexual character was subversive of morality, and I have contended, that to render the human body and mind more perfect, chastity must more universally prevail, and that chastity will never be respected in the male world till the person of a woman is not, as it were, idolized, when little virtue or sense embellish it with the grand traces of mental beauty, or the interesting simplicity of affection."

The first sentence is erroneous in fact and in reasoning: it is contradicted by the experience of ages, the practice of different nations.

The second sentence is a curious one—How can she be supposed to co-operate (we *suppose* in the progress of knowledge) unless she know why she ought to be *virtuous?* Virtuous! Here must be some mistake: what has virtue to do with the progress of knowledge? As to freedom, strengthening the reason, &c. we see no occasion for metaphysical investigation on this subject: that virtue is connected with prosperity and happiness, and vice with misfortune and misery, she might learn, not from Locke, but the New Testament. The concluding sentence of the first paragraph is still more strange. Patriotism may be very properly instilled by a *father*; and we must beg leave to differ in opinion from this lady in another point: we are confident, from frequent and extensive observation, no arguments can confute the opinion that we have formed, and we must still persist in thinking, that the education and situation of women, *at present*, really and effectually *inspire* the *love* of *man*kind. We do believe with miss Wollstonecraft, that chastity will be respected more, when the person of a woman ceases to be idolized, and the grand traces of mental beauty are principally conspicuous.

The pathetic address ad hominem[1], on the injustice and cruelty of subjugating women, is interesting and well expressed. It is true, that women cannot "by *force* be confined to domestic concerns:" it is equally true, that "they will neglect private duties, to disturb, by cunning tricks, the orderly plans of reason;" and sometimes, we may add, even for worse purposes. We agree too, that no coercion should be established "in society, and *the common law of gravity prevailing, the sexes will fall into their proper place:*" nor shall we object to another passage, that "if women are not permitted to enjoy *legitimate rights*, they will render both men and themselves vicious to obtain *illicit privileges.*" But to be serious.

We should despise ourselves, if we were capable to garble sentences, in order to make them bear a different or a double meaning. The meaning of miss Wollstonecraft must be obvious, and we have only marked the equivocal nature of her language by Italics. If the

---

1   As we write this article professedly for the service of the lady, we ought to apologise for the Latin word: It may be englished "*personal* address;"—but "hominem" is a word, in this instance, peculiarly happy, for it means man or woman—either exclusively man, or those *manly females* who endeavour to imitate men.

whole was not as defective in reasoning as in propriety, we should not for a moment have indulged a smile. The object of this dedication, and indeed of her whole work, is to show that women should participate in the advantages of education and knowledge, that they may be more suitable companions for their husbands, better tutors in the earlier periods of their children's lives, and more useful active citizens.

When she steps from the stilts of patriotism, and omits the last object, she reasons with accuracy and propriety; not always indeed in a regular method, or by a well compacted chain of argument, but sometimes with a force carrying conviction. When we proceed to examine the subject more closely, and enquire into the degree of education and mental improvement necessary, we suspect that we must greatly differ. Are the mental powers to be regulated only, and generally informed, or are the sciences to be regularly taught? If a young woman be led to examine a subject coolly, to compare different arguments, to estimate the different degrees of evidence which each subject admits of, and to trace with some attention the evolutions of the human mind: above all, if she indulges a habit of reflection, and is neither afraid nor ashamed to look at her own errors, and investigate their source, she will be a more pleasing companion, a better wife and mother, a more useful member of society. All this a frequent reflection, and the conversation of a sensible man, will teach better than books, if we except those general essays, which, while they improve the mental faculties, add to the stock of ideas; and those works, which instruct the mind by the experience of former ages, or trace its exertions in different circumstances; we allude to history and travels, for we, *at present*, exclude the more elegant works of entertainment.

If we examine the sciences to be taught, it will be necessary to consider a previous question, how far there is a sexual difference in minds. Physicians have told us, and we have reason to think their account, as it is derived from the observation of succeeding ages, true, that different bodily constitutions are connected with minds of different faculties and powers. They have distinguished the volatile, choleric, temperament from the slower and more steady melancholic, the one which rapidly attains and soon loses, from the other more capable of attention, requiring greater diligence, and more carefully retaining the ideas acquired. Even a poet, no common observer of men and manners (we mean Horace), has distinguished the volatile youth from the more steady adult. If then there are similar constitutional differences in women, must we deny that there is not some difference in their minds? To examine facts: France boasts the marquise de Chatelet, and Mademoiselle Keralio; England Mrs. Carter, and Mrs. Macaulay; in criticism each nation has produced a madame Dacier and Mrs. Montague.[1] Their works deserve praise; but we seek in vain that profound spirit of investigation, those deep comprehensive views, that calm intuitive penetration, which have distinguished the works of *many* men on similar subjects. It is usual, we know, on the strength of these names, to challenge the men; but they need not fear the contest. If those, who have spent their lives in their peculiar studies, do not rise to superior excellence, unless compared with women, we must suppose some constitutional defect; if we cannot blame the culture, the soil must be less fruitful. If miss Wollstonecraft means only that the understandings and intellectual attainments of some men are superior to those of some women, the contest is at an end, and we freely confess that we know women who would excel in the office of premier, even (with deference be it spoken) some members of the house of commons. But this forms no exception; for, if the general change, which our author recommends in national education were to take effect, the state would lose 10,000 useful domestic wives, in pursuit of one very indifferent philosopher or statesman. With these premises then before us, we shall proceed to examine our author's work, and let us only add, in excuse of the ludicrous turn we have given to some of this lady's sentences, that she has herself a little too freely alluded to the communication of sexes. Even in the Dedication, she speaks of the "essence of sensuality" having been extracted in France "to regale the voluptuary, and that a kind of sentimental lust has prevailed;" of the calls of *appetite*, &c. Nor is this fault confined to the Dedication: it pervades the whole. Surely Mrs. Cowley did not tacitly allude to these improprieties, when, in the preface to her last comedy, she spoke of

---

1 [Gabrielle-Émilie, marquise du Châtelet (1706-49) was a mathematician, physicist, philosopher, lover of Voltaire and popularizer of Newton and Leibniz; Elizabeth Carter (1717-1806) was a poet and translator of Epictetus; Anne Dacier (1654-1720) translated Homer; Elizabeth Montagu (1720-1800) was a critic and leader of the Bluestockings.]

the work before us as containing "a *body* of mind."[1]

In the Introduction miss Wollstonecraft explains more particularly her object. She allows the physical superiority of the males, but wishes to give the ladies strength of body and mind, to induce them to look on "refinement of taste," "delicate sentiments," and "susceptibility of heart" as weakness and the means of slavish dependence. Such beings she thinks objects of pity, and the kind of love which these qualities inspire, contemptible.—To acquire habits of reflection, self-command, firmness, and resolution, are undoubtedly proper: to discard the softer feelings, refinement of taste, and delicacy of sentiment is, we think, to be no longer women. We are sure we speak the sense of mankind, when we say it is to be no longer amiable, attractive, or interesting.

The first chapter contains the consideration of the rights and involved duties of mankind. Its object is to show the disadvantages which flow from the superiority of distinction, from monarchy and hereditary honours. Miss Wollstonecraft falls into the error which we noticed in our review of her first pamphlet, viz. vague inconclusive reasoning from imperfect ideas, and the want of a well-digested plan. The observations we shall transcribe relate to Rousseau's defence of a state of solitude; and the following is the reasoning, and the language, that is to defend the Rights of Women.

"When that wise Being who created us and placed us here, saw the fair idea, [he] *willed*, by *allowing it to be so*, that the passions should *unfold our reason*, because he could see that present evil would produce future good. Could the helpless creature whom he called from nothing break loose from his providence, and boldly learn to know good by practising evil, without his permission? No.—How could that energetic advocate for immortality argue so inconsistently? Had mankind remained for ever in the brutal state of nature, which even his magic pen cannot paint as a state in which a single virtue took root, it would have been *clear*, though not to the *sensitive unreflecting wanderer*, that man was born to run the circle of life and death, and adorn God's garden for some purpose which could not easily be reconciled with his attributes.

---

1    [Hannah Cowley, *A Day in Turkey; or, The Russian Slaves* (London: G.G.J. and J. Robinson, 1792) iii.]

"But if, to crown the whole, there were to be rational creatures produced, allowed to rise in excellence by the exercise of powers implanted for that purpose; if benignity itself thought fit to call into existence a creature above the brutes[1], who could think and improve himself, why should that inestimable gift, for a gift it was, if man was so created as to have a capacity to rise above the state in which sensation produced brutal ease, be called, in direct terms, a curse? A curse it might be reckoned, if all our existence was bounded by our continuance in this world; for why should the gracious fountain of life give us passions, and the power of reflecting, only to imbitter our days and inspire us with mistaken notions of dignity? Why should he lead us from love of ourselves to the sublime emotions which the discovery of his wisdom and goodness excites, if these feelings were not set in motion to improve our nature, of which they make a part, and render us capable of enjoying a more godlike portion of happiness? Firmly persuaded that no evil exists in the world that God did not design to take place, I build my belief on the perfection of God."

First, the creature produced is not rational, and yet he is to reflect, and to discover what is within the powers of reason only. Next he is rational, and what does his reason lead him to? to a future state: certainly, but what is the connection of this part of the subject with the gregarious nature of animals, or the social qualities of man? The philosopher will smile at the note, when he perceives that animals, not gregarious, are supposed not to *pair*, since to pair is mentioned as the distinction of being gregarious. Might we venture? No, we dare not hint at the *unpaired* state of this advocate of the social nature of man. The comparison between the weak, insipid minds of *some* officers (our author must allow us to limit her position) and fashionable women, is very just: similar causes will generally produce similar effects, and the boasted strength of mind, even of lordly man, is not proof against the enervating causes; the lion, that has been stinted in his growth, either by accident or design, will never become the terror of the forest.

---

1    "Contrary to the opinion of anatomists, who argue by analogy from the formation of the teeth, stomach, and intestines Rousseau will not allow a man to be a carnivorous animal. And carried away from nature by a love of system, he disputes whether man be a *gregarious* animal, though the long and helpless state of infancy seems to point him out as particularly *impelled to pair*."

Our author next discusses the prevailing opinion of sexual character[1]. This title does not convey a proper idea of the two chapters in which the subject is contained. The object is to show that women have been unfairly treated. Instead of the sweet attractive grace, mild, docile, blind obedience, tenderness, affection, and all the softer passions of the mind, the severer studies should have been inculcated, and the firmer virtues cherished. To a certain extent, we can agree with our fair author. Women have been considered too frequently as the idols of the senses, as the objects of amusement in the moments of pleasure. Their minds have been looked on as barren wastes, the cultivation of which would be useless, or unprofitable. This conduct is undoubtedly erroneous: women are the companions of man, and the companions of a rational creature should possess reason not totally uncultivated. Yet, on the other hand, man is not merely rational: sense and judgment are requisite for his conduct, and the softer affections claim their share; affections which women feel more acutely, in which their sensibility is more refined, and their taste more exquisite. These affections are equally a part of man, and, in these, if we understand miss Wollstonecraft rightly, woman is to have no share. Reason and virtue are to form the whole of both characters.—As we have already stated our opinion of the sexual differences of mind, we may venture to produce the following attack on Rousseau, with commendation. The few exceptions we should make will be easily perceived; and these are certainly not against the moral virtues, of which women in general feel the force more acutely, and even practise more severely than men.

[Quotes "Women are, therefore, ... their true subordinate light" (134).]

Miss Wollstonecraft attacks Dr. Gregory also with some success. His system of reserve and dissimulation we think evidently wrong; and, though Dr. Gregory possessed the more amiable virtues in the

---

1   Miss Wollstonecraft has not been explicit in defining the meaning of sexual character; and we therefore do not fully understand the meaning of her assertion in the "Summary," that there are no *sexual virtues*, not even *modesty!*

highest degree, his system of female excellence was formed in consequence of confined views, and a state of society, neither the best, nor
the most eligible. Two passages of a different nature we shall transcribe.

> [Quotes "Of the same complexion ... common appetites of
> human nature" (141-42), and "How women are to exist ... he
> chooses to be amused" (143-44).]

Of such vague inconclusive reasoning, strung together with little
art, and no apparent plan, do these chapters consist. The whole is an
indignant invective against treating women merely as toys, as the
amusement of an idle moment, and as gratifying (our author sets the
example of the language), the calls of appetite. We might cull some
passages, so inconsistent is our author, in which she supports our
opinions; and some writers, particularly Shakspeare, whose nervous
mind she commends, might be adduced, as by no means agreeing
with this author in his opinion of women. But this would be a petty
warfare. We want not to prove miss Wollstonecraft inconsistent, either
in her doctrines or her example. We wish to take up the question on
its most solid ground—Have the qualifications of the two sexes been
mistaken? Are the ladies entitled from their natural powers, taken collectively, to lead, or even to rival the men in scientific pursuits, in the
labours of the mind? We have shown, in general, what must be the
answer to these questions; and we find, in our comprehensive view,
we have anticipated several remarks which had occurred to us in
perusing particular passages of these chapters. [4: 389-98]

W o m e n are supposed to be degraded; for, possessing rights coequal,
*almost* coeternal, with man, they are sunk, in our fair author's opinion,
unjustly and improperly *below* him. I have often erred, says Hogarth,
in his Analysis of Beauty, in the drawings: look not on these, but on
the precepts.[1] Yet it is strange, that an analyser of beauty could not
express it in correct drawings: it is more surprising, that this contender
for the equality of women, cannot defend the cause in a correct sen-

---

1 [William Hogarth, *The Analysis of Beauty. Written with a view of fixing the fluctuating
IDEAS of TASTE* (London: Printed by J. Reeves for the author, 1753) 2.]

tence, or with accurate ideas. Women we have often eagerly placed *near* the throne of literature: if they seize it, forgetful of our fondness, we can hurl them from it. A sentence that occurs early in the 4th chapter, has drawn this opinion almost reluctantly from us. The *"stamina* of immortality, if I may be allowed the phrase, *is* the *perfectibility* of human reason"—Why? the explanation is not more singular: "for was man created perfect, or did a flood of knowledge break in upon him when he arrived at maturity, that precluded error, I should doubt, whether his existence would be continued after the dissolution of the body." This is the old absurd proposition quaintly and aukwardly expressed, viz. because our reason is imperfect, there must be a future state; for reason must be perfected. We may as well say, because apples are not as large as pumpions, there must be future orchards in the other world. The reasoning, which follows in the same page, is equally untenable; and, if miss Wollstonecraft had wished to give a practical instance of the inferiority of the female mind, she has completely effected it. Again, "but dismissing those fanciful theories, and *considering woman as a whole, let it be what it will, instead of a part of man,* the enquiry is, whether she has reason or not." Why? because, if she has, she was not intended merely as the solace of man.—This is literally uniting the mechanical powers in a machine to cut cabbages: dear lady, you *may* be a *pleasing* companion, but, depend on it, we will allow you other merits. We only wish that you would not so rashly resign the power of pleasing; for be assured your different qualifications without it, will not be very impartially weighed.

The power of generalizing ideas is the only rational acquirement, it is said, of the divine being, and this acquisition has by some been denied the ladies; and the causes that degrade the sex, and prevent woman from this operation of the mind, are next pointed out. We never yet met with a lady who was not able to generalize or decompound ideas. An instance? Well, you shall have one. A young lady, with a full flow of health, and a vivid glow of colour, looks well at a ball with ribbons of an apple green. It is a simple observation, but the rival beauty immediately renders it a general one, and fixes in her mind, the propriety of suiting the colour of the dress to the complexion. On her next appearance, knowing that an olive beauty will look disadvantageously with the apple green, she politicly adopts the lilac or the brown. How then are the ladies degraded? The operation of the mind is the same, whether the subject be the colour of a ribbon, the source of moral virtue, or the connection of any cause with the effect.

From the remotest antiquity, woman, our author tells us, has either been a slave or a despot, and either situation retards the progress of reason. Some pages are employed to show that minute attention to woman weakens their minds, and miss Wollstonecraft wishes "to see the distinction of sex confounded in society, unless"—Do our eyes deceive us?—unless—where LOVE animates the behaviour. Is it so then? Our fair author objects not to the lover; and reason may, she thinks, be degraded with such an object in view.

[Quotes "In the regulation of a family, in the education of children, ... sensibility is not reason" (180-81).]

This reasoning, for want of a few necessary distinctions, might easily be rendered ridiculous, but we have disclaimed this petty warfare. We have selected this passage from the desultory inconclusive chapter before us, to show with how much labour miss Wollstonecraft erects her trifling buildings. We allow that women must have reason for these pursuits, and, in general, the sounder the judgment, they will execute them better. But how is this connected with the subject? or does it prove that the lady who is never suffered to stoop for her handkerchief cannot be either a good wife or a good mother.

The degrading sensibility, attained by these indulgences, is supposed to be the source of error in another view, by unfitting the mind for the most early and delightful office, "teaching the young idea how to shoot." People of sensibility infallibly spoil the child's temper, it is said; but it may be added, that the severity of reason, independent of sensibility, breaks the spirit; and that the heart dictates a thousand nameless endearing attentions, which the reason is a stranger to: besides, that the human mind possesses social affections, as well as reasoning powers, which must be checked by such conduct. But the absurdity of the remark will be, in a moment clear, or, if it is not, the reduction to an absurdity soon appears. "I have followed, says the author, this train of reasoning much further, till I have concluded that a person of genius is the most improper person to be employed in education either public or private." Follow it, dear lady, a little farther; and with your singular talents, you will soon perceive these premises lead to a farther conclusion, that the very best person, to whom education can be entrusted, is an idiot.

[Quotes "It would almost provoke a smile of contempt, ... the exercise of a duty is sacrificed to its indulgence" (191–92).]

These remarks require not a comment; but that they should fall from a female pen, is a little surprising. If to be loved, degrades the sex, we suspect our author's plan of reformation will be less successful, than even that of her great coadjutor Mr. Thomas Paine. In the conclusion, she is more rational, and we shall transcribe it.

[Quotes "In tracing the causes ... in which women have never yet been placed" (196–97).]

As we have now ascertained the outline of our author's system, and adduced the principal arguments brought in support of it, and a few (indeed a few only) of the very peculiar opinions and expressions, we must step on more rapidly, lest the Rights of Woman seem to preclude the great *privileges* of man. The 5th chapter contains "animadversions on some of the writers who have rendered women objects of pity, bordering on contempt." This is the language of the present author, and our readers can now understand it without a comment. The first of the writers examined is Rousseau, and he is reprehended for making Sophia the tender victim of love and sensibility. Fordyce is blamed for inculcating, in his system, female meekness and artificial grace; for the farrago of affected sentiment and unnatural refinement; for extravagant unmeaning compliment, and its doctrines of abject submission. We own that to Fordyce's Sermons much may be objected; nor can we deny that many of the observations, in this section, are just. Dr. Gregory comes next under review; and our author a little petulantly objects, in the midst of some judicious and well-turned compliments, to the concise elegance of the style, scarcely suitable to the affectionate father, with his tenderness and solicitude tremblingly alive. Miss Wollstonecraft knew not Dr. Gregory, and we forgive her;

she will, however, excuse us for remarking, that the tender elegance of his mind, his habit of thinking and speaking with feeling and propriety, were so firmly rooted, that his most careless convivial language had often the elegance of a finished composition. The great objection to the "Last Legacy" seems the system of dissimulation, which pervades the whole; but on the subject we have already given our opinion. Some of Mrs. Piozzi's opinions; those of the baroness de Stael, of madame Genlis, Mrs. Chapone, and Mrs. Macaulay, are mentioned with respect or with an ardor of esteem; yet with Mrs. Chapone our author adds, that she cannot always agree in opinion; some general observations on education, introduced with strictures on lord Chesterfield's system, conclude the chapter.

The sixth chapter is on the effect which an early association of ideas has on the general character. The proposition, as a general one, is unexceptionable. We object only to the application, as connected with our author's system: if the manners of women are not so essentially wrong, as they are represented in this volume, the early association of ideas is not injurious.

[Quotes "Modesty! sacred offspring ... they supinely sleep life away!" (252).]

This pretty poetical address introduces the chapter, of which a "comprehensive consideration of modesty," in general, is the subject—not considering modesty as a "sexual virtue." How this is done may appear surprising; we have seen such instances in legerdemain tricks—hey presto, pass, be gone! was any thing ever executed more dexterously. See; modesty is no longer modesty: it is something else, and that something, a lady who can write like miss Wollstonecraft, who can discuss anatomical subjects with men, and the proportions of naked statues (p. 278), is of very little importance. Let us, however, give a short abstract of the power which thus transmutes words and things. Modesty is either the purity of mind, which is the effect of character, or it is that soberness of mind which sets a *proper* value on our powers and abilities. In the common systems of vulgar souls this last quality is styled confidence. A modest man is steady, a humble man timid, and a bashful one timid from ignorance. This is a trifling jargon: modesty when applied to women is, as miss Wollstonecraft states, purity of mind. This purity may not be alarmed at the learned discussions of anatomy, the sexual system of botany, or the proportions of the Farnese Hercules.[1] She has, however, unfortunately forgotten that the imagination, which the severity of study, or the profoundest investigations cannot wholly suppress, will connect these subjects with others, which a pure mind should not admit. Unfortunately, on these enquiries the imagination, for reasons which it is unnecessary to state, is peculiarly active. In this disquisition then, respecting modesty, she has in some respects changed the terms, and in others misrepresented them. If she had adopted the first distinction of purity of mind, and added a corresponding propriety of behaviour, she would have come nearer to the truth, and she would have found modesty to be peculiarly a female virtue. We know, indeed, that many men are truly modest; that others can, for a time, guard their conduct, and appear so; but women, in consequence of their peculiar sensibility, feel more quickly and with more pain any offensive hint. This is, however, the source of our author's error: women *must* not have more sensibility, because it is a weakness, consequently they must not possess, in a peculiar degree, modesty. What are virtue, purity and modesty, compared with a system? what are even the lives of all the men and women that ever existed?

The difficulties and inconsistencies we mentioned pervade the whole chapter, and produce either confusion or error in the reasoning. Some parts of it contain representations not the most delicate: they are, however, the errors of women, and should have been respected by a woman. Swift's picture of a lady's dressing-room is indefensibly indelicate:[2] it would have been disgusting from a female pen, and yet we have often the door left a-jar, and we see too much.

In the 8th chapter, miss Wollstonecraft endeavours to show, that "morality is undermined by sexual notions of the importance of a good reputation." The first proposition startled us. "It has long since occurred to me, says this levelling lady, that advice respecting behaviour, and all the various modes of preserving a good reputation, which

---

1   [A statue by the ancient Greek sculptor Glykon, found in the Baths of Caracalla, Rome, in 1546, and exhibited in the Palazzo Farnese until 1787.]
2   [Jonathan Swift, "The Lady's Dressing Room" (1730).]

have been so strenuously inculcated on the female world, were *specious* poisons, that, incrusting morality, eat away the substance." The foundation of the reasoning, in support of this curious proposition is that, from the present state of the arguments, women are led to prefer reputation to chastity, and are not unwilling to err, if they think their errors will be concealed. The reasoning is perfectly consistent with the rest of the work, for it can only have any force, when the preliminary is admitted, that modesty is no sexual virtue. These are propositions that cannot be treated with ridicule: it is enough to adduce them to raise the contempt and indignation of man, and of her own sex. The concluding reflections on the chastity of man, are more nauseously disgusting and indelicate, than a reader, without some specimens of the style and language of this volume, can conceive.

Our author next proceeds to consider "the pernicious effects which arise from the unnatural distinctions established in society." But the first part is "meat thrice sodden,"[1] the repeated observations on the necessity of rendering woman independent, and no longer an idol on account of her beauty, no longer the enervated victim of sensibility and indulgence; the second part is more purely political, a trifling declamation of a levelling reformer: to which is added some enquiry on the proper employment for women.—The two following chapters on parental affection and filial duty are scarcely in a different style. The precepts are calculated to form such women as we hope never to see; such as we are certain would waste their days in joyless celibacy, their sweets upon the desert air.

Our author's observations on "national education" are not distinguished for extensive views, or just reasoning. The declamation on the danger of public schools is trite and trifling; the remarks on female boarding-schools have a better foundation: we suspect, that the unpleasing picture is a likeness. The outline of the new plan we shall transcribe.

[Quotes "To render this practicable, ... which would not exclude polite literature" (310-11).]

---

1 [Possibly a variant on the proverb "Beware of meat twice boil'd, and an old foe reconcil'd" (e.g., Benjamin Franklin, *Poor Richard's Almanac*, September 1733.)]

One of the good effects of this indiscriminate association, is said to be early marriages; but how far this is a national advantage may be doubted: a more frequent one would we fear be, seduction; for the reader will perceive little time allotted to, and less stress laid on religion, while morality is not once mentioned. Indeed, we afterwards hear of the effects of this plan on the moral character, and that these would be schools of morality. The only danger is, that the mischief would be done before the lesson of morality in the marriage-bed would begin. Would a person put a child asleep on a precipice, and trust to its discovering its danger when it awakes?

The volume concludes with "some instances of the folly which the ignorance of woman generates, and reflections on the moral improvement, that a revolution in female manners might naturally be expected to produce." The instances of folly derived from ignorance are taken from their superstitious belief in divination or animal magnetism; the *sentimental* turn of the female mind, in their fondness for novels; their partiality for dress; their great sensibility and sexual attraction; and their indulgence of children. The concluding reflections are such as our readers may easily anticipate. Their chief merit depends on the force and propriety of the prior reasoning.

On the whole, we cannot praise this work, or look for the continuation with eagerness. It is, in our opinion, weak, desultory and trifling. Some parts of its subject have given it a splendor in the eyes of individuals; before whom prejudice has interposed a fallacious medium, or whose views party has limited or distorted. If miss Wollstonecraft means it as a trial of skill with the stronger sex, she has wholly failed: she has betrayed her own cause by defending it, and has lost that credit which female authors have sometimes claimed. What shall we say of her language? it is flowing and flowery; but weak, diffuse, and confused: of the indelicacy of her ideas and expressions? Here we must draw the veil, though it was our attention to have collected a bouquet from the parterre. We have desisted, from a respect to *our* readers, which the lady has not paid to her's; and we have blushed to copy in the closet, what she has openly published. We call on men therefore to speak, if they would wish the women to be pupils of this new school? we call on the women to declare, whether they will sacrifice their pleasing qualities for the severity of reason, the bold unabashed dignity of speaking what they feel, of rising superior to the vulgar prejudices of decency and propriety.—We may easily antici-pate the answer; and shall leave miss Wollstonecraft at least to obliv-ion: her best friends can never wish that her work should be remembered. [5: 132-41]

iii. *Monthly Review* ns 8 (1792): 198-209

PHILOSOPHY, which, for so many ages, has amused the indolent recluse with subtle and fruitless speculations, has, at length, stepped forth into the public walks of men, and offers them her friendly aid in correcting those errors which have hitherto retarded their progress toward perfection, and in establishing those principles and rules of action, by which they may be gradually conducted to the summit of human felicity. Inveloped as mankind at present are with the mists of prejudice, and encumbered on every side with institutions and cus-toms, which prevent the free expansion of their intellectual and moral powers, it is the interest of private individuals, and the duty of those who are entrusted with the care of the public welfare, where-ever, or in whatever character, this divine Instructress appears, to give her an honourable reception, and an attentive hearing. Among the most enlightened people of antiquity, Wisdom, as well as Beauty, was dei-fied under a female form; and in modern language it is still usual to give Philosophy and Wisdom a female personification. What is this but a tacit concession in favour of the female part of the species, that they are no less capable of instructing than of pleasing?—and how jealous soever WE may be of our *right* to the proud pre-eminence which we have assumed, the women of the present age are daily giv-ing us indubitable proofs that mind is of no sex, and that, with the fos-tering aid of education, the world, as well as the nursery, may be benefited by their instructions.

In the class of philosophers, the *author* of this treatise—whom we will not offend by styling, authoress—has a right to a distinguished place. The important business, here undertaken, is to correct errors, hitherto universally embraced, concerning the female character; and to raise woman, from a state of degradation and vassalage, to her prop-er place in the scale of existence; where, with the dignity of independence, she may discharge the duties and enjoy the happiness of a rational Being. The fundamental principle, on which the whole argument of this work is founded, is that, except in affairs of love, sexual distinctions ought to be disregarded, and women be considered in the light of rational creatures; who, in common with men, are placed in this world to unfold their faculties, and whose first object of ambition ought to be to obtain a character as a human Being. It is acknowledged that more attention has lately been paid to the education of women than formerly: but it is at the same time maintained, that the method, in which they are commonly educated, only tends to enfeeble both the body and the mind, and to render them insignificant objects of desire. In order to correct this error, which is considered by Miss Wollstonecraft as a gross violation of justice against one half of the species, and as prolific in mischief to the whole; and after some general observations on the rights and duties of human beings, and on the causes of the present imperfect state of human society; the prevailing opinion of a sexual character is discussed, and its influence on female education and manners is, with equal solidity of reasoning, and strength of colouring, represented at large. [198-99]

[Summarizes the book, with quotations.]

From the copious extracts which we have made from this truly original work, a better judgment may be formed of its merit, than from any summary of its leading sentiments which we could have given. It will be easily perceived that the author is possessed of great energy of intellect, vigour of fancy, and command of language; and that the performance suggests many reflections, which well deserve the attention of the public, and which, pursued under the direction of good sense and sage experience, may greatly contribute to the improvement of the condition and character of the female world. We do not, however, so zealously adopt Miss W.'s plan for a REVOLUTION in female education and manners, as not to perceive that several of her opinions are fanciful, and some of her projects romantic. We do not see, that the condition or the character of women would be improved, by assuming an active part in civil government. It does not appear to us to be necessary, in order to enlighten the understandings of women, that we should prohibit the employment of their fingers in those useful and elegant labours of the needle, for which, from the days of Penelope, they have obtained so much deserved applause.[1] Certain associations, now too firmly established to be easily broken, forbid us to think that women are degraded by the trivial attention which the men are inclined to pay them; or that it would be any increase of the pleasures of society, if, "except where love animates the behaviour, the distinction of sex were to be confounded." This distinction, we apprehend, will never be overlooked, till the time arrives, "when we shall neither marry nor be given in marriage, but be as the angels of God in heaven."[2] Notwithstanding all this, however, we entirely agree with the fair writer, that both the condition and the character of women are capable of great improvement; and that, by means of a more rational plan of female education, in which a judicious attention should be paid to the cultivation of their understanding and taste, as well as of their dispositions and manners, women might be rendered at once more agreeable, more respectable, and more happy in every station of life. Both men and women should certainly, in the first place, regard themselves, and should be treated by each other, as human beings. It might, perhaps, in some measure, contribute to this end, if, beside the sexual appellations of man and woman, we had some general term to denote the species, like [*Anthropos*] and *Homo* in the Greek and Roman languages. The want of such a general term is a material defect in our language.

What practical measures may be reasonably adopted, in order to produce the improvement so strongly recommended in this work, we expect to be more distinctly informed in the second part; in which we are promised a more minute consideration of the laws relative to women, and of their particular duties.

---

1　[Penelope, the wife of Odysseus, put off her suitors during his long absence by promising to marry one of them as soon as she had finished weaving a shroud for her father-in-law. Every night, she undid the work she had done the previous day.]
2　[Matthew 22: 30.]

# Works Cited/Recommended Reading

## Primary Texts

Equiano, Olaudah. *The Life of Olaudah Equiano, or Gustavus Vassa the African. Written by Himself.* 1789. Isaac Knapp, 1837. Rpt. New York: Negro Universities Press, 1969.

Gouges, Olympe de. *Les Droits de la femme.* Paris, 1791.

Gregory, John. *A Father's Legacy to his Daughters.* London: W. Strahan and T. Cadell, 1774. Rpt. New York: Garland, 1974.

Hays, Mary. "Memoirs of Mary Wollstonecraft." *The Annual Necrology for 1797-1798.* London: Phillips, 1800.

——. Obituary of Mary Wollstonecraft. *Monthly Magazine* 4 (1797): 232-33.

——. Letter. *Monthly Magazine* 4 (1797): 245. An acknowledgment of the authorship of the obituary.

Light, Launcelot, and Laetitia Lookabout. *A Sketch of the Rights of Boys and Girls.* London: J. Bew, 1792.

Macaulay Graham, Catharine. *Letters on Education. With Observations on Religious and Metaphysical Subjects.* London: C. Dilly, 1790. Rpt. New York: Garland, 1974.

——. *Observations on the Reflections of the Right Hon. Edmund Burke, on the Revolution in France, in a Letter to the Right Hon. the Earl of Stanhope.* London: C. Dilly, 1790.

Polwhele, Richard. *The Unsex'd Females: A Poem, Addressed to the Author of The Pursuits of Literature.* London: Cadell and Davies, 1798. Rpt. New York: Garland, 1974.

Price, Richard. *A Discourse on the Love of our Country, Delivered on Nov. 4, 1789, at the Meeting-House in the Old Jewry, to the Society for Commemorating the Revolution in Great Britain. With an Appendix, Containing the Report of the Committee of the Society; an Account of the Population of France; and the Declaration of Rights by the National Assembly of France.* London: T. Cadell, 1789.

Talleyrand-Périgord, Charles Maurice de. *Rapport sur L'instruction publique, fait au nom du Comité de Constitution.* Paris, 1791.

Taylor, Thomas. *A Vindication of the Rights of Brutes*. London: Edward Jeffery, 1792. Rpt. Gainesville, Fla.: Scholars' Facsimiles and Reprints, 1966.

Wollstonecraft, Mary. *The Female Reader; or Miscellaneous Pieces in Prose and Verse; Selected from the Best Writers, and Disposed under Proper Heads; for the Improvement of Young Women*. "By Mr. Cresswick, Teacher of Elocution." London: Joseph Johnson, 1789. Rpt. Delmar, N.Y.: Scholars' Facsimiles and Reprints, 1980.

——. *Posthumous Works of the Author of a Vindication of the Rights of Woman*. Ed. William Godwin. 4 vols. London: Joseph Johnson, 1798. Rpt. New York: Garland, 1974.

——. *A Vindication of the Rights of Men, in a Letter to the Right Honourable Edmund Burke; Occasioned by his Reflections on the Revolution in France*. London: Joseph Johnson, 1790.

——. *A Vindication of the Rights of Men, in a Letter to the Right Honourable Edmund Burke; Occasioned by his Reflections on the Revolution in France*. Second edition. London: Joseph Johnson, 1790.

——. *A Vindication of the Rights of Woman: with Strictures on Political and Moral Subjects*. London: Joseph Johnson, 1792.

——. *A Vindication of the Rights of Woman: with Strictures on Political and Moral Subjects*. Second edition. London: Joseph Johnson, 1792.

——. *A Vindication of the Rights of Woman: with Strictures on Political and Moral Subjects*. Third edition. London: Joseph Johnson, 1796.

## Contemporary Reviews: *A Vindication of the Rights of Men*

*Analytical Review* 8 (1790): 416-19.

*Critical Review* 70 (1790): 694-96.

*English Review* 17 (1791): 59-61.

*General Magazine and Impartial Review* 4 (1791): 26-27.

*Gentleman's Magazine* 61.1 (1791): 151-54.

*Monthly Review* ns 4 (1791): 95-97.

*New Annual Register* 11 (1790): 237.

*Universal Magazine and Review* 5 (1791): 77-78.

*Walker's Hibernian Magazine* 1 (1791): 269-71 [copied from the *Gentleman's Magazine*].

## Contemporary Reviews: *A Vindication of the Rights of Woman*

*Analytical Review* 12 (1792): 241-49; 13 (1792): 481-89.

*Christian Miscellany* 1 (1792): 209-12.

*Critical Review* ns 4 (1792): 389-98; 5 (1792): 132-41.

*General Magazine and Impartial Review* 6.2 (1792): 187-91.

*Literary Magazine and British Review* 8 (1792): 133-39.

*Monthly Review* ns 8 (1792): 198-209.

*New Annual Register* 13 (1792): 298.

*New-York Magazine* 4 (1793): 77-81.

*Scots Magazine* 54 (1792): 284-90.

*Sentimental and Masonic Magazine* 1 (1792): 63-72.

*Town and Country Magazine* 24 (1792): 279.

## Modern Editions

Burke, Edmund. *The Correspondence of Edmund Burke.* Ed. Thomas W. Copeland. 10 vols. Chicago: U of Chicago P, 1958-78.

———. *A Philosophical Enquiry into the Origin of our Ideas of the Sublime and Beautiful.* Ed. Adam Phillips. Oxford: Oxford UP, 1990.

———. *The Works of the Right Honourable Edmund Burke.* 12 vols. London: John C. Nimmo, 1887.

———. *The Writings and Speeches of Edmund Burke.* Gen. ed. Paul Langford. 17 vols. Oxford: Clarendon P, 1981-.

Coleridge, Samuel Taylor. *Biographia Literaria; or, Biographical Sketches of My Literary Life and Opinions.* Ed. George Watson. Rev. ed. London: Everyman, 1975.

Condorcet, Marie-Jean-Antoine-Nicolas de Caritat, Marquis de. "On the Admission of Women to the Rights of Citizenship." Trans. Alice Drysdale Vickery. *The First Essay on the Political Rights of Women.* Letchworth: Garden City Press, 1912. 5-11.

Equiano, Olaudah. *The Interesting Narrative of the Life of Olaudah Equiano, or Gustavus Vassa, the African. Written by Himself. The Classic Slave Narratives.* Ed. Henry Louis Gates, Jr. New York: Mentor, 1987. 1-182.

Godwin, William. *Memoirs of the Author of "The Rights of Woman."* Holmes 201-77.

Hume, David. *Enquiries Concerning the Human Understanding and Concerning the Principles of Morals*. Ed. L.A. Selby-Bigge. Oxford: Oxford UP, 1975.

Locke, John. *Some Thoughts concerning Education*. Ed. John W. and Jean S. Yolton. Oxford: Clarendon P, 1989.

——. *Two Treatises of Government*. Ed. Peter Laslett. 2nd ed. Cambridge: Cambridge UP, 1967.

Rousseau, Jean-Jacques. *The Confessions*. Trans. J.M. Cohen. Harmondsworth: Penguin Books, 1953.

——. *Emile; or, On Education*. Trans. Allan Bloom. New York: Basic Books, 1979.

——. *The First and Second Discourses*. Ed. Roger D. Masters. Trans. Roger D. Masters and Judith R. Masters. New York: St. Martin's Press, 1964.

——. *Politics and the Arts: Letter to M. d'Alembert on the Theatre*. Trans. Allan Bloom. Ithaca: Cornell UP, 1968.

Sidney, Philip. *The Countess of Pembroke's Arcadia (The New Arcadia)*. Ed. Victor Skretkowicz. Oxford: Clarendon P, 1987.

Smith, Adam. *The Theory of Moral Sentiments*. Ed. D.D. Raphael and A. L. MacFie. The Glasgow Edition of the Works and Correspondence of Adam Smith, 1. Oxford: Clarendon Press, 1976.

Wollstonecraft, Mary. *Collected Letters of Mary Wollstonecraft*. Ed. Ralph M. Wardle. Ithaca: Cornell UP, 1979.

——. *A Critical Edition of Mary Wollstonecraft's A Vindication of the Rights of Woman: With Strictures on Political and Moral Subjects*. Ed. Ulrich H. Hardt. Troy, NY: Whitston, 1982.

——. *Mary and The Wrongs of Woman*. Ed. Gary Kelly. Oxford: Oxford UP, 1976.

——. *Political Writings: A Vindication of the Rights of Men, A Vindication of the Rights of Woman, An Historical and Moral View of the French Revolution*. Ed. Janet Todd. Toronto: U of Toronto P, 1993.

——. *A Short residence in Sweden, Norway, and Denmark*. Holmes 57-200

——. *A Vindication of the Rights of Men with A Vindication of the Rights of Woman and Hints*. Ed. Sylvana Tomaselli. Cambridge: Cambridge UP, 1995.

——. *A Vindication of the Rights of Woman*. Ed. Carol Poston. 2nd ed. New York: Norton, 1988.

——. *A Vindication of the Rights of Woman.* Ed. Miriam Brody. Rev. ed. London: Penguin, 1992.

——. *The Works of Mary Wollstonecraft.* Ed. Janet Todd and Marilyn Butler. Asst. Emma Rees-Mogg. 7 vols. London: William Pickering, 1989.

Wordsworth, William. *The Poems.* Ed. John O. Hayden. 2 vols. London: Penguin, 1977.

——. *The Prelude.* Ed. J.C. Maxwell. Rev. ed. London: Penguin, 1972.

## Secondary Texts

Alexander, Meena. *Women in Romanticism: Mary Wollstonecraft, Dorothy Wordsworth and Mary Shelley.* London: Macmillan, 1989.

Bate, Jonathan. *Romantic Ecology: Wordsworth and the Environmental Tradition.* London: Routledge, 1991.

Boulton, James T. *The Language of Politics in the Age of Wilkes and Burke.* London: Routledge and Kegan Paul, 1963.

Butler, Marilyn, ed. *Burke, Paine, Godwin, and the Revolution Controversy.* Cambridge: Cambridge UP, 1984.

Conger, Syndy McMillen. *Mary Wollstonecraft and the Language of Sensibility.* London: Associated University Presses, 1994.

Coole, Diana H. *Women in Political Theory: From Ancient Misogyny to Contemporary Feminism.* Sussex: Wheatsheaf Books, 1988.

Guralnick, Elissa. "Radical Politics in Mary Wollstonecraft's *A Vindication of the Rights of Woman.*" *Studies in Burke and his Time* 18 (1977): 155-66.

——. "Rhetorical Strategy in Mary Wollstonecraft's *A Vindication of the Rights of Woman.*" *Humanities Association Review* 30 (1979): 174-85.

Holmes, Richard, ed. *Mary Wollstonecraft, A Short Residence in Sweden, Norway and Denmark and William Godwin, Memoirs of the Author of "The Rights of Woman."* London: Penguin, 1987.

James, C.L.R. *The Black Jacobins: Toussaint L'Ouverture and the San Domingo Revolution.* New ed. London: Allison and Busby, 1980.

Janes, R.M. "On the Reception of Mary Wollstonecraft's *A Vindication of the Rights of Woman.*" *Journal of the History of Ideas* 39 (1978): 293-302.

Johnson, Claudia L. *Equivocal Beings: Politics, Gender, and Sentimentality in the 1790s: Wollstonecraft, Radcliffe, Burney, Austen*. Chicago: U of Chicago P, 1995.

Jump, Harriet Devine. *Mary Wollstonecraft: Writer*. New York: Harvester Wheatsheaf, 1994.

Kates, Gary. *Monsieur d'Eon Is a Woman: A Tale of Political Intrigue and Sexual Masquerade*. New York: Basic Books, 1995.

Kelly, Gary. *Revolutionary Feminism: The Mind and Career of Mary Wollstonecraft*. London: Macmillan, 1992.

Levy, Darline Gay, Harriet Branson Applewhite, and Mary Durham Johnson, eds. *Women in Revolutionary Paris 1789-1795: Selected Documents Translated with Notes and Commentary*. Urbana: U of Illinois P, 1979.

Lorch, Jennifer. *The Making of a Radical Feminist*. Oxford and New York: St. Martin's Press, 1990.

Macdonald, D.L. "Master, Slave, and Mistress in Wollstonecraft's *Vindication*." *Enlightenment and Dissent* 11 (1992): 46-57.

Maclean, Marie. "Revolution and Opposition: Olympe de Gouges and the *Déclaration des droits de la femme*." *Literature and Revolution*. Ed. David Bevan. Amsterdam: Rodopi, 1989. 171-82.

Myers, Mitzi. "Impeccable Governesses, Rational Dames, and Moral Mothers: Mary Wollstonecraft and the Female Tradition in Georgian Children's Books." *Children's Literature* 14 (1986): 31-59.

——. "Politics from the Outside: Mary Wollstonecraft's First *Vindication*." *Studies in Eighteenth-Century Culture* 6 (1977): 113-32.

——. "Reform or Ruin: 'A Revolution in Female Manners.'" *Studies in Eighteenth-Century Culture* 11 (1982): 199-216.

——. "Sensibility and the 'Walk of Reason': Mary Wollstonecraft's Literary Reviews as Cultural Critique." *Sensibility in Transformation: Creative Resistance to Sentiment from the Augustans to the Romantics: Essays in Honor of Jean H. Hagstrum*. Ed. Syndy M. Conger. Rutherford: Fairleigh Dickinson UP, 1989. 120-44.

Nussbaum, Martha C. *Poetic Justice: The Literary Imagination and Public Life*. Boston: Beacon Press, 1995.

Paulson, Ronald. *Representations of Revolution (1789-1820)*. New Haven: Yale UP, 1983.

Poovey, Mary. *The Proper Lady and the Woman Writer: Ideology as Style in the Works of Mary Wollstonecraft, Mary Shelley, and Jane Austen*. Women in Culture and Society. Gen. ed. Catharine R. Stimpson. Chicago: U of Chicago P, 1984.

Poston, Carol H., and Janet M. Todd. "Some Textual Variations in the First Two Editions of *A Vindication of the Rights of Woman*." *Mary Wollstonecraft Journal* 2.2 (May 1974): 27-29.

Reiss, Timothy J. "Revolution in Bounds: Wollstonecraft, Women, and Reason." *Genre and Theory: Dialogues on Feminist Criticism*. Ed. Linda Kauffman. Oxford: Blackwell, 1989.

Sapiro, Virginia. *A Vindication of Political Virtue: The Political Theory of Mary Wollstonecraft*. Chicago: U of Chicago P, 1992.

Schrîder, Hannelore. "The Declaration of Human and Civil Rights for Women (Paris, 1791) by Olympe de Gouges." *History of European Ideas* 11 (1989): 263-71.

Sunstein, Emily W. *A Different Face: The Life of Mary Wollstonecraft*. New York: Harper and Row, 1975.

Thomas, Keith. *Man and the Natural World: A History of the Modern Sensibility*. New York: Pantheon Books, 1983.

Todd, Janet M. *Mary Wollstonecraft: An Annotated Bibliography*. New York: Garland, 1976.

Tomalin, Claire. *The Life and Death of Mary Wollstonecraft*. New York: Harcourt Brace Jovanovich, 1974.

Tyson, Gerald P. *Joseph Johnson: A Liberal Publisher*. Iowa City: U of Iowa P, 1979.

Wardle, Ralph M. *Mary Wollstonecraft: A Critical Biography*. Lincoln: U of Nebraska P, 1951.

Woolf, Virginia. "Mary Wollstonecraft." *The Second Common Reader*. New York: Harcourt Brace, 1932.

Woshinsky, Barbara. "Olympe de Gouges' *Declaration of the Rights of Woman* (1791)." *Mary Wollstonecraft Newsletter* 2.1 (December 1973): 1-6.

Yaeger, Patricia. *Honey-Mad Women: Emancipatory Strategies in Women's Writing*. New York: Columbia UP, 1988.

·

# *Index to* A Vindication of the Rights of Men, A Vindication of the Rights of Woman, *and "Hints"*[1]

---

1 The Introduction and Appendices are not indexed, except for Appendix C.

stonecraft and: 200
animal magnetism: 326-28
animal spirits: 188, 202, 225, 233, 244, 306
animals: 73, 102, 133, 144, 146, 153,
167n., 188, 189, 293, 304, 317, 321, 336;
cats: 259n., 300, 319; cruelty to: 316,
317; dogs: 47, 144, 204, 278, 281, 309,
316-17; horses: 184, 285, 316, 317, 337,
343, 411; humans as: 39, 56, 81, 89, 112,
119, 120n., 127, 142, 179, 197n., 205,
214, 319; immortality of: 63n., 158, 180;
inferiority to humans: 43, 63, 66, 73, 87,
95, 109-10, 117, 120, 146; kindness to:
315
anorexia: 156
antiquity: 38, 44, 51, 63, 74, 78, 84, 123,
135, 169, 262, 274, 283, 314
appetite(s): 39, 65, 72, 140, 142, 156,
181n., 204, 236, 263, 272, 273, 300, 326,
328, 331, 341; sexual: 105, 146, 151, 152,
160, 181, 185, 190, 191, 203, 224, 238,
248, 256, 257, 273, 274-75, 304, 319,
340, 409-10
Arcadia: 92
Argus: 266
aristocracy: 40, 124-25, 166, 179, 187,
210; see also: feudalism, nobility, rank
Aristotle, Politics: 50n.
army: 52, 123, 132; see also: soldiers
art(s): 137, 151n., 168n., 174, 202-3, 205,
206, 208, 227, 228, 232, 246, 281, 320,
333; civilized: 94, 133, 152n., 208, 286,
322; deceiving: 69, 92, 138, 147, 151n.,
206, 207, 222, 230, 265, 266, 322, 342;
erotic: 105, 138, 141, 164, 208, 213, 248,
266, 273; fine: 92, 134n., 152n., 308,
339, 411n., 412; see also: nature
astrology: 324-26
astronomy: 269, 311
atheism: 38n., 80, 129, 200
Atlas: 226
Augustus, Gaius Julius Caesar Octavianus: 412

authority: 50, 51, 62, 68n., 88, 92, 93, 97,
104, 123, 124, 171-72, 175, 191, 210,
212, 213, 242, 247, 295, 310, 335, 343;
arbitrary: 46, 49, 210, 296; divine: 43;
parental: 230, 296; of reason: 165, 226,
340; revolt against: 40, 204; subjection
to: 203, 205, 209-10, 226; submission to:
43, 132, 174, 226, 295, 335; Wollstonecraft's textual: 152, 203, 268
authors: 91, 121, 127, 130, 181, 221, 245,
265, 415; God as: 159, 239
avarice: 93

Bacon, Francis, Essays: 127, 180
barbarism: 42, 43, 67, 124, 274; Rousseau
and: 121
Barbauld, Anna Laetitia: 168n., 171, 243n.
bashfulness: 162n., 187, 253, 254, 260,
262-63, 305, 306
Bastille: 58
beauty: 35, 38, 77, 82, 83, 91, 130, 141,
212, 217, 218, 252, 279, 315, 317, 333n.;
artistic: 314, 315, 414-15; and cleanliness: 259, 261, 315; evanescence of: 113,
163, 213, 220, 229, 247, 250n., 279, 287,
288; feminine: 36, 80, 126, 153, 168n.,
171n., 187, 188, 201, 207, 208, 212, 219,
247, 288, 334-35; literary: 200, 262, 413;
masculine: 175, 187, 188; mental: 80,
103, 188, 248, 288, 315, 414; mistaken
notions of: 156, 207, 246, 278-79; of
nature: 38, 95, 237, 309, 315; power of:
127, 129, 157, 170-71, 250; respect paid
to: 173, 224, 229, 279; and strength: 131,
314; and the sublime: 35, 79, 160, 234,
414; and virtue: 80, 81, 83, 193, 234; and
weakness: 80-81, 109, 112, 130, 147,
152, 153, 202, 204, 245, 314
benevolence: 48, 49, 52, 54, 78, 88, 89,
166n., 182, 185, 231, 233, 282, 286, 299,
302, 307, 316, 329; Wollstone-craft's:
280, 288, 314
Berkenhout, John: 254

character: 37, 61, 86n., 94, 122, 127, 142, 145, 165, 173, 180, 187, 188, 223, 232n., 233, 242, 244, 252, 268-69, 269-70, 278, 285, 312, 318, 321-22, 342; of the century: 128-29, 286; clerical: 71, 72, 86; degradation of: 72, 151-52, 157, 190, 224, 272, 293, 310, 312; dignity of: 55, 62, 98, 153, 260, 284; fictional: 133, 318; of a gentleman: 131, 149; of God: 154-55, 158, 159, 200, 234; human: 110, 111, 112, 157, 165, 167, 220, 280, 293, 309, 322; individual: 123, 188, 222, 244; maternal: 161, 321, 322-23; of men: 185, 197, 219, 245; moral: 140, 245, 259, 273, 300, 305, 307, 311, 324, 338; national: 67, 102, 170, 176; professional: 124, 157, 195, 283; public and private: 36, 53, 303-4; respectability of: 140, 190, 233, 272; sexual: 103, 112, 126, 168, 169, 173, 200, 203, 245, 249; simplicity of: 232, 263, 300, 410; strength of: 147, 163, 174; weakness of: 53, 97, 129, 172, 330; of women: 111, 134, 155, 156-57, 164, 173, 177, 198, 199, 217, 219, 245, 246, 290, 291, 317, 342, 343, 410; written: 217, 239

charity: 39, 79, 190; endearing: 55, 189, 341; Wollstonecraft's: 79, 86

Charlotte Sophia, Queen of Britain: 59

chastity: 103, 191, 255, 262, 410; in men: 103, 113, 258, 274, 275, 306, 342; and modesty: 252, 254, 256, 262, 275, 342; and reputation: 266, 267-68, 270, 272, 333; in women: 137, 184, 190, 210, 213, 218, 227n., 229, 256, 272, 273

Chesterfield, Philip Dormer Stanhope, Earl, Letters to his Son: 172, 232

children: 47, 53, 58, 133, 140, 153, 161, 164, 180, 184, 187, 189, 195, 201, 202, 213, 217, 236, 240, 259, 274, 279, 291, 292, 321, 322, 327, 337, 338; affection for: 164, 192, 289-91, 295, 296, 309, 317; affection of: 47, 204, 291, 296, 297,

298, 317, 336; as bonds between parents: 213, 263, 273, 279, 291; books for: 152, 230; breastfeeding: 55, 192, 274, 279, 284, 291, 324, 339; duty of: 292-97; education of: 88, 102, 128, 145, 152n., 180-81, 195, 211, 229, 232n., 241, 242, 284, 286, 293, 294, 295, 296, 298-324, 341; exercise for: 153, 411; humans as God's: 89, 226, 254, 328; ignorance/innocence of: 64, 127, 236; inheritance: 55, 162, 182, 267; maintenance of: 94, 189, 196, 284, 285; men as: 130; neglect of: 54, 105, 290, 294, 338; obedience of: 128, 294, 411; oppression of: 52-53, 161, 294, 295, 316, 337-38; rights of: 43, 182; sexualization of: 203, 246; spoiled: 128, 290, 338; women as: 111, 112-13, 127, 140, 178, 246, 266, 309, 332, 340

China: 37, 148, 153

chivalry: 61, 179, 222

Christianity: 62, 69, 79, 86, 262, 326, 412

church: 54, 69, 184, 326, 327; see also: clergy, liturgy, priests, property, religion, sermons, tithes

Church of England: 49, 52, 67, 68, 69, 70, 78, 84, 97, 123, 163, 301

Cibber, Colley, Tragical History of King Richard III: 78

Cicero, Marcus Tullius: 78, 211

Cincinnatus: 281

Circassia: 208

citizens: 44, 53, 78n., 95, 104, 121, 180, 275, 280, 282, 284, 288, 300, 303, 304, 307, 312, 319, 323; fellow-: 70, 102, 174

civilization, personal: 47, 53, 73, 93, 109, 177, 196, 215, 283, 285, 335; social: 39, 48, 61, 65, 74, 95, 109, 118, 119, 121, 125, 132, 158, 170, 173, 222, 282, 283, 287, 334, 335; see also: arts, Europe

class: 277, 303, 310; lower: 45, 51, 285, 286, 315; middle: 54, 69, 111, 197; upper: 47n., 111, 196; see also: rank

248

207, 215, 229; women as: 130, 143, 147,
158, 160, 165, 169, 204, 257, 281, 290,
337; to men: 104, 111, 133, 134, 146,
157, 171, 196, 207, 215, 220, 229, 249,
273, 282, 288, 295, 306, 309-10, 318; to
themselves: 156, 157, 178, 227, 282, 318
Smellie, William: 187n., 204, 415
Smith, Adam, *Theory of Moral Sentiments*:
173, 174-75, 214, 268, 270, 336, 337n.
social compact: 37, 55, 75, 317
society: 45, 55, 73-74, 85, 104, 119, 122,
132, 139, 165, 172, 184, 190, 211, 250n.,
277, 292, 299, 305, 330, 334; civil: 81,
113, 160; education by: 128-29, 176,
194, 203; enlightened/improved: 94-95,
122-23, 124, 277, 303, 307, 308, 312,
322, 339, 343n.; hunted out of: 102,
144; ideal: 118, 284, 312; infancy of: 40,
124, 413; licentiousness of: 151-52, 307;
of men: 124, 187, 263n., 298; none
among unequals: 72, 128; not properly
organized. 180, 221-22, 278, 297; order
of: 140, 147; present state of: 117, 130,
131, 170, 194, 283, 315; surveys of: 87-
88, 111, 133; usefulness to: 54, 56, 87,
129, 183, 340; whole circle/mass of: 62,
111, 151-52, 285, 323; women in: 112,
131, 177, 179, 244, 286, 343; of women:
110, 213-14, 298, 309-10, 318, 410
Socrates: 77n., 311, 327n.
soldiers: 123-24, 131-32, 246, 253n., 280,
283-84, 309
solitude: 73, 134n., 174, 183, 245, 250n.,
313; Rousseau and: 119, 214
Solomon: 138
sons: 43, 53, 55, 68, 83, 162, 226, 230, 237,
243, 273, 286-87, 293, 303; *see also*: primogeniture
sons-in-law: 343
sorrow(s): 45, 58, 91, 95, 162, 164, 178,
225, 240, 269; Wollstonecraft's: 109
soul(s): 56, 58, 62, 113, 123, 133, 137, 142,
150, 193, 217, 223, 254, 301, 327, 412;
and body: 81, 169, 201, 255; immortali-

ty of: 46, 134-35, 138, 141, 154, 161,
167, 169, 180, 194, 236, 255; iron in: 64,
335; and matter: 54, 161, 181n.;
Rousseau's: 121, 141, 214; sex ascribed
to: 145, 176; Wollstonecraft's: 57, 67,
147, 254, 271, 309, 312; of women: 80-
81, 126, 138, 142, 158, 162, 167, 180,
185, 281, 313, 335
Sparta: 81, 121, 133
speculation: 76, 84, 92, 131, 150n., 188,
233, 284, 294
speech: 71, 208-9, 299, 305, 331-32, 413
spirit(s): 55, 56, 69, 71-72, 79, 90, 93, 124,
127, 137, 155, 190, 193, 227, 250, 255n.,
266, 284, 287, 294, 302, 327, 332, 337,
342, 415; animal: 188, 202, 225, 233,
244-25, 306; and body/matter: 50, 65,
95, 145, 178, 179-80; Burke's: 70; of
chivalry/romance: 61, 123, 222; God as:
72, 160-61; of independence/freedom:
16, 76n.; of the laws: 265, 301; party: 38;
public: 275; of tyranny: 38, 91-92; Wollstonecraft's: 101, 109, 146, 271
Staël, Anne-Louise-Germaine, baronne
de: 228-29
state(s): 35, 55, 67, 68, 70, 74, 78n., 83-84,
123, 222, 287, 322; future: 81, 88-89,
137, 143-44, 191, 215, 237, 412, 413; of
nature: 119-20, 121
statesmen: 58, 280, 281
statues: 228, 314-15
Steele, Richard: 236n.
Sterne, Laurence: 91, 335n.
storms: 73, 168n., 215, 235, 242, 335
strength: 55, 113, 154, 183, 186, 214, 226,
230, 231, 232-33, 239, 252, 268, 295,
296, 316, 325, 336, 415; of affections:
188n., 278, 282, 307-8; of argument: 46,
81, 194; Burke's: 71, 85; and beauty:
109, 112, 130, 155-56, 201, 207-8, 314;
of body: 111, 129, 138-39, 149-50, 152,
158, 163, 173-74, 180-81, 184, 187, 202,
216, 241-42, 262, 274, 411; men's superior: 110, 113, 135, 148, 150, 151, 161n.,